ENCYCLOPAEDIA OF WOMEN IN SOUTH ASIA (INDIA)

ENCYCLOPAEDIA OF WOMEN IN SOUTH ASIA

(In 8 Volumes)

India

(Volume 1)

Editors :

Sangh Mittra, Bachchan Kumar

KALPAZ PUBLICATIONS

Delhi-110052

Encyclopaedia of Women in South Asia *(India)*
(International Studies, Women)

Rs. 7000 (Set)

ISBN: 81-7835-187-0 (Set)
ISBN: 81-7835-188-9 (Vol. 1)

Published in 2004 in India by
Kalpaz Publications,
C-30, Satyawati Nagar, Delhi-110052
E-mail : Kalpaz@hotmail.com

Laser Typesetting at : Shree Vaishnavi Creations, Delhi
Printed at : Mehra Offset Press, Delhi

Contents

Preface

The Encyclopaedia of women in South Asia has deep bearing on numerous aspects of eight neighbouring countries including the Indian sub-continent. In fact it includes the Himalayan countries, Nepal and Bhutan and others are Bangladesh, Pakistan, Afghanistan, Sri Lanka, and Maldives. There had been several developmental changes during the last few decades and these were thought to be for the benefit of the common woman.

The theme has been weaved into eight comprehensive chapters in which useful details have been given. They deal with historical background, geography and the people of the country, their religious status, right to property, national policy for the development of education, progress through the phased programmes, education as fundamental and basic human right, resources provided by the Government, the formal education, training of treachers, welfare of students, open schools and centres of higher education, technical education, emphasis on elementary education, curricula and vocationalisation of education.

Emphasis has been laid down on the changing social status of women. Such a policy has significant basis on malnutrition, poor health and the ways for its improvement, Kerala as a model state, national sociao-demographic roles, leading causes of mortality , gender bias, expenditure on health devices, discrimination against women, abortion, sexual assaults and offences, and dowry related violence.

Two chapters have been devoted on the role of women in politics and government service. They have begun participating in active politics although such a number is fairly small, on account of lack of education. India indeed has greatly cared for the political; and cultural development of women. In South Asia, as a whole women are being provided with opportunities to join government service. The fact is that the women movement is becoming conscious of their basic rights and she is showing eagerness to mobilise her faculties beyond domestic environments. This kind of awakening has paid her sizeable dividends.

We have collected the material from several academic centres, viz, Nehru Menorial Museum and library, Delhi University Library Jawahar Lal Nehru University Library, Sapru House Library, Central Secretariat Library and Indian Council of Historical Research Library. We have used the extracts of writings of eminent scholars in order to build up a readable draft. We are indeed grateful to them for their scholarly support during our researches.

1

Historical Background, Geography and People

Location and Area

India, the second largest country in Asia, is located in the Indian subcontinent in South Asia. Including the Andaman and Nicobar Islands in the Bay of Bengal and Lakshadweep (formerly, the Laccadive, Minicoy and Amindivi Islands), the total land area is 3,287,588 sq km (1,269,341 sq mi), extending 3,214 km (1,997 mi) N to S and 2,933 km (1,822 mi) E to W. The length of the total coastline on the Bay of Bengal, Arabian Sea and the Indian Ocean is 5,110 km (3,175 mi).

Weather

India is a tropical country but is subject to a wide range of climates, from subfreezing Himalayan winters to 50°C (122°F) in the shade in the Indo-Gangetic Plain, from the highest annual rainfall in the world (1,096 cm, 428 in.) in Cherrapunji in Maghalaya to almost permanent rainlessness in the Thar Desert. Four fairly distinct seasons are common to all regions: a relatively cool winter monsoon season, a hot and rainless transitional season, a rainy monsoon season, and a humid season, during the retreating monsoon.

Population

The population of India was estimated in 1980 at 673,659,000, on the basis of the last official census held in 1971 when the population was 548, 154, 562. With 14% of the world's population, India ranks second only to China in size of population. According to 2001 Census its population is 1,027,015,247.

Ethnic Composition

Ethnically, India is one of the great melting pots of the world, and its racial diversity is perhaps the most complex to be found anywhere outside of Africa. From prehistoric times the subcontinent has absorbed several waves of conquering peoples. On its basic racial stock, a Caucasoid people who moved into the Indus (from which the name India has been derived) Valley from Central Asia and established a flourishing civilization around 2500 B.C., there has been grafted Proto-Mongoloid, Australoid and Negrito elements. The great majority of the population belongs to the Caucasoid family. The Dravidians of South India are believed to be the descendants of the Alpines, the Mediterranean branch of the Caucasoids, while most North Indians are believed to be Indo-Nordics. The former constitute 25% of the population and the latter 72%.

Language

According to the 1961 census, 1,652 languages and dialects are spoken in India. Of these, 15 are recognized in the constitution as regional languages and one, Hindi, written in the Devanagiri script, is designated as the official language.

Religion

Almost all the major religions of the world are represented in India and four of them have originated in the country: Buddhism, Jainism, Sikhism and Hinduism.

Hindus form majority of population in all areas except Jammu and Kashmir (where Islam is dominant) and Negaland (where Christians are in the majority). Hinduism is less a monolithic creed than a conglomeration of loosely related but interwoven cults and traditions. It has no unifying creed of pristhood, no founder, no ecclesiastical organization and no concept of heresy. Relatively tolerant, it encompasses differing theologies and spans religious spectrum.

In our ancient texts while great care has been taken to classify men in detail, women are generally treated as a uniform category, and unambiguously equated with the Sudras.[1] Even the *Gita* places women, Vaisyas and Sudras in one category and describes them all as beings of sinful birth.[2] According to another text, the punishment for killing either a woman or a Sudra is identical.[3] As a daughter she should be under the surveillance of her father, as a wife of her husband and as a widow of her son.[4]

Women even composed some of the hymns of the *Rigveda*.[5] After finishing their education, they could either enter married life or devote themselves to religious and metaphysical studies just like men.[6] They took part in the sacrifices performed by their husbands and the term *patni*, which is applied to a wife, indicates this participation.

Manu[7] takes a low view of women's intelligence which may be inferred from a verse wherein he observes that the understanding of women is apt to waver and they do not make good witness. According to him, "the two sexes are unequal in strength, stamina and psychology."[8] Such a view was bound to lead to a decline in women's education. However, there were some *Smrti* writers who protested against this low view of women.[9]

From the 4th century B.C. onwards, writers of the *Dharmasutras* advise that marriage of a girl should not be delayed for long after her puberty.[10] Manu[11] and Kautilya[12] concur with them. Vasishtha and Baudhayana prefer to give a time of three years after puberty but Gautama and Vishnu insist that marriages must be celebrated within three months after puberty. The *Kamasutra*, which belongs to the end of this period, indicates that when it was composed both the post-puberty and pre-puberty marriages were prevalent.[13] The stories of the *Kathasaritsagara* refer both to child-marriages and love-marriages.[14]

From about 200 A.D. pre-puberty marriages became order of the day. Yajnavalkya, who wrote about this time, insists that the girls should be married before puberty.[15] Yama, who lived about 400 years later, states that a girl should be married before she comes of age, even to an unsuitable husband.[16] *Smriti* writers of the period 500-1000 A.D. They held that a girl should be regarded as having attained puberty at the age of 10 and, therefore, her marriage should not be postponed beyond that age.[17]

Women in the Household

The creation of the universe was ascribed by the Aryans to the union of *Prakrti* and Purusha.[18] Woman is supposed to be *Prakrti* and man Purusha; the union of these two created the home and made the world. According to ancient ideals, the wife is half of man and hence as long as he does not obtain her he is incomplete.[19] The Epic literature also lays down that a man's half is his wife; therefore, she is called *ardhangini*. It may also be observed that although Manu did not entertain a very high opinion of the female intellect, he insisted that women should be honoured. Manu assigns them the highest position of respect[20] and says that a mother is in no case to be forsaken even if she has fallen from moral rectitude.[21]

Divorce

A Hindu marriage in ancient India was held to be indissoluble; it was supposed to subsist even after death.[22] The *Sutra* literature condemns the practice of divorce.[23] The *Apastamba* says, "If the marriage vow is transgressed, both husband and wife certainly go to hell."[24] Manu also did not cherish the idea of divorce. There is only one verse[25] in which he provides a clear reference to remarriage of women, but there is enough internal material in the *Manu Smriti* to prove that by and large it is against their remarriage. However, Manu and Yajnavalkya both lay down that a man may abandon his wife if a serious disease of her was not disclosed by her parents before marriage or if there is a loss of chastity on her part.[26] Manu also does not object to a women abandoning her husband if he is insane (*unmatta*), impotent (*kliba; abija*) or suffering from an incurable or contagious disease (*paparogi*).[27]

Narada[28] and Parasara[29] have laid down that marriage can be dissolved if the husband is impotent (*kliba*). According to the *Smritis*, there are five cases of legal sanction wherein a wife is allowed to take a second husband, i.e., if he is missing (*nashta*), or dead (*mrta*), or becomes an ascetic (*pravrajita*), or is impotent (*kliba*) or is degraded from the caste (*patita*).[30] Kautilya also speaks of divorce (*moksha*), which could be obtained only in case of mutual enmity and hatred between husband and wife.[31] But he maintains that marriages of the Brahma, Daiva, Arsha and Prajapatya forms cannot be dissolved at all.[32]

Widow

About the remarriage of widows, there is no clear or definite reference in the *RV*, but the widow could live with her late husband's younger brother to get a son for her husband, if she so chose[33] *Niyoga* was a common practice in the Sutra age also.[34] In the age of *Dharmasastras*, Manu[35] is not very clear about it; he approves of the practice at one place and disapproves it at another.

The growing importance attached to physical chastity

explains the gradual discouragement of widow-remarriage, divorce and levirate, and encouragement of the system of *sati*. The rules about remarriage in the *AS* closely follow those laid down in the *Dharmasastras*.[36] They permit remarriage of a woman whose husband is dead, has become an ascetic or has gone abroad, after a period of waiting which varies according to circumstances. The *Dharmasastras* of Manu[37] and Yajnavalkya[38] forbid the marriage of widows[39] but Narada[40] permits it. Following it, even later texts like *Parasara Smrti* and *Agni Purana* lay down that a woman can remarry even during the life-time of her husband if he is lost (i.e., unheard of), has become an ascetic, is impotent or is an outcaste. Such a remarried woman was called *punarbhu*.[41]

Sati

As briefly mentioned above, custom of *sati* was another interesting aspect of a widow's life in ancient India. It is contended by some[42] that the practice of burning of widows was prevalent even in the early Vedic and post-Vedic age. But, is Altekar has maintained, 'we find no traces of it whatsoever down to C/. 400 B.C.'[43] It was after this that the practice of *sati* became prevalent first among the Kshatriyas and later on among all sections of the Hindu community.

The customs of *niyoga* and remarriage became unpopular gradually from the beginning of the Christian era. However, some widows, not inclined to lead a celibate life, still took recourse either to *niyoga* or remarriage down to 500 A.D. Thereafter, it became difficult for them to do so, though remarriage of child widows continued to be permitted till about 1000 A.D.

A widow did not receive much sympathy in society. If she continued to live in the family of her husband she had to work as a drudge. If she lived separately, she was given a pittance as her maintenance.[44] She was treated as an outcaste on festive occasions. She was looked upon as a bad omen, her very sight being regarded as most inauspicious.[45] The Rama. says, that the greatest suffering that a woman can have is widowhood.[46]

Religious Status

A wife in ancient India was known as *sahadharmini*.[47] In other words, she was held to be one with her husband not only physically but spiritually as well. In the Vedic age, women enjoyed all the religious rights and privileges which men possessed. Her presence and co-operation were regarded necessary in religious rites and ceremonies.[48] The *RV* refers to Ghosha and Lopamudra as well-versed in the mantras.[49] Man could not become a spiritual whole unless he was accompanied by his wife.[50] A bachelor was not considered competent to offer oblations or perform sacrifices.[51] Thus in the age of the Samhitas and Brahmanas the religious status of women was as high as that of men.

In the Upanishadic period, the intellectual classes diverted their attention from the active to speculative life. To them riddles of universe were more attractive than the monotonous transactions of daily rituals. The sages spent their lives in quest of the supreme truth and in solving the mystries of creation, occasionally through discussions as well. In the *Brhadaranyaka Upanishad*,[52] there is reference to a certain ritual for a father who desires his daughter to be a scholar (*Pandita*) and the same *Upanishad* mentions Maitreyi, the wife of Yajnavalkya, discussing problems of deepest philosophical and metaphysical import with her husband.[53] Apparently in this period also the religious, status of women was not inferior to that of men as it became in the later ages.

In the Vedic age the initiation ceremony (*upanayana*) of girls used to take place as regularly as that of boys.[54] After a few centuries, however, writers like Manu, began to advocate that girls' *upanayana* may be performed but no Vedic mantras should be recited on the occasion.[55] Manu also explicitly forbids a girl and a married woman to offer an *agnihotra*.[56] No sacrifice, no vow, no fast was to be observed by women separately from their husband.[57] Even the recitation of Vedic hymns is forbidden in the case of women.[58] Yajnavalkya is forthright in prohibiting altogether the *upanayana* ceremony in the case of girls.[59] He is of the opinion that all religious rites in the case of a woman must be carried out in silence. The marriage ceremony alone should be conducted with recitation of the sacred texts.[60]

Though the prohibition of *upanayana* affected women's position in family and society, the prohibition of Vedic sacrifices by them did not produce any permanent hardships,[61] for these sacrifices themselves soon lost much of their, popularity. It may also be noted that exclusion of women from Vedic studies and sacrifice was not a deliberate attempt to lower their status; rather lowering of marriage age left women with little time for the study of the Vedic *mantras*.

In Jainism and Buddhism marriage was not compulsory for women; rather it was regarded as a fetter which women were advised to avoid. They were urged to become nuns without entering the matrimonial bond. Among the nuns of the *Therigatha,* the majority consists of women who had renounced the world during their maidenhood. The career thus opened for women by Jainism and Buddhism attracted a large number of talented ladies and offered a somewhat freer status of those who entered the *Samgha.* The Pali Vinaya refers to the nun Sundarinanda as beautiful, clever and of scholarly disposition (*dassaniya, pasadika, pandita, medhavini, dakkha*).[62]

As early as the 3rd century B.C. women were already performing a number of vows and fasts (*vratas*) which were unknown to the women of the Vedic age. They are referred to by Asoka in his Rock Edict IX. *Vratas,* it appears, were quite common even before the beginning of the Christian era. The epic-Pauranika religion made ample provisions for the religious requirements of women, most of whom at this time were not educated and, therefore, incapable of understanding or appreciating intellectual arguments. The new religion mostly relied on faith (*sradhha*) and devotion (*bhakti*) and appealed to women immensely.[63] The Tantrika religions of the early medieval period also accepted the equality of women in religious sphere.[64]

Political Status

As regards the political status of women, we find two parallel streaks[65] on the one hand the political condition of women was seemingly quite degraded, and on the other, because of the compulsions of dynastic rule we find many examples of women administering kingdoms in various capacities and exercising immense political authority under special circumstances. As a general rule succession to the throne was confined to males.[66] The Aryan society, being patriarchal, does not furnish many names of female rulers. In the Vedic and post-Vedic literature we seldom find a reference to a reigning queen.

In the *Rama.,* at one place a proposal is made to offer the crown to Sita when Rama was banished,[67] but it could not materialise owing to Sita's determination to accompany her husband in his banishment. In the *Mbh.* Bhishma advises Yudhishthira to sanction the coronation of the daughters of those kings who had died in the war.

In a *Jataka* story[68] we find a king of Varanasi renouncing the world and his queen assuming the reins of administration at the request of the subjects. During the captivity of king Udayana of

Kausambi his mother took full charge of the administration. The way in which she discharged her duties elicited admiration even from experienced ministers.[69] Megasthenes mentions lady rulers of the Pandya country.[70] In the second century B.C. queen Naganika was the head of the administration of the extensive Satavahana empire during the minority of her sons.[71]

The rise of the Imperial Guptas is attributed to their matrimonial alliance with the Lichchhavis. It is generally believed that Kumaradevi, whom Chandragupta I married, was perhaps heiress of the Lichchhavi state. This fact is reflected in the Chandragupta-Kumaradevi type of coins which suggest that the Gupta kingdom was jointly ruled by the Lichchhavis and the Gupta.[72] In the seventh century Yuan Chwang found two *strirajyas* (women's kingdoms) in India. Inscriptions also testify to several queens and princesses taking active part in administration, particularly in the Decean.

Thus Vijayabhattarika, the senior-queen of king Chandraditya of the Chalukya dynasty, ruled over a portion of Bombay in the middle of the 7th century.[73] In 786 A.D. we find Sila Mahadevi, the queen of the Rashtrakuta king Dhruva, making a land grant on her own authority.[74] Revakanammadi, a daughter of the Rashtrakuta king Amoghavarsha I and wife of Erraganga, was the governor of the district of Edetore in 837 A.D. Altekar has quoted many more instances of this type.[75]

In the 9th century A.D. Tribhuvana-Mahadevi I (known as Siddha Gauri), a widowed queen of the Kara dynasty of Orissa, was requested by the feudatory chiefs to accept the throne, on the example of Devi-Gosvamini who belonged to the same family and had administered her kingdom under similar circumstances. In compliance with their request she ascended the lion-throne. Queen Trihuvana-Mahadevi II, also known as Prthivi-Mahadevi, wife of King Subhakara IV, ascended the throne on the death of her husband's younger brother, King Sivakara III. The third great queen, who ascended the throne after the death of the last king Subhakara V of this dynasty, was Gauri-Mahadevi. She was succeeded by her daughter Dandi-Mahadevi.[76] The last known ruler of the Bhaumakara dynasty was Dharma Mahadevi, wife of Santikara III.[77] Tribhuvana-Mahadevi I and Dandi-Mahadevi issued charters and also bore the titles Paramabhattarika Maharajadhiraja Paramesvari.[78]

Under the Rajput dynasties there are several instances[79] of widowed queens efficiently administering the kingdoms of their respective deceased husbands during the minority of their sons.[80] In 1139 A.D., for example, Kumaradevi, on the death of her husband Samarasi of Mewar, undertook the administration of the state in her own hands.[81]

Women as Warriors

In the Vedic times we find reference to Vispala as the one who had fought in wars.[82] Mudgalani or Indrasena, the wife of the sage Mudgala, helped her husband in pursuit of robbers; taking up her husband's bow and arrow she gave them battle, defeated them and rescued the state-property.[83] Again, in the *RV* Sarasvati, the goddess of speech, has been described as Vrtraghni or the slayer of Vrtra and is said to have taken part with Indra in his fight against that demon.[84] In the Devisukta of the same scripture the goddess Vak is mentioned as representing the primordial force of the universe.[85] In the *Taittiriya Brahmana* an allusion is made to Indrani, who is said to be a goddess of army. In the *Rama.*[86] Kaikeyi is said to have accompanied her husband in a battle against the enemies of Indra. In the *Mbh.*, however, there is no reference to women taking part in the historic war. In the days of Rajput chivalry, however, in 1178 A.D. when Gujarata was invaded by Mohammad Ghori, Najikadevi, taking her infant son Chalukya Bhima II in her lap, led the army against the invaders and inflicted a severe defeat on them while queen Kumaradevi of Mewar fought at the head of her troops against Qutb-ud-din. But these are all examples of personal bravery and may be taken as exceptions only. In general, women were treated as property of men, to be protected against agression.[87]

Women as Political Advisers and their Role in Judicial Matters

Ancient Indian law-givers do not suggest the appointment of women as advisers to king or as members of King's Council. Of the eight executive officers of the king or crown mentioned by Sukra,[88] not even one is suggested to be a woman. It was thought that women tend to divulge secrets of the state and are incapable of offering any sound advice in complex matters of government. Kautilya also does not recommend that women should be entrusted with the duties of the state.

In judicial matters, women were not called upon as witnesses. Both Yajnavalkya[89] and Vasishtha[90] are not in favour of women appearing as witnesses; only Manu[91] grants the right of giving evidence to women but only in exceptional cases when male witnesses are not available. However, both Manu[92] and Sukra lay down that women may appear as witnesses for women, especially in disputes involving female matters.

It is against this background of the general status of women in ancient India that their economic status should be studied. We propose to begin our study of the same from the next Chapter.

The Classical Age of Indian history was followed by the rise of the Middle Ages. The early medieval period may be divided into two parts, the age of the Pratiharas which was, from the point of view of the present problem, the age of decline in the status of Indian women, and the post-Pratihara period which was marked by some revivalist trends in the condition of the women folk. The age of decline covers quite a long period from 650 to 1000 A.D. In this period there were no original *Smrti* writers, excepting Devala. It is, however, noteworthy that though this period did not produce any original *Smrti* literature, it abounds in commentaries; even some of the *Puranas* were given a fresh look. In this connection particular mention must be made of the *Varaha Purana,* which got a section of *stridhana* interpolated into it, probably in the tenth century. Similarly, we find that while commenting on the original texts of the *Smrtis* the various commentators gave new interpretations to earlier laws by expanding or limiting their scope.[93] On the basis of their observations we may surmise that the commentators were either influenced by their age or they were just trying to give interpretations which they considered proper. It is, however, highly gratifying to note that the age witnessed the birth of commentators with high intellectual creativity, which is a fact of great historical importance. Besides the commentators, this period is also rich in digest writers.

Before making a detailed analysis of the subject of the property rights of women during this period, it will not be out of place to mention briefly the Smrti writers and commentators who have written on this subject in some detail.

The Sources : Devala

Devala is the only *Smrti* writer of this age. The original *Devala Smrti* is now lost and is available only in citations in various commentaries, e.g. *Krtyakalpataru, Smrti Chandrika* and Apararka's commentary on Yajnavalkya. Most probably, Devala lived in Sindh and witnessed the onslaughts of the Arab invaders. His main theme is devoted to the re-admission of such women into society as had been molested by and had suffered at the hands of the invaders. As Apararka and the *Smrti Chandrika* cite verses from Devala on partition and inheritance of woman's right over *stridhana,* he must have flourished before them and certainly just after Arab invasion. He may, therefore, be safely placed in the first half of the 8th century. No other information about him is available.

Smrti Samgraha

The period witnessed the writing of a few digests of which *Smrti Samgraha,* an important work, is available in citations. Its writer is unknown. According to Kane it was compiled probably between the 8th and 10th centuries A.D.[94] The writer of the *Samgraha* has criticized various earlier writers, like Gautama, on the question of inheritance. However, he is unique in allowing absolute right of succession to the childless widow of a separated family, if she submitted to *niyoga* at the behest of her elders. Similarly, enumerating the order of heir's he states that the paternal grandmother takes the property after the mother and before father.[95]

Bharuchi

Bharuchi is another digest writer whose work is also available in citations only. The earliest mention of Bharuchi is found in the *Mitakshara,* a fact which places him in the 9th century A.D. It appears that Bharuchi did not write any original commentary of his won; he either commented upon the *Vishnudharmasutra* or wrote some work in which he took great pains to incorporate explanations of several sutras of Vishnu.[96] Whatever information we have upon the subject is only through numerous references contained in works like *Sarasvati-Vilasa* and some commentaries. According to Bharuchi, unmarried sisters were entitled only to a provision for their marriage and were not entitled to a fourth share as provided by Asahaya and Medhatithi.[98]

Srikara

Srikara is the last of the digest writers who paid particular attention to explaining the code of Yajnavalkya. He may be assigned to the early 9th century A.D., since he has been quoted by Vijnānesvara and other later writers.[98] According to Kane, he probably belonged to Mithila.[99] As regards his views for succession he bases them on spiritual benefit theory. Srikara was a voluminous writer who classified and condensed the doctrines promulgated by the jurists before him and adopted them to the circumstances of the province in which he lived.[100]

Asahaya

After digest writers we may probe a little about the prolific commentators of whom Asahaya is the first. He most probably lived in the 8th century A.D. He commented upon various *Smrtis,* namely, *Manu Smrti, Narada Smrti, Sankha-Likhita Smrti* and the *Gautama Dharmasutra.* Asahaya speaks affectionately of Pataliputra as Sripataliputra and mentions 'Thokkuras', a term common only in Bengal and Mithila. These facts are indicative of his place of activity. He perhaps lived in Bengal and graced the court of Dharmapala. However, in spite of having been a resident of Bengal, he regards it as the right of unmarried sister to have one-fourth share by way of the provision for her marriage which is the same as in the *Mitakshara.* On the succession to the *sulka* of a woman, Asahaya held that even step brothers should be given something, though the major portion goes to full brothers.[101]

Visvarupa

Visvarupa is an important commentator on *Yajnavalkya Smrti.* His work is called the *Balakrida.* Kane thinks that he probably lived during the first quarter of the 9th century and perhaps belonged to the Deecan and graced the court of some early Chalukya king. He has written elaborately on *achara* and *prayaschitta,* which is of not much use for us. But he also makes a detailed study of the question of partition, and here he anticipates Vijnanesvara in holding that ownership does not arise for the first time on partition, but that partition takes place of what is already jointly owned. Commenting on Yajnavalkya he allows father the freedom to distribute property among his sons during his life-time.[102] It seems that his provision about father's freedom refers to self-acquired property. Further, he held that if father makes equal division then he will give equal shares, like that of the sons, to the widow whose husband or fathers-in-law have not given them any share of property.[103] The noticeable point of Visvarupa is that he does not mention two kinds of property : *sapratibandha* (obstructible) and *apratibandha* (unobstructible).

Medhatithi

Medhatithi is one of the few commentators whose work has not only survived, but is still reckoned as one of the pre-eminent authorities on all the questions relating to inheritance. His opinions are held in the highest esteem and his interpretation of the law of the country before the age of Vijnanesvara is valuable. We can usefully refer to Medhatithi to see what the state of the law in question was before the time of the author of the *Mitakshara*. The commentary of Medhatithi is of utmost value in throwing light on the obscure portions of the *Mitakshara* law. He is the oldest commentator on the *Manu Smrti,* wherein he compares its various provisions with other *Sutra* and *Smrti* writers such as Gautama, Baudhayana, Narada, Brhaspati and others. Since he quotes Asahaya and Kumarila, he most probably lived between 825-900 A.D.[104] There are two divergent opinions about the place to which he belonged. According to one opinion he was Southerner while according to the other he was a Kashmiri.[105] Medhatithi's importance lies in the fact that he has modified the opinion of Manu in accordance with his own times. While commenting on an unknown authority of Manu, Medhatithi writes that Manu's dictum that the eldest son should get an additional share in his father's property belongs to an earlier age and should not be applied to the present age. Manu was certainly the basis of Medhatithi's law, but the great commentator knew how to impart Manu's laws a contemporary meaning and relevance. But he too did not touch upon many a controversial points of the *Manu Smrti*.

Generally speaking, the period under review was one of decline and decadence in all the spheres of cultural activity. By this time, Buddhism and Jainism had lost their dominant position and had become confined to some particular regions. The rise of the Tantrika cults had brought corruption both in Buddhism and Brahmanical religion. Literature had become less creative and more artificial. The pursuits of science were now less active. The age of the original *Smrtis* had passed away, ushering in the age of the commentaries. It was felt that the era of authoritative creation in the field of religion, philosophy, law, manners and moral was now over and all that remained for the people was to understand the past and follow it as scrupulously as possible.[106] Nevertheless the commentators of this period were outstanding intellectuals whose views were, and still are, held in high esteem.

Women's Right to Own Property : Wife

There is little evidence of any change in the status of wife. Nearly all the writings and commentaries of this period expect absolute obedience and devotion of wives to their husbands. Medhatithi[107] says that husband and wife differ only in their bodies but are one entity in their functions. Ancient jurisprudence shows little deviation from this position but prescribes minimum rights in succession or inheritance to a wife. A woman, a slave, and a son, are said to be poor in the *Matsya Purana,* for the wealth acquired by them belongs to their master.[108] Such a statement is quite similar to the age-old saying of Manu wherein he equates wife, son and slave as far as their right to property was concerned.[109]

Commenting on the above verse of Manu, Medhatithi[110] states that these three may have property but not ownership. Indeed property acquired by the said three persons is owned or possessed by the one to whom they themselves belong. Thus the property of the wife belongs to the husband, that of the son to the father, and that of the slave to the master. It means that the said persons are dependent and subservient. The wife should not use her property for any purpose except with the sanction of the husband, nor the son without the sanction of the father, nor the slave without the sanction of the master. He further states that according to other *Smrtikaras,* in times of distress, the master may take what belongs to his slaves, just as a father can take what belongs to his son and a husband can take what belongs to his wife.[111] Further, according to Manu, a wife could not have any share in the property during the life-time of her husband but she was to be maintained in case she was faithful.[112] All this went a long way in restricting the right of inheritance by woman. Medhatithi held that the above views hold good and clearly mean that a wife is to be maintained under various circumstances which he elaborated at great length. According to a verse attributed to Manu and quoted by Medhatithi,[113] "the virtuous wife is to be maintained even by committing a hundred bad acts."[114] The wife, even though guilty of grievous sins, must not be turned out of the house, says Medhatithi. The punishment by confiscation prescribed by Manu for a wife is most probably intended to be a warning to her to reform herself, for he does not sanction to confiscation of all her belongings. Medhatithi[115] also makes it obligatory on the husband going abroad to make provision for his wife in his absence. This is not surprising, as according to Medhatithi the husband must not take to journey abroad leaving his wife behind, except for the specific purposes mentioned by Manu. The law on the subject of the wife's maintenance is summed up by

Medhatithi in another context wherein he says, "faithful wife must not be abandoned, even though she may be disagreeable in looks, or harsh in speech, and the like."[116] On the other hand, the unfaithful wife may be confined to a room when she is guilty of a single act of transgression; but if she repeats the offence she is to be abandoned. Referring to Yajnavalkya's text allowing a mere subsistence to an unfaithful wife, Medhatithi observed that the above provision applies when the husband is able and willing to maintain her but if he is not willing, she may be abandoned.[117] "The wife", concludes Medhatithi, "must be maintained even if she hates her husband, but if she becomes outcaste she may be abandoned." However, he has nothing to comment on the verse where Manu lays down that a woman could not take anything from the family property which is common to many or out of her own property, without the permission of the husband.[118] Thus it is clear that the wife's position existed only by virtue of her relationship with her husband.

Similar views are expressed by Visvarupa while commenting on the *Yajnavalkya Smrti.* Yajnavalkya allows a share to wife at the time of partition, while the husband and children are all alive; she is eligible to receive a share equal to that of the sons in case she has received no *stridhana.* Visvarupa[119] further states that the wife over whose head the husband has married a second time should be given an amount equal to what has been spent in the second marriage. If *stridhana* has been already been given, then only half shall be given to her. This has to be given only in case where there has been 'suppression' without sufficient reason. Visvarupa[120] also pointed out that the wife was not free to use the family property according to her own wishes, but had to take the permission of her husband.

Stridhana

Notwithstanding what been stated above, women from the earliest times have been given not only the right of maintenance but also a right over a portion of assets termed as *stridhana. Stridhana* has been variously defined in different periods by *Smrti* writers, as well as by commentators. In the process they have limited or expanded the scope of *stridhana.* From about the 7th century A.D. we find a general tendency to enlarge the scope of *stridhana.* According to Devala, "maintenance, ornaments, *sulka* and profits, these would be a woman's property."[121] Thus we can guess the reason why in some place '*sulka*' which was originally a price to the bride's father for giving away the bride, became the bride's perquisite. Even *asura* marriage was grudgingly recognised. The selling of girls, which was the practice in such marriages, began to be condemned in unequivocal terms. It is possible that a section of people among whom *asura* marriage prevailed, the bride's price (*sulka*) was handed over to the bride by her father. Thus *sulka* may have come to be regarded as the bride's portion in the same way as 'Melier' became the bride's property in Semitic societies.

In the *Agni Purana,*[122] *stridhana* is defined as "The estates given to a woman by her father, mother, husband or brother as well as those presented to her near the nuptial fire or those which fall under the denomination of *adhivedanika* are the four classes of *stridhana* recognised by law."

However, Visvarupa[123] describes *stridhana* as what was received before the fire or received at the time of marriage, called '*adhivedanika*', and what is given to wife who has been superseded or what is given for the purpose of suppression. Commenting on Yajnavalkya, he observes that ornament and such other things, mentioned in other *Smrti* texts, given by the father and other relations are also included in the *stridhana*. Even those articles given to the daughter for engagement before marriages are included in it.

Women's Right Over Stridhana : It is gratifying to note that Devala and commentators accord full right to the wife over her *stridhana*. According to Devala,[124] "property given for maintenance, ornaments, fees and gifts, the woman alone can enjoy, and the husband is not entitled to spend it except in distress." In case he spends anything frivolously or enjoys it, he should repay it to the woman with interest but for the treatment of the son he can make use of the woman's property. If he spends the money with her permission and in a loving manner, he should be made to repay only the principal amount from his own property.

Devala further states that the money given by the wife on knowing the husband to be ill or in trouble or harassed by creditors, should be repaid of his own accord.[125] Like Katyayana, Devala believes that the *stridhana* that had been promised by the father should be given by the sons in the same way as his debts are paid by them if the widow stays in the house of her husband and does not go to live in that of her father.

Commenting on Yajnavalkya (II. 146), Visvarupa[126] states that "Having received money from the bridegroom and having given away the maiden, if one takes her back, he should be punished by the king, and be made to pay the bridegroom the expenses incurred by him with interest. On her death the husband should take back what he had given after having cleared off the expenses incurred on both sides." He further says that if a person other than the husband, such as the brother and the like, were to take the property, even at the time of distress—such as famine and the like—he would have to make it good. When a debtor is forced to pay off the debt it is called *sampratirodhaka.* If the husband has taken his wife's money when the city is under a siege or during famines or for performance of religious rites or during illness, he need not repay it to her.[127]

In the *Agni Purana*[128] it is stated that, "A husband is not bound to repay or restore to his wife an estate or a property forming her *stridhana* which he has appropriated in the time of famine, or sold for his medical treatment, or for the purposes of religious acts, or in the event of its being stolen by thieves. A husband marrying a second wife in the life-time of the first, and without having assigned any separate property to her (*stridhana*), should settle on her a *stridhana* equal in value to that had been settled on his first wife, or a half thereof in the event of the first wife having not been similarly provided for."

About the father taking his daughter's property, it is stated in the same *Purana*[129] that "A man by taking back a property or an estate, formally assigned and made over to his daughter, should be liable to punishment, whereas he is bound to defray the expenses incidental to her marriage and maintenance."

Succession to Stridhana : As to the succession to *stridhana,* the texts of various *Smrti* writers are in apparent conflict with each other and the commentators have laid down arbitrary rules. As daughters took nothing from the paternal estate when there were sons, it was thought just that the *stridhana* of the mother should be taken by the daughters and their children. Among daughters, the maiden daughters come before married daughters and among the latter indigent daughters before others. We have seen earlier that Vishnu, Yajnavalkya, Narada and Katyayana all agree in giving this property to the maiden daughter(s) and failing her (them) to other daughters and failing them, according to Narada, to their children.

But during the age of decline women's right in this respect

came to be restricted.[130] Devala states : "When a woman dies her *stridhana* belongs in common to her sons and unmarried daughters who have equal right over all kinds of their mother's *stridhana.*" This provision of Devala is nearer to Manu's distribution scheme of *stridhana,* rather than that of the preceding age, where we find Yajnavalkya and others assigning equal share to daughters only, sons getting only in their absence.

Commenting on Yajnavalkya,[131] Visvarupa says, "Just as sons inherit equal shares in the father's property so the daughters inherit in the mother's property. They shall divide among themselves only what remains after the debts have been paid off; but they shall not pay her debts if the mother has left no property." He, however, did not say that sons have nothing to do with the mother's property. He observes that "in the absence of the daughters the *anvaya,* i.e., sons come in for property." The *Smrtikaras,* however, have explained this sentence to mean that in the absence of daughters, the sons of the daughters get the property. Visvarupa does not agree with it. He says that only in the absence of the daughter, the property should go to the son. Still further he says, '*bandhudatta*', '*sulka*' and '*anvadheya*' gifts go to daughter's *bandhavas,* i.e., uterine brothers and the rest, if the woman dies without an off-spring.[132] However, this rule becomes applicable only after the death of the mother. In the case of *stridhana* of a kind other than the above three, if the woman has been married according to any of the four forms of marriage beginning with the *Brahma* (i.e., *Brahma, Daiva Arsha* and *Prajapatya*), her *stridhana* goes to her husband if she had no child; if she had children then to her daughters.[133]

Medhatithi[134] commenting on Manu says, "The term '*yautaka*' is usually applied to the separate property of a woman, of which she alone is the owner others; apply it only to what she receives at the time of marriage and not to all her belongings, as it is only over the former that she has absolute right and which on that account can be called absolutely her own. It has also seen been declared that what a woman makes out of what she receives from her husband for her clothing and ornaments and for the daily household expenses is the share of the unmarried daughters alone." Since the texts add the qualification 'unmarried', it is clear that what is said here does not apply to one who has been married. Similarly, it does not apply to the appointed daughter (*putrika*)[135] Asahaya held that as regards the succession to the *sulka* of a woman, even step-brothers should be given something though the major portion would go to full brothers.[136] Commenting on Narada (I. 20) he states that when the widow having a son, possessing *stridhana,* blinded by sexual passion forsakes the son and takes to another husband with her *stridhana,* her *stridhana,* is taken by the other husband and not by the sons from the former husband. Those having no *stridhana* but possessing property left by the former husband, that property is not taken by the other husband.

It is mentioned in the *Agni Purana*[137] that "The *bandhus* of a woman dying without any issues, should inherit the estate presented by her friends and relations as well as those Anvadheyaka. Husbands of all castes should inherit the *stridhana* left by their respective wives dying without issue, while their daughters should be deemed as the legal heir to such properties in the event of their having any female child; otherwise the property would revert to the father of the deceased."

Widow

It has been discussed in the previous Chapter that the introduction of widow as an heir and settling her place in the series of heirs seems to have been a matter which was accomplished only after a log controversy amongst the authors of the *Smrtis.* Vrdha-Manu,[138] Vishnu,[139] Brhaspati,[140] and Yajnavalkya[141] are clear and definite that the first heir of a sonless man in his widow. On the other hand, Narada[142] states that when a sonless man died his wife (or wives) is entitled only to maintenance and that the heirs are his brothers who should take the property. Sankha[143] puts the wife in the list of heirs but says that her place is after brothers and parents. Katyayana[144] remained ambiguous. There were thus texts of *Smrtis* which favoured the widow's claim though they differed as to her exact place in the list of heirs.

In the north-western region, Muslim invaders penetrated quite deep into the Punjab; yet it seems that the Hindu law codes continued to be accepted and as such *Devala Smrti* has much information for us on this point. According to Devala[145] a sonless widow had the right of maintenance. In case a man died sonless, his property was to be inherited in order of priority by his brothers, the daughters of the same caste, the father if he was living, the half-brothers of the same caste, and lastly the mother. The widow came last, only in the absence of the above claimants. But the widow was given the right of maintenance whoever succeeded to the property.

It is clear from the above order of succession that a widow was considered almost an outsider in the family as compared to the above-mentioned inheritors. In practice there was little possibility left for her inheriting even a little property left by the deceased.

Besides Devala, there are two important commentators of this period, viz., Medhatithi and Visvarupa. Since Manu had not given even remote right of inheritance to the widow, Medhatithi had nothing to comment or add on it. This is confirmed by Kulluka who states that Medhatithi held that the widow is prohibited from inheriting her husband's wealth.[146] However, Medhatithi, too, allows the maintenance to the widow. According to him a widow, who remains faithful to her husband's memory, deserves to have her property looked after by the king, but in a contrary case (i.e. unfaithfulness) she is not only to be disqualified from possessing property but also to be banished.[147]

The commentators, who were opposed to women taking the *daya,* tried to explain it in such a way as to whittle down her right. They said that a wife could get the *daya* not independently in her own right but only in conjunction with her son or with her husband. Thus the texts of *Smrtis,* which said that the wife was an heir to a sonless husband, should be understood, as explained by Visvarupa, to mean that the widow of a sonless man would be his heir if she was pregnant at the time of the death of her husband, or if she intended to produce a son for her husband by cohabiting with his brother according to rules of the ancient practice of *niyoga.*[148] He also quotes a verse from Vasishtha in support of his view wherein it is stated that brothers should postpone partition till those widows who are childless, obtain sons.[149] This shows that the pregnant widow also gets some inheritance. In case a female child is born, she becomes a *putrika.* Again Visvarupa quotes a verse from Gautama in support of his views and holds that the word 'wife' indicates the pregnant widow.

He further holds that father distributing his property in his life-time has absolute discretion in giving equal or unequal shares to the sons. Here he also implies that the father giving equal shares to the sons shall allow the husband's share to the wife as also to the widow of his predeceased sons and grand-sons, who have not been provided with *stridhana.* Visvarupa here seems to anticipate modern legislation as her states that the widow of predeceased sons and grand-sons should also be given the shares that could have been taken by their husbands, if they were alive at the time of partition.

The *Smrti Samgrahakara* also maintained that the wife would take the estate of her sonless husband if she submitted to *niyoga* and procured a son for her husband. The *Samgrahakara*[150] allows only that the widow, whose husband was a separated coparcener dying childless, would inherit his whole estate if she submitted to *niyoga* at the behest of her elders. This view of *Smrti Samgrahakara* derives support from earlier writers, Gautama,[151] Vasistha[152] and Manu,[153] who had supported *niyoga,* except where it was resorted to because of the greed of wealth.

Bharuchi also allows *niyoga* to a childless widow and thereby gives her some right in the property till a male issue was born. But Srikara held the view that the widow succeeded to her deceased husband's estate if it was small, and was given maintenance only if it was large.

An interesting order of succession is found in the *Agni Purana,* which is perhaps more reliable in the face of the contradictory views of the commentators. According to the *Agni Purana,*[154] the wife, daughter, parents, brothers, their sons, persons belonging to the same gotra, bandhus, disciples (in the case of Brahmacharin) should be successively deemed as heirs to a sonless man. This rule and order of succession applied to all castes.

A king would manage the property of a widow, who is the mother of a minor child or of those who have not legitimate guardians or relations of their own to protect them in their period of widowhood. Property settled on widow, who had been faithful as wife during the covertures of her marriage and who was unable because of ill health or incapacity to manage her estate to her own benefits, shall also pass under the wardenship of the sovereign. And any attempt on the part of their relations to rob or encroach upon a portion of this should be meted out punishment as for an act of theft.[155]

We may conclude from the above discussion that the tendencies of limiting the right of a sonless widow of the preceding period persisted during this age also. The liberal outlook of Yajnavalkya did not seem to have a significant effect as it is stated in the *Agni Purana* only. The orthodox views of Manu and Narada formed the basis of the ideology of the commentators of this age. Medhatithi, Visvarupa, Bharuchi and the *Smrti Samgrahakara* all represented the conservative philosophy. Bharuchi and the *Smrti Samgrahakara* allowed the widow to be an heir only if she submitted to *niyoga*. This virtually amounted to denying her the right of inheritance, for *niyoga* had fallen into disrepute by the 7th century A.D. And even if a woman resorted to *niyoga* her ownership would be short-lived as it would be terminated with the birth of a child. Srikara's proposal was also a half-way measure, as he stated that the widow could succeed to her husband's estate if it was small.

Daughter

In the previous Chapters we have studied the rules regarding the daughter's right to succession and inheritance. It is recalled that the daughter's right was limited to a portion required for her marriage and that the married daughters had no share. The process of evolution passed through a difficult struggle before daughter's right to inheritance was recognised. Let us now consider her position from various stand-points during this period.

Daughter with Brothers : The feeling that a woman could not be the receiver of *daya,* persisted in this age. Some commentators and digest writers of this age began to question the explanation of the text of Yajnavalkya where he said that one-fourth share should be given to a daughter. Some thought that daughter as woman could not take the *daya* or any part of it; what was given to her was to be treated as a gift and not as inheritance from her father. Some thought that what Yajnavalkya meant was that the provision should be made for her maintenance and marriage, and that when Yajnavalkya said that a daughter was an heir he meant that the daughter should be given as much as was necessary for her maintenance and marriage. As soon as she was married she went away to another family, and henceforth the responsibility for maintaining her lay with her husband and his family. Thus, the right given to her by Yajnavalkya was restricted by some commentators only to gifts. Commenting on Yajnavalkya, Visvarupa[156] remarks that the brothers should perform the marriage ceremony of their sisters and for that purpose if there was no money set apart by the father then only they should give one-fourth part of their share. From his interpretation it would appear that the commentator was not in favour of giving one-fourth part as a rule, for it was to be given in the event of non-availability of any means for the purpose of marriage, which obviously tended to curtail the rights of the daughter.

Commenting on Manu, Medhatithi[2] says that the term *kanya* as a rule is used in the sense of unmarried girl; in another *Smrti* text the term *amudha* is used for an unmarried girl. The share that is to be set apart should be taken as relating only to the unmarried daughters of the same caste. Each of the brothers should give to the sister of the same caste as himself the fourth part of his own share; that is to say, in case where the father has left several unmarried daughters, the share allotted to each of them should be the fourth part of the portion of the brother belonging to the same caste as himself. The upshot, therefore, appears to be that the three parts of the property shall be taken by his sons and the fourth part shall be set apart for the marriage of the unmarried daughters. The allotment of the one-fourth share clearly indicates that in marriage unlimited expenses are not to be incurred.[157]

Medhatithi further observes that to some people the only benefit to which the girl is entitled is that her marriage should be performed, as is the custom also. But the direct assertion of the *Smrti* is definitely more authoritative than custom; moreover, the custom referred to is by no means universal. Another view that has been held is that the daughter shall receive just enough property to suffice for the performance of her marriage; and not exactly the fourth part of share. But this would make the rule indefinite; their being no specific understanding as to what is required for the performance of the marriage. Then again we have Yajnavalkya's text[158] laying down, "That the brothers who have had their sacramental rites already performed, should perform the same for the unmarried girls, and sisters should receive from their brothers the fourth part of their share." The term *bhratarah* or brothers has often been taken to mean uterine brothers. But if that were so, then the girl who has no uterine brother would have to go without a share in the property; the would not be any chance for a dowry being provided for her. It might be argued that her step-brother would provide for her; but in the absence of such a rule, he may not do it. In reality, the term 'brother' has been used in the sense of sons of the same father, though they may have been from different mothers.

Medhatithi's discussion leads to the conclusion that the brothers would commit sin by not giving a fourth share of their property, but there is no legal force to compel them to give it except that those not inclined to give would be outcastes. Devala[159] states that out of the father's property that amount of wealth shall be given to the daughters which may be needed for their marriage. It is also clear from the words of Devala that emphasis was not so much on assigning a share to the daughter as on providing sufficient provision for her marriage.

Bharuchi was also of the opinion that the unmarried sisters were only entitled to a provision for their marriage and not to a fourth share.[160] The *Parasaramadhaviya* and the *Sarasvativilasa* also confirm his views. The *Mitakshara,*[161] however, says that the explanation of "the fourth share" to be given to the unmarried sisters of fered by Asahaya and Medhatithi was the proper one and not that of Bharuchi.

Thus it may be inferred that the main anxiety of the law-givers was to make a provision for the marriage of the unmarried daughters and for this purpose the allotment of one-fourth share by the brothers was propounded by them. In this context it would not be improper to add that the marriage was considered obligatory for girls, and if by ill-luck, the parents could not perform it in their life-time, it was the sacred duty of the brothers to perform their marriage. It was naturally laid down that any reasonable expenses in connection with their marriages should be a charge on the family property.

Brotherless Daughter : A brotherless daughter was taken into the scheme of kinship and inheritance only through the institution of *putrika,* and a series of statements of Manu referred to in Chapter 4 seem to represent the evolution of her rights in her father's property in the correct historical order. After a study of the *Smrti* literature along with its commentaries and digests, we find that perhaps the daughter's rights were recognised earlier than those of the widow. The daughter entered the family by birth whereas the wife entered it after marriage. This caused a great difference between them. The daughter, just like the son, was born of the body of the father and if the son was heir by the right of his being born of the father, the daughter too should have the same right. If a son was the source of future generations, the daughter also was such a source, though it is true that the issues of the son would remain in the father's family, whereas the issues of the daughter would go to her husband's family.

We have seen that in the first stage a daughter is given away in marriage by a sonless father with the hope that a son born of her marriage would be as good as his son. It may be noted that the right of inheritance is given to the son of the *putrika* alone. The next stage comes when the daughter qualifies to succession by mere intention of the father to make her a *putrika.* At this stage the *putrika* herself steps into the position of a son till she gives birth to her own son. The next stage is when the daughter, *putrika* or no *putrika,* is deemed to be the heir in her independent right and the son of the daughter as heir is definitely placed after the daughter. This stage is already reached in the texts of Yajnavalkya, Vishnu and Brhaspati[162] and continued upto C. 7th century A.D. As the position of the daughter of a sonless father declined, the commentators again resorted to stricter interpretation of the verses of Yajnavalkya, Vishnu and Brhaspati[163] in favour of *putrika* only. Similarly, Visvarupa also restricts the inheritance by pushing the order of succession of daughter into the background and it is only *putrika* who can inherit, according to him.

Among the Brahmanas, the duty of offering oblations to a deceased grand-father was laid upon both the son's son and the daughter's son. A man with only a daughter or daughters as his issues could make a declaration that the daughters or one of the daughters who is appointed as *putrika,* was like a son and her sons were like son's sons. Even without declaring a daughter to be a *putrika,* the father could give the daughter in marriage to a person with the condition that the son born to the daughter would be his son. Thus commenting on Yajnavalkya,[164] Visvarupa states : "Daughter means appointed daughter." He quotes the verse of Manu to support his view. Manu bestowed the right only upon the appointed daughter. Visvarupa says, "the son is as one's ownself and the daughter is like the son. How could another person take the property when there is likelihood of a son being born to her ? She takes in default of the son. The plural here is used to mean plurality of appointed daughters. The word *Cha* (and), though means jointly, indicates here to taking the wealth at option. The word *cha* (and) indicates that the rule is a general one."

When brothers were living in a joint family and one of them died leaving no child but a pregnant wife, and a daughter was born to him posthumously, Visvarupa suggests[165] that the daughter would be regarded as a *putrika* and equal to a son, and would be a member of the joint family or coparcenary with all the rights of a son along with her uncles. Thus gradually the claim of the daughter as an heir to the father became established.

Commenting on Manu, Medhatithi[166] interprets the word

'*duhita* as applicable to the *putrika* only. He states that "the father shall declare that the son born of her (*putrika*) shall be mine" and that her son shall inherit his property when the father dies. If the daughter too had no son, it would seem that she could not inherit her father's property. Therefore, commenting on Manu he lays down that the daughter shall inherit it.

According to the *Brahma Purana* "That daughter alone is known as appointed daughter who is made like a son by her sonless father, either in his mind, or in the presence of the king, fire and relations, or anywhere else." Whoever in given to the bridegroom without taking the bride-price or married after her father's death, she is known a *putrika*. Such a daughter receives an equal share from the paternal estate.

Srikara, like Visvarupa, holds the view that *duhitarah* in Yajnavalkya refers to the *putrika* only. According to the *Smritisamgraha,* the widow comes first in order of succession to a sonless man, and then comes a daughter who is a *putrika.*[167]

Thus all we can say is that the commentators of this period are of the view that only the appointed daughter is entitled to inherit the property of a sonless man. Kane[168] says that as the usage of appointing daughter as son became obsolete, the ordinary daughter came to be recognised by analogy as an heir to a sonless man after the widow. However, his contention is not tenable in view of the large commentaries on Visvarupa and Medhatithi who influenced quite a large part of the society as is confirmed by later commentators. Thus it may be concluded that the earlier custom of appointing *putrika* seemed to have been revived by the commentators of this age.

It is, however, surprising to note that when Brhaspati, Yajnavalkya, and Narada declare the daughter as an heir they meant an ordinary daughter. It is declared by Vasistha that the *putrika* comes third in order of priority among the different kinds of sons. *Putrika* thus being in the category of sons inherits like the son, even when the widow exists. And thus while the *putrika* is the heir on failure of *aurasa* son, her right of inheritance in default of the widow, as mentioned by the *Smrtikaras* of the age of progress, was not accepted by the early commentators. Kane[169] states that though the words of Yajnavalkya, Vishnu and Brhaspati were clear enough, the ancient commentators were not prepared to accept them in their literal sense. However, Devala's views are quite emphatic as to the right of a legitimate unmarried daughter of the same caste in the same way as the son.[170]

Mother

Mother occupied a very high position in the ancient Indian society. Even in this age her position did not decline.[171] We learn from a copper plate inscription found from Nalanda that Devapala's mother Rannadevi was honoured as an incarnation of the Goddess of Fortune, the Earth Goddess in a visible form, an embodiment of king's glory and tutelary deity of the royal household.[172] Among the Smrti writers, as we have already seen there are divergent opinions as to the preference about the inheritance of parents. Manu[173] at one place prefers father to mother and at another[174] place mother to father. Thus Manu was not definite about the preference among the parents. Katyayana[175] prefers father among the parents, while Brhaspati[176] is the only *Smrtikara* who preferred mother when a son died without leaving his own wife or issue. However, during the period under review it is only Devala, who places the mother after the half-brothers. He gives the following order of succession, i.e., full brothers, daughters, father, half-brothers, mother and widow.

Commenting on Yajnavalkya, Visvarupa[177] states that the mother, who has no *stridhana* of her own, shall receive a share equal to that of her son. The word 'mother' here stands for the father's wives in general, as all such wives would be equally related to the dead father. Visvarupa[178] further explains another verse of Yajnavalkya that '*pitarau*' means mother and the father. Though both have joint rights, yet the fact that they have been mentioned in a copulative compound shows that each one of them is entitled to inherit. Yet, the mother comes first, since this has been clearly stated in the text that 'the mother shall inherit the property of her childless son.'[179] Visvarupa further states that we have also the text declaring, "*Pita haredaputrasya riktham*"[180] i.e. the father shall take the property of her sonless son. The latter text is taken as applying to cases where the mother is dead.[181] Srikara holds that both parents, if alive, succeed together. But the *Dayabhaga, Smrti Chandrika* and others criticise this view, as discussed in the next Chapter.

Medhatithi, however, did hot comment on these verses of Manu,[182] in which he has mentioned the mother's right to inherit the property of her childless son.

Taking an over-all picture of this age we find that the general position and proprietary rights of women declined. As regards the position of the wife the scope of *stridhana* was enlarged by Devala, but in times of distress the husband could take away her *stridhana* without returning it in future.

Similarly, while in the earlier age even an ordinary daughter could inherit her father's property, in this period only a *putrika* has such rights, implying that eventually only her son would get the property even in mother's *stridhana.* She had to share the assets with her brothers.

As for the widow, she got her husband's property only in case she submitted to *niyoga,* again implying that only her son or daughter (*putrika*) would get the property ultimately. Finally, the position of the mother was not better, since her priority in the order of succession declined too; now it was put after half brothers.

However, women's right of maintenance as wife, daughter, widow and mother remained in tact. In case of partition during the husband's life-time, wife would get a share equal to that of sons if, ofcourse, she did not have *stridhana*; if she had, her share would be reduced to a half only. To make her position further secure, the former wife would get maintenance from her husband equal to the expenses incurred in the second marriage. The principle of spending one-fourth of inheritance from the father's property on sister's marriage also continued more or less.

The commentaries and Nibandhas served the very useful purpose of giving a detailed account of the different texts as written in various periods in ancient India. As a matter of fact, the existence of many ancient texts would not have been known had they not been referred to, or quoted by different commentators. Indeed, the Nibandhas and commentaries have played an important part in the development of the Hindu Law. The period under study is incidentally the point of conflux of the ancient law and the new law as it evolved then. It was a remarkable period from the point of law of partition and inheritance. When find two special schools on them developed through the commentaries, one, the *Mitakshara* and the other, the *Dayabhagta.*[183]

The Sources : Jitendriya

Jimutavahana in his *Kalaviveka, Vyavaharamatrka* and *Dayabhaga* refers to Jitendriya's comments on the subject of partition and succession.[184] Jitendriya lived in Bengal, probably between 1000 to 1050 A.D. It appears that he was one of the immediate predecessors of Jimutavahana and his work, though now lost, was a fairly comprehensive one. It seems that his importance was completely eclipsed by the brilliant Jimutavahana.[185] Jitendriya laid down that the daughter's son should succeed immediately after the daughter. He also held that the sonless widow of a deceased person, whether living separately or in a joint family, shall succeed her husband's estate. Further, while elaborating the general rule, he lays down that whatever a person acquires by his own abilities, that is, without using the means or materials jointly owned by other members of the family, becomes his exclusive property.

Balaka

The next commentator in importance is Balaka,[186] who is also known only from the citations in the works of Jimutavahana, Raghunandana and Sulapani. Like Jitendriya he also advocated the right of the succession of a daughter's son.[187] He is most likely identical with Valoka, who is mentioned six times in the *Prayaschitta Prakarana* of Bhatta Bhavadeva.[188] Balarupa, another writer, is also taken by Kane[189] to be the same as Balaka on the basis of the evidence given in *Dayabhaga*. This is, however, debatable. However, in all probability, Balarupa belonged to Bengal and flourished before 1100 A.D. Basing his views on Parasara, Balarupa held that the unmarried daughter of a sonless man is to be preferred to the married one as an heir. According to him, the order of succession is as follows : (1) *Atmabandhus* (one's own relatives), (2) *pitrbandhus* (father's cognates), and lastly (3) *matrbandhus* (mother's cognates).[190]

Yogloka

Yogloka is a writer whom we know only from the work of Jimutavahana and Raghunandana. He was perhaps a native of Bengal and may have lived between 950 A.D. and 1010 A.D. There is not much to be said of his views on inheritance. He held with Srikara that if the owner is present, adverse possession of movable property for ten years and immovable property for twenty years entails loss of title.[191] Yogloka wrote at least one *Kala* and one *Vyavadhara,* and composed two treatises on *Kala.*

Dharesvara

Dharesvara Bhoja Deva is identified with Bhoja Paramara, the famous king, who ruled for 40 years from 1005 A.D. to about 1045 A.D. He is remembered as the king who is supposed to have called an assembly of eminent Panditas to make the first authentic digest of law which, it seems, is lost. Whether Bhoja composed one or two books on *Dharmasastra,* or whether his work was a commentary or an independent digest, is difficult to say. However as he is quoted by every commentator as Dharesvara (Lord of Dhara, the capital of Malwa) his law must have been the law of Northern India. There are several points on which the *Mitakshara* disagrees with Dharesvara. We may particularly mention here the instances of the widow's and the grand-mother's right of succession. Dharesvara held ownership to be known only from *sastra* (i.e., spiritual) while the *Mitakshara* held it to be *laukika* (i.e., of this world). Dharesvara held that the word *'duhitrah'* in Yajnavalkya stands for *putrika* in the order of succession. However, on some other points, the views of Dharesvara coincide with those of the *Mitakshara,* namely, on the right of succession of the daughter's son, on father's inability to give a greater share to his sons on partition during his life-time, etc.

Haradatta

Haradatta's fame rests on the commentaries over *Gautamadharmasutra* and *Apastambadharmasutra.* The former is more concise than the latter. Various references indicate that Haradatta may have been an inhabitant of Southern India. *Viramitrodaya* counts Haradatta and Devannabhatta among the southern *nibandhakaras.*[1] He must have lived before Vijnanesvara. Kane places him between 1100-1300 A.D.[193] Like Medhatithi, Haradatta also denies the widow's right to inheritance.[194] After Vijnanesvara, hardly any writer assigns the same position to the widow as Haradatta does.

Vijnanesvara

Vijnanesvara, the writer of the *Mitakshara,* is recognised as an authority on law all over India except in the Punjab, Malabar, Bengal and Asam. The *Mitakshara* is a commentary over the *Yajnavalkya Smrti.* The date of the composition of this book, as surmised by Kane, is between 1070 and 1100 A.D.[195] Vijnanesvara was a religious mendicant. In the concluding verses of the *Mitakshara,* he styles himself as 'Vijnanayogi'. The later writers also frequently refer to him as such. Vijnanesvara prominence as a learned ascetic enabled him to overrule the great commentaries of Visvarupa and Dharesvara. In all, he has referred to over eighty *Smrtis* and *Smrtikaras* in his *Mitakshara,* but it stands to his credit that he was able to present a compact compendium.

Govindaraja

Govindaraja was one of the commentators on *Manu Smrti.* He wrote *Smrti Manjari* which deals with all the main topics of *Dharmasastra.* Govindaraja lived on the holy banks of the river Ganga. Kane assigned him to the period 1000-1110 A.D., since he has mentioned Dharesvara Bhoj Raja and is himself mentioned in the *Kalpataru* and the *Dayabhaga.*

Apararka

Apararka was the author of the *Apararka-Yajnavalkya Dharmasastra Nibandha,* a commentary or rather a digest, as the very name implies. He was a Silahara king and profusely quotes from the *Grhyasutra* and the *Dharmasutra.* Some of the views usually associated with Jimutavahana were really propounded by Apararka. Apararka bases the right of a claimant to take a deceased person's property on the spiritual benefit conferred by the former on the latter.[196] But in several other respect, he differs from the *Mitakshara.* Apararka prefers a father to a mother as an heir to a sonless son.

The *Mitakshara* and the work of Apararka belonged to the same period but neither of them makes any reference to the other. The doctrine propounded by both the authors are often the same, but it is not clear which one of them borrowed from the other or whether both of them were indebted to a common source.[197]

Jimutavahana

Jimutavahana, the author of the *Dayabhaga,* perhaps lived in the last quarter of the eleventh and the first half of the twelfth century of the Christian era. He is the most popular and the leading authority among the later commentators and writers of digests in Bengal.

In Bengal the *Dayabhanga,* the most famous work of Jimutavahana, is the main source of Hindu law on subjects such as inheritance, partition, *stridhana* and re-union. Jimutavahana brushed aside the archaic convention of two kinds of properties. viz., obstructed and unobstructed,[198] and enunciated only one course of succession, whether the family was divided or undivided or the property was ancestral or self-acquired.[199] Unlike Vijnanesvara he defines *stridhana* in a strictly technical sense as that which a woman can give, sell or enjoy independently of her husband.[200] He lays down his rules of succession to a woman's *stridhana.* He says that such property would equally devolve upon the sons and unmarried daughters.[201]

Devannabhatta

Devannabhatta belonged to southern India and lived between 1150-1225 A.D. He wrote a very extensive commentary called *Smrti Chandrika*[202] quoting profusely numerous authors. He examines their views and offers his own interpretation. Though duly respectful towards the general theory of the *Mitakshara* that a son acquires by the birth the ownership of ancestral property, he criticises many views of the *Mitakshara* in detail. The *Smrti Chandrika* does not accept the definition of the word *daya* as given in the *Mitakshara.* It also does not countenance the unequal distribution of ancestral property,[203] or that the mother should be preferred to the father in the case of succession to the property of a sonless deceased son. The *Smrti Chandrika* enjoins that both the parents should succeed together[204] and advocates spiritual benefit as the guiding principle of succession.[205]

Kullukabhatta

Kulluka's commentary on *Manu Smrti* called *Manvarthamuktavali* is the most famous of all the commentaries on Manu. He avoids all unnecessary discussions and is unequivocal. He is not original, and draws upon the commentaries of Medhatithi and Govindaraja. He was very proud of his achievement and said that neither Medhatithi nor Govindaraja, nor any other commentator explained in the way he did, and that explanatory material like his would be difficult to find elsewhere.[206] He not only criticized Govindaraja severely, but also points out the mistakes of Medhatithi. According to Kane, he flourished between 1150 A.D. and 1300 A.D. and probably wrote in c. 1250 A.D.[207]

After this brief survey of the works of the writers of digests[208] and commentaries belonging to the period under study, we may now discuss the main rules regarding the property rights of women.

Wife

The *Smrti* writers and commentators of this age are not unanimous as to the right of succession by a woman. The lawgivers, who disapprove it, have based their opinion on two ancient texts[209] which declare the general in competency of women to inherit. The *Dayabhaga*[210] upholds these texts and agrees that women, other than those mentioned in the *Smrti* texts, cannot have a claim to inheritance.

Jimutavahana, in support of the Smrti texts, argues that the daughter, the widow, the mother, and the paternal grand-mother have a right to succession to the property of the paternal grand-father. The text of Yajnavalkya[211] regarding succession agrees with the above statement. The term *gotraja* occurring there, means 'those born in the family', and the female *sapindas* are hence excluded, as they are not born in the family.[212] According to the text of *Dayabhaga,* as the word used in *gotraja* and it occurs in masculine singular form, it precludes the notion of any female *gotraja* entitled to succession.[213] Kulluka and Apararka follow the version of *Dayabhaga.* Vijnanesvara treats *gotraja* as a plural form in his *Mitakshara.* He gives a different interpretation of *gotraja* and includes all the blood relatives belonging to the same family (*gotra*) and this definition of the term, while including the wives, excludes the daughters of the *gotraja* on the pretext that they are transferred to different *gotras* after marriage, which is essential for a girl according to law-givers. However, daughters are included as *bandhus* by him.[214]

The *Smrti Chandrika,* on the other hand, argues that the plural term applied to *gotraja* denotes both male and female. But Devannabhatta clings to the old interpretation that as the general incapability of women to succession has been declared by the Smrti itself, the passage of Yajnavalkya must relate only to men. As regards Manu's (VIII. 416) version that the wife, the son and the slave are paupers since whatever they earn belongs to the master, Davannabhatta comments that this does not mean that the wife is really without property; all that it means is that as far as spending is concerned, she is not entirely independent. She can make use of the property with the permission of her husband.[215] Vijnanesvara said with respect to the wife that it was true that a woman was unfree but this lack of freedom did not come in the way of her acquiring property.[216]

Kulluka holds the opinion that Manu's well-known position regarding property right cannot be accepted literally. Indeed Manu has himself enumerated six kinds of *stridhana* for women. He also entitles her to the performance of sacrifices, which she can do out of her own property with the permission of her husband.[217]

Haradatta,[218] however, excludes women from inheritance on the basis of a passage of the Vedas. He says that though the Vedic text is very sweeping and general, it is meant to exclude women other than those explicitly mentioned in the *Smrtis*. Devannabhatta, in the *Smrti Chandrika,* says that the Vedic passage must be taken as not referring to those women who are explicitly mentioned.[219] Apararka holds that the Vedic text excludes women only when there is a son.[220] The *Dayabhaga* quoting Baudhayana remarks that the wife is entitled to inherit because of the references found in the *Yajnavalkya* and *Vishnu Smrtis* in her favour.[221]

A great deal of injustice has been done to women by not keeping in view the great distinction between the early law contained in the codes, and its later development by commentators in respect to their disabilities and rights. There cannot be any doubt that women were originally disqualified from owning and holding property and this disability continued as a highly generalised rule.

Stridhana

Scope and Definition : Of all the commentators, the author of the *Mitakshara* has been the most favourable one towards women's proprietory rights. The prevailing tendency in his writings shows that a woman may acquire property precisely in the same way as a man does and no distinction is made about the property obtained by her on the basis of the mode of acquisition. Even inheritance is not excluded from *stridhana*. There can be no doubt that Vijnanesvara wanted to extend the original scope of *stridhana* and has in fact given an unlimited expansion to their capacity for holding property. He supports his theory by the text of Yajnavalkya to which he gives the highest importance. Commenting on the text he says "that which is given by the father, by the mother, by the husband or by a brother and that which is presented (to the bride) by the maternal uncles and the rest of them, at the time of wedding before the nuptial fire, and a first or second marriage or gratuity on account of suppression, as will be subsequently explained (to a woman whose husband marries a second wife, let him give an equal share as compensation for the supersession) likewise, as indicated by the word *adyam* (etc.), property which she may have acquired by inheritance, purchase, partition, acceptance or finding." All these kinds of property are denominated as women's property by Manu and other ancient sages also.[222]

The first portion of the above definition is a repetition of the definition of *stridhana* as given by Yajnavalkya. The second part of the above definition is the expansion by Vijnanesvara of the word *adyam* which occurs in Yajnavalkya's definition of *stridhana* so as to include in *stridhana* five distinct kinds of property which were not recognised as *stridhana* by the early sages. Manu recognised only six kinds of *stridhana*, but Vijnanesvara explains this restriction by saying that all that was meant by Manu's text was that the number could be more but not less than six. He further says that the term *'stridhana'* conforms in its import with its etymology and is not technical. Thus, according to the *Mitakshara* law, the property of any description belonging to a woman is *stridhana* and also property vested in her by any legal means earned or otherwise received through inheritance, purchase or partition.[223]

Vijnanesvara is supported in this view by a large number of commentators of medieval times, such as Kamalakara, Balabhatta, Nandapandita, Rudradeva and Apararka.[224]

Apararka also adopts a liberal interpretation of *stridhana.* He includes other kinds of *stridhana* such as are mentioned in the texts of Yajnavalkya,[225] Manu,[226] and Vasistha.[227] This proves that Apararka, who followed a different reading, also arrives at the same conclusion as Vijnanesvara, by a different process of reasoning.[228] What is particularly important is that he explicitly includes in the term *stridhana* all property obtained by partition or inheritance by a woman whether in her maidenhood, or during covertures or as widow. It should also be mentioned that Apararka, commenting on the text of Katyayana, which deals with the maximum amount of donations of *stridhana,* 2,000 *panas,* says that it relates to donations made in the course of one year. This liberal interpretation, which has been adopted by most other commentators, illustrates the prevailing tendency to extend the original scope of *stridhana.*[229]

Among those who refused to recognise this interpretation are Devannabhatta and Jimutavahana. The latter restricts the application of the term to certain kinds of property belonging to woman. Jimutavahana first examines the various definitions, or rather descriptions, of *stridhana* given in the old *Smrti* texts. He alters the text of Yajnavalkya by substituting explicit *eva* for *adya* so as to confine the term *stridhana* to the kinds of property specifically enumerated by Yajnavalkya.[230] He rejects the definition of *stridhana* given in the *Mitakshara* and defines *stridhana* thus : "That alone is *stridhana* which she (a woman) has power to give, sell, or use independent of her husband's control."[231]

Jimutavahana does not say what kinds of property can be disposed of by a woman without her husband's consent but imme diately after defining *stridhana,* he cites the texts of Katyayana[232] and Narada.[233] In the light of these texts, he says in the chapter on *stridhana,* that all gifts from relatives constitute *stridhana* except the gift of an immovable property made by the husband, and gifts from strangers also constitute *stridhana,* if made before the nuptial fire or at the bridal procession. However, according to *Dayabhaga,* that property inherited by a woman, or obtained by her on partition, or gifts from strangers except those made before the nuptial fire or at the bridal procession, and also those acquired by her mechanical arts are not considered *stridhana.*[234]

The *Smrti Chandrika,* however, does not define *stridhana,* nor does it adopt the definition of *stridhana* given in the *Mitakshara.* According to the *Smrti Chandrika,* the following kinds of property are included in *stridhana* :

> The *adhayagni* or gifts before the nuptial fire; and *adhyavahanika* or presents at the bridal procession (both of which may be gifts from any person); the *pritidatta* or gifts through affection or as a token; gifts obtained from the husband, the parents or son, or from kindered; the *adhivedanika* or presents on supersession and the *sulka* or gratuity and the *anvadheya* or subsequent gifts as defined by Katyayana, are supposed to be a woman's *stridhana.*[235]

But he excludes from the category of *stridhana* gains from mechanical arts, conditional gifts, and gifts from strangers.

These differences, in the opinions of the jurists, show that society was following no uniform practice in the matter of the scope of *Stridhana.* We have, however, not found any written records which prove whether or not the items mentioned by Vijnanesvara were actually included within the scope of *stridhana,* or were restricted to those as prescribed by Jimutavahana. Still one can surmise that the society of that time, by and large, was following the rules as laid down in the *Mitakshara* since we find a large number of his successors upholding his opinions and interpretations.

Rights of Woman Over Stridhana : Woman's rights over her *stridhana* depended upon her status in relation to marriage, as well as on the nature of the property. Properties for this purpose may be divided into three kinds : (1) over which she had absolute power of disposal, (2) over which she did not have any such power, and (3) over which her power of disposal was restricted during covertures. The husband also had, under certain circumstances, a qualified right to use her *stridhana.* These different cases require detailed consideration. For the convenience of treatment, we shall consider separately the two classes of restrictions, namely, those depending on a woman's status, and those attaching to the nature of the property.

Restrictions Emanating from Status of Woman : Though the role of a Hindu female is that of a perpetual tutelage, yet this lack of independence does not disqualify her from exercising independent control over her own property.

(a) Maidenhood : During maidenhood, the Hindu female was under no restriction as regards her power over her *stridhana;* and, except in the capacity of a guardian, her father or her other relatives had no control over it. The *Mitakshara* explicitly declares that the father or other kinsmen, have no right over a woman's *stridhana.*[236]

(b) Coverture : During coverture, a woman's right over her *stridhana* is subject to certain restrictions. *Smrti* writers have placed a number of restrictions in this regard.[237] However, these restrictions have been considerably removed by other texts as well as by the rules as expounded by other commentators. The dominion of the husband was limited to only some types of the wife's property; as regards the rest, he was allowed only a qualified right of use under certain circumstances, which were specifically defined.

Here, there is a difference between the *Dayabhaga* and the *Mitakshara* schools Vijnanesvara says that "in certain circumstances (emphasis added) a husband is allowed to take his wife's goods in her life-time, even if she has an issue", irrespective of the find of property.[238] However, if "he seizes up in any other manner (or under other circumstances) he must make it good." But Jimutavahana, following a text of Katyayana, observes that the property obtained by the wife as gift from strangers or earned by her by mechanical arts was always subject to her husband's control and that he had a right to take it even though no distress exists.[239]

Devannabhatta suggests that the nature of 'distress' must be such that could not be overcome without the help of *stridhana.*[240] Thus, he prescribes the taking over of the woman's property only in the case of extreme necessity. He is of the view that the husband had to repay the principal even if he obtained it with the permission of his wife. The husband could use the wife's *stridhana* (i.e., her *saudayika stridhana*, her ornaments and the like) as a matter of right without her consent, only in cases of extreme distress, and in that case, repayment was optional. If he used it in any other circumstances without her consent, he was guilty and was bound to restore it with interest. If, however, he used it with her consent, he was bound to make good the principal only when he was able to do so. Finally, even if he used the *stridhana* with the consent of his wife, he was bound to restore her property in case he neglected her for the sake of another wife. Evidently, according to Devannabhatta, the husband could neither exercise independent power nor claim ownership over his wife's separate property. It can be inferred that the wife, by virtue of her marriage, had the right of ownership over her husband's property, though not of an independent nature. The husband could not claim the same right over his wife's property.[241] It may further be pointed out that the right to use the property in distress was given only to the husband and not to any other member of his family.[242]

(c) *Widowhood* : During widowhood, a woman's rights over her *stridhana* became much more stringent and no kinsman was entitled to use it. As regards her power of alienation, movable property given by her husband, which was required to be spent frugally during his life-time, became absolute after his death, says Jimutavahana.[243] Further, property acquired by a woman during widowhood by her skill and labour, or by gifts from strangers, becomes her *stridhana*, according to the commentators.

Restrictions According to the Nature of the Property

(a) *Property Received Through Gifts* : Gifts as a gesture of affection from the kindred, called in technical terms *saudayika stridhana*, constitute a woman's absolute property over which she had at all times an independent power of alienation. Her husband has only a qualified right over it, namely, the right of using it in times of distress.[244]

(b) *Gifts Received from the Husband* : The widow's rights over gifts from her husband when he is alive were not absolute. During coverture, she had no right to alienate such property, and even after the death of her husband her right became absolute only on the movables.[245] But nothing is explicitly said in the commentaries about the power of alienation over the immovable property obtained as gift from her husband.

(c) *Gifts from Strangers* : The *Mitakshara* says nothing explicitly on this point, but according to the *Dayabhaga* and the *Smrti Chandrika*, gifts from strangers do not rank as *stridhana* and are always subject to the husband's dominion.[246] But during maidenhood and widowhood, a woman's ownership over gifts received from strangers is absolute.

(d) Property Acquired by Mechanical Skill or Purchase : While the *Mitakshara* remains silent here as well, according to the *Dayabhaga,* the same rule as above applies to wealth earned by mechanical skill or acquired by purchase, and to gifts received from strangers.[247] However, if property is acquired by a widow by her personal exertions, she has absolute power of disposal over it. Here, there is no distinction between movable and immovable property so acquired.

(e) Property Acquired by Inheritance : The law regarding property acquired by inheritance is not stated clearly in all cases. The Bengal school states that the inherited property of the woman cannot be termed *stridhana.* Interest of a woman in property, whether it was inherited from the father or the husband or any other male relative, was of a qualified nature. This general rule, deduced by Jimutavahana[248] from Katyayana's text[249] relating to the widow, is *a fortiori* applicable to the daughter and the rest, because their claims were inferior to the widow's. In the same text, the word 'wife' is employed with a general import. It implies that the rule must be understood as applicable generally to the case of woman's succession by inheritance.

(f) Stridhana Promised by the Husband : A woman is not only entitled to enjoy what is given by her husband, but also to claim from the heirs of her husband what had been promised by him. Katyayana declares : "what has been promised to woman by her husband as her exclusive property, must be delivered by her sons provided she remains with the family of her husband, but not if she lives in the family of her father."[250] Devannabhatta explains that the term sons includes the grandsons also.

Taking an over-view, we may observe that various definitions and interpretations of *stridhana* as given by the Hindu jurists reveal that a widow had more powers over her *stridhana* than a wife during coverture. During widowhood, whatever a woman acquired by her skill or labour or as presents from non-relatives came under the caption of *stridhana* and she had full control over it, while during coverture the husband was the sole authority in this regard. It may be understood that when the control of her husband was not effective, she had the right of exercising full control over such property.

The restriction on the use of property depended upon the nature of gifts and the status of women in relation to marriage. Some kinds of property were under the full control of the wife, while over certain other things she did not have the same control and over some other kinds of property she could exercise her right only during coverture.[251]

Succession to Stridhana : Various schools of the Hindu law differ from each other more widely on this subject than on any other. The law of succession applicable to *stridhana* differs from the law of succession applicable to the property of a male. Probably, daughters were preferred as heirs to *stridhana* as a sort of equity, where sons were allowed to exclude daughters in inheritance to the father's wealth.[252] Gooro Dass Banerjee is of the opinion that the true reason is, perhaps, to be found in the natural desire to make an equitable distribution of the effects of the parents among children, both male and female. For a variety of reasons, some of which are not peculiar to the Hindu law, the sons exclusively took the property of their father; and as a sort of compensation, the daughters were allowed preference in the order of succession to their mother's estate.[253]

Succession to Sulka : According to the *Mitakshara,* there were two lines of succession to *stridhana,* one for *sulka* and the other for all other kinds of *stridhana. Sulka,* according to the *mitakshara* (following Gautama), devolved first on all the brothers, then on the mother.[254] Haradatta[255] holds that it devolved first on the mother and then on the brothers. The *Mitakshara* and *Smrti Chandrika* lay down that in default of the uterine brother and mother, the property devolved upon the father and then on the father's heirs, i.e., his *sapindas, samanodakas* and *bandhus.* But the *Dayabhaga* differs on the point and says that after the father, the property devolved on the husband instead of the father's heirs.

Succession to the Property of a Maiden : A maiden's property, according to all the commentators, passed first to the uterine brothers; on their failure, to the mother; on her default, to the father; and on his default, to the father's heir in order of propinquity and failing them to the kinsmen of the deceased, i.e., her mother's heir in order of propinquity.[256]

Where a girl promised in marriage died before marriage, all presents received from the bridegroom were to be returned to him, after deducting all expenses incurred by the bride or her parents or guardians. Similarly, presents received by the bridegroom must be returned.

Succession to Stridhana According to the Mitakshara : The *Mitakshara* lays down a simple order of succession to *stridhana* which is based upon the texts of Yajnavalkya, Manu, Gautama and Narada. From the text of Yajnavalkya,[257] Vijnanesvara deduced the rule that on the death of a woman, her daughters took over the property in the first instance.

As regards married and unmarried daughters, the unmarried one's preceded in the first instance, and it was only on their failure that the married daughters took the inheritance. Among the married, again, preference was given to the unprovided, and then to the provided ones. By the word unprovided, Vijnanesvara means indigent or childless.[258]

On failure of daughters, the succession devolved on the daughter's daughters.[259] In default of daughter's daughters, daughter's sons succeeded. Although Yajnavalkya's text contains no provision regarding the rights of a daughter's son, Vijnanesvara propounds the above rule of succession from the text of Narada.[260]

On failure of a grandson by the daughters, the sons took the property.[261] This rule is easily deduced from the text of Yajnavalkya.[262] But it is not equally easy to reconcile this rule and the text upon which it is based with the writings of other sages on the same subject.

Finally, if a woman died without any issue, i.e., leaving no daughter, nor daughter's daughter nor daughter's son, nor son's son, her kinsmen namely, her husband and the rest took her property.[263] The rule that kinsmen took a woman's *stridhana* if she died issueless was deduced by Vijnanesvara from Yajnavalkya.[264]

On failure of heirs leading down the ladder to a woman's son's son, the order of succession ceased to be uniform and begins to vary with the form of marriage. There is one order of succession if her marriage took place according to one of the four superior forms of marriage, namely the *Brahma,* the *Daiva,* the *Arsha* and the *Prajapatya,*—and a different order of succession if her marriage took place according to one of the remaining four, regarded as the inferior forms. Where the marriage was according to an approved form, the *stridhana* went to the husband and his heirs. When the marriage was according to an unapproved form, the *stridhana,* in default of issue, went to the mother, father and father's heirs,[265]—the same order as in the case of *stridhana* be longing to a maiden.

Succession to Stridhana According to Smrti Chandrika : According to the *Smrti Chandrika*,[266] *stridhana* includes only those kinds of property that are so described in the *Smrtis* only (*sulka, yautaka, bhartrdatta* and *anvadheyaka*) and some other kinds of technical *stridhana. Sulka* devolves in the same way as laid down by the *Mitaksara.* As regards the succession to the *yautaka,* it devolves first on the unmarried daughters and then on the sons. Another type of *stridhana,* the *bhartradatta* and *anvadheyaka* were inherited in equal shares both by the sons and the daughters.

If the woman died without any issue, her *stridhana* of all types, with the exception of *sulka,* passed to her husband if she was married in approved form ; and if she was married in an unapproved form, to her mother, and then to her father. The *Smrti Chandrika* made no provision for the succession on *yautaka, bhartradatta,* and *anvadheyaka stridhana* in the absence of sons and daughters.

Succession to Stridhana According to Dayabhaga : The *Dayabhaga* provides for a re-adjustment of the order of succession, which was originally confined to the family, by the recognition of consanguity to some extent, in addition to the agnatic relationship. *Dayabhaga's* rules[267] on the subject are not simple. As regards *sulka,* Jimutavahana[268] follows the rules which were propounded by the *Mitakshara.* For the *yautaka* type of *stridhana,* Jimutavahana quoted the verse of Manu that the property which was given to the mother on her marriage (*yautaka*) was to go to her unmarried daughters.[269] Accordingly (since the term signifies wealth received at the time of the marriage) Vasishtha says 'Let the female share the nuptial presents—*parinaya* of their mother—for *parinaya* signifies wealth received at marriage. He was of the opinion that in the text of Gautama, the right of the female heir was indicated by the term daughters and the specific mention of the term *apratta* (poor) and *apratishthita* (unmarried) suggested the order of succession. Quoting the views of Yajnavalkya, Jimutavahana propounded that whatever was given to a woman at the marriage went to her daughters. The right to inherit was to be devolved first on the unmarried and unbetrothed daughters, then on the betrothed ones, and in their default, the married ones. But in the case of non-availability of daughters, the son was to get it.[270] The separate property of an issueless woman, if married according to approved forms, went to her husband.[271] If a woman was married according to unapproved form, her property first went to her mother and then to her father.[272]

As regards the property given to a woman, after her marriage, by the family of her father and mother and the family of her husband, it devolved in the same order as *yautaka,* except where the sons got priority over the married daughters. In case the woman died without any issue, it devolved on brothers; then first on the mother and then on the father; on their failure, the husband could take it.[273]

In respect of the fourth and the last category of *stridhana,* i.e., *ayautaka,* Jimutavahana quoted the views of Manu, Brhaspati, Sankha-Likhita[274] and Devala[275] on the subject. He concluded that sons and unmarried daughters inherited jointly.[276] In default of either of them, the other would succeed, and if both of them were not available, then the married daughter, who had a son or who was likely to have one, was entitled to inherit it. But on failure of the daughters, the daughter's son could inherit the property; and if there were daughter's sons as well as the son's sons, the latter possessed the exclusive rights over such property. In default of all the above-mentioned heirs, the barren and widowed daughters were considered eligible to inherit their mother's estate as they were also her offspring's. It may be remarked that the mention of the barren and widowed daughters as the last heir was due to the fact that they could not offer an oblation, either personally or through their issues.

The order of succession to the *stridhana* as given by these law-givers was very ambiguous and complicated, and it varied according to the different schools. In brief, it may be stated that *stridhana* usually consisted of ornaments and clothes, which could be used by women alone, so it was deemed to be in the fitness of things that it was to be inherited by daughters. Among daughters, unmarried ones were to be preferred to married ones and among the latter, the first claim was of those who were not well-to-do. It was in their absence that the sons were to inherit.

Widow

The ancient *Smrtis* generally treat woman as inferior to man and do not give them any right to hold property. During the Brahmana period the primary obligation of a person holding property as successor was to perform religious rites and ceremonies, as he was considered a sort of trustee for their performance. Hence the woman's claim to succession began to be restricted. It need not be stated that the *Smrtis* are unanimous in declaring the son as the first heir of a man; in case of the son's default, came the grandson, and in the default of a grandson came the great grandson.[277]

In the *Smrtis,* there is no indication that a widow was entitled to inherit the separate or self-acquired property of her husband. Later, the *Smrtis* dealt with restrictions on the property itself. The only inference that can be drawn from the *Smrtis* is that she was entitled to inherit her husband's or father's property only under certain conditions.[278]

There was no unanimity over the rules of inheritance of a widow in this period also. The *Mitakshara*[279] says that Dharesvara tried to reconcile the conflicting texts about the right of widow of her husband's estate by saying that she succeeded if her husband was separate and if she was willing to submit to *niyoga.* Thus, Dharesvara gives only a grudging recognition to the rights of a widow. Vijnanesvara,[280] Apararka and Devannabhatta[281] oppose the above view.

The doctrine of the *Mitakshara* marked the second epoch in the history of the widow's right of succession. The first epoch may be placed in the earlier period when the widow was declared ineligible for succession and was allowed simply maintenance as long as she lived.

The reason for the change in the attitude was that while in the earlier period, property was meant for religious uses (women could not perform the religious rites), the *Mitakshara* contended that religious observances were not the sole object of wealth[282], wealth was also intended for other pious or charitable purposes. As such he seems to advocate for the widow's right in inheritance. The ancient custom of *niyoga* was, at one time, generally prevalent and was approved by writers like Dharesvara.[283] But now there was a strong public opinion against such a practice. Vijnanesvara in his commentary declared such a custom as immoral and disreputable.[284] Quoting Manu, he pointed that *niyoga* should not be permitted at all. He reasoned that if a widow, who submitted to *niyoga,* could be an heir to her husband, then what is the fault of a chaste and virtuous widow in laying such a claim ? He further pointed out that a widow who wanted to produce a son by *niyoga* was not the heir but the son so produced was the heir.[285]

The *Mitakshara* recognized the widow's right of inheritance only if her husband had been separated from the joint family before his death.[286] An examination of the context of the verse of Yajnavalkya, which is quoted, mentions a widow as the next heir. It is intended to recognize her right only if her husband was not a member of the joint family at the time of his death. Yajnavalkya laid down that were the members of the family get reunited after separation, the surviving male co-parceners would succeed the deceased, and not the wife.[287] Thus Vijnanesvara is correct in holding that according to Yajnavalkya, only the widow of a separated co-parcener can become an heir to her husband.

It may be observed that the text of Yajnavalkya is not clear on the condition imposed on a widow's succession as stated by Vijnanesvara. The author of the *Mitakshara* lived at a time when the current public opinion was in favour of the widow's right. At the same time, he found that there was still a considerable opinion arrayed against the widow. So he took to a middle course. He established to widow's claim with the proviso that a woman could inherit as the widow of a separated parcener. In those times, joint hold was the rule and separate hold was exceptional. By initiating this doctrine he did the least violence to established authorities.[288] He based the right of a widow to inherit the whole estate of her sonless husband on the basis of Yajnavalkya, Brhaspati, Vishnu, Vrddha-Manu, and Katyayana[289] and refuted opinions of Manu, Sankha and Devala, who denied the right of inheritance to a widow.[290] He had included that inherited property under *stridhana* and was probably reluctant to sanction a scheme of succession where property would had automatically and very frequently passed out of the family to the female *stridhana* heirs.

Apararka, another commentator of this period, was also against the custom of *niyoga.* He said that the desire to raise an issue by *niyoga* was only an alternative to inherit the estate of the sonless husband. Apararka,[291] taking support from Vrddha Manu, observes that she, who had been faithful to her husband who had himself acquired wealth without the aid of the father's estate, should take his entire estate, even when the husband's younger bothers are alive; but where there is a possibility of adultery, the estate should go to the husband's brother and not to the widow. If the deceased acquired wealth jointly with the brothers without detriment to the father's wealth, the brothers took the wealth. If the property was ancestral, then the parents took it and not the brothers. Therefore, in the above two cases, the property of a person, who had died without having a son, should be taken by the wife only to the extent necessary for her maintenance and no more.

The author of the *Smrti Chandrika* also mentions that the widow was entitled to inherit the whole property, including the immovables of her sonless deceased husband, provided she was chaste and where the husband had been a 'divided' number of the family. Such property should be used in performing all such acts as *sraddha,* works of public utility, charities and so forth which are conducive to her husband's spiritual welfare.[292] In case the husband did not belong to a 'divided' family, the property should go to his father, brother and other co-residents, provided the wife had no daughter and she was unchaste. The immovable property being meant for the maintenance of her offspring, a woman would be entitled to receive it only when she had daughters.[293]

To Jimutavahana, the founder of the *Dayabhaga* school, belongs the credit of liberalising the law still further in favour of the widow. He did not include the inherited property under *stridhana* because he wanted the widow to be an heir to her husband, even when the latter was a member of the joint family at the time of his death. He undoubtedly took one step further in expansion of the widow's rights. He suggested that the widow of the deceased who belonged to the joint family was also eligible to get her husband's share. He took the incentive from the text of Brhaspati,[294] and concluded that the whole wealth, movable and immovable, of the deceased man who had no male issue, belonged to; his widow. He further pointed out that even when brothers were still living as members of the joint family, each one had got his own share, though formally separated. Hence it was fair that the wife should get her husband's share. He argued that there was nothing to prove the wife's co-ownership in her husband's property that arose at the marriage, which automatically terminated at his death, if it happened while the family was still joint.[295] It is, therefore, but fair that she should be allowed to inherit he husband's share, irrespective of the consideration as to whether he had separated from the joint family or not. Jimutavahana relied on the text of Brhaspati which was silent whether the family was joint or separated. Jimutavahana went a step further than Vijnanesvara who denied the right to the widow of a man belonging to the joint family.

It seems that Kulluka, a commentator of Manu, was inclined to give right to the widow to inherit her husband's property in default of a son. He argued that the rule of providing maintenance to the widow was for the concubines and unchaste widows only. The father and others were entitled to get the property of a sonless man only when he left no widow and daughter behind. It may be argued that no word in the verse of Manu (IX, 185) indicates the meaning *'patni duhitrahitasya'* as suggested by Kulluka.[296] So we can justifiably say that the commentator himself was of the opinion that the widow should get the right to inherit the property of her husband.[297]

It cannot be inferred from the ideas of Jimutavahana that he gave an absolute right to the widow in the property of her husband. He was of the view that the widow's right of inheritance should be limited for her life-time. She could use its income in any way she liked, but she could not gift, sell or mortgage it.[297] It may, however, be noted that there was some relaxation in this rule in case of legal necessity. The author of the *Dayabhaga* put the expenditure incurred for the benefit of the late husband under the category of 'legal necessity'. Any expenditure beneficial to the late owner would come within the category of legal necessity and would justify the widow's right to dispose of the property.[299] This category also includes her own maintenance, the maintenance of the family of her husband, the maintenance of the unmarried daughters, and also that of the childless widowed daughter who has no provision for her maintenance, and the marriage expenses of the unmarried daughters.[300]

From the above account it may be inferred that down to the twelfth century A.D., the widow could enjoy only a limited power over her estate. However, it was Devannabhatta who, relying on the text of Brhaspati, declared that his denial to the sale or mortgage of the immovable property only indicated that the gifts should not be made to the persons of questionable conduct like singers, dancers and actors.[301] But his views did not seem to have gained any currency as we find that widows continued to be limited heirs since it is proved by the testimony of an inscription according to which the permission of reversioners was also taken in the transaction of a deal. One South Indian inscription says that gifts of land were made by the widow with the sanction of her brother-in law, who was the next reversioner.[302] Another inscription of the twelfth century A.D. indicates that sometimes the permission of the whole caste was also essential for the transaction.[303]

It appears that the widow's right of inheritance was not recognized in actual practice in Gujarat and the adjoining regions till the twelfth century A.D. since the kings wished their rich citizens to die issueless so that they could acquire their property. On the other hand, we have king Kumarapala's (1143-72 A.D.) example who is said to have forfeited his right in favour of a sorrowful widow.[304]

Daughter

Daughter with Brothers : The general opinion of the Hindu society was that sisters should get no share in patrimony if they had brothers, and the same is reflected in the works of the jurists of this period. The theory behind this was that marriage completely transfers the bride to the new family and, consequently, the jurists held that she should be provided for from the assets of the groom's family. There were many difficulties in giving a daughter the right of inheritance along with her brothers. For instance, if she was given a share in the immovable property, it would be difficult for her to look after it after her marriage, as she went off to some other place and would, therefore, be an absentee landlord. Thus she might not benefit materially from a share in the immovable property of her father. Sukra[305] was the only jurist who championed the cause of a daughter's share in patrimony, even if she had brothers.[306] A Mysore inscription dated[307] 1188 A.D. refers to a gentleman, named Machi, partitioning his landed property among both his sons and daughters. From the *Kathasaritsagara,* we come to know that Vagvati, the sister of Mahavanga got half of her father's kingdom, the other half being given to her brother.[308]

From the records quoted above it should not be inferred that the daughter was generally assigned a share in patrimony. The *Smrtis* and inscriptions which give the daughter a right in patrimony are exceptions and not the rule. The general opinion of society was that women should get a share, directly or indirectly, in the property of their husbands and not in that of their fathers. Since girls had to get married, it was laid down that reasonable expenses in connection with their marriage should be a charge on the family property. If the daughters were not married during their father's life-time, the sons were required to spend a reasonable amount for their marriages out of the family property. The precise amount that a brother ought to spend for his sister's marriage could not be laid down in the law books, and it varied with the circumstances and status of each family. The only general rule however, was that a brother should spend for his sister's marriage an amount equal to a one-fourth share.[309]

Kulluka[310] also pointed out that the one-fourth part must be spent by the brothers on the marriage of their sisters and suggested that each brother should give this share to his uterine sister.

A difficulty would have arisen in the case where a girl had no uterine brother Kulluka tried to solve this problem by adding that the duty of providing for sisters devolved in the first instance, on the full brother, and on his default on the half-brothers.[311]

Referring to the text of Manu, Devannabhatta[312] stated that the meaning of the words as indicated by the repetition of '*svat, svat*' is that "the brothers shall give to the girls as many quarter shares as there may be full shares of the brothers." But seeing that the text pertains to the cases where there are several girls, discrepancy would be involved if a single sister were to receive the fourth part of the shares of all the brothers. What is meant is that the fourth part of the whole property is to be divided equally among all the sisters.

It is said in the *Smrti Chandrika*[213] that if the family property is quite extensive and the one-fourth share allotted to the daughter is so much that some of it remains unspent after the performance of the marriage, then the daughter cannot take it to her new home. While anxious to make adequate provision for the marriage of a sister, the Hindu jurists have disapproved the principle that she should inherit a share along with her brother, and carry it away with her after her marriage. Jimutavahana held the opinion that if ancestral wealth was small, the provision for the marriage of the unmarried daughter should be made by giving her a fourth share but if the wealth was ample then she should get only as much as was necessary for her marriage.[314]

If the father had no son and if he died without performing his daughter's marriage, the widow was bound to spend one-fourth part of her husband's property on the marriage expenses of her unmarried daughters.[315]

Apararka, while commenting on Yajnavalkya,[316] cited the verses of Narada, Vyasa and Manu and said, "As for the sisters who have not been already married each of them shall be given away in marriage by the brothers, after the latter have given to each of the sisters the fourth part of the share that may have come to each of them."

It was Vijnanesvara only who strongly recommended a share to the daughter in the property of her father. Commenting on Yajnavalkya,[317] he recommended that when a man left both sons and daughters, a daughter got a share which was equal to one-fourth of what she would have got if she had been born as a son. He said that a daughter is also an heir and is entitled to a share after her father's death.[318]

As regards the one-fourth share, his view was that the brothers of the same caste should give a share equal to their own fourth share to their uterine sister. He prescribed that if a certain person had one wife, a son and a daughter, then after his death, the whole paternal property should be divided into two, one to be given to the wife and the other to the son. Son's part should further be divided into four parts and one of it should be given to his sister.[319]

Vijnanesvara further added that one should not take the word 'one-fourth' literally and that the unmarried sister gets only as much as is necessary for her marriage. Indeed, she is entitled to one-fourth of her brother's share.[320]

Brotherless Daughter : According to Yajnavalkya,[321] Vishnu,[322] and Brhaspati[323] the daughter comes next in succession to the widow. As mentioned in the previous Chapter, early commentators of the 8th to 10th centuries A.D. were not prepared to accept the view of the *Smrtikaras* in their literal sense. E.g. Visvarupa[324] held that Yajnavalkya recommends only the *'putrika'* as successor to a sonless person and employs the plural in order to convey that several daughters may be appointed as sons. Later, Madhatithi, Srikara and the *Samgrahakara* also agreed with the views of Visvarupa. During the period of our study, the *Smrti Chandrika*[325] informs us that the similar opinion was held by Dharesvara, Devasvamin and Devavrata while Apararka, Vijnanesvara and Devannabhatta held different opinions.

Disagreeing with the views of those who interpreted the daughter as *putrika,* Apararka says that the father of *putrika* cannot be called sonless since *putrika* is considered as a son. For his views he depended on the opinion of Vasishtha. Further, Vijnanesvara reasoned that *putrika* is a son (not as good as a son) and hence she cannot be included in the category of a brotherless daughter.

Thus, according to the above commentators, the daughter of a sonless man as *'putrika'* takes precedence over the widow. Hence where the *Smrtikaras* speak of daughters taking after the widow, they did not mean *"putrika'* but ordinary brotherless daughters. As such, we may now discuss the position of a brotherless daughter not included under the category of a *'putrika'*.

Vijnanesvara cited Brhaspati where the wife is pronounced as successor to the wealth of her sonless husband; and in her default the daughter.[326] Further, Vijnanesvara[327] also cited a text of Katyayana to the effect that the widow should succeed her husband's wealth provided she was chaste; and in default of her, the daughter inherits. Though Yajnavalkya makes no distinction between married and unmarried daughters, yet Vijnanesvara had ordained that the unmarried daughter inherited in preference to a married one.[328] In order to elaborate his views, he referred to the text of Gautama who laid down that a "woman's separate property goes to her unmarried and unprovided daughters."[329] Vijnanesvara further laid down that if the alternative was between an unprovided and a rich one, then the unprovided inherited ; of course, on her failure the rich one succeeded. He said that the text of Gautama was equally applicable to the paternal as well as the maternal estates. But no preference is given to the daughter who has or is likely to have a male issue over a daughter who is barren or a childless widow. Vijnanesvara based the daughter's right of succession on consanguinity rather than on her capacity to offer funeral oblations and held that such inheritance would not be in conflict with his general doctrine of sapindaship.[330]

In the *Smrti Chandrika,* the principle of religious efficacy is introduced as an additional reason for inheritance. Devannabhatta held that barren daughters were not at all entitled to inherit their deceased father's estate, they being incapable to confer on him the spiritual benefits through the medium of their offspring.[331] Devannabhatta clearly states that daughters inherited in default of the widow and that on the failure of the daughters, the daughter's son inherited. With regard to the order of precedence amongst daughters, *inter se*, the *Smrti Chandrika* lays down the rule that where there in competition between a poor daughter and unmarried one, both being of the same class, the unmarried one should get priority. On the failure of such a daughter, the unprovided should receive the property. In default of unprovided daughters, the rich daughter should inherit the property.[332]

Jimutavahana also introduced the rule of spiritual or religious efficacy in determining the rules of daughter's inheritance to their father's estate. The daughter's right of succession was accepted on failure of the wife.[333] Jimutavahana said that a daughter's right to succession to the property of her father was founded on her offering the oblation through her son. To support this he said. "It is the daughter's son who is the giver of a funeral oblation not the son's son nor daughter's daughter, for the funeral oblation ceases with him, i.e. the daughter's son."[334] Therefore, he contended that a daughter, who was the mother of a male issue or who was likely to become so, was competent to inherit, not the one who was a widow, or was barren, or failed to bring male issue.

The above discussion is sufficient to show that the right of the daughter to inherit was dependent on the spiritual capacity, meaning thereby the capacity to produce a son who could offer oblation to the deceased father.

We have seen how the right of the widow was hemmed by later commentaries to a limited benefit of the usufruct with a further limitation that on her death the property went to her husband's heirs and not to her daughters. This rule applied to the joint property left by the husband. However, there is no *Smrti* text placing any such restriction on the daughter's rights. A daughter was entitled to succeed her father's estate even if she was unchaste at the time of her father's death, except in cases governed by the *Dayabhaga*. According to the *Dayabhaga*,[335] Brhaspati declared "a daughter equal in caste to the father and married to a husband of the same caste as her own, who is virtuous and intent on serving her husband inherits her father's property." Implication also seem to be that an unchaste daughter could not inherit.

Jimutavahana restricted the right of the daughter on a somewhat curious argument, *a fortiori*, because according to him, daughter being inferior (*jaghanya*) as heir to the widow, her right could not be higher than that of a widow. A daughter succeeded, not because she was the daughter, but because she satisfied all conditions laid down by Brhaspati. Jimutavahana further said that the word 'wife' in the *Dayabhaga* was merely illustrative and whatever restrictions were imposed on the wife applied to all women as heirs.[336]

Mother

In the previous Chapter it has been discussed that early commentators were not unanimous as regards the order of preference of inheritance by the parents. Visvarupa stated that the wealth of a childless son was taken by the mother if the deceased had no wife. Srikara held that both the parents, if alive, succeed together. During the period under study, Vijnanesvara prefers the mother before the father. Commenting on Yajnavalkya[337] he observed that between the parents the mother came first to inherit than did the father. A father may have several wives and sons and, therefore father may be common to all the sons while the mother may not be common. The mother was directly related to her own son only, and not to the other sons of her husband.

In accordance with the text of Manu,[338] he contended that the proximity of relationship is the determining factor in the claim to inheritance. The mother's right to succession was not made to depend upon her capacity to perform any ceremonies. It was based rather upon the ground of nourishing the son in the womb. The *Mitakshara* based the mother's right to take the inheritance before the father consequent to her nearer relationship to the deceased. Of course, on her failure the father was to be the successor to the property.

Dharesvara also preferred the mother. He had taken the text of Manu (IX. 217) to mean that if the mother died, the property went to the father's mother and not to the father.

Apararka, who belonged to the South, did not state clearly as to who should inherit an issueless man's property who left behind no wife. The word *pitarau* indicates that the heritage of the sonless son vested in the parents. In support of his view, he quoted a verse of Brhaspati wherein it is stated that when man died without leaving a widow and a son, his mother took his wealth or his brothers with her permission. He also quoted Manu (IX. 217) to support his views.

Coming to Kulluka, we find a different interpretation of Manu's text wherein he has tried to strike a compromise between the two verses of Manu. At first Manu suggested that the father took the estate of an issueless son[338] and a little later suggested that the mother took the wealth of such a son.[339] Kulluka, commenting on the above two verses, suggested that in the absence of a sonless person's widow and daughter, his mother and father inherit jointly.[340] The consequences of such an interpretation of the rule are rather serious. If the son having separated from his father earned a certain amount of property with his own labour and died issueless and, if his wife had also died earlier (or he had not married at all), his property would go to his parents, who would divide it between themselves equally. The result would be that the mother's share would become her *stridhana* which after her death would devolve upon her specific successors entitled to her property while the father's share would go to his agnates. This would not be in keeping with the spirit of the Hindu law of succession.

Coming to the *Dayabhaga,* here the situation is found reversed. Jimutavahana makes the mother come after the father because in comparison to the male, a female is pronounced as inferior. Here again as in the case of the daughter, the author introduced religious of spiritual merit as the test of succession. He rejected the notion that superior title to veneration was the reason for a right of inheritance on the ground that, if it were so the succession would devolve on the spiritual preceptor before the father, for the former was more venerable of the two.[342] He explained in the same strain the passage of Manu[343] as well as those of Brhaspati[344] which must be understood as related to the case of failure of heirs down to the father. The mother came after the father in the order of inheritance.

Devannabhatta, however, mentioned three different views in the *Smrti Chandrika* on the mother's rights and control over property, because they were opposed to the texts of Vishnu and Katyayana. He also refuted the opinion of Srikara that both the parents may divide between them and share the inheritance. Devannabhatta contended that in default of the wife, the daughter and the daughter's son, the estate went to the father.[345] If the father also failed, only then the mother inherited.[346]

Mother's Share on Partition : Apararka stated that after the father's death, the mother shall also receive a share equal to that of the sons. The term 'mother' stood for all co-wives. The *Mitakshara* and the *Smrti Chandrika*[347] also agreed with his view. They, however, add that her share should be equal to that of her sons only if no *stridhana* had been given to her; in case *stridhana* had been given she should receive only half of a share. Jimutavahana agreed with their opinion but excludes the step-mother from inheritance.

Thus, all the commentators unanimously agreed with the view that when partition took place after the demise of the father, the mother was an equal sharer with the sons; however, when the mother was in possession of *stridhana,* the share should only be half of the son's share.

Grand Mother's Rights

The grand mother's rights to succession on partition were recognised since the time of Manu. Kulluka states "if the mother is dead, then the property shall go to father's mother provided the wife, the father, the brother and nephews are not there."[348]

Dharesvara had taken this text to mean that even when the father was there, if the mother died, the property went to the father's mother, because if the father inherited it, there were possibilities of its going to such of his sons who belonged to different castes. While if it were taken by the father's mother, it would go only to the persons of the same caste.[349]

The *Mitakshara* lays down that in the absence of brother's son, the property goes to sagotras. Sagotras are paternal grand mother and sapindas and samanodakas; among these the father's mother comes first.[350]

These general improvements in the property rights of women were recognised due to a number of factors. The Muslim invasion introduced an entirely new element in the Indian social order. The central authority broke down and a large number of small states came into existence. Various local traditions began to influence the law of inheritance in different regions of the country. The moral fibre of society became weak and women became confined to the household more than ever. They needed protection of their rights in a more formal way. In such a situation liberal views of yajnavalkya became popular. His commentator Vijnanesvara, who belonged to South, increased women's property rights. Even in the *Dayabhaga* school liberal tendencies emerged.

References

1. *Manu,* IX. 153.
2. *Bhagavadgita,* IX. 32.
3. *Parasara,* VI. 16.
4. *Manu,* IX. 3.
5. *RV,* I. 145, 179; V. 28; X. 86, 145, 179.
6. *Ibid.*
7. *Manu,* VIII. 77.
8. Aiyangar, K.V. Rangaswamy, *Aspects of the Social and Political System of Manusmriti,* p. 162.
9. *Harita,* XXI. 20.
10. *Vasishtha Dharmasutra,* XVII. 59; *Gautama Dharmasutra,* XVIII. 20.
11. *Manu,* IX. 90.
12. *Arthasastra,* IV. 21.
13. *Kamasutra,* III. 2-4.
14. *Kathasaritsagara,* 24, 124.
15. *Yaj.,* 1. 13.
16. Yama quoted in *SCS,* p. 216.
17. *Brhad Yama,* III. 21-22. Adoption of young age for marriage of girls was prevalent in other countries as well. Westermark has

remarked, "The stipulation of the Roman Law, according to which a man may marry at the age of twelve, was adopted by the Church and is, under the influence of' canon law, still preserved in various countries," Westermark, *A Short History of Marriages,* p. 46.

18. *RV*, X. 124, 5.
19. *Satapatha Brahmana*, V. 2. 1. 10.
20. *Manu*, II. 145.
21. *Ibid.*, XI, 60.
22. Aiyangar, *op. cit.*
23. *Ibid.*
24. '*Jayapatyo no vibhago* asti' (*Apastamba*, II. 10.27.6).
25. *Manu*, IX. 175.
26. *Ibid.*, IX. 72; *Yaj*, I, 73.
27. *Ibid.*, IX. 79.
28. *Narada*, XII. 16.
29. *Parasara*, IV. 28.
30. *Narada*, XII. 97; *Parasara*, IV. 28.
31. *As*, III. 155.
32. *AS* (Shamasastry's trans.), p. 177.
33. *RV*, X. 40.2; X, 18.7.8.
34. *Gautama*, XVIII. 9-14.
35. *Manu*, IX. 67-68.
36. *AS*, p. 201.
37. *Manu*, V. 156-7.
38. *Yaj*, I. 75.
39. Bar both of them sanction such marriage, in certain cases (*Manu*, IX. 176; *Yaj.*, I. 67).
40. *Narada*, XII. 45 ff., 96 ff.
41. *Manu*, IX. 175; *Narada*, XII. 46; *Vas.*, XVII. 20.
42. At the time of the legal prohibition of the *sati* custom by William Bentick, it was argued that the funeral hymns of the *RV* refer to widows ascending the funeral pyre. For refutation of the contention of the Vedic sanction to *sati*, see, Altekar, A.S., *The Position of Women in Hindu Civilization*, p. 117.
43. *Ibid.*, p. 118.
44. *Brhaspati Smrti*, 487.
45. *Skanda, Purana*, III, 7. 51.
46. *Rama.*, VII. 45, 43.
47. Sayana, commenting on *RV*, V. 61.8, says. "The wife and husband, being the equal halves of one substance are equal in every respect and take equal part in all works, religious and secular."
48. *RV*, VIII. 31 5.
49. *Ibid.*, I. 179 and IX. 30-40.

50. *AB*, I. 2.5.
51. *SB*, V. 1.6.10; V. 2.1.10.
52. *Br. Up*., VI. 4.17.
53. *Ibid*., II. 4.
54. Altekar, *Position of Women in Hindu Civilisation*. p. 202.
55. *Manu*, III. 66.
56. *Ibid*., XI. 36.
57. *Ibid*., IX. 22.
58. *Ibid*., II, 66; also IX, 96.
59. *Yaj*., I. 13.
60. Altekar, *op. cit*.
61. *Ibid*.
62. Cf. Misra, G.S.P., *The Age of Vinaya*, p. 175.
63. Cf. Goyal, S.R., *A Religious History of Ancient India*, II, Meerut, 1986, Chapter 17, p. 414 ff.
64. *Ibid*., p. 414.
65. Altekar, *op. cit*.
66. Cf. Joshi, M.C., *Princes and Polity in Ancient India*, Meerut, 1986; cf. also Goyal, S.R., *Kautilya and Megasthenes*, Meerut, 1985, Ch. 6, pp. 39-41.
67. *Rama*., II. 37, 38.
68. *Jataka*, IV, p. 487.
69. *Pratijnayaugandharayana*, Act. I.
70. See, Altekar, *PWHC*, p. 186.
71. Vide, Goyal, S.R., *Prachina Bharatiya Abhilekha Samgraha*, Jaipur, 1982, p. 424 ff.; see H.C. Raychaudhari, *Political History of Ancient India*, p. 369.
72. Altekar, *PWHC*, p. 186; *Coinage of the Gupta Empire;* Contra, Goyal, S.R., *A History of the Imperial Guptas*, p. 85 ff.
73. *IA*, VII, p. 163.
74. EI, *XXII*, p. 98.
75. Altekar, *PWHC*, p. 190 ff.
76. *JBORS*, II, pp. 422-23; cf. *The Age of Imperial Kanauj*, p. 66 f.
77. *Ibid*.
78. *Ibid*.
79. See, Altekar, *PWHC*, pp. 187-91.
80. Tod, *Annals*, I, pp. 303-04.
81. For details vide Sharma, D., *Rajasthan Through the Ages*.
82. *RV*, I. 112. 10.
83. *Ibid*., X. 112. 2.
84. *RV*, V. 61. 7.
85. *Ibid*., X. 125. 6.
86. *Rama*., *Ayodhya Kanda*.

87. *Sukra,* IV. 7. 300.
88. *Ibid.,* II. 73.
89. *Yaj.,* VIII. 77.
90. *Vasishtha,* V. 1.2.
91. *Manu,* VIII. 76.
92. *Ibid.,* VIII. 78.
93. Majumdar, R.C., *The Age of Imperial Kanauj,* p. 248.
94. Kane, *op. cit.,* p. 540.
95. Majumdar, R.C., *The Age of Imperial Kanauj,* pp. 253-54.
96. Kane, *HDS,* Vol. I, Part I, p. 564.
97. *Ibid.,* p. 567.
98. *Ibid.,* p. 573.
99. *Ibid.,* p. 572.
100. Sarvadhikari, *Hindu Law of Inheritance,* p. 257.
101. *Mit.* on *Yaj.,* II. 124.
102. Visvarupa on *Yaj.,* II. 118.
103. *Ibid.*
104. Kane, *op. cit.,* p. 583.
105. *Ibid.,* pp. 574-81.
106. *The Age of Imperial Kanauj,* Preface, p. xxxvi.
107. Medhatithi on *Manu.,* I. 32.
108. *Matsya Purana,* I. 31.
109. *Manu.,* VIII. 416.
110. Medhatithi on *Manu.,* VIII. 416.
111. *Ibid.*
112. *Manu.,* IX. 95.
113. Medhatithi on *Manu.,* IV. 25.
114. *Ibid.,* IX. 77.
115. *Ibid.* IX. 74.
116. *Ibid.,* IX. 95.
117. *Yaj.,* I. 70.
118. *Manu.,* IX. 199.
119. Visvarupa on *Yaj.,* II. 148.
120. *Ibid.,* II. 119.
121. Devala quoted in Apararka, p. 755.
122. *Agni.,* 256. 30.
123. Visvarupa on *Yaj.,* II. 144, 145.
124. Devala as quoted in Apararka, p. 755.
125. Devala as quoted in *Vivada Chintamani,* p. 220.
126. Visvarupa on *Yaj.,* II. 146.
127. *Ibid.,* II. 147.
128. *Agni P.,* pp. 256. 30-36.
129. *Ibid.*

130. Devala, quoted in *Viramitrodaya*, p. 694.
131. *Yaj.*, II. 144.
132. Visvarupa on *Yaj.*, II. 145.
133. *Ibid.*, II. 146.
134. Medhatithi on *Manu.*, IX. 131.
135. Because a daughter was made a *putrika* at the time of marriage.
136. Asahaya quoted in the *Smrti Chandrika*, p. 384.
137. *Agni P.*, 256. 30.
138. Vrdha Manu quoted in Apararka, p. 742.
139. *Vishnu.*, XVII. 4-7.
140. *Ibid.*, XV. 46-55.
141. *Yaj.*, II. 135-136.
142. *Narada.*, XIII. 52.
143. Sankha quoted in Apararka, p. 741.
144. Katyayana quoted in *Mit.*, p. 727.
145. Devala quoted in Apararka, p. 741.
146. Kulluka on *Manu.*, IX. 187.
147. Medhatithi on *Manu.*, IX. 76.
148. Visvarupa, on *Yaj.*, II. 135.
149. *VDS*, XVII. 41.
150. *Samgrahakara* quoted in *Smrti Chandrika*, p. 681.
151. *GDS*, XXVIII, 19. 20.
152. *VDS*, XVII. 65.
153. *Manu.*, IX. 146. 190.
154. *Agni Purana*, 253. 12-13.
155. *Agni Purana*, 223. 17-21.
156. Visvarupa on *Yaj.*, II. 124.
157. Medhatithi on *Manu.*, IX. 118.
158. *Yaj.*, II. 124.
159. Devala quoted in *Smrti Chandrika*, p. 615.
160. Bharuchi quoted in *Parasaramadhaviya*.
161. *Mitakshara* on *Yaj.*, II. 124.
162. *Yaj.*, II. 136; *Vishnu.*, XVII. 4; *BDS*, XXV. 56.
163. *Ibid.*
164. If a man of undivided family dies leaving daughters only, Visvarupa suggests, commenting on the plural number in the word 'daughters' in *Yaj.*, II. 136-137, that all daughters may be treated as *putrikas*.
165. Visvarupa on *Yaj.*, II. 136. 137.
166. Medhatithi on *Manu.*, IX. 130. Also see, Jha, *Hindu Law and its Sources*, pp. 481-82.
167. *Samgrahakara* quoted in the *Smrti Chandrika*, p. 656.
168. Kane, *op. cit.*, p. 714.

169. Kane, *op. cit.*, p. 715.
170. Devala as quoted in the *Dayabhaga.*
171. *OBPK*, p. 153.
172. *EI*, IV, p. 248.
173. *Manu.*, IX. 217.
174. *Ibid.*, IX. 185.
175. Katyayana quoted in the *Smrti Chandrika*, p. 693.
176. *BDS*, XXV. 63.
177. Visvarupa on *Yaj.*, II. 123.
178. *Ibid.*, II. 136.
179. *Manu.*, IX. 217.
180. *Ibid.*, IX. 185.
181. Visvarupa on *Yaj.*, II. 136.
182. Medhatithi on *Manu.*, IX. 217.
183. Kane, P.V., *op. cit.*, Vol. I, p. 595.
184. *Ibid.*
185. *Ibid.*
186. *Ibid.*, p. 597. Balaka is sometimes ridiculed by Jimutavahana as holding childish views.
187. Colebrook's *Dayabhaga*, p. 382.
188. Vide, *JASB*, 1912, p. 336. Valoka is apparently a rendering of some Bengal scribe for Balaka.
189. Kane, P.V., *op. cit.*, pp. 595-98.
190. *Ibid.*
191. Yogloka quoted in *Vyavaharatattva* (Jivananda, Vol. II), p. 217.
192. *Viramitrodaya*, p.705.
193. Kane, P.V., *op. cit.*, I, p. 746.
194. Ghose, J.C., *Hindu Law*, Introduction, p. xv.
195. Kane, P.V., *op. cit.*, Vol. I, pp. 607-10.
196. Apararka, *Yajnavalkya, DS*, pp. 244-45.
197. Sarvadhikari, *Hindu Law of Inheritance*, p. 292.
198. *Mit.*, I. 1. 20.
199. Dutta, B.N., *Hindu Law of Inheritance*, p. 122.
200. *Mit.*, IV. 1. 11.
201. This procedure served a very useful purpose.
202. *SCV*, p. 297.
203. *Ibid.*, p. 295.
204. *SCV*, p. 297.
205. *Ibid.*, p. 295.
206. Last verse of Chapter XI.
207. Kane, *op. cit.*, p. 759.
208. We may mention that Lakshmidhara was also a digest writer of this period and wrote *Kalpataru*. He, however, did not write

anything new or original. He only compiled the information available in other *Smrtis,* commentaries and digests.

209. *T S,* VI. 5. 8. 2; *Manu.,* VIII. 416.
210. *Daya.,* XI. 2. 31; XI. 1. 56.
211. *Yaj.,* II. 136.
212. See, *Hindu Law of Partition, Inheritance and Adoption,* p. 217
213. *Ibid.*
214. *Ibid.,* p. 218.
215. *Smrti Chandrika,* pp. 653-54.
216. The *Mit.* on *Yaj.,* VI. 135-36.
217. Kulluka on *Manu.,* VIII. 416.
218. Haradatta, on *GDS,* XXVII. 19 and *ADS,* II. 6. 14. 1.
219. *Smrti Chandrika,* p. 294.
220. Apararka, P. 743.
221. *Daya.,* IX. 6.11.
222. *Mit.* on *Yaj.,* II. 143.
223. *Ibid.*
224. Jolly's, *Hindu Law and Custom,* pp. 248-50.
225. *Yaj.,* II. 144-45.
226. *Manu.,* IX. 118.
227. *VDS,* XVII. 46.
228. Here in the text of Yajnavalkya *cha* stands for *adi* so that the other kinds of women's property is included.
229. J. Jolly, *op. cit.,* pp. 250-51.
230. *Daya.,* IV. I. 18.
231. Katyayana cited in the *Dayabhaga,* IV. 1. 18.
232. *Daya.,* pp. 73-76.
233. *Narada.,* IV. 28.
234. *Daya.,* IV. 1.
235. *Smriti Chandrika,* p. 281.
236. *Mit.,* II. XI. 33.
237. *ADS,* II. VI. XIV. 16-18.
238. *Mit.* on *Yaj.,* II. 146.
239. *Daya.,* IV. I. 20.
240. *Smrti Chandrika,* p. 658.
241. *Ibid.,* p. 656.
242. *Ibid.*
243. *Daya.,* IV. I. 23.
244. *Smrti Chandrika,* pp. 654-55.
245. *Daya.,* IV. I. 23.
246. *Ibid.*
247. *Daya.,* IV. I. 19. Macnaghten's *Precedents of Hindu Law,* Ch. VIII.
248. *Daya.,* XI. II. 30, 31.

249. Katyayana cited in *Daya.*, XI. I. 56.
250. Katyayana quoted in the *Smrti Chandrika*, p. 656.
251. Benerjee, G.D., *Hindu Law of Marriage and Stridhana*, pp. 323-24.
252. *Mit.* on *Yaj.*, II. 117.
253. Banerjee, G.D., *op. cit.*, pp. 355-56.
254. *Mit.* on *Yaj.*, II. 145.
255. Hardatta on *Gautama.*, XXVIII. 23.
256. *Mit.* on *Yaj.*, II.146.
257. *Yaj.*, II. 117.
258. *Mit.* on *Yaj.*, II. 145.
259. *Manu.*, IX. 193.
260. *Naranda* cited in *Mit.* on *Yaj.*, II. 145.
261. *Yaj.*, II. 117.
262. *Ibid.*
263. *Mit.* on *Yaj.*, II. 145.
264. *Ibid.*
265. *Ibid.*
266. *Smrti Chandrika*, p. 285.
267. Jimutavahana divides *stridhana* property into four categories, viz. *sulka, Yautaka, anvadheyaka* and *ayautaka. Daya.*, Ch. IV.
268. *Daya.*, IV. 3. 29.
269. *Manu.*, IX. 131.
270. *Daya.*, IV. 2, 22 and 25.
271. *Ibid.*, III. 2-3.
272. *Ibid.*, III. 6.
273. *Ibid*, IV. 3-29.
274. Sankha-Likhita cited in *Daya.*, IV. 2. 4.
275. Devala cited in *Daya.*, IV. 2-6.
276. *Daya.*, IV. 2, 1-2; 9, 11-12.
277. *Manu.*, IX. 137, which is the same as *VDS*, XVII. 5; *Vishnu.*, XV. 46; *Manu.*, IX. 186 and *Yaj.*, I. 78.
278. *Yaj.*, II. 136-137 and *Vishnu.*, XVII. 4-15.
279. *Mit.* on *Yaj.*, II. 136.
280. *Mit.*, II. I. 15.
281. *Smrti Chandrika*, II, p. 294.
282. *Mit.*, II. I. 22.
283. *Ibid.*, II. I. 23.
284. *Mit.*, II. I. 24.
285. *Ibid.*, II. I. 15.
286. *Mit.* on *Yaj.*, II. 136.
287. *Yaj.*, II. 138.
288. Mitra, T.N., *The Law Related to the Hindu Widow*, p. 130.
289. *Mit.* on *Yaj.*, II. 136.

290. *Ibid.*, II. 117.
291. Apararka on *Yaj.*, II. 136.
292. *Smrti Chandrika*, p. 675—as translated by G.N. Jha, *Hindu Law in its Sources*.
293. *Smrti Chandrika*, p. 676 as translated in Jha, *op. cit.*
294. *Daya.*, II. 1. 2.
295. *Daya.*, XI. 1. 3.
296. Kulluka on *Manu.*, IX. 185.
297. *Ibid.*, IX. 187.
298. *Ibid.*, XI. I. 56.
299. *Ibid.*
300. *Ibid.*, XI. I. 62-66.
301. *Smrti Chandrika*, p. 677.
302. *EC*, Vol. IX, No. 33.
303. *Ibid.*, Vol. X, No. 100-A.
304. *Kumarapala Pratibodha*, p. 43.
305. *Sukraniti* as a whole is as late as about 1300 A.D.
306. *Ibid.*, IV. 5. 299-300.
307. *EC*, VI, Mudgere, No. 24.
308. *KSS*, 106 Panchalambaka, 14 Taranga, verses, 139-141.
309. *Yaj.*, II. 124; *Manu.*, IX. 118.
310. Kulluka on *Manu.*, IX. 118.
311. *Ibid.*
312. *Smrti Chandrika*, IV. 4-6
313. *Ibid.*, p. 628.
314. *Daya.*, III. II. 36-39.
315. *Ibid.*, XL. I. 66.
316. Apararka on *Yaj.*, II. 124.
317. *Yaj.*, II. 124.
318. *Ibid*
319. *Yaj.*, II. 124.
320. *Ibid.*
321. *Ibid.*, II. 136, 137.
322. *Vishnu.*, XVII. 4.
323. *Brh.*, XXV. 55-56.
324. Visvarupa on *Yaj.*, II. 136. 137.
325. *Smrti Chandrika*, p. 295.
326. *Mit.*, II. II. 2.
327. *Ibid.*
328. *Mit.*, II. II. 2.
329. *GDS*, XXVIII. 22.
330. *Mit.*, II. II. 4.
331. *Smrti Chandrika*, p. 662.

332. *Ibid.*, p. 663.
333. *Daya.*, XI. II. 2.
334. *Ibid.*, XI. II. 3.
335. *Ibid.*, XI. II. 8. 13.
336. *Ibid.*, XI. II. 31.
337. Because the term used in the text of *Yajnavalkya*, II. 136. 137 is *pitarau* which is treated as a compound word meaning *'mata cha pita cha'* wherein the mother comes first. The other form of the same compound is *mata pitarau'* where also the mother comes first.
338. *Manu.*, IX. 187.
339. *Manu.*, IX. 185.
340. *Ibid.*, IX. 217.
341. Kulluka on *Manu.*, IX. 185 and 217.
342. *Daya.*, XI. III. 1.
343. *Manu.*, IX. 217.
344. *Brhaspati.*, XXV. 63.
345. *Daya.*, XI. III. 2.
346. *Smrti Chandrika*, p. 691.
347. *Ibid.*
348. Kulluka on *Manu.* IX. 217.
349. Dharesvara quoted in *Mitakshara*, p. 729.
350. *Mit.*, II. V. I.

2

Education and Employment

Women have played crucial role in social reforms, economic development and also in the political process. They make the most effective providers of healthcare, be it grandmothers mother, nurses non-formal teacher and managers of the local environments As a wife and mother, she is the most influential member in determining the stability of her family and the development of her children's personality. Women are the real treasure of any nation. They are the principal architects of the family, the nation and the world. It is they who give birth to new generations. Education provides the foundation for this. Women's education is not only the key to development, but also for bringing up peace, prosperity, harmony and co-operation in the society.

There is a strong correlation between several developmental indicators and level of literacy of the population. Correlation is particularly strong with the level of female education It is found that the relation between the age of marriage of a girl and her achievement in education is positive. On the other handy infant mortality rate, birth rate and total fertility rate are negatively correlated, The lower the educational level of the mother, the more number of children born to her, the greater are the risks of reproductive mortality/ morbidity.

Despite persistent efforts of the Government of India, illiteracy though declining in percentage continuos grow in absolute numbers. The World Bank has estimated that in 2000 A.D. there will be 500 million adult illiterates in India constituting 54,8 percent of world's illiterate population in the age group 15-19 years. Since Independence, determined efforts have been made towards the achievement of the Universal Literacy in India. Over the years there has been a very impressive increase in the number and spread of Institutions as well as enrolment of girls. But, the lowest amount of literacy of women is found in the Hindi-belt states of Rajesthan, Bihar, Madhya Preadesh and Uttar Pradesh. These states account for the majority of illiterate women in India.

The Problem of unbalanced development of female literacy in comparison with men and with women between different states. Region and social groups is not a very simple issue. These p oblems needs to be classified on the basis of age, sex. Class and caste because the problems at each category are different for women's literacy.

Thus, the Integrated Learning Programmes for women have to be universalised which will riot only emphasis on literacy but also on empowering women through awareness building on the necessity of educating girls, social issues. bring about attitudinal change, promoting skill training for employment. providing information on healthcare, nutrition b hygiene and small family norm, The growing availability of communication media should be directed towards Keeping up information flows and inculcating positive image of women in non-conventional roles,

Mass scale Adult education programme for women in the age group 15-35 years, Non- formal education for the age group 6-14 years and the formal school system- these three systems of education have to be integrated and co-ordinated to eradicate illiteracy among females. Continuing education centres should be strengths to provide training and for retention of literacy skills.

National Policy for Education

The National Policy for Education document made a strong commitment to 'a well conceived edge in favour of women' as 'an act of faith and social engineering'. These commitments have been translated into concrete guidelines, and have resulted in a number of interventions which focus on the empowerment of women as the critical precondition for their participation in the educational process. The impact of these programmes is reflected in the decennial growth rate in female literacy of 9.54 per cent (Census 1991) which is significantly higher than the corresponding figure for males (7-76 per cent).

The following special provisions for women have been incorporated in the existing schemes:

(i) Operation Blackboard scheme now provides that at least 50 per cent of the teachers recruited in the future should be women. Out of the 1.27 lakh posts of the teachers filled under the scheme, 47 per cent are by women;

(ii) An innovative approach taken up in Rajasthan to improve access to education is the Shiksha Karmi Project. It envisaged substitution of the primary school teacher in single teacher schools by a team of two locally resident educational workers called Shiksha Karmis, of whom 10 per cent are women;

(iii) Under the scheme of Non-Formal Education, 90 per cent assistance is given for NFE centres exclusively for girls. The scheme has recently been revised so as to provide more facilities for educating girls by increasing the ratio of NFE centres exclusively for girls from 25 per cent to 40 per cent of the total;

(iv) Efforts are being made to ensure that at least one-third of the students in each Navodaya Vidayalayas are girls. In Navodaya Vidayalayas and Kendriya Vidyalayas, free education is imparted to girls up to Class XII;

(v) Free education is provided to girls up to class VIII in Punjab (Government schools), Manipur, Rajasthan (Government schools), UP, Delhi, Meghalaya and Chandigarh and up to secondary stage in Andhra Pradesh, Assam, Bihar (Government schools), Himachal Pradesh (Government schools) ' Karnataka, Tamil Nadu (Government schools), Mizoram and Lakshadweep and up to senior secondary stage Class XII in the states of Arunachal Pradesh, Goa, J and K, Kerala, Sikkim (Government schools), Tripura, West Bengal, A and N Islands, D and N Haveli, Daman and Diu, Pondicherry, Gujarat and Madhya Pradesh;

(vi) Under the Centrally-sponsored programme, at+2 level vocational programmes with emphasis on entrepreneurship are being designed to cater to the needs of girls who drop out of schools. Efforts are also on to consciously encourage participation of girls in the non-traditional and emergent technologies;

(vii) Women's education at the -university and college levels have been diversified and re-oriented in tune with the changing requirement of society, industry and trade. The number of women enrolled institutions of higher education increased from 40,000 in 1950-51 to about 20,65,000 in 1995-96, an increase of more than 51 times over the 44 year period;

(viii) The enrolment of women students at the beginning of the year 1993-94 was 15.90 lakh, as against 15.12 lakh in the previous year. At the postgraduate level the enrolment of women was 34.09 per cent of the total enrolment;

(ix) The UGC has been providing assistance to universities for undertaking research projects in women's studies; a number of research projects have been approved for assistance. Also assistance has been provided to 22 universities and 11 colleges for setting up women's studies/cells. The UGC has also created 40 positions of part-time research associateships for women candidates; and

(x) The participation of women in technical and professional streams has also shown a marked increase from a little over 6,000 in 1950-51 to 1.46 lakh in 1986-87, an increase of 23 times. There was also noticeable growth in the number of women students in the engineering and technology streams (in IITs and Polytechnics). As against 40 women students in 1950-51 (0.3 per cent) it rose to 16.67 thousand in 1986-87 (7.7 per cent) and 78.3 thousand in 1993-94 (13.1 per cent).

The process of mobilising and organising women is facilitated by a *Sahayogini* (a cluster coordinator in charge of 10 villages). She is a crucial link between the village sangha and the district implementation unit of the programme. The latter provides resource support and inputs to meet the needs of the women. The district units in turn are supported by a State Office which ensures a facilitative environment and brings in necessary resource inputs for the programme.

Role of Project Director

At the state level, an autonomous registered society as an empowered body has been set up to oversee the programme. At the national level the programme is coordinated by a Project Director. A National Resource Group, an advisory committe of eminent women activists, academics, development workers and bureaucrats, supports the programme bringing in new concepts, experiences and advises on programme policies and strategies.

Mahila Samakhya has expanded its coverage to 40 districts and over 6,876 villages in the States of Uttar Pradesh, Karnataka, Gujarat, Andhra Pradesh, Bihar, Madhya Pradesh and Assam. During 1998 the programme was expanded into a new State, i.e., Kerala where it would cover two districts. The effectiveness of the MS strategy in mobilising women for education has resulted in it being adopted by other basic education projects.

Through the International Development Agency assisted UP Basic Education Project, six districts have been additionally covered in Uttar Pradesh. The programme is being implemented in seven districts of Bihar as part of the Bihar Education Project and in three districts each of Madhya Pradesh and Assam the programme is supported by the District Primary Education Programme.

The sangha, which is a nodal point of the programme, has emerged as an effective women's collective at the village level. The *sanghas* address a wide range of issues relating to their livelihood, education, health, to accessing resources among others. At the village level, sanghas have carved out a niche for themselves by actively participating in village affairs and are recognised by the communities as a force to reckon with.

Adult and children's education continue to be of central concern to the sanghas. Sanghas have taken an active lead in enrolling children primarily girls in the village schools. Monitoring the functioning of schools and encouraging parents to send their children to school has become part of sangha agenda. Campaigns, Melas, Participatory Rural Appraisals have been some of the strategies through which issues of girls education have been brought centre-stage. In all the States, strategies for a functional convergence with the DPEP programme are being undertaken.

Non-formal Education

Non-formal education centres for drop-outs of school girls continue to grow in numbers bearing testimony to the growing importance of girl child education within the programme as well as with the *sanghas*. The Mahila Shikshana Kendras (16 in number) are a unique residential learning opportunity for adolescent girls and young women. The curriculum based on a holistic approach includes imparting basic literacy, life skills, and a preparation to play a leadership role in the development of their communities. The Mahila Shikshan Kendra is evolving as an innovative strategy to address the learning needs of adolescents and young women.

Under the Mahila Samakhya programme, health education has received considerable attention primarily because it is of great concern and interest for the sanghas. Baroda Unit of MS in Gujarat has opened two Jasod Health Centres in which use of herbal medicines, home-made remedies are propagated. Baroda Unit has also initiated necessary plantation of medicinal plants as part of dealing with health problems as well as economic development programme in collaboration with State Forest Department.

The biggest challenge before the Government and NGO's is to create awareness and Sentization among people to all levels, specially in rural areas, about the special needs of women and girls, and that imparting education to women is a great service to society. as this vital section of society remainder deprived and neglected from the very past. There is a need for affirmative and real action in favour of women which will ensure the women to right to food, Shelter, Health, education and employment.

Women Literacy Development in Kerala

The higher the level of literacy and education of women, the faster would be the development process. In this context, it would be illuminating to examine the experience of Kerala which has the highest level of women's literacy and education and a unique pattern of development. The empowerment of women as a concept was introduced at the International Women's Conference 1985 at Nairobi and development with empowerment has become the slogan for the 1990. The Government of India made a commitment at Nairobi for uprooting gender discrimination at the earliest.

The National Policy on empowerment of women 1986 drafted by the Department of Women and Child Development, Ministry of HRD, Govt. of India declares that empowerment of women is possible by giving them complete and equal access to and control over factors contributing to such empowerment, particularly health, education, information, life-long learning for self-development, vocational skills, employment and income earning opportunities. It would be interesting to know that in Kerala this kind of an approach was in vogue much before independence. A system of non-formal education organised around temples prevailed in Kerala even before 18th century. Because of the matriarchal system in the Nair community, one of the dominant castes, women enjoyed respectability and status in their families and they got the opportunity to learn in the indigenous local 'Kudippallikkudoms' run by 'Asans' (Master). Thus, traditionally women in the Nair community had equality in many ways and education was one among them. However, with the commencement of modern education by Christian missionaries in the 19th century, female education received a greater emphasis.

The first Girl's School in India was started by the missionaries in the State of Travancore in 1819 and this was followed by another school by the Government in 1859. By the end of the 19th century, the state had several girls schools. The relatively high literacy level among women in Kerala is the result of these early efforts . The female literacy rate was 31.5 in Kerala in 1951 as against just 7.9 in India as a whole. The high female literacy undoubtedly, facilitated the state to achieve remarkably high status in health as evidenced from indicators like life expectancy, infant mortality etc. The life expectancy at birth in Kerala was always higher among females.

In 1951, the life expectancy at birth among females was 42.30 as against 39.90 among males. Both these were higher in Kerala, compared to that in India. Similarly the lower infant mortality rate, birth rate and death rate in Kerala, compared to all India rates in 1951 were also partly attributable to the higher level of female literacy in the State.

The relatively high literacy and education level in Kerala, particularly among women paved the way for several socio-cultural movements in the State that created widespread social awareness and sowed the seeds of radical thinking among the people.

In Kerala, Adult and Non-formal Education activities began with the formation of the Kerala Gandhasala Sangham (Kerala State Library Council) by organising 47 rural libraries in 1945 under the initiative of Shri. P.N. Panicker and subsequently the number of libraries have increased to 6000. They served as good community centres by organising discussion, seminars, symposiums etc.

The Kerala, Grandhasala Sangham submitted a proposal in 1970 to Govt. of India to open 7000 Literacy Centres in the State. The Govt., of India sanctioned a pilot project to start 20 centres each in two districts. Later sanction was accorded to start 20 more centres in two other districts. In appreciation of the creditable work the Grandhasala Sanghom won the Krupskaya award from UNESCO, in 1975. A number of voluntary agencies came into being during this period, KANFED (Kerala Association for non-formal Education and Development) was the leading one in the field of Non-formal and Adult Education.

Subsequently Rural Functional Literacy Programme (RFLP) was started in five districts Trivandrum, Alappuzha, Thissur, Palakkad and Kannur in 1982-83. The Programme was implemented at the block level and managed by Assistant Development Commissioners. Later RFPL was extended to 11 districts. Simultaneously the Universities of Kerala and Calicut started centres for Adult Education and Extension and they also had literacy centres. National Service Scheme Volunteers were also pooled in to the activities of Adult Education.

The People's Education and Literacy Campaign, Kottayam (PELCK) was started in Kottayam town with the intention to make the town fully literate within a period of 100 days. This venture was commenced with the help of N.S.S. Volunteers of Mahatma Gandhi University. An idea of the campaign for total literacy in Ernakulam, was mooted by Shri.K.R.Rajan, the then District Collector. The proposal was approved by NLM and entrusted the District administration to implement it with the co-operation of Kerala Sastra Sahitya parishad (K.S.S.P) and subsequently District Literacy council was registered for the purpose. The programme commenced on 26th January 1989 and ended on 25th January 1990.

The experiments in Ernakulam and its achievement gave an impetus to enlarge the campaign throughout the state. The total Literacy Programme was formally inaugurated by the then Prime Minister Shri.V.P.Singh on 4th February 1990. The Kerala Saksharatha Samithy (K.S.S.) sponsored by the Govt. of Kerala steered the programme under the Chairmanship of the Cheif Minister. The Project was duly endorsed by the NLM. By using all available infrastructure with the Co-operation of people and the administrative machinery, Kerala was declared as a totally literate State on April 18,1991. The successful culmination of the TLC in produced over 12 lakhs neo-literates. The Post Literacy Campaign which was aimed at consolidating the gains of TLC and sustaining the achievements of literacy launched on 2nd October 1992. Out of the target group of 12.2 lakhs neo-literates, 4,16 lakhs neo-literates dropped out in the first phase.

The post literacy activities lacked momentum and were becoming a dead-weight. It was in this context the Government ordered in 1996 that the District Saksharatha Samiti this will be handed over to the elected District Panchayaths which were already in position. However, as the PLC had veased to exert any influence, this handing over had not become effective.

In January 1997, a new project for Continuing Education was drawn up, taking into account the changed attitudes and expectations of the community. A successful TLC has made people aware of their rights and privileges and therefore Continuing Education has to suit the socio-economic milieu.

Continuing Education has thus been designed as a major Human Resource Development initiate, covering all sections of the society like the neo-literates, rural artisans, women and drop-out children. Besides, the implementation of the programme will follow a highly decentralised model, utilising fully the potential of the 3-tier Panchayaths.

A systematic effort encompassing all areas of women development was made in the mid sixties. In the 1970's however, it became evident that unless women's development needs were specifically addressed, they will continue to lag behind in social and economic sectors and become increasingly marginalised.

The report of the Committee on Status of women in India, which made a comprehensive analysis of women's status in developmental framework came out with a series of recommendations for improving the status of women. This has resulted into the creation of separate Bureau of Women's Development in the Department of Social Welfare and in setting up a National Committee with Prime Minister as the Chairman. We now have a separate Department of Women and Child Development, which acts as a nodal point on matters relating to women development.

The Sixth Plan

The Sixth Plan (1980-85) for the first time presented an integrated strategy for women development which emphasised a multi-sectoral approach to the development of women and gave specific attention to inter-linkages. The seventh plan continued the strategy. In recent years, a National Perspective plan for women has been prepared which provides direction for the development of women in various fields.

The National Policy of Education 1986, which updated in 1992 is considered to be a land mark in education, because the policy envisages a dual track approach designed to promote simultaneously adult literacy and primary education with a focus on girls and other disadvantaged groups. There is a pronounced policy shift from equal education opportunity to 'education for gender equality'. It enjoins that the education system should play a positive interventionist role in the empowerment of women, foster the development of new values through revised curriculum and text books provide systematic training and orientation of teachers, decision makers and administrators all through the active involvement of education institutions. Thus very high priority continued to be given for education and literacy, particularly for female education in Kerala during the post-independence period. Consequently the female literacy rate went up to 86.9 in Kerala by 1991 as against only 39.4 at the All India level. Also, the disparity in the literacy rates of males and females narrowed down to just 7.6, the male literacy rate being 94.5 percent in 1991. While there is a gap of 24.5 percent between the literacy rates of males and females in the country as a whole.

Kerala's development in the post-independence period is characterised by several unique features, and the one single most important and fundamental factor that contributed to these features has been the high literacy and education level in Kerala, without much gender differences. The achievement of the state in the area of health and family welfare programme have been remarkable and almost at par with the level achieved in developed countries. Among the Indian states Kerala has the highest life expectancy at birth, the lowest birth rate and death rate, the lowest infant mortality rate, the highest PQLI and the highest Human Resource Development Index (HRDI).

Further Kerala could implement the most successful Land Reforms build up a widespread public distribution system, reduced the urban-rural disparities in social development and implementation of welfare programmes and above all could arouse the political and social conscience of the people.

All these commendable progress in health, social amenities,

agrarian relations, distributive justice, equality of life etc. which contributed to substantial improvement in the living conditions and status of the people, particularly of women and the poor. This could have achieved only because of the high literacy and education level in the state.

The mid-seventies witnessed the emergence of several women's groups and organisations which have taken up feminist issues from a new perspective. Their activities were not restricted merely to assert women's rights but also made serious attempts to articulate their thoughts on the roots of oppression of women. Moreover, these groups were not guided by any political leader or party. Young educated women took the initiative to form autonomous women's groups. These organisations generated feminist cultural groups and as a result of their strenuous efforts, they could get favourable amendments in the laws relating to women.

The Muslim and Christian women have come out challenging their respective personal laws based on religions. More than that, their attention has been turned to the problems of women, social customs, responsibilities of house-work and patronising attitude of male trade union leaders. The high literacy and education level of women is mainly the driving force behind all these developments related to women.

The experience of Kerala provides a number of lessons for future actions. We have seen from Kerala's experience that it was the wide-spread literacy and education among women that made possible the state to achieve a unique pattern of development with a humanistic face. It was the commendable achievements of the state in the areas of education, health, public distribution, land reforms and in other service sectors at a relatively low per capita income level that made Kerala's model of development notable and famous and attracted world-wide attention.

The greatest challenge before us therefore is to find enough resources for undertaking massive literacy and education programmes for women during the next one decade with a view to achieve. (i) Cent percent literacy level for all women in the county and (ii) to educate and equip the women with necessary skill not only to take up gainful employment, but also to participate actively and effectively in the planning and development process of the county. It is really an ambitious task to achieve 100 percent literacy in another one decade's time. But it is not impossible, as can be seen from the experience of Kerala, if we can find enough resources to launch massive programmes in this area. Taking into consideration the urgency and need for achieving such a target, we should definitely commit ourselves to such a programme. In fact the greatest challenge before us is to get ourselves committed to this noble objective.

There are several other specific challenges before us when we enter into the 21st century. Some of them are delineated below :

1. The 73rd and 74th amendments in the constitution, empowering the local bodies for self-governance under a three-tier Panchayati Raj system, provide provisions for women's reservation in one third of the seats in the Panchayats. This means that from now onwards the women have to play a much bigger role in the nation-building process. One of the important challenges is to prepare them for undertaking new responsibilities. The first pre-requisite for this is to give them suitable education. Their effective participation in Grama Sabha and in other decision making bodies at local level in development matters and day to day governess can be ensured only if they are properly educated and trained. The post-literacy and continuing education programme in the country, particularly in Kerala, should be chalked out with this end in view.
2. A time bound programme for universalisation of primary education among women is an immediate need of the hour. This is the first step for integrating women with the country's development process.
3. The existing scenario of Continuing Education demands diversification and need-orientated programmes for women literacy and development. The process of diversification requires conscious formulation of cultural policy for women and its implementation, keeping in view the expected changes and challenges in the 21st century. Needless to say the literacy and post-literacy projects in India have been resorted to the traditional or conventional

method of propaganda and extension education. What is required in Kerala is the introduction of continuing Education Programmes with more thrust on vocationalisation for producing enough technical man power. This is essential for taping the opportunities provided for women in starting self-employment enterprises. There is the need for evolving the intervention strategy suited to the long-felt needs of the different women's group like casual labourers, seasonal labourers, fish-marketers, farm labourers etc. It is desirable to consider the following in this context

(i) Women resource Unit may be started in the State Resource Centre for vocational training and extension support for women groups in terms of seeking assurance from other government agencies. This women Resource Unit should be equipped with a comprehensive and computerised date bank for policy making and for co-ordinating all women development projects

(ii) Work centres for women on a co-operative basis in the rural areas should be encouraged by women's Resource Units with the help of counsellors in Women's Resource Unit.

(iii) A large majority of women, both rural and urban work in the unorganised sectors of the economy where their plight is deplorable. Hence to safe-guard the interests of these less privileged women it is desirable to start Women's Co-operative and credit societies.

(iv) Suitable continuing education programme should be formulated and implemented to articulate and improve necessary skills in women who organise themselves on 'Self-Help' groups for improving their living conditions.

(v) Equal Remuneration Act in both organised and unorganised sectors may be effectively enforced.

(vi) The diverse traditions, cultures, ideals, habits ethnic consciousness and life style of Indian women pose a challenge while planning and implementation development oriented Literacy programme for women.

(vii) The changing value system, expectations, perceptions of religion/ caste groups and linguistic and regional consciousness among people at large and women in particular, are the challenges to be addressed through educational programme.

(viii) Special continuing education programmes for the benefit of the neo-literates SC/ST communities are to be introduced on a time-bound basis to liberate them from further exploitation.

(ix) In Kerala, which already achieved about 100 percent literacy among women, the emphasis in the coming decades should be on programmes that would integrate them with the process of development. Such an integration of women with development process and their active participation in this process are all the more important in Kerala, particularly in the context of the decentralized planning experiment under implementation in the state, known popularly as 'Peoples planning'. The women members of the local bodies in the three-tier system in Kerala awefully need educational inputs to improve themselves and to discharge their new responsibilities effectively. Also, the women in the society, whose active participation and involvement are expected in the 'grama Sabhas' the basic forum of the people's planning, badly need minimum level of understanding, skill and communication capability. The greatest challenge in the continuing education programme in Kerala is how to address this most vital and crucial issue. This challenge could be met only through massive programmes for which Kerala needs necessary resources.

The CSWI viewed women's education from the point of view of the individual as well as the society - that is, its value in the development of the personality of the individual and the usefulness of the educated individual to society at large. The educated individual commanded a high status in society because of the innate value of rationality and learning and due to acquisition of qualifications to fulfill economic, political and cultural functions. Such enhancement of status would bring about reduction of inequalities between individuals. In this view, the CSWI referred to education being recognised in the Universal Declaration of Human Rights as a basic right of every human being and to the Constitution of the UNESCO directing efforts to achieving equality of educational opportunities without regard, *inter alia*, to sex.

The emancipators of the 19th century wanted education to be given to women more on humanitarian grounds and to strengthen them in the performance of their traditional roles in families. Though change in this view came about during the post independence period, ambivalence about the purpose of women's education persisted at least in traces amongst individuals and even among official agencies. The CSWI called for an understanding of this ambivalence in the context of proper academic planning, allocation of resources and analysis of quantitative indices of educational development like enrolment, institutional infrastructure, literacy rates etc.

Having referred to the Constitutional directive for Universalisation of Elementary Education (UEE) within ten years of the promulgation of the Constitution and to the non fulfillment of this directive as brought out in the Report of the Indian Education Commission (1966), the CSWI attributed it mainly to the slow progress of education among girls.

While women's education expanded more rapidly during the post independence period relative to earlier times, expansion by itself was not satisfactory and wide gaps existed between the enrolment of boys and girls. The National Committee on Women's Education (1959) had found that even the targets fixed for the First and Second Plans tended to widen the disparity between the education of men and women; and had recommended: "...a bold and determined effort be made ... to close the existing gap between the education of men and women in as short a time as possible; ... and the funds required for the purpose should be considered to be the first charge on the sums set aside for the development of education."

Fifteen years later, disparities still continued. In 1973-74 enrolment of girls relative to that of boys was 62 per cent at the Primary stage, 43 per cent at Middle level, 36 per cent at Secondary stage and 31 per cent at the Tertiary stage. In professional education, women had substantial enrolments in teaching, fine arts and medicine, but their enrolment in other courses like agriculture, commerce, law and engineering was rather small. Women's entry in the fields of research was satisfactory and at the University level particularly, the performance of girls in all subjects including mathematics and science often outstripped that of the boys. However, higher education in general seemed to be a preserve of the urban upper and middle classes. The CSWI also identified six States, namely, Bihar, Madhya Pradesh, Rajasthan, Uttar Pradesh, Orissa and Andhra Pradesh as lagging behind in women's education.

Enrolment by itself would not be adequate to capture the level of educational advancement. Factors such as 'dropouts' and 'wastage', 'retention', 'out turn' etc., were crucial too. Educational advancement also depended upon whether enrolled children attended schools even for a short time, whether they did not drop out causing wastage. In the case of girls, social factors such as marriage, betrothal and parental apathy played significant part in causing wastage.

There had been expansion of educational institutions including by establishment of a large number of institutions exclusively for girls. However, a large number of them turned out to be single teacher schools at the primary level. When the teacher was not able to attend, the school had to remain closed. This caused dropout of girls. At the middle and secondary levels, teaching facilities were not adequate. Enrolment in women's colleges was low. Academic standards were often diluted: The supply of women teachers fell far short of demand. A substantial number of them were also untrained. School inspections were also inadequate.

In this backdrop the CSWI presented wide ranging and crucial recommendations covering areas relating to values, access, content and process and system of education.

MAJOR DEVELOPMENTS/EVENTS SINCE CSWI REPORT

Progress through Five Year Plans

Women's education was made a major programme under

"Women and Development" in the Sixth Plan (1980-85). This was, indeed, a direct outcome of the CSWI Report. Universalisation of elementary education, creation of Balwadis-cum-Creches, appointment of women teachers especially in rural areas, strengthening of science teaching for girls, streamlining admission policies to promote greater access for girls including to professional courses in higher education, etc., were given special importance in the Sixth Plan.

In the Seventh Plan (1985-90), emphasis was on restructuring of educational programmes, removal of gender bias through curricular reform, incentives and scholarships, non-formal and open learning systems, etc.

In the Eighth Plan (1992-97), education remained a core sector. In fact, the main focus of the Eighth Plan was human development of which educational development was a part.

One of the basic objectives spelt out in the Ninth Plan (1997-2002) is empowerment of women. Apart from free and compulsory education for children, emphasis was also on initiative by the Government in upgradation of education and skill development.

National Plan of Action, 1976

This was prepared keeping in view the deliberations and debate during the International Women's Year and the subsequent World Plan of Action and other recommendations and suggestions. Education was one of the priority areas identified under this Action Plan.

National Policy on Education (NPE), 1986 and Programme of Action

The most important development since the CSWI Report was, of course, the formulation of a new Educational Policy, "National Policy on Education:' (NPE) 1986. The Policy and the Programme of Action (POA) framed thereunder were reviewed in 1991 by a National level Committee and with reference to this review, they were further fine-tuned by the Government in 1992. The basic work on the formulation of the Policy, the commencement of its implementation as well as its mid-term review spanned between the Seventh and Eighth Plans.

NPE, 1986 laid special emphasis on "Education for Women's Equality." In fact, women's education was presented by the policy in the perspective of an overall strategy for securing equity and social justice. Paras 4.2 and 4.3 of the Policy in particular strongly brought out the "intervening and empowering" role of education. The parameters and strategies specifically envisaged in the Policy were:-

- Gearing the entire education system to play a positive interventionist role in the empowerment of women.
- Encouraging educational institutions to take up active programmes to enhance women's status and further women's development in all sectors.
- Widening women's access to vocational, technical and professional education levels, breaking gender stereotypes.
- Creation of dynamic management structure that would respond to the challenges posed by the mandate on enhancing women's status.

The POA viewed the empowering role of education in terms of several value/ skill parameters – enhancing the self esteem and self confidence of women, building up positive image about them by due recognition of their contribution to society, polity and economy, capability to think critically, making informed choices in areas like education, employment and health including reproductive health, equal participation in developmental processes, acquisition of information, knowledge and skill for economic independence, legal literacy, etc.

The POA also spell out various specific activities to be undertaken in the area of education for women's equality. Programming for addressing gender related concerns on a continuous basis by the various government agencies cutting across departments at the Central and State levels, creation of monitoring mechanisms to watch progress, submission of Annual Reports, *inter alia,* dealing with women's and girls' access to education, gender sensitizing the content and progress of education a well as curricula, specialised training for teachers and instructors, promoting research and women's studies in higher educational institutions, etc. were specific measures stipulated by the POA.

Special emphasis was laid on reaching out to the girl child as an integral part of the process of achieving Universalisation of Elementary Education. This concept of "reaching out" was to be articulated through Non-Formal Education (NFE) for girls and open school distant education systems. Support services were also to be provided in co-ordination with other Ministries/Departments to enhance their participation in education - for example, to take care of domestic supplies of fuel fodder, water, etc. so as to release girls from this responsibility and thereby enhance their entry into the world of education. It was stipulated that fifty percent of the teachers recruited for provision of elementary education would be women.

Women's access to vocational, technical and professional education and existing and emerging technologies was emphasised. Specific measures suggested in this area included science and mathematics teaching in girls schools, recruitment of more teachers of these subjects, development of vocational technology oriented curricula, etc. Revamping of Polytechnics and Industrial Training Institutes and diversifying their disciplines, courses and trades was to be organised. The Apprenticeship Scheme was to be geared to enhance the coverage of women and they were to be given access to information on credit, banking and entrepreneurial skills.

The POA further called for creation of an environment for equal opportunities for women and girls through the electronic print and traditional Media. Use of the Radio was given special importance as a strategic measure because of the strength of its outreach into rural areas.

In terms of NPE 1986 and the POA, more than a dozen centrally sponsored schemes have been under implementation commencing from 1987-88. An amount of more than Rs. 7,000 crore has been released to the State Governments up to the year 1998-99 for the, implementation of these schemes. Year-wise, NPE scheme-wise data on release of funds to the States is presented in Table 1.

While considerable lot of monies are being released by the Centre to the States, implementation of crucial schemes would seem to leave much to be desired, as would be brought out in detail later.

SAARC Workshop on the Girl Child, 1988

India actively participated in regional level as well in the matter of promoting the cause of education of girls. The Government of India (Ministry of Human Resource Development, Department of Women and Child Development) hosted a SAARC Workshop at New Delhi. In the country presentation on India in this workshop, it was observed : In the area of education, the scenario presents a depressing trend. The national goal of universalisation of primary

Table 1. Release of Funds to States/ UTs under Centrally Sponsored Schemes on Education (1987-88 to 1998-99).

Years	OB	NFE	TE	RTF	VE	SCE	ET	IEDC	CLASS	RELP	JSN	SAS	AHT	HTTI	En.Ed.	PL&CE	Yoga	DPEP	LJ	M.Edn.	Total
1987-88	110.61	35.52	32.48	3.19	32.26	29.27	7.15	2.26	0.51	32.99	9.48	3.52	1.93	0.08	–	–	–	–	–	–	301.25
1988-89	135.73	30.65	36.57	9.21	49.64	29.02	11.19	1.94	0.69	45.97	10.65	4.63	3.27	0.29	1.60	–	–	–	–	–	371.05
1989-90	126.98	26.28	35.69	7.11	43.72	21.33	10.61	2.39	0.65	41.37	11.63	5.93	1.94	0.24	1.10	–	–	–	–	–	336.98
1990-91	150.09	34.93	19.74	–	72.87	20.38	11.66	3.43	–	28.85	–	6.91	3.07	–	1.59	8.20	0.31	–	–	–	361.98
1991-92	175.63	40.02	42.90	–	56.57	18.23	9.47	3.78	–	15.10	–	4.93	2.13	–	1.09	8.88	0.25	–	–	–	378.96
1992-93	154.91	45.17	82.93	–	77.14	24.55	9.07	3.80	–	1.37	–	8.53	1.97	–	1.00	6.20	0.18	–	–	–	416.82
1993-94	178.70	86.26	68.02	–	82.72	21.45	14.98	4.50	23.30	7.23	–	9.98	5.70	–	0.31	9.03	0.54	–	–	–	512.72
1994-95	214.70	106.37	63.23	–	66.77	22.00	16.09	5.17	23.03	7.62	–	12.12	5.75	–	0.71	11.05	0.19	–	–	–	554.80
1995-96	267.93	153.41	78.30	–	67.55	23.17	4.18	6.70	21.99	0.28	–	11.00	4.10	–	0.04	9.34	0.10	–	–	–	648.09
1996-97	291.17	158.20	79.30	–	51.29	14.46	5.80	20.54	0.32	–	11.59	4.40	–	1.06	17.71	0.12	179.42	22.20	–	867.74	–
1997-98	297.69	179.15	71.48	–	2.66	2.94	6.23	9.99	10.30	0.40	–	4.00	2.15	–	1.27	23.94	–	545.56	16.33	2.15	1174.09
1998-99	227.70	119.57	142.58	–	4.95	1.00	8.49	–	1.00	–	5.00	5.86	–	1.79	23.32	–	547.80	37.50	13.53	1144.11	–
Total	2331.70	1015.53	753.22	19.51	608.14	230.96	111.79	58.25	101.01	182.50	31.76	88.14	42.27	0.61	11.56	117.67	1.69	1272.78	76.03	15.68	7068.59

Source : Progress of Centrally Sponsored Schemes in Education 1996; Annual Financial Statistics of Education Sector 1996-97 and 1997-98; Ministry of Human Resource Development, Department of Education.

OB – Operation Blackboard   NFE – Non-Formal Education   TE – Teacher Education   RTF – Refund of Tuition Fees
VE – Vocational Education   SCE – Science Education   ET – Education Technology   IEDC – Integrated Education of Disabled Children
CLASS – Computer Literacy and Studies in Schools   RELP – Rural Functional Literacy Project   JSN – Jan Sikshan Nilayam
SAS –   AHT – Appointment of Hindi Teachers
HTTI –   En.Ed. – Environment Education PLCE   DPEP – District Primary Education

education by 1995 appears impossible to achieve, as vast numbers of girls are out of school or drop out in the school going age. The Government for the last three decades been trying to make nutritional and educational interventions through various programmes and strategies on behalf of women and girls. More specific and focused efforts are needed to bring about significant changes in the health, nutritional and educational status of the girl child".

Prescriptions of the NDC Committee for Universalisation of Elementary Education 1992-93

- In Districts in which access and enrolment are almost universal, bringing the residue into the fold of UPE (Universal Primary Education)/UEE;
- Strong intervention for a total coverage of all eligible children in all Total Literacy Campaign (TLC) Districts in which community mobilization for literacy and education has been successfully done under the National Literacy Mission;
- Socio political and community mobilization in low literacy Districts in which provision of educational facilities is unsatisfactory - block by block and even parts of the block;
- Replication of successful practices in externally aided project districts, based on feed backs on innovations;
- Publicising innovative and successful area specific methodologies evolved by voluntary agencies and research organisations;
- Considering that enforcement of compulsion at the primary stage has not been very successful even in sixteen States which have enacted Primary Education Acts to ensure full attention and retention, provision of incentives such as attendance scholarships, mid-day meals, weekly supply of grain, provision of uniforms, free supply of text books and minimum learning materials etc, apart from alternative channels of schooling;
- Recruitment of women teachers such that they constitute 60 to 80 per cent in most States; and
- Provision of support services in the form of child care facilities, attachment of pre-primary sections to primary classes and assistance to voluntary organisations for

running Early Child Care and Education (ECCE) Centres.

National Development Council (NDC) Committee on Literacy, 1992-93

Another important development after the Report of the Committee on the Status of Women was the submission of a Report on Literacy by a Committee on National Development Council in 1993. This Committee was chaired by the Chief Minister of Uttar Pradesh and consisted of four other Chief Ministers (West Bengal, Mizoram, Punjab and Bihar), apart from the Union Minister of Human Resource Development.

The Committee examined the status of literacy in the country from the point of view of universalisation of elementary education as well as adult literacy.

The terms of reference of this Committee included, *inter alia*—

- "To suggest measures for reduction of social, gender and regional disparities in literacy achievement during the Eighth Plan."
- "To suggest structures and modalities for efficient administration, monitoring and evaluation of literacy activities so as... to integrate the literacy movement with child care, child development, women's economic empowerment, population limitation and reduction of IMR (Infant Mortality Rates) and maternal mortality, etc:"

In the presentation of the literacy perspective in its Report; the Committee took note of the relevance of women's literacy in the following words:

> "World Bank studies in 29 developing countries have shown that infant and child mortality rates are in inverse proportion to the level of education of mothers and that each year schooling for girls and women's literacy means further reduction of IMR and lower birth rate. A study conducted by ICMR (Indian Council of Medical Research) in 1990-91 on Immunization Programme and Maternal and Child Health in the States of UP, MP, Rajasthan and Bihar has shown that immunization status of children of literate mothers is better than that of illiterate mothers both in urban and rural areas. Reduction of sickness arising from lack of hygiene, malnutrition and superstitious practices has also been noticed in families,

which have literate women members. This improvement in health leads to reduction of national cost on health services while providing to the country more capable human resources. The conclusion that literacy and education of women lead to a higher pace of population control and to greater economic productivity has awakened the world to the need to focus upon literacy and elementary education programmes not simply as a matter of social justice but more pertinently as a matter of economic growth, social well being and social stability."

Reviewing the elementary education scenario in terms of quantitative dimensions, access and disparities. the Committee found, particularly with reference to the Fifth All India Educational Survey (1986), that in about six percent of the rural habitations with a population of 300 or more, primary schools were not available within a distance of 1 km; and that in about 16 per cent of the rural habitations with a population of 500 or more, middle schools were not available within a distance of 3 km. (Figures deduced from data on percentage of such habitations covered by primary schools within 1 km./middle schools within 3 km.). The Committee further noted the major problem in providing primary schooling facilities within a distance of 1 km. in 1,20,480 habitations, which have a population of less than 300. In absolute numbers, there were 2,36,986 habitations with a population of, 500 or more, which were unserved by middle schools with a distance of 3 km. In areas where upper primary schooling facilities were not available within convenient walking distance, children tended to drop out of education after completing primary schooling.

Yet another important factor taken note of by the Committee was the relatively low increases in Gross Enrollment Ratio (GER) for girls. Between 1986 and 1990 it increased only by about 6 per cent at the primary stage (from 79.81 per cent to 85.97 per cent) and by less than 11 per cent (from 35.65 to 46.13 per cent) in the upper primary stage.

The Committee was concerned also about the male female disparities in literacy achievements. It observed; "the literacy rate in the case of females during 1981-91 increased by 9.6 per cent as compared to 7.5 per cent in the case of males. Though the progress rate of literacy in 1981-91 in respect of females was better, yet a huge disparity between male and female literacy rates continued to exist. As against the literacy rate of 63.9 per cent for males, literacy rate for females was 39.4 per cent. Females form 60 per cent of illiterate population though they constitute 48.1 per cent of the population in Bihar SC (Scheduled Caste) literacy rate was ... 2.51 per cent for females ... in Rajasthan female ST (Scheduled Tribe) literacy rate was 1.2 per cent".

Dwelling on the adverse impact, on universalisation of primary education, of inadequate participation of girls, the Committee observed:

> "Conservatism of tradition-bound families and illiterate groups, the practice of early marriage despite preventive legislation, reluctance to release girls from domestic chores, rapid population growth which compels girls to look after younger siblings, need for girls to release older women in the household for wage-employment, need for girls themselves to work for wage-employment increasingly seen among the rural poor, traditional preference to sons as providers for the parents in old age and looking upon daughters as economic burden, and the overall low status of women, are parts of the cluster of reasons for the educational deprivation of girls in India. Such administrative measures as reservation of seats for women in teacher-training institutions, selection of women teachers especially for handling lower primary classes, construction of quarters for women teachers etc., have been tried out in the past as blanket provisions for tackling the problem of girls' enrolment without a critical attention to the feasibility of implementing such measures in a predominantly rural and tradition-bound society which is largely illiterate and male-dominated. The inability of urban-educated women to work as primary teachers in an isolated manner in the rural areas, the lack of educated women in the rural areas themselves, the orthodoxy and outdated customs which treat women as a lower order of citizens, and uncharitable male attitudes have led to the failure of these schemes based on urban viewpoints. Disregard of the Constitution in the case of SC/STs, and girls has been most noticeable

all along. Such are the factors that have been the major hurdles in the path of universal primary education. Dependence on mere administrative efforts will not solve this problem. Mobilizing public opinion against this social injustice and finding specific solutions to the predicament of different disadvantaged groups, State by State, district by district, block by block and even habitation by habitation is now most essential. Disaggregated micro-level planning which treats each rural and tribal household and each habitation as the basic unit for planning and socio-political action for implementation has been (*sic*) the major thrust if equality of educational opportunity at the primary stage is to be realized before the year 2000."

Education as Fundamental Right

A significant development in the judicial front since the report of the CSWI is the Supreme Court pronouncement that equality of access in education is an integral part of fundamental rights.

In their judgement in Mohini Jain Vs The State of Karnataka, in 1992, the Supreme Court ruled that education including higher education is a fundamental right. They reasoned too that the preamble of the constitution mentions about assuring the dignity of every individual; that Article 38 refers to a social order in which Justice – social, economic and political – shall inform all the institutions of national life; that Article 38 talks about minimising inequality of income and status and Article 41 about the right to work; and that as for all these education is essential, right to education should be construed as constant to fundamental rights enshrined in Part-III of the Constitution, though it may not be a fundamental right in itself. Equality of access in education is subsumed in fundamental rights.

"Educational for All" Summit of Nine 'High Population' Countries, 1993

This Summit hosted by India focused on primary education and universal adult literacy; financial, technical and political commitment; decentralised management of education; and mobilisation of community participation.

The Fourth World Conference on Women, Beijing, 1995

In the Platform for Action brought out by the Fourth World Conference on Women, Beijing, 1995, one of the Critical Areas of Concern identified was "Inequalities and inadequacies in and unequal access to education and training".

The basic strategies spelt out in the Platform for Action to address this concern were :

- ensuring equal access to education;
- eradication of illiteracy amongst women;
- improving women's access to vocational training, science and technology and continuing education;
- development of non-discriminatory education and training;
- allocation of sufficient resources for and monitoring of educational reforms; and
- promoting life long education and training for girls and women.

National Perspective Plan, 1998

This Plan observed "the strategies spelt out in the National Policy of Education, 1986, the Programme of Action for its implementation and the National Literacy Mission and the successful achievement of the goals imposed in these documents would be important for improvement in the status of women".

It also laid emphasis. *inter alia,* on generation of awareness about importance of educating girls; establishment of import with community; uniform pattern of education in terms of structure, curriculum and mobility actions States without differences between boys and girls; involvement of Mahila Mandals; 50 per cent reservation for women in recruitment of primary teachers; open learning school system; diversification of secondary education courses; vocationalisation, counseling and guidance; reservation of 30 per cent seats for girls in higher education, 50 per cent reservation of seats for women in pre-service courses in all teacher training institutions; and formation of village clusters for improving delivery of educational services.

Expansion of Educational Institutions

There was improvement in access to education in terms of increase in the umber of educational institutions since CSWI Report. Between 1970-71 and 1998-99, the number of recognised educational institutions increased in large numbers, the increases being 1.19

lakh primary schools, 1 lakh upper primary schools, 75,000 higher secondary level institutions, 5,209 Colleges and 155 Universities (Table 2).

Table 2. Growth of Recognised Educational Institutions

Year	*Primary*	*Upper Primary*	*Higher Secondary*	*Colleges for General Education*	*Colleges for Professional Education*	*Universities*
1950-51	2,09,671	13,596	7,416	370	208	27
1955-56	2,78,135	21,730	10,838	466	218	31
1960-61	3,30,399	49,663	17,329	967	852	45
1965-66	3,91,064	75,798	27,614	1,536	770	64
1970-71	4,08,378	90,621	37,051	2,285	992	82
1975-76	4,54,270	1,06,571	43,054	3,667	3,276*	101
1980-81	4,94,603	1,18,555	51,573	3,421	3,542*	110
1985-86	5,28,872	1,34,846	65,837	4,067	1,533*	126
1990-91	5,60,935	1,51,456	79,796	4,862	886	184
1991-92	5,65,786	1,52,077	81,747	5,058	950	196
1992-93	2,72,541	1,53,921	84,086	5,334	989	207
1993-94	5,72,923	1,55,707	88,411	5,639	1,125	213
1994-95	5,81,305	1,63,605	92,252	6,089	1,230	219
1995-96	5,90,421	1,71,216	98,134	6,569	1,354	226
1998-99	6,26,737	1,90,166	1,12,438	7,494	2,113	237

Source : Selected Educational Statistics, 1998-99; Ministry of Human Resource Development.

* These figures were inclusive of Post-Matric Courses.

Summation of Developments since CSWI Report

Despite considerable lot of targeted efforts taken, fairly comprehensively covering the various suggestions made by the CSWI and resources deployed for the purpose, the basic problems highlighted by the CSWI continue to persist. The ambivalence regarding the importance of women's education still continues in

Table 3. Gender Gaps in Education

Name of the Country	*Female Adult Literacy*		*Female Primary Net Enrolment Ratio*		*Female Secondary Enrolment Ratio*		*Female Tertiary Students*		*Female Tertiary Science Enrolment*
	Rate % 1997	*As % of male rate 1997*	*As % of relevant age group 1997*	*As % of male rate 1997*	*As % of relevant age 1997*	*As % of male rate group*	*Per 10,000 Women 1997*	*As % of males 1996*	*As % of female Tertiary Students 1995*
Bangladesh	27.4	55.0	69.6	87.0	15.6	58.0	–	–	–
Bhutan	30.3	52.0	12.3	88.0	–	–	–	–	–
India	54.2*	71.4*	71.0	91.0	48.0	68.0	481	61	–
Pakistan	25.4	46.0	–	–	–	–	–	–	–
Sri Lanka	87.6	93.0	99.9	100.0	79.3	109.0	388	69	–
Indonesia	79.5	88.0	98.6	99.0	53.4	91.0	812	53	23
Malaysia	81.0	90.0	99.9	100.0	68.5	115.0	–	–	–

(Contd.)

(Contd.)

Name of the Country	Female Adult Literacy		Female Primary Net Enrolment Ratio		Female Secondary Enrolment Ratio		Female Tertiary Students		Female Tertiary Science Enrolment
	Rate % 1997	As % of male rate 1997	As % of relevant age group 1997	As % of male rate 1997	As % of relevant age 1997	As % of male rate group	Per 10,000 Women 1997	As % of males 1996	As % of female Tertiary Students 1995
Philippines	94.3	99.0	99.9	100.0	78.5	102.0	3404	133	27
Singapore	87.0	91.0	89.5	98.0	74.8	98.0	2250	81	–
Thailand	92.8	96.0	89.2	103.0	36.9	97.0	–	–	23
Vietnam	89.0	94.0	99.9	100.0	54.2	97.0	–	–	–
Republic of Korea	95.5	97.0	99.9	100.0	99.9	100.0	4182	60	16
China	74.5	82.0	99.9	100.0	65.1	88.0	327	54	–

Source : UNDP, Human Development Report, 1999 quoted in ESCAP's "Overall Review of Regional implementation of the Beijing Platform for Action.

* Figures as per Census 2001.

Table 4. Illiterate Population 15 Years and above by Sex, 1980, 1990 and 1995

Name of the Country	*Years*	*% of Illiterates*		*Total*
		Females	*Males*	
Bangladesh	1980	82.8	52.8	70.4
	1990	76.8	58.7	64.8
	1995	73.9	53.3	62.0
Bhutan	1980	85.1	58.9	72.0
	1990	76.8	48.8	62.8
	1995	71.9	43.8	57.8
India	1980	74.7	44.7	59.2
	1990	66.5	37.6	51.6
	1995	62.3	34.5	48.0
Nepal	1980	92.7	69.2	80.9
	1990	88.6	62.8	75.9
	1995	86.0	59.1	72.7
Pakistan	1980	85.3	61.6	72.9
	1990	79.1	53.7	65.8
	1995	75.6	50.0	62.2
Sri Lanka	1980	20.5	9.1	14.7
	1990	15.2	7.4	11.3
	1995	12.8	6.6	9.8
Indonesia	1980	42.3	22.5	32.6
	1990	24.7	11.7	18.3
	1995	22.0	10.4	16.3
Malaysia	1980	40.3	20.4	30.4
	1990	26.4	13.1	19.7
	1995	21.9	10.9	16.4
Philippines	1980	11.3	9.4	10.4
	1990	6.8	6.0	6.4
	1995	5.7	5.0	5.4

(Contd)

(Contd)

Name of the Country	*Years*	*% of Illiterates*		*Total*
		Females	*Males*	
Singapore	1980	26.0	8.4	17.1
	1990	17.0	4.9	11.0
	1995	13.7	4.1	8.9
Thailand	1980	16.0	7.7	11.9
	1990	8.8	4.4	6.6
	1995	8.4	4.0	6.2
Vietnam	1980	22.4	10.0	16.6
	1990	13.0	5.2	9.3
	1995	8.8	3.5	6.3
Republic of Korea	1980	9.9	2.6	6.3
	1990	4.8	1.0	2.9
	1995	3.3	0.7	2.0
China	1980	47.3	21.4	34.0
	1990	31.9	13.0	22.2
	1995	27.3	10.1	18.5

Source: UNESCO, Compendium of Statistics on Illiteracy, 1995; United Nations Population Division, World Population Prospects; Quoted in ESCAP's "Overall Review of Regional Implementation of Beijing Platform for Action."

the minds of large masses of people due to patriarchal attitudes. Social and political mobilisation of a fairly significant order has not yet resulted in neutralisation of these basic attitudes. Therefore, male-female disparities continue to get reflected in access to, retention in and quality of education. The very same States which were identified by the CSWI as backward in this regard continue to be so even now.

Even universalisation of primary education appears capable of being achieved – in the light of the present trends – much later than certain South East Asian/East Asian countries. According to the world Bank, India would achieve uviversalisation of primary education only three decades later than the Republic of Korea and two decades later than Malaysia and Indonesia.

In the "Overall Review of Regional Implementation of the Beijing Platform for Action" made by Economic and Social Commission for Asia and Pacific (ESCAP) in a high level inter-Governmental meeting, the gender gaps in terms of literacy, enrolment, and the illiteracy rates prevailing in various countries of the South, South Eastern and East Asian region have been brought out with impact. The data based on this review, which speak for themselves are presented below in Tables 3 and 4. It can be seen that India lags much behind several South East Asian and East Asian countries.

Resources for Education

School enrolment, retention and achievement are all closely linked to economic development, household incomes and poverty.

Ever increasing and all round awareness has, indeed, been generated about the need for a significantly higher share of household incomes being invested in education. After CSWI Report, National Institutions have also come to closely and targetedly scrutinizing educational investment issues, especially with reference to their implications for women's education.

Data generated by NSSO 42nd round, revealed that :

- Households spend about one-third of total (government plus household) expenditure on primary education in the country;
- Where household expenditures on education are high, the tendency to never enroll increases and attendance tends to decline;
- High gender disparities are also evident in households with high expenditure on education;
- Expenditure on education of girls is lesser than for boys at all income levels, in rural and urban areas, in government and private schools, in many of the States;
- Among students receiving free primary education without tuition-fee, girls are better placed;
- Number of boys receiving partial or total exemption from payment of tuition fee is proportionately higher than girl students;
- A smaller proportion of girls receives scholarship than boys in rural areas; and
- Scholarship per student was only Rs. 67 for girls, compared to Rs. 103 for boys.

The Department Related Parliamentary Committee on Human Resources Development in its 94th Report on Demands for Grants, 2000-2001 in respect of the Department of Secondary and Higher Education has observed: "..... The Committee was given to understand that even though several Committees have suggested for 6 per cent of the GDP to be made available for Education sector, yet the present allocation is only 3.4 per cent of the GDP which is still less by 2.6 per cent. The Committee in this respect is of the considered view that when there is a general trend for disinvestment of the public sector and cuts in subsidies, it should be the effort of the Government to prioritize the social sector, especially Education and Health which stand as the heart and the soul of human development".

Despite the significant and diversified steps taken through Five Year Plans, achievements have continued to be offset by population growth.

Progress in the status of the educational advancement of women (and of men) has to be evaluated in the context of the growth in their population as well. Growth in the size of the clientele for education would obviously render targeted efforts at advancement so much more difficult, straining the financial, manpower and infrastructure resources.

Between 1971 and 1991, there was an increase of around 298 million (143 million females) in the total population, 58 million (23 million females) in Scheduled Caste population and 30 million (15 million females) in Scheduled Tribe population (Table 5).

As per the 1991 census, the clientele for elementary education (children in the age group of 714) was 153 million of which girls were 78 million (there are difficulties in working out the increase in this clientele since 1971 because data available in respect of 1971 are for 5-14 age group whereas 1991 data relate to 7-14 age group. These data based on different age-groups are not comparable).

WOMEN'S EDUCATIONAL PROGRESS VIS-A-VIS SPECIFIC CSWI RECOMMENDATIONS

General Approach to Educational Development of Women

Since the submission of Report by CSWI, conscious and sustained efforts have been made to remove male female imbalances. NPE 1986 and the various schemes framed thereunder give special attention to "Education for Women's Empowerment". Gender

Table 5. Growth of Population, All, Scheduled Castes and Scheduled Tribes

(In million)

Year	*Category*	*Persons*	*Males*	*Females*
Growth of Population, All				
1971	Total	548.16	284.05	264.11
	Rural	439.04	225.32	213.72
	Urban	109.11	58.73	50.38
1991	Total	846.30	439.23	407.07
	Rural	628.69	324.32	304.37
	Urban	217.61	114.91	102.70
Growth of Scheduled Caste Population				
1971	Total	80.00	41.34	38.66
	Rural	70.45	36.27	34.18
	Urban	9.56	5.08	4.48
1991	Total	138.22	71.93	61.29
	Rural	112.34	58.34	54.00
	Urban	25.88	13.59	12.29
Growth of Scheduled Tribe Population				
1971	Total	38.02	19.19	18.83
	Rural	36.72	18.50	18.22
	Urban	1.29	0.68	0.61
1991	Total	67.76	34.36	33.40
	Rural	62.75	31.76	30.99
	Urban	5.00	2.60	2.40

Source : Selected Educational Statistics, 1998-99; Ministry of Human Resource Development. Based on Census Data.

disaggregated data are being regularly collected in the education sector covering all levels of education. Special focus on the education of girls and women is designed integrally in general as well as special education projects. The public authorities as well as local communities are being increasingly involved in general awareness generation about the importance of women's educational development, in mobilisation to enhance recipients of education amongst the girls and women and in monitoring the progress achieved. Special attention is also given for creation of girls/women-specific infrastructure facilities for access to and retention in education. The ultimate objective is removal of male-female imbalances in education.

> **Observations/Recommendations of the CSWI on General Approach to Educational Development**
> Educational development of women should be based on removal of malefemale imbalances, which would call for attention, by public authorities with reference to the factors responsible for these imbalances. These imbalances are to be seen in terms of social attitudes militating against girl's education; gap in the enrolment of boys and girls; inadequate facilities for girls; significantly higher rate of illiteracy amongst them, etc.

Equality of Sexes

On account of the past practices which often flow from sub-conscious indifference to the concerns of females in having access to education, school textbooks have tended to be marked by sexist bias in content and language.

> **Recommendation of the CSWI on equality of sexes**
> The educational system as a whole should inculcate the value of equality of sexes through reflection on traditional prejudices as well as through the curricula.

A computer-aided content analysis of 21 English and 20 Hindi language-instruction textbooks, prescribed yearly for more than 1.3 million students of Haryana, Punjab, Rajasthan, U.P. and Delhi, has reflected the following:

- The texts had a majority of male characters;
- In 75 per cent of the lesson plots, men emerge as the dominant figures;
- There are 47 biographies of men, as opposed to only seven biographies of women;
- In most lessons men venture out to seek fame and fortune while women stay home to attend to household chores;
- Males are projected as engaged in high-prestige occupations;
- Both in and outside the home, men appear to be the

dominant decision-makers in a wide range of activities;

- Most women are relegated to low-prestige, low-income positions;
- Of the 465 occupations held by the characters in the plots, women are completely excluded from 344;
- Women's authority to make decisions is generally shown as restricted to domestic matters ; and
- As it catering to a male readership alone, the authors and editors use nouns and pronouns that exclude females.

Now a conscious and all out effort is being made for removal of gender bias from all textual material. Removal of gender bias is, indeed, the core of the work of Department of Women's Studies of the National Council of Education Research and Training (NCERT).

Recommendations of CSWI on Sex Education

(a) Introduction of sex education from middle school.

(b) Appointment of an expert group by the Ministry of Education to prepare graded teaching materials on the subject; an inclusion of mass media experts in the group to advise on the use of the media including films for the purpose.

Sex Education

As part of the exercise in undertaking revision of the curricular framework, the National Council of Educational Research and Training is examining inclusion of matters relating to sex education, reproductive processes, etc.

Formal Education

Co-education has virtually become a norm. The practice in the country of having exclusive educational institutions for girls or boys has essentially been an urban phenomenon and the number of such schools at the elementary level would not constitute more than one per cent of the total number of schools in the country. At higher levels also, the number of such schools is not very significant.

The common structure of education (10+2+3 years) and the common curricular framework that have come under implementation help girls access education of same standards and quality.

Affirmative actions in terms of policy, programmes, projects and schemes have been designed to ensure that there is no discrimination against girls and that whatever discrimination has been there in the past are specifically targeted for removal.

Recommendations of CSWI on Formal Education

(a) Co-education should be adopted as a general policy, especially at the primary level.

(b) At the middle and secondary levels separate schools for girls could be provided where there is a demand for the same, efforts to pursuing co-education being continued simultaneously.

(c) At the University level opening of new colleges exclusively for girls should be discouraged.

(d) There should be no prohibition on admission of girls in boys' institutions.

(e) Wherever separate educational institutions are provided for girls, it should be ensured that in terms of quality of staff, facilities, courses and co-curricular activities, the required standards are maintained.

(f) Provision for mixed staff should be made a condition for recognition of mixed schools, the provision being reviewed a few years after initial implementation on account of the apprehension that girls might get excluded from some schools.

(g) In mixed schools separate toilet facilities and retiring rooms for girls should be provided.

Curricula

As already stated, what is now applicable for boys and girls equally is the common curricular framework.

Since 1993, in order to ensure Minimum Levels of Learning (MLL), in elementary education, attention has been devoted to development of better text books, supplementary reading materials, teachers' handbooks and improvement of pupil's evaluation.

At the school stage, girls and boys are also being allowed equal access to what is understood as "socially useful productive work" (SUPW). While this inculcates positive values in terms of hands-on-work, it helps in the development of one's interest in productive work in accordance with one's aptitudes. Conscious gender stereotyping is avoided. Vocational stream in school education and technical courses are also accessible by girls without any discrimination.

At the University stage too, facilities for, and access to, various courses of education are commonly available for boys as well as girls though, of course, girls' profiles in professional and technical courses in higher education is rather low, especially relative to boys. Specific data based situational analysis is presented in respect of these matters later.

Recommendations of the CSWI on Curricula

(a) There should be a common course of general education for both sexes till the end of Class-X.
(b) At the primary stage simple needlecraft, music and dancing should be taught to both sexes.
(c) From the middle stage, differences may be permitted under work experience.
(d) At the post secondary level (Classes - XI & XII), girls should have full opportunity to choose vocational and technical courses according to local conditions, needs and aptitudes.
(e) At the University stage there is a need to introduce more relevant and useful courses for all students.

Universalisation of Elementary Education

Access: Coverage of Villages and Habitations by Schools

The number of recognised educational institutions has increased at all levels of education. Since 1970-71, the increase was more than one lakh primary schools, about a lakh of upper primary schools and 75,000 high schools. However, significant number of inhabited villages are not yet serviced by schools (Table 6).

As per the Sixth All India Education Survey 1995, in terms of habitations (not villages), coverage by schools is only 50.31 per cent (Primary), 13.76 per cent (Upper Primary) and 5 per cent (Secondary).

There are more than 30,000 habitations with a population of 300 and above which do not have primary schools within one kilometre.

Table 6. Coverage of Inhabited Villages* by Schools

	Primary	*Upper Primary*	*Secondary*
No. of villages covered	5,11,849	1,27,863	48,262
Percentage of villages covered	87%	12%	8%
No. of villages not covered	75,398	4,59,384	5,75,605
Percentage of villages not covered	13%	78%	92%

* Total number of inhabited villages in the country is 5,87,247.
Source : Census 1991.

Recommendations of CSWI on Universalisation of Elementary Education

(a) Primary schools should be provided within walking distance from home of every child within five years.

(b) Establishment of ashram or residential schools should service clusters of villages scattered in difficult terrains.

(c) Mobile schools should be provided for children's of nomadic tribes, migrant labour and construction workers.

(d) Parents, community leaders, officials and non-officials should make concerted efforts and sustained propaganda for cent per cent enrolments of girls in Class I.

(e) The phenomenon of dropouts should be tackled by provision of incentives – mid day meals, free school uniforms, scholarships/ stipends, free supply of books and study materials, etc.

(f) At least 50 per cent of the teachers at the elementary level should be women.

(g) Provision of at least two teachers in all schools and conversion of single teacher schools accordingly.

(h) Provision of part-time education for girls at times convenient to them.

(i) Provision of facility of multiple entry system for girls who had to leave before becoming functionally literate.

(j) Provision of additional space in schools for girls to bring their younger siblings to be looked after either by the girls themselves or by some local women.

(k) Opening of schools and greater flexibility in admission procedure in middle schools to help girls complete their schooling.

Residential Ashram schools are run by State Governments, like, for example, in Andhra Pradesh - especially in tribal areas.

An Education Guarantee Scheme is run now by the Government of Madhya Pradesh where the parents and other local people mobilise and bring children for education, the State Government takes the responsibility for providing teachers. Space to accommodate the schools is provided by the community.

Mobilisation by officials and non-officials, parents, community leaders etc., for promoting enrolment of children, especially girls, is done under some of the special programmes like the Mahila Samakhya, Lok Jumbish, Siksha Karmi etc., projects about which reference is made in some detail later.

Incentives

Extension of incentives for school going children has been recommended as a measure of improving enrolment and school attendance. Provision of Mid-Day Meals (MDM) to children has been construed as a strong motivation for the parents, particularly among poorer sections, to send them to schools and for children themselves to attend classes. For long, many individual States like Tamil Nadu, Gujarat and even Kerala though not always regularly, have been giving this incentive. However, huge numbers of children and heavy financial commitments had often inhibited the universalisation or regular implementation of a programme for MDM.

A National Programme of Nutritional Support to Primary Education (NP-NSPE) was commenced in 1995 — designed to cover all Government, Govt. aided and local body schools. Linked to 80 per cent attendance, central support is being given to States, where cooked meals are provided, for supply of free foodgrains to children at the rate of 100 grams per student per day. Where cooked meals are not provided (that is, where the foodgrains only are distributed) support has been on the scale of 3 kgs. per month per student. Gujarat, Kerala, Orissa, Tamil Nadu and Madhya Pradesh are the States where cooked meals are provided. The programme is reported to have enhanced enrolment/improved attendance and retention. Since the inception of the programme, till early 2000, the quantity of foodgrains distributed under the programme was 2.7 million tonnes at a cost of over Rs.1000 crore. The number of beneficiaries has risen from over 3 crore (1995) to about 10 crore in 1999-2000.

Preference for appointment of women teachers, flexi-time and flexi-admission procedures are also being encouraged and practiced under specific schemes, projects and programmes.

Enrolment of Girls

The picture regarding progress in enrolment of girls and boys and totals at all levels of education updated to 1998-99 are presented in Table 7.

Gross enrolment ratio of girls has increased between 1970-71 and 1998-99 by 22.4 percentage points at the primary level, 28.3 percentage points at the upper primary level, 26.2 percentage points at the elementary level as a whole. The enrolment ratio for girls at the secondary and post-secondary level has increased by 13.5 per cent between 1970-71 and 1994-95. Nonetheless, girls' gross enrolment ratio still (1998-99) continues to be well below 100 per cent. It is only 82.9 per cent at the primary level, 49.1 per cent at the upper primary level, 70.6 per cent at the elementary level as a whole and 23.3 per cent at the secondary and post-secondary level. It is significant to point out that the gross enrolment ratio of girls over the last 30 years has continued to reflect the trend of steep decline at each subsequent stage of education.

Time sequence data on girls' enrolment relative to boys are presented in Table 8. The relative gap in girls enrolment, while coming down over the years at all levels of school education, is still Significant and higher the level, higher is the gap.

Drop-out Phenomenon

A factor continuing to militate against educational advancement of women is the persistent phenomenon of "drop-outs" at all levels of school education, primary, elementary (and secondary). This phenomenon continues to slow down universalisation of elementary education and causes wastage. During 1996-97, the drop-out rates for girls were 39.37 per cent at

Table 7. Gross Enrolment Ratios@

Year	*Primary* I - V (6-11 years)			*Upper Primary* VI - VIII (11-14 years)			*Elementary* I - VIII (6-14 years)			*Secondary/Hr.Sec* IX - XII (15-18 years)			
	Boys	Girls	Total	Boys	Girls	Total	Boys	Girls	Total	Boys	Girls	Total	Total
1970-71	95.5	60.5	78.6	46.5	20.8	33.4	75.50	44.40	61.90	26.80	9.80	18.50	61.9
1992-93	95.0	73.5	84.6	72.5	48.94	67.5	87.70	65.70	77.15	40.10	21.77	31.20	77.2
1998-99	100.9	82.9	92.1	65.27	49.08	57.8	87.63	70.56	79.43	*41.50	*23.31	*32.64	79.3

Source: Selected Educational Statistics, 1998-99; Ministry of Human Resource Development.

@ Percentage of enrolment to the estimated child population in the respective age groups as indicated in the Table.

* These figures relate to the year 1994-95.

Table 8. Number of Girls per 100 Boys Enrolled in Schools

Year	*Primary (I-V) Classes*	*Middle (VI-VIII) Classes*	*Secondary (IX-X) Classes*
1950-51	39	18	16
1955-56	44	25	21
1960-61	48	32	23
1965-66	57	37	30
1970-71	60	41	35
1975-76	62	46	39
1979-80	62	48	41
1980-81	63	49	44
1981-82	63	49	43
1982-83	64	51	41
1983-84	64	51	43
1984-85	65	52	44
1985-86	67	54	44
1986-87	69	54	46
1987-88	69	55	47
1988-89	70	55	50
1989-90	70	56	50
1991-92	71	58	50
1992-93	72	61	51
1993-94P	75	65	55
1994-95P	75	64	55
1995-96P	76	64	57
1996-97P	77	66	59

Source : Ministry of Human Resource Development, Department of Education, New Delhi.

P: Provisional

@: Excludes professional, technical and special courses

There are very wide disparities in gross and net enrolment ratios as between States (Table 9).

Table 9. State-wise Gross/Net Enrolment Ratio (1997-98) at Primary Level (6-11 years)

State/UT	*Gross Enrolment Ratio*			*Net Enrolment Ratio*		
	Total	*Boys*	*Girls*	*Total*	*Boys*	*Girls*
Andhra Pradesh	89.6	92.3	86.8	68.6	71.1	66.1
Arunachal Pradesh	97.2	114.5	82.1	69.3	81.7	58.4
Assam	109.1	113.8	104.3	98.4	102.5	94.2
Bihar	76.0	90.9	59.5	75.9	90.9	59.4
Goa	86.1	97.1	76.8	61.2	68.3	55.2
Gujarat	117.6	119.9	114.5	86.4	87.7	84.7
Haryana	83.9	83.1	84.9	73.4	72.5	74.4
Himachal Pradesh	90.1	98.6	82.7	68.1	74.3	62.9
Jammu & Kashmir	67.2	82.7	53.4.	55.2	68.1	43.7
Karnataka	113.2	120.7	105.5	88.6	94.2	82.8
Kerala	90.1	91.3	88.8	71.5	72.5	70.4
Madhya Pradesh	102.4	114.5	89.4	88.1	97.4	78.2
Maharashtra	112.9	115.7	110.0	84.4	86.2	82.5
Manipur	85.9	99.7	74.1	67.8	77.7	59.5
Meghalaya	93.4	101.9	86.1	50.3	54.5	46.8
Mizoram	113.6	123.0	104.6	72.6	77.7	67.6
Nagaland	94.3	103.6	86.3	58.5	64.0	53.6
Orissa	90.5	104.5	76.1	69.7	81.0	58.0
Punjab	81.6	80.4	83.1	70.6	68.8	72.7
Rajasthan	97.0	111.3	81.0	71.6	82.6	59.3
Sikkim	113.3	116.7	110.0	61.4	63.4	59.3
Tamil Nadu	108.6	109.8	107.3	84.6	85.7	83.6
Tripura	88.4	103.4	75.3	79.5	92.0	68.6
Uttar Pradesh	62.3	74.1	49.0	46.8	56.0	36.4
West Bengal	92.2	98.6	85.6	55.6	59.2	51.8
A&N Islands	86.9	99.6	76.2	63.8	72.1	56.7
Chandigarh	79.5	85.9	73.2	60.1	65.1	55.2

(Contd.)

(Contd.)

State/UT	*Gross Enrolment Ratio*			*Net Enrolment Ratio*		
	Total	*Boys*	*Girls*	*Total*	*Boys*	*Girls*
D&N Haveli	96.2	111.0	81.3	70.2	79.0	61.4
Daman & Diu	99.1	110.9	88.8	74.2	81.6	67.8
Delhi	89.1	97.2	81.6	67.6	74.0	61.7
Lakshadweep	104.5	112.8	96.3	72.8	77.2	68.4
Pondicherry	93.5	105.8	83.0	73.6	83.4	65.2
India	90.3	98.5	81.5	71.1	77.7	64.0

Source :
1. Selected Educational Statistics 1997-98, Ministry of Human Resource Development
2. Sixth All India Educational Survey, National Council of Educational Research and Training
3. State Directorates of Education, 1997-98.

the primary level, 51.89 per cent at the elementary level as a whole and 66.82 per cent at the secondary level. Of course, these are considerably lesser rates of drop-outs, compared to the figures respectively of 66.18 per cent and 82.80 per cent for primary and elementary levels in 1975-76 (the year of the CSWI Report). That is, in 1996-97, the drop-out phenomenon amongst girls was only 591 per cent of what it was in 1975-76 at the primary level and 71 per cent of what it was that year at the elementary level as a whole (Table 10). Nonetheless, the incidence of dropouts is quite high even at reduced levels and is a matter of serious concern.

Among the children of the age group 5-9, the school attendance rate, according to the 50th round of the NSSO (1993-94), was 66 per cent for boys and 56 per cent for girls in rural areas. It was 84 per cent and 80 per cent for boys and girls respectively in urban areas. Among the children of the age group 10-14, the corresponding ratios were — 76 per cent and 56 per cent for boys and girls in rural areas and 87 per cent and 82 per cent for boys and girls respectively in the urban areas, 74.4 million boys and 53.5 million girls were at the elementary level according to the NSSO figures 1993-94.

The major reason for drop-out is "not interested in education" for both boys and girls in urban and rural areas. "Participation in household economic activity" or "other economic reasons" are

Table 10. Drop out Rate (Percent) at Different Stages of School Education

Year	*Primary (I-V Classes)*		*Elementary (I-VIII Classes)*		*Secondary (I-X Classes)*	
	Girls	*Boys*	*Girls*	*Boys*	*Girls*	*Boys*
1960-61	70.93	61.74	–	–	–	–
1965-66	70.49	36.17	–	–	–	–
1970-71	70.92	64.48	83.40	74.60	–	–
1975-76	66.18	60.21	82.80	74.30	–	–
1980-81	62.50	56.20	79.40	68.00	86.60	79.80
1981-82	57.30	51.10	77.70	68.50	86.81	79.44
1982-83	56.30	49.40	74.96	66.04	86.24	78.21
1983-84	53.96	47.83	75.27	66.10	84.79	76.41
1988-89	49.69	46.74	68.31	59.38	79.46	72.68
1989-90	50.35	46.50	68.75	61.00	77.72	70.99
1990-91	46.00	40.10	65.13	59.12	76.96	67.50
1991-92	44.30	40.30	62.40	56.10	75.87	68.55
1992-93P	43.20	40.07	60.06	53.99	74.89	68.15
1993-94P	39.05	36.07	56.78	49.95	74.54	68.41
1994-95P	37.79	35.18	56.53	50.02	73.78	67.15
1995-96P	41.31	37.92	61.70	54.99	74.07	66.36
1996-97P	39.37	38.35	51.89	52.77	66.82	73.04

Source : Ministry of Human Resource Development, Department of Education; Education in India, (Various Years)

Note: Total drop out during a course (stage) has been taken as per cent of intake in the first year of the course (stage).

significant causes in the case of boys. In the case of girls, "domestic chores" and "other economic reasons" are other significant reasons. For both boys and girls in both urban and rural areas, "failure" is a very important reason for discontinuing school education. The perception of irrelevance of education is a pertinent point. The classification of drop-outs according to the reasons for discontinuance is given in Table 11.

Table 11. Percentage Distribution of Drop-outs by Reason for Discontinuance

Reasons	*Rural*			*Urban*		
	Boys	*Girls*	*All*	*Boys*	*Girls*	*All*
1. Not interested in education/further studies	26.57	33.25	26.26	23.62	28.47	25.60
2. Participated in household economic activity	26.80	9.38	19.17	22.80	6.71	16.28
3. Other economic reasons	20.63	14.97	17.11	24.15	15.42	20.58
4. Domestic chores	2.01	14.25	5.54	2.20	15.93	7.77
5. Failure	18.43	16.68	16.29	21.28	18.77	20.27
6. Others	5.56	11.47	15.63	5.95	14.70	9.50

Source : Sarvekshana, Vol. 14, Nos. 3 & 4, Jan-June 1991, Issue 46, NSS 42nd Round, Table 7, p. 37.

The analysis of the earlier National Sample Survey Data from the 42nd round (for 1986-87), had highlighted economic factors for boys in both urban and rural areas as the major reason for not getting enrolled in schools. The second reason was their not being interested. In the case of girls, the reason for not getting enrolled in schools is 'not being interested in education' and 'economic factors' coming second in urban areas and both these factors being equally important in the rural areas. This is explained in Table 12.

Table 12. Percentage of Children (Aged 6 and above) Never Enrolled, by Reason for Non-enrolment in Schools in India, 1986-87

Reasons for Non- Enrolment	*Boys*	*Girls*	*All*
Rural			
Economic factors	50.0	32.6	39.6
Domestic chores	1.3	9.9	6.4
No schooling facilities	9.9	10.5	10.3

(Contd.)

Reasons for Non-Enrolment	*Boys*	*Girls*	*All*
Not interested	25.2	32.3	29.5
Urban			
Economic factors	51.9	29.4	37.4
Domestic chores	0.9	10.7	7.2
No schooling facilities	5.9	9.0	7.9
Not interested	23.5	32.9	29.6

Note : * Includes code numbers (4 and 5): household economic activities, and economic reasons. Other reasons ('too young to go to schools', 'waiting for admission' and 'others') are not included here.
Source : NSSO (1991: Table 21.2; pp. S70 and S119) cited in Tilak (1996).

The National Council of Applied Economic Research (NCAER) conducted in-depth interviews of 32 girls and 30 boys in age group 10-14 years, who are recent dropouts from school, belonging to Madhya Pradesh, Maharashtra and Tamil Nadu. The study observed that the lack of conveniently located and/or adequately equipped schools seem to be playing a major role in influencing the drop-out rate of village children. Parents educated the girls up to whatever level the village school provided. They were afraid of sending the girls away to other villages, specially crossing the fields. This element of danger was felt more acutely once girls attained puberty. Because of the high dropout rate among girls, the lack of female company for those remaining in school beyond class eight is another discouraging factor. Further, the phenomenon of drop-out from schools was heavily influenced by:

- Low parental interest and support for further schooling especially for girls
- Lower educational aspirations among girls as compared to boys
- Weak public commitment to the promotion of education
- Indifferent teachers stifle students desire to learn

Data on State-wise rates of efficiency presenting a composite

Picture of promotion rates, drop out rates and 'years input per graduate' are presented in Table 13.

Recommendations of CSWI on Pre-School Education

(a) The system should provide for a three year pre-school education for all children; in this context, in rural areas and urban slums, the number of balwadies should be increased.

(b) Pre-school education facilities should be situated, as far as possible, near the primary and middle schools of the localities.

Pre-school Education

Universalisation of elementary education pre-supposes laying a firm foundation at the pre-primary stage itself. What is understood as Early Childhood Care and Education (ECCE) - for the children at age group of 0-6 years - is an area which has to be given foremost attention. NPE, 1986 not merely laid special emphasis on this but its integration with the programme of Integrated Child Development Services (ICDS) an important component of which is pre-school education and which is implemented by the Ministry of Human Resource Development, Department of Women and Child Development. The beneficiary children are of the order of 18 million. The ICDS programme has been universalised, covering all the community development blocks in the country. However, the programme itself has a number of deficiencies - lack of provision of basic minimum facilities, varying performance, especially of the educational component, of the ICDS centres, lack of a gender inclusive approach, etc.

Special importance needs to be given in the matter of improving pre-school education of children to the training of the aganwadi workers (ICDS functionaries), especially in handling the educational component, ECCE would also need to be built into the training curriculum of primary teachers.

Operation Blackboard

This was a scheme started in 1987-88 with a view to improving primary school environment by providing basic infrastructure - at least two class rooms, an additional teacher to single teacher schools, preferably a female teacher, teaching - learning materials, furniture for teachers, equipment, separate toilet facilities for girls, etc. A third

Table 13. State-wise Rates of Efficiency (1997-98)

State/UT	Promotion Rate			Dropout Rate			Years Input Per Graduate		
	Boys	Girls	Total	Boys	Girls	Total	Boys	Girls	Total
Andhra Pradesh	72.6	72.8	72.7	27.4	27.2	27.3	7.3	7.9	7.6
Arunachal Pradesh	61.6	61.6	61.6	23.4	23.3	23.4	8.2	8.4	8.3
Assam	63.1	62.5	62.8	23.6	24.7	24.1	5.8	8.2	6.7
Bihar	66.3	64.8	65.4	25.9	26.0	25.9	8.3	9.8	8.8
Goa	74.1	75.3	74.7	22.5	22.3	22.4	5.1	5.3	5.2
Gujarat	69.1	69.7	69.4	18.8	17.2	18.1	7.4	7.1	7.3
Haryana	70.5	73.5	71.9	22.1	19.1	20.7	6.0	6.3	6.1
Himachal Pradesh	60.7	67.2	63.8	28.1	22.0	25.2	6.8	5.6	6.2
Jammu & Kashmir	67.1	65.4	66.4	27.0	29.2	27.9	6.1	6.4	6.2
Karnataka	78.7	77.9	78.3	20.8	21.5	21.5	6.9	7.6	7.2
Kerala	74.8	75.5	75.2	18.5	19.7	19.1	4.7	4.8	4.7
Madhya Pradesh	72.7	73.7	3.1	19.3	18.1	18.8	5.5	6.2	5.8
Maharashtra	70.9	70.8	70.9	19.6	19.9	19.7	5.9	6.1	6.0
Manipur	77.5	77.0	77.3	19.6	20.2	19.9	5.2	5.1	5.1
Meghalaya	60.7	61.3	61.0	30.6	30.9	30.7	8.9	9.8	9.3
Mizoram	63.2	63.2	63.2	25.9	26.6	26.2	6.2	6.4	6.3
Nagaland	71.4	69.5	70.5	23.4	25.9	24.6	8.4	8.6	8.5
Orissa	63.0	59.9	61.7	22.8	25.7	24.0	7.5	8.2	7.8

(Contd.)

(Contd.)

State/UT	Promotion Rate			Dropout Rate			Years Input Per Graduate		
	Boys	Girls	Total	Boys	Girls	Total	Boys	Girls	Total
Punjab	71.1	73.8	72.4	19.3	18.1	18.7	5.4	5.6	5.5
Rajasthan	63.9	61.7	63.0	32.7	34.8	33.5	6.2	7.5	6.6
Sikkim	50.9	50.6	50.7	25.1	27.5	26.3	8.5	10.0	9.2
Tamil Nadu	70.6	71.9	71.2	19.3	18.0	18.7	6.2	6.1	6.2
Tripura	59.0	59.2	59.1	22.0	22.1	22.1	7.7	7.4	7.6
Uttar Pradesh	59.5	55.1	57.8	38.8	42.9	40.4	13.4	21.2	15.7
West Bengal	58.6	53.4	56.1	35.8	41.3	38.4	12.2	17.3	14.3
A&N Islands	73.1	73.1	73.1	21.8	22.7	22.2	5.1	5.5	5.3
Chandigarh	84.9	85.9	85.4	13.3	12.8	13.1	3.8	3.8	3.8
D&N Haveli	60.3	59.5	60.0	12.9	13.9	13.3	6.0	6.4	6.1
Daman & Diu	72.1	72.1	72.1	15.9	18.1	17.0	5.4	5.6	5.5
Delhi	80.3	78.2	79.3	14.0	14.2	14.1	4.5	3.8	4.1
Lakshadweep	65.3	68.3	66.7	17.2	19.1	18.1	6.1	5.4	5.8
Pondicherry	74.3	75.6	74.9	19.6	18.7	19.2	4.6	4.5	4.5
India	**67.8**	**67.3**	**67.6**	**25.6**	**26.0**	**25.8**	**7.2**	**8.0**	**7.5**

Source : 1. Selected Educational Statistics 1997-98, Ministry of Human Resource Development.
2. Sixth All India Educational Survey, National Council of Educational Research and Training.
3. State Directorates of Education, 1997-98.

teacher is also sought to be provided where enrolment has exceeded 100. Finances for the implementation of the scheme is jointly provided by the Central and State Governments. The Ministry of Human Resource Development, Department of Education, in co-ordination with the Ministry of Rural Areas and Employment provides funds under the Jawahar Gram Samridhi Yojana to the extent of 75 per cent.

Non-formal Education (NFE) for Women

Non-Formal Education (NFE) with a special focus on girls gained momentum after the International Women's Year, 1975 and after the CSWI Report. In 1979-80, a programme of NFE for children in the age group of 6 to 14 was started. Amongst out of school children, the girl child was given special attention in the programme, considering the societal practice of thrusting on her domestic responsibilities such as fetching fuel, fodder and water which has continued all along seriously inhibiting her formal schooling. The design of implementation of the programme has also been one of focusing on educationally backward States and hilly, tribal and desert areas, apart from urban slums.

Currently, the programme is being implemented in 24 States/ Union Territories. As of 1999-2000, 297,000 NFE Centres (118,000 of them exclusively for girls) had come into existence, servicing nearly three quarters of a million children. The Centre and the States share the financial commitment under the programme in the ratio of 3:2. In the case of running co-educational centres and centres exclusively for girls, the pattern of sharing financial commitment is in the ratio of 9:1. The entire expenditure is borne by the Government of India in the case of NFE Centres being run by voluntary organisations and where innovative and experimental projects are taken up.

Recommendations of CSWI on Non-Formal Education

(a) Through non-formal education, meaningful basic education should be provided to those who remain outside reach of the formal system.

(b) This kind of education should be such that its usefulness is immediately perceived.

(c) The content of non-formal education should have

literacy as its core but has to be functional.

(d) Sponsorship and organisation of non-formal education should be rather panchayats and other local bodies, government's role being limited to providing technical guidance and advice, apart from literature and reading material.

Alternative and Innovative Education Scheme

Based on review of performance of the NFE Scheme by the Parliamentary Standing Committee and on evaluation conducted by the Planning Commission, a new scheme under the nomenclature Alternative and Innovative Education Scheme is proposed to be established. Emphasis under this Scheme would be on providing elementary education centres within one kilometre in habitations where there are none; conduct of school mapping; quality of education being made comparable to that of formal system; and active involvement of the community in implementation. This Scheme which is sought to replace NFE Scheme is being designed to be flexible and non-prescriptive such that several ways of teaching would be facilitated.

Sarva Shiksha Abhiyan (National Elementary Education Mission (NEEM)

Universalisation of Elementary Education is proposed to be approached in terms of a Mission, with special focus on the girl child, SCs, STs and slum dwellers. Some of the more important features of the Abhiyan are shifting attention from States to Districts, curricular reforms to promote life skills, involvement of Panchayati Raj Institutions in management etc. This idea was thrown up in a Conference of State Education Ministers. Accordingly, a committee was constituted under the Union Minister of Human Resource Development to work out its contours. Convergence of resources, human, financial and institutional to achieve universalisation by year 2010 in a cost effective and decentralised manner is the approach.

District Primary Education Programme (DPEP)

The DPEP is a special initiative launched in 1994 within the broader objective frame of universalisation of elementary education. This programme also has a marked gender focus. As the nomenclature indicates, the programme is based on district specific planning. Decentralised management of the programme is a special feature. The processes followed in this style of management are participatory. Implementation is through State level registered societies. The programme is further driven by grassroots level disaggregated target orientation - reduction of primary drop-out rate to less than 10 per cent, reducing gender gap and that between social groups to less than 5 per cent and enhancing primary level learning attainment by at least 25 per cent.

Selection of the districts for coverage by this programme is principally done with reference to educational backwardness characterised by female literacy below the national average level.

Activities under the programme include upgradation and creation of school infrastructure, provision of teachers, production of teaching learning material etc. As of 1999-2000, the programme has covered 219 districts in 15 States. Coverage of 23 more districts in three States is also envisaged.

Expenditure on the programme is shared between the Centre and the States in the ratio of 85:15, funds being passed on to the respective registered societies. Funding of the programme is supported by multilateral and bilateral external sources (Table 14).

According to the Ministry of HRD, as per data collected/ surveys and studies conducted, in the phase-I districts, the gross enrolment ratio "is near universal"; and in the Phase-II and Phase-III districts the ratio has reached 85 per cent. It is also reported by the Ministry that at least in Phase-I districts there has been perceptible reduction in dropout rates and in the overall repetition rate of children, apart from appreciable increase in learning achievements. Further, the Ministry has observed: "Gender gap in enrolment is closing rapidly. Enrolment of girls has been faster than boys....... Index of Gender Equity (IGE) in 23 districts, as against 15 in 1995, out of the 42 Phase-I districts is about 95 percent, which is the goal to be achieved by the end of the project period. One district has IGE below 85 per cent as against six in 1995. Out of 75 districts in Phase - II/III covered in the study, 35 have IGE greater than 95 as against 31 in 1997 and eight have less than 85 compared to 14 in 1997."

Mahila Samakhya (Education for Women's Equality)

Mahila Samakhya is basically an empowerment programme.

Table 14. Funding of District Primary Education Programme

Name of the Agency	*Assistance*	*Coverage*
World Bank	US$260.3 million	Phase I (1994-2001)
European Community	ECU 150 million	Madhya Pradesh 1994-2001
IDA	US$ 425.2 million	Phase II (1996-2002)
The Netherlands	US$ 25.8 million	Gujarat
DFID (UK)	Pounds Sterling	
	42.5 million	Andhra Pradesh
	31.7 million	West Bengal
IDA	US$ 152.4 million	Phase III Bihar
UNICEF	US$ 10 million	Phase III Bihar
IDA	US$ 137.4 million	Andhra Pradesh
IDA	US$ 85.7 million	Phase IV Rajasthan (1999-2003)
IDA	US$ 182.4 million	Uttar Pradesh
DFID	Pounds Sterling 30.0 million	West Bengal

Source : Government of India, Ministry of Human Resource Development, Annual Report 1999-2000.

It was started in 1989. As of 1999-2000, the programme was under implementation in over 7000 villages in 51 districts of eight States of the country- Assam, Bihar, Madhya Pradesh, Uttar Pradesh, Gujarat, Andhra Pradesh, Karnataka and Kerala. Mobilisation of women is the basic strategy. Adoption of innovative approaches with emphasis on processes rather than on targets, is part of this strategy. This is a major departure from any Government initiative. Education is understood not merely as a route for acquiring basic literacy skills but as a process for building up a spirit of inquiry that would lead to analysis of issues and problems to seek solutions.

At the grass-roots level, village "sanghas" (women's groups) are organised for facilitating mobilisation. A "sahayogini" each is provided for a cluster of ten villages. She provides the link between the sanghas and district level implementation units. These units provide resource support and inputs and are coordinated by a State level autonomous registered society. At the national level, there is a

Project Coordinator guided by an advisory body of academics, women activists etc.

One of the crucial areas of mobilisation under the programme is basic education. The village sanghas play the role of change agents, inter alia, in the areas of school enrolment of children, especially girls, parent motivation for the purpose, monitoring the functioning of schools. Mobilisation of adolescent girls for education through kishori sanghas and of women for adult education is also part of the work schedule under the programme. Mahila Samakhya also functions coordinately with the District Primary Education Programme, so as to provide convergent services.

Shiksha Karmi Project

This project commenced in 1989 is designed to cover remote, arid and socially backward areas of Rajasthan with special emphasis on girls' education. Considering the serious problem of teacher absenteeism due to remoteness of the areas, an innovative approach has been followed in the implementation of this project. Less qualified teachers intensely trained under induction and refresher courses have been pressed into service.

The project is implemented with the association of voluntary agencies under the overall guidance and direction of a State Shiksha Karmi Board. In order to cater to the requirements of out of school children, a large number of "prehar pathasalas"(schools of convenient timings) have been established. In these schools, more than 20,000 girls (71 per cent of the enrolled) are reported to be studying. Six-fold increase in enrolment has also been reported.

The project has gone through two phases (1989-94 and 1994 - 99) and the third phase(1999-2004) has commenced. The Swedish International Development Agency (SIDA) has supported the Government of Rajasthan in the implementation of this project in the first two phases - to the extent of 90 per cent in the first phase and 50 per cent in the second phase. The third phase has been sought to be supported by the Department of International Development (DID) of the United Kingdom. In the first phase, over Rs. 2 crore was spent and in the second phase Rs. 72 crore. The outlay for the third phase is Rs. 240 crore.

Till 1999 the Project has covered 2715 villages in 146 Blocks of 32 Districts, the number of "prehar pathasalas" being 4829 and enrolment being over 200,000. By the end of the third phase, the project is expected to have covered over 4000 villages with over 7000 "prehar pathasalas", enrolment reaching over 300,000.

Lok Jumbish (Peoples' Movement for Education for All)

This programme has been under implementation in Rajasthan since 1992. The basic objective of the programme is to concentrate on primary education with focus on girls. Special attention is given to school attendance such that enrolled children complete primary education. Mobilisation of people and their participation in supporting the programme are secured, bringing home to them that education sets in motion processes that would empower women and thus is an instrumentality for women's equality.

The programme is run by the Lok Jumbish Parishad, an autonomous registered society. Between 1992 and 1999, the programme has gone through two phases and a third phase has been commenced so as to end in 2004.

Financial support to the extent of over Rs. 20 crore for the first two phases was obtained from the Swedish International Development Agency (SIDA). The third phase has an outlay of about 35 million pounds to be provided by the Department of International Development of the Government of the United Kingdom.

Seventy-five blocks of Rajasthan have been covered under the programme. For non-formal education of out of school children, especially girls, over 3000 centres have been run under a sub-programme known as "Sahaj Shikshan Programme".

It has been reported by the Ministry of Human Resource Development that quality improvement has been achieved in primary education under the programme, especially through development of text books based on MLL (Minimum Level of Learning) and teacher training in a cascade model.

Provision of Teachers, Teacher Training and Education

Teacher-pupil ratio is a prime factor which has considerable impact on the quality of education. The standard norm is that it should not exceed 1:25. Higher the ratio, the lower would be the quality. With higher demand for education consequent on increasing population and with establishment of larger numbers of educational institutions, the demand for teachers has increased too. But on the supply side, growth in the supply of teachers, especially in the rural areas as already stated, has not kept pace with the demand for education. The teacher-pupil ratio has, therefore, increased between 1970-71 and 1998-99 at all levels of education. In rural areas, at the primary level, the ratio was 1:48. The ratio is appallingly dismal in several States - 1:78 in Bihar, 1:.72 in Karnataka, 1:60 in Gujarat, 1:54 in Andhra Pradesh and Maharashtra, 1:49 in West Bengal, 1:46 in Assam,1:45 in Madhya Pradesh and 1:43 in Haryana and Uttar Pradesh. Exhaustive State-wise data are presented in Table 15.

Table 15. State-wise Enrolment and Teachers in Primary Schools (1997-98)

State/UT	*Total Enrolment*	*Total Teachers*	*Teacher Pupil Ratio*	*Per cent of Trained Teachers*	*Per cent of Female Teachers*
Andhra Pradesh	83,70,079	1,54,194	54	95.4	33.2
Arunachal Pradesh	1,49,719	4,295	35	50.3	28.6
Assam	38,16,603	82,091	46	47.5	25.0
Bihar	1,02,66,989	1,30,822	78	90.4	19.5
Goa	1,25,717	4,445	28	92.6	67.3
Gujarat	60,03,862	99,543	60	96.5	47.0
Haryana	20,96,106	48,905	43	96.5	51.7
Himachal Pradesh	6,94,412	23,985	29	88.0	38.6
Jammu & Kashmir	8,93,005	30,286	29	63.5	37.2
Karnataka	69,12,100	95,495	72	100.0	47.3
Kerala	27,49,535	74,784	37	97.4	69.6
Madhya Pradesh	1,01,61,269	2,27,154	45	67.8	27.4
Maharashtra	1,18,79,899	2,21,475	54	95.6	50.3
Manipur	2,51,651	11,735	21	34.8	34.8
Meghalaya	3,02,518	10,550	29	42.5	45.4
Mizoram	1,34,091	5,210	26	67.6	47.4

(Contd.)

(Contd.)

State/UT	*Total Enrolment*	*Total Teachers*	*Teacher Pupil Ratio*	*Per cent of Trained Teachers*	*Per cent of Female Teachers*
Nagaland	2,03,689	9,376	22	50.8	39.3
Orissa	39,45,000	1,12,876	35	98.9	25.9
Punjab	21,21,310	57,011	37	98.6	61.0
Rajasthan	68,60,625	1,34,061	51	97.6	28.8
Sikkim	84,986	5,092	17	46.4	45.5
Tamil Nadu	68,14,039	1,55,349	44	99.8	44.1
Tripura	4,40,886	20,653	21	33.1	21.0
Uttar Pradesh	1,37,07,742	3,18,769	43	97.3	25.0
West Bengal	89,07,736	1,81,710	49	67.2	24.8
A&N Islands	39,967	1,969	20	97.7	47.7
Chandigarh	65,978	1,773	37	100.0	96.4
D&N Haveli	25,003	483	52	98.1	34.2
Daman & Diu	14,868	424	35	97.6	57.1
Delhi	12.61,359	37,532	34	100.0	62.4
Lakshadweep	8,362	284	29	100.0	42.3
Pondicherry	1,03,798	3,408	30	97.0	58.6
ALL INDIA	10,94,12,903	22,65,739	48	87.7	35.8
Rural	8,17,09,398	16,89,980	48	87.7	35.8
Urban	2,77,03,505	5,75,759	48	87.7	35.8

Source : Selected Educational Statistics 1997-98, Ministry of Human Resource Development

Availability of adequate number of teachers, especially female teachers is indispensable for advancement of women's education. Since the submission of the Report of CSWI, there has been improvement in this regard as well.

- The total number of teachers registered increased at all these levels during this period as shown in the Table 16.
- Compared to 1975-76, the index of female teachers went up to 224 at the primary level, 207 at the upper primary

Table 16. Index of Growth of Institutions and Female Teachers Between 1975-76 and 1998-99

Year	*Primary*			*Upper Primary*			*High/ Higher Secondary*		
	Schools	*Teachers*	%	*Schools*	*Teachers*	%	*Institutions*	*Teachers*	%
1975-76	4,54,270			1,06,571			43,054		
Index of institutions	(100)			(100)			(100)		
Total		12,48,000	100		7,78,000	100		7,59,000	100
Male		9,55,000	76.5		5,54,000	71.2		5,59,000	73.6
Female		2,93,000	23.5		2,24,000	28.8		2,00,000	26.4
Index of female teachers		(100)			(100)			(100)	
1985-86	5,28,872			1,34,846			65,837		
Index of institutions	(116.4)			(126.5)			(152.9)		
Total		14,96,000			9,68,000			11,32,000	
Male		10,94,000	73.1		6,63,000	68.8		7,93,000	70.0
Female		4,02,000	26.9		3,05,000	31.2		3,39,000	30.0
Index of growth of female teachers		(137%)			(136.1%)			(169.5)	

(Contd.)

(Contd.)

Year	Primary			Upper Primary			High/ Higher Secondary		
	Schools	Teachers	%	Schools	Teachers	%	Institutions	Teachers	%
1998-99	6,26,737			1,90,166			1,12,438		
Index of growth of institutions	(137.9)			(178.4)			(261.2)		
Total		19,04,000			12,78,000			17,47,000	
Male		12,46,000	65.4		8,14,000	63.7		11,68,000	66.9
Female		6,58,000	34.6		4,64,000	36.3		5,79,000	33.1
Index of growth of female teachers		(224%)			(207%)			(289.5%)	

Source : Selected Educational Statistics, 1998-99; Ministry of Human Resource Development.

level and 289 at the high/higher secondary level in 1998-99.

- Relative to increases in the total number of teachers as well as male teachers, increases in the number of women teachers registered higher levels.
- The proportion of female teachers to total teachers at all levels has registered an increasing trend and is more than 30 per cent, ranging between 33 and 36 per cent in 1998-99, but has not reached the 50 per cent level envisaged in the Report of the CSWI or in NPE 1986 which specifically calls for an endeavour to recruit female teachers to the extent of 50 per cent.
- The index of growth of female teachers is higher than the index of growth of institutions at all levels, and more significantly higher at high/higher secondary levels.

Women teachers are in significant short supply in rural areas. This phenomenon adversely impacts on educational participation of girls. It also causes high dropout rates amongst girls around the time they are to switch over from primary to middle level of education, that is, around the time they are 11 to 12 years of age. Girls dropping out at such early stage and not remaining in the educational system to complete 12 years of schooling which is the qualifying requirement for primary teacher training virtually excludes rural areas from being recruiting grounds for women teachers.

Women teachers, in 1993-94, constituted only 23 per cent of the total number of teachers in rural areas at the primary and secondary levels. At the middle level they accounted for 25 per cent of the total number of teachers. In urban areas, the presence of women teachers was of a significantly higher profile (Table 17).

Table 17. Rural-urban Distribution of Female Teachers at School Stage (1993-94)

(percentage)

Area	*Primary*	*Middle*	*Secondary*	*Total*
Rural	23.0	5.0	23.0	18.0
Urban	60.0	59.0	54.0	41.0

Source : Selected Educational Statistics, 1998-99; Ministry of Human Resource Development.

Teacher training is yet another factor which impacts on quality of education. In 1995-96, untrained teachers were 12 per cent at the primary and middle levels and 11% in secondary level against 23 per cent (primary), 17 per cent (middle) and 19 per cent (secondary) in 1973-74. Thus there has been some improvement in teacher training at the All India level. Variations as between States are quite wide and striking as of 1997-98. While 100 per cent of the teachers are trained in Karnataka, Delhi, Chandigarh and Lakshadweep, five States (Assam, Manipur, Meghalaya, Sikkim, Tripura) have less than 50 per cent trained teachers. Arunachal Pradesh and Nagaland are very near this situation with just a little over 50 per cent trained teachers. Primary education in virtually the entire North East of the country is serviced by teeming numbers of untrained teachers (Table 15 supra).

Quality of teacher education has been sought to be enhanced by providing teacher training infrastructure all over the country. The basic objective has been one of improving the pedagogical skills of teachers at all levels. Between 1987 and 1998-99, 451 District Institutes of Education and Training (DIETs) for elementary education, 76 CTEs for secondary education and 34 IASEs for collegiate education have been established in different parts of the country with the support of the Central Govt. A project on Networking for Institutional Capacity Enhancement (NICE) has been under implementation since 1997-98. Under the project, networking with DIETs, etc. was facilitated through five identified institutes of education including the Assam University, Kakathiya University, Warangal and Gujarat Vidyapeeth, Ahmedabad.

For providing resource support for teacher education, the institutional structures have been strengthened - with NCERT at the national level and State Councils of Educational Research and Training in the States (SCERTs). Development of instructional materials and orientation of teachers in the use of these materials have been the principal tasks of these institutions. Interactive in service training of teachers through the distance mode on the TV has been tested successfully in 1996. This strategy is proposed to be followed for mass orientation of teachers during the Ninth Plan.

Secondary Education

Many State Governments have come to provide free education for girls beyond elementary level.

The centrally sponsored schemes brought under implantation under the NPE about which reference has been made earlier included several schemes relevant to Secondary education - science education, education technology, environment education, Computer Literacy and Studies in Schools (CLASS), vocational education etc. While these schemes were not exclusively meant for girls, they are also beneficiaries of the schemes equally with boys.

Vocationalisation of School Education

Para-10.4.13 of the POA of 1992 states "The involvement of girls in the vocational educational programmes is crucial. Under the centrally sponsored programme at +2 level girls have equal access to vocational courses as the boys. Efforts should be made by the States/UTs to consciously encourage the participation of girls in the non-traditional and emergent technologies. The non-formal vocational programmes with emphasis on entrepreneurs should be specially geared to the needs of the out of school-girls. Facilities for guidance should be made available."

Recommendations of CSWI on Secondary Education

(a) Provision of free education for all girls up to the end of the secondary stage.

(b) Improving the quality of teaching and provision of facilities for teaching important subjects like Science, Mathematics and Commerce.

(c) Introduction of job oriented work experience, keeping in view the local needs and resources and employment potential of the region. For example, such courses could be on nursing, commercial practices, operation relating to agriculture and animal husbandry, etc.

(d) Provision of mixed schools, separate toilet facilities, co-curricular arrangements etc.

(e) Provision of need cum merit scholarships and hostel facilities for girls.

A programme for vocationalisation of higher secondary education was started in the year 1976 - to provide employment orientation to education. Till the year 1986 only 2.5 per cent of the students in higher secondary level opted for vocational education.

So, in 1988 a centrally sponsored scheme for vocationalisation of secondary education was launched under which 194 vocational courses have been introduced; 94 of them have been notified under the Apprenticeship Act. Policy co-ordination and guidance for the scheme is being provided by a Joint Council for Vocational Education (JCVE) established in 1990. In 1993 pre-vocational course at lower secondary stage was introduced too. By 1996-97 the ratio of students in vocational courses increased to 11.51 per cent against the target of diverting 25 per cent of secondary school students to vocational stream by year 2000. As of 1999-2000, vocational sections have been introduced in about 6500 schools creating capacity for diversion of a million students to vocational stream.

Open School

Inter alia, girls are a special target group in the National Open School (NOS) with its accredited institutions numbering over 1000 and an aggregate enrolment of 4.5 lakh students. NOS runs, inter alia, courses for out of school girls and women and even employed among them for facilitating completion of 10 year/secondary level education. Courses include traditional, non-traditional and vocational subjects. Paripurna Mahila Yojana course run by NOS is meant for adolescent girls and women so as to impart legal literacy and health, nutrition and general awareness. States like Tamil Nadu and Haryana also have started State Open Schools which could be availed of by girls and women.

Boarding and Hostel Facilities for Girls Students

In order to facilitate participation of girls from rural areas and weaker sections in school education, assistance is granted to voluntary agencies in running boarding and hostel facilities for girls students studying in Classes-IX-XII. Priority is given in the implementation of this scheme in backward districts, especially in areas of SC/ST concentration. Assistance is given in terms of a one-time grant of Rs. 1500/- per girl student for purchase of furniture etc. and Rs. 5000/- per annum per girl student for food, salary of cook and of warden. As of 1998-99, 3000 girls are beneficiaries under this scheme.

Navodaya Vidyalayas

This scheme which was started in 1985-86 has been designed to provide residential coeducational schools upto plus two level, boarding, lodging, uniform etc. being free - to cater mainly to rural children. The Navodaya Vidyalaya Samiti, an autonomous organisation under the Chairmanship of the Union Minister for Human Resource Development has by now established 410 schools, the students on rolls being 1.21 lakh. A special feature of the scheme is that efforts are made to see that at least one-third of the students selected are girls.

In terms of performance, as reported by the Ministry of Human Resource Development, girls are doing as well as, and even better than, boys in secondary and post secondary education. In the 1999 CBSE exams for Class-X, pass percentage for boys was 64.6 per cent and for girls 64 per cent. In Class-XII exam, pass percentage for boys was 71.01 per cent as against 79.75 per cent for girls.

Inadequacies in Implementation of NPE Schemes

The following are some of the observations made by the Department related Parliamentary Standing Committee on Human Resource Development in its 93rd report on Demand for Grants 2000-2001 in respect of Department of Elementary Education and Literacy:

"The Committee observes (in the case of Operation Blackboard) that lack of initiative on the part of many States has resulted in unspent balances lying with them. As on 10.3.2000, out of Rs. 2590.16 crore released under Operation Blackboard, an amount of Rs. 378.69 crore is lying unutilised with different State Governments. This calls for serious review of the Scheme........"

The Committee has also deprecated implementation problems in respect of the following schemes as noted against them :

Sarva Siksha Abhiyan	Inordinate delay (3 years time) in sanctioning the scheme
Operation Blackboard	Teachers appointed under the Scheme not taking charge of their offices in tribal areas.
National Council for Teacher Education (NCTE)	Allocated funds not being spent
Mid-day Meal Scheme (National Programme	40% of the foodgrains allotted for running the scheme not being lifted (the

for Nutritional Support of Primary Education)	Committee would suggest that it would be better to serve cooked meals than distribute foodgrains).
DPEP	Delay in release of funds to the States, delays in recruitment of teachers due to litigation, frequent transfer of project directors, etc.
Navodaya Vidyalayas	Allocated funds not being fully spent.
Vocational education	Uncertainty about the scheme pending its review based on the finding of the Operation Research Group that the scheme has not yielded the desired results.
Computer Literacy and Studies in Schools (CLASS)	Significant scaling down of budget allocations in revised estimates since 1997-98 to 1999-2000; uncertainty about the scheme pending review by a sub-committee of the National Development Council.
Education Technology	Delays in purchase of equipment and release of funds from time to time after adjusting unspent amounts; by implication, allocated funds not being spent adequately.
Promotion of Science	State Governments exhibiting unspent balances frequently.
Laboratories Technical Education	Low enrolment for apprenticeship training; unspent balances; non-approval of Schemes for student counseling, creation of Research Information Centre, etc.

Higher Education

Girls' Enrolment in Higher Education

In higher education, both general and professional, girls' enrolment has been significantly of low proportion of total enrolment (including that of boys) since 1970-71, though the enrolment index for girls relative to the overall index has shown steeper increases as

Table 5.18. Indices of Girls' Enrolment in Higher Education

Category of Higher Education		*1970-71*		*1975-76*		*1993-94*	
		Number (000)	*Index*	*Number (000)*	*Index*	*Number (000)*	*Index*
General Education							
(a) Graduation	Total	1436	**100**	1731	**121**	4192	**292**
	Female	338	**100**	472	**140**	1504	**445**
(b) Post Graduation	Total	144	**100**	193	**134**	477	**331**
	Female	39	**100**	51	**131**	177	**456**
(c) Research	Total	11	**100**	15	**137**	52	**470**
	Female	2.6	**100**	4.2	**160**	20.5	**784**
(d) Diploma/Certificate	Total	18.8	**100**	19.6	**104**	43.4	**231**
	Female	3.8	**100**	4.7	**123**	11.4	**300**
Total for General Education	Total	1610	**100**	1959	**122**	4764	**296**
	Female	383	**100**	532	**139**	1712	**447**
Professional Education							
(a) Graduation	Total	310	**100**	416	**134**	939	**302**
	Female	41	**100**	54	**132**	191	**465**

(Contd.)

Category of Higher Education		*1970-71 Number (000)*	*Index*	*1975-76 Number (000)*	*Index*	*1993-94 Number (000)*	*Index*
(b) Post Graduation	Total	17.2	**100**	26.8	**156**	73.1	**425**
	Female	2.7	**100**	3.9	**145**	17.2	**632**
(c) Research	Total	2.1	**100**	3.1	**145**	9.9	**467**
	Female	0.14	**100**	0.29	**205**	2.3	**164**
(d) Diploma/Certificate	Total	14.3	**100**	21.4	**150**	31.2	**219**
	Female	3.9	**100**	4.9	**126**	8.7	**222**
Total for Professional Education	Total	334	**100**	467	**138**	1054	**316**
	Female	47.8	**100**	63.1	**132**	219	**458**
Grand Total for General and Professional Education	Total	1954	**100**	2426	**124**	5817	**298**
	Female	431	**100**	595	**138**	1931	**448**
		(22%)		(24.5%)		(33%)	

Source : Based on data of University Grants Commission, New Delhi, quoted in National Seminar and Workshop Report of NCERT on 'Fifty Years of Women's Education in India', (1947-97).

Figures in brackets indicate % of women to total enrolment

shown in Table 18. The steepness is due to the comparatively lower participation of girls in higher education in earlier years. In specific terms, the proportion of women in higher education increased from 22 per cent in 1970-71 to 33 per cent in 1993-94. Yet it is very significant, as it is an increase in absolute terms from less than half a million to about two million.

Bulk of women's enrolment in higher education even after 25 years of efforts after the GSWI report, continues to be on softer courses like Arts, Commerce, Science, Education etc. Enrolment in professional courses is rather low (Table 19).

Table 19. Enrolment of Women in Higher Education by Courses

Courses	*Total No. of Women Students enrolled in 1970-71*	*Total No. of women students enrolled in 1995-96*
Arts	4,21,850	11,91,774
Commerce	12,675	3,09,830
Science	1,68,540	4,40,354
Education	20,799	85,699
Law	2,626	39,551
Engineering and Technology	910	26,368
Others including medicine, agriculture, veterinary science, music, fine arts/social work, physical education etc.	28,422	97,562
Total	6,55,822 (21.9% of all enrolment, men and women students)	21,91,138 (34.1% of all enrolment, men and women students)

Source : University Grants Commission.

In Kerala, Punjab and Goa women account for more than 50 per cent of total enrolment in higher education. Bihar receives the lowest rank with just 18.6 per cent women's enrolment.

"Career orientation" of courses at the first-degree level was started in 1994-95. Thirty-five vocational subjects have been identified. And, 26 Universities and over 1000 colleges have introduced vocational subjects.

University Grants Commission (UGC) and Women's Education

The University Grants Commission gives assistance to the extent of 60 per cent of construction cost for construction of women's hostels. About a dozen universities have availed of this facility.

The UGC also gives assistance for Centres/cells for women studies and for research and development of curricula.

Other UGC programmes with a focus on women include assistance for day-care centres for women students/teachers, scholarships for women in professional courses and in gender sensitivity programmes.

The project for creation of Population Education Research Centres (PERCs) implemented by the UGC is funded with the assistance of United Nations Funds for Population (UNFPA). Seventeen such Centres have been already started. They are engaged in curriculum development and production of teaching learning materials to project women related issues - family size, quality of life, gender equity, reproductive health, AIDS, etc.

The UGC has also started, in 1998-99, a new scheme of introducing technical courses for women in Women's Universities. Assistance under this scheme is given for a period of five years for under-graduate courses in engineering and technology. Five Universities have been identified for implementation of the scheme and assistance has already been granted to SNDT University.

Open Universities and Distance Education

In the country's context of cultural barriers and vast spread of population in rural areas which particularly inhibit women's participation even in lesser levels of education, open and distance education becomes crucial for women's participation in higher education. The advantages of distance education are flexible timings, facility for part-time and low cost access, open admission policy without restrictions of minimum entry qualifications or minimum percentage marks, absence of opportunity costs of lost work, etc.

Provision of higher education services through open universities has been a major step forward in this context. The Indira Gandhi National Open University (IGNOU) was established in 1985. It has come to offer in 15 years 50 programmes at masters, bachelors, advanced diploma, post-graduate diploma and certificate levels for nearly 200 thousand students. Data (including gender disaggregated) on performance of IGNOU are presented in Table 20.

Table 20. Distribution of IGNOU Students by Gender, Social Status and Rural Urban Division

(Percentages)

Variables	*1995*	*1996*	*1997*	*1998*	*1999*
Gender (%)					
Male	77.75	77.98	77.18	71.52	73.53
Female	22.25	22.02	22.82	28.48	26.47
Social Status (%)					
SCs	4.16	3.88	4.32	NA	3.14
STs	2.12	1.57	1.69	NA	1.46
General	93.72	94.55	93.99	NA	95.30
Rural/ Urban (%)					
Rural	18.81	8.77	16.48	17.89	22.40
Urban	81.19	91.23	83.52	82.11	77.60
Employment status (%)					
Employed	61.52	57.00	67.54	NA	NA
Un-employed	38.48	43.00	32.46	NA	NA

Source : Dr. Vijayshri, Reader and Prof. Suresh Garg, Director, School of Sciences, IGNOU; Conference Papers – "Reaching the Un-reached Through Open and Distance Learning", 27-29 April, 2000; Conference organised by IGNOU.

IGNOU has established 45 Special Study Centres of which 9 are meant for exclusively for women, 18 are for remote and rural areas and 5 for SCs/STs.

IGNOU programmes are telecast daily on the National Channel of Doordarshan. Interactive radio, phone-in counseling is aired on 21 AIR Stations.

IGNOU has also started working on DD Gyandarshan, an educational TV channel.

Technical Education

Para-15.14.1 of the POA, 1992 states "Opportunities for

technical education for women at all levels will be suitably increased. Additional polytechnics for women will be established under the World Bank assisted Technician Education Projects and concerted efforts will be made to increase the proportion of girls enrolling in polytechnics and engineering courses. Adequate hostel facilities will be provided to the girl students in technical and management institutions. Guidance seminar for girls at the 10+2 stage will be organised through the State Governments, Boards of Apprenticeship Training and other selected institutions to make them aware of opportunities in technical education and potential for employment and self-employment.

An important area in technical education relevant to women's participation is polytechnic education. The Ministry of Human Resource Development, Department of Education, runs a scheme for community polytechnics supported by direct central assistance. Assistance is granted in terms of a one time nonrecurring grant of Rs.10 lakhs and of a recurring grant of Rs.7 lakhs per annum to polytechnics approved by the All India Council for Technical Education (AICTE). So far 442 community polytechnics have been organised. Another 100 are proposed to be added.

Community polytechnics functions through extension centres (five per institution), each centre covering ten to twelve villages. The special focus of community polytechnics is training young women in employable skills. The Luther Committee for review of the scheme of community polytechnics has recommended (1994) that a special women's programme be organised by these institutions with functional linkages to the development schemes of Central and State Governments.

One of the thrust areas of the World Bank assisted Technician Education Project has been enhancing women's participation in polytechnics. Under the project, the overall percentage of women students in polytechnics has gone up from 11.29 per cent to 29 per cent. Sixty-eight new coeducational polytechnics, women's polytechnics and women's wings have been organised.

The Canada-India Institutional Co-operation Project (CIICP) and Canada-India Institute - Industry Linkage Project (CIIILP) implemented with the assistance of Canadian International Development Agency (CIDA) has, as one of its principal objectives enhancement of women's involvement in technical education. These projects are under implementation in 25 diploma granting polytechnics in Karnataka, Kerala and Tamil Nadu. The three State Directorates of Technical Education, the Technical Teachers Training Institute, Chennai and ISTE are the institutions which are coordinately involved in the projects.

Special Schemes for Girls of SC/ST/OBC/Minority Communities

As already brought out in several contexts, educational disparities are very prominent in the case of SC/ST girls. Several of the schemes also have special focus on SC/STs, especially girls among them. The Ministry of Social Justice and Empowerment runs several schemes exclusively meant for the benefit of SC/ST/OBCs and Minorities (Table 21). In many of those schemes special provisions have been made for affirmative action for girls amongst them.

Table 21. Special Schemes for Girls of SC/ST/OBC/ Minority Communities

Hostels for SC boys and girls	Meant to help students from remote and rural areas for provision of hostels in the middle, higher secondary, college and university levels (in fact, this scheme has been under implementation even from Third Five Year Plan)
Book Banks for SC/STs	Meant for helping students who cannot afford costly text books and who therefore often drop-out. Book Banks facilities are made available for medical, engineering, agriculture. veterinary, polytechnic, law, chartered accountancy and MBA courses. 30 per cent of the beneficiaries should be girls.
Special Education Development Programme for Girls belonging to very low literacy levels	This is meant to facilitate establishment of residential schools; package of inputs is provided for scheduled caste girls in class I only; The scheme is implemented through Zila Parishads/ voluntary organisations. Forty-eight Districts having

	literacy levels below 2 per cent are covered.
Upgradation of merit of SC/ST students	This scheme is meant to enhance capability of SC/STs to access professional courses like engineering and medical by availing of the quotas reserved for them; 100 per cent Central Assistance is given to States/ UTs for remedial coaching of students in classes IX to XII; there is 30 per cent reservation for girls in these special coaching courses.
Pre-examination coaching for OBCs	Meant for enhancing capabilities of students to be successful in competitive examinations for Public Services and entrance tests; implemented through Universities or State level Professional Coaching Institutions; there is 30 per cent reservation of seats in these courses for girls.
Boys' and Girls' Hostels for OBCs	Hostels are put up in States/UTs with large OBC population; Hostel facilities are meant for students in middle, secondary, college and University levels; one-third of the hostels are for girls.
Moulana Azad Education Foundation	Financial support is given for establishment of residential schools for girls to raise their educational standards of educationally backward minorities; for opening of multi stream residential higher secondary schools for girls where science, commerce and vocational courses are run; implementation agencies are to be registered organisations, societies or Trusts.

Source : Ministry of Social Justice and Empowerment: Schemes and Programmes

Literacy

The overall scenario of female literacy in the country continues to be marked by low attainments as well as male-female imbalance, features which the CSWI had projected strongly.

The CSWI also pointed out that the formal system of education had very serious limitations and that in spite of all expansion, the system covered only 10 per cent of the total female population. There has since been some improvement over this situation. In 1991, in terms of levels of attainment, 23% of the total female population could gain out of the formal system by availing of the same (Table 22). Still, the female literacy situation is quite dismal.

Table 22. Female Population by Level of Educational Attainment

(in Million)

Age-Group	*Primary*	*Middle*	*Secondary*	*Post Secondary & Above*	*Total*
10-14	14.01	5.24	0.25	0.03	19.53
15-19	4.99	6.88	4.28	2.16	18.31
20-24	4.22	3.99	2.90	3.40	14.51
25-29	3.92	3.12	2.21	2.40	11.65
30-34	3.10	2.22	1.63	1.54	8.49
35-39	2.69	1.77	1.24	1.08	6.78
40-44	1.82	1.06	0.75	0.65	4.28
45-49	1.47	0.74	0.48	0.37	3.06
50-54	1.02	0.47	0.29	0.22	2.00
55-59	0.76	0.32	0.18	0.12	1.38
60-64	0.60	0.23	0.11	0.07	1.01
65-69	0.39	0.14	0.06	0.04	0.63
70-74	0.23	0.07	0.03	0.02	0.35
75 plus	0.26	0.08	0.03	0.03	0.40
Age unknown	0.22	0.09	0.04	0.07	0.42
	39.7	26.42	14.48	12.2	92.8*

* This figure of 92.8 million as a percentage of the total female population (1991) of 407.07 million works out to 22.8%.

Source : Selected Educational Statistics, 1968-99.

Time sequence data on distribution of population by educational level are presented in Table 23.

Table 23. Distribution of Population by Educational Level (Percent)

Educational Level	*1971*		*1981*		*1991*	
	Female	*Male*	*Female*	*Male*	*Female*	*Male*
Illiterate	81.3	60.6	75.2	53.1	67.83	47.25
Literate without educational level	6.8	12.2	8.6	14.4	8.94	12.53
Primary	7.1	13.7	8.1	13.6	10.09	14.37
Middle	3.0	7.5	4.2	8.4	6.55	11.19
Matriculate/ Secondary	1.5	4.9	2.3	5.9	3.59	7.57
Higher secondary/ Intermediate/ Pre-University	–	–	0.8	2.2	1.39	3.18
Non-technical diploma or certificate not equal to degree	–	0.1	–	–	0.06	0.10
Technical diploma or certificate not equal to degree	–	0.1	0.1	0.3	0.11	0.40
Graduate and above	0.3	0.9	0.7	2.1	1.44	3.40
All levels	100	100	100	100	100	100

Source : Registrar General, India, Census of India, Social and Cultural Tables (1.971 and 1.981)

Note : The figures for 1981 exclude Assam where the census could not conducted that year. The figures for 1991 excludes J & K where census could not be conducted that year.

The sluggish progress in educational levels for females as well as males, especially at the higher levels, is self-evident from this table.

Education attainments of women have been associated with the different classes of the Indian society. Women from middle and upper classes acquire education as opposed to those from the lower classes. This is mainly due to poverty coupled with the low valuation of the benefits of education. The literacy programmes are specially meant to make a dent in promoting literacy amongst illiterate rural women and girls in India.

Overall female literacy in the country **(not by levels of attainment),** however, has risen up to 54.16 per cent (2001), compared to 21.97 per cent in 1971 registering an increase of 32-19 per cent points. The ranking of the States according to female literacy rates as per the 2001 Census is presented in Table 3.7 in Annexure III. Despite increase in the level of female literacy over the decades including since 1971, it has continued to be far below male literacy. This disparity which is 21.69 per cent points in 2001 is only slightly lesser than that in 1971 which was 23.98 per cent points (Table 24). The rate of female literacy has generally tended to grow faster than male literacy. However, the male female literacy

Table 24. Literacy Rates India: 1951-1998

Relative Male Female

Literacy Growth		*Year*	*Persons*	*Males*	*Females*
Male	*Female*				
13.24	6.48	1951	18.33	27.16	8.86
5.55	6.63	1961	28.31	40.40	15.34
10.45	7.88	1971	34.45	45.95	21.97
7.65	9.44	1981*	43.67	56.50	29.85
9.00	11.00	1991*	52.21	64.13	39.29
–	–	1997@	62.00	3.13	50.29
–	–	1998@	64.00	–	–
11.72	14.87	2001*	65.38	75.85	54.16

***Source*:** RGI, Census of India.

Note : Literacy rate for 1951, 1961 and 1 971 related to population aged five years and above. The rates for the years 1981, 1991 and 2001 related to the population aged seven years and above.

* Census could not be conducted in Assam in 1981 and in J&K in 1991.

@ An analysis based on NSSO Survey 1998, National Literacy Mission.

gap does not seem to be narrowing towards closure at a significant pace. This trend could be attributed basically to two factors; first, men having reached a far higher level of literacy than women, further growth is coming about less fast; and two, targeted attention to women is having a positive impact on the pace of their literacy growth rate.

The male-female literacy divide manifests itself more starkly amongst the Scheduled Castes and Tribes, though relative to 1971, there has been improvement. In 1991, in rural areas, female literacy for all persons was 30.62 per cent against 64.05 per cent in urban areas and against the overall national average of 39.29 per cent. Rural female literacy for scheduled castes was 19.45 per cent and for Scheduled Tribes 16.02 per cent. In 1971, rural female literacy for all persons had been 13.17 per cent and 5.06 per cent and 4.36 per cent respectively for scheduled castes and scheduled tribes. In

Table 25. Literacy Rates of SCs/STs by Sex and by Rural/Urban Classification

Years/Persons/ Males/Females	*Scheduled Castes*			*Scheduled Tribe*		
	Total	*Rural*	*Urban*	*Total*	*Rural*	*Urban*
Persons						
1961	10.27	8.89	21.81	8.53	8.16	22.41
1971	14.67	12.77	28.65	11.30	10.68	28.84
1981	21.38	18.48	36.60	16.35	14.92	37.93
1991	37.41	33.25	55.11	29.60	27.38	56.60
Males						
1961	16.96	15.06	32.21	13.83	13.37	30.43
1971	22.36	20.04	38.93	17.63	16.92	37.09
1981	31.12	27.91	47.54	24.52	22.94	47.60
1991	49.91	45.95	66.60	40.65	38.45	66.56
Females						
1961	3.29	2.52	10.04	3.16	2.90	13.45
1971	6.44	5.06	16.99	4.85	4.36	19.64
1981	10.93	8.45	24.34	8.04	6.81	27.32
1991	23.76	19.45	42.29	18.19	16-02	45.66

Source : Selected Educational Statistics, 1998-99 based on Census of India documents.

1997, female literacy for all persons in rural areas was 43 per cent against 72 per cent in urban areas and against the national average of 50 per cent (urban/rural female literacy figures for Scheduled Castes and Scheduled Tribes as of 1997 are not yet available) [Table 25].

Adult Female literacy (15 years and above) in 1997 was 43 per cent against the male literacy of 70 per cent and national average of 57 per cent. In 1971 these figures were 19.36 per cent, 47.69 per cent and 34.08 per cent. In absolute numbers, there were 123.25 million **adult female literates** in 1997 against 29.55 million in 1971. During these years **adult female illiterates** were 163.40 million and 123.13 million respectively. Continuing high numbers of female literates is to be seen in the light of the increase of adult female population by 133.96 million between 1971 and 1997 (from 152.68 million to 286.64 million) [Table 26].

Table 26. Adult Literacy 15 Years and Above

(in million)

Particulars	*1961*	*1971*	*1981*	*1991*	*1996*	*1997*
I. Total Population						
Male	133.60	165.14	207.98	273.48	301-91	309.59
Female	125.24	152.68	193.86	252.72	279.52	286.64
Total	258.84	317.82	401.84	526.20	581.43	596.23
II. Illiterates						
Male	78.22	86.37	93.78	104.21	98.87	92.87
Female	108.77	123.13	144.03	166.56	165.84	163.38
Total	186.99	209.50	237.81	270.77	264.71	256.25
III. Literates						
Male	55.38	78.76	114.19	169.26	203.04	216.71
Female	16.47	29.55	49.82	86.15	113.68	123.25
Total	71.85	108.31	164.01	255.41	316.72	339.96
IV. Illiteracy %						
Male	58.55	52.31	45.09	38.11	32.75	30.00
Female	86.85	80.64	74.30	65.91	59.33	57.50
Total	72.24	65.92	59.18	51.46	45.68	43.00
V. Literacy %						
Male	41.45	47.69	54.91	61.89	67.25	70.00
Female	13.15	19.36	25.70	34.09	40.67	43.00
Total	27.76	34.08	40.82	48.54	54.32	57.00

***Source*:** Selected Educational Statistics - 1998-99 based on NSSO 52nd and 53rd Rounds.

There was significant increase in adult female literacy between 1991 and 1997 by about nine percentage points, and one percentage point higher than for males. The increase, however, varied for different States and Union Territories (UTs). The increase was highest for A&N Islands at 35 per cent and negative for Chandigarh at (-) 0.2 per cent. It was between 25 and 30 per cent for one State, between 20 and 25 per cent for 6 States, between 10 and 20 per cent for 13 States, between 5 and 10 per cent for 7 States, and less than 5 per cent for 2 States. The States, which had high levels of female literacy like Kerala have registered lower rates of increase in the 1991-97 period and States, which had lower levels of literacy in 1991, have registered, generally higher rates of increase in this period with the exception of Orissa.

Adult literacy data indicate that the older age groups have lower levels of literacy compared to the younger age group of women who reach up to middle school. This pattern is uniform for rural and urban areas though the percentage of literacy for both males and females is higher in the urban areas. Table 27 highlights the literacy levels of males and females in rural and urban areas.

Table 27. Age-Wise, Sex-Wise and Area-Wise Distribution of Population by Literacy, All India

Age Group	*Total*		*Rural*		*Urban*	
	M	F	M	F	M	F
15-19	75.25	54.89	70.96	45.82	86.40	78.34
20-24	71.55	43.83	65.86	33.99	84.41	69.65
25-29	65.86	38.31	59.29	28.30	82.16	64.30
30-34	63.32	34.59	55.86	24.44	81.31	61.82
35+	53.33	22.99	45.36	14.94	75.56	47.65

Source : Compiled from Census of India, 1991, C-Series.

Age-wise, sex-wise, time sequence data on literacy are presented in Table 28

The CSWI had pointed out, based on data for 1968-69, that

Table 28. Literates by Age and Sex (per cent)

Age Group (Years)	*1961*			*1971*			*1981*			*1991*		
	Female	*Male*	*Total*	*Female*	*Male*	*Total*	*Female*	*Male*	*Total*	*Female*	*Male*	*Total*
5 - 9	14.4	25.5	19.8	18.9	27.2	23.1	25.6	34.7	30.2	51.0	62.6	56.9
10 - 14	28.4	54.4	42.3	38.2	59.8	49.6	44.8	66.8	56.4	59.7	77.0	68.8
15 - 19	23.8	52.0	3.8.4	37.7	63.3	51.3	43.3	66.1	55.4	54.9	75.3	65.8
20 - 24	18.2	49.8	33.6	28.7	60.7	44.7	37.1	66.6	52.0	43.8	71.6	57.8
25 – 34	13.9	42.5	28.5	19.3	50.1	34.8	28.9	60.7	45.1	36.6	64.7	50.8
35 plus	7.7	35.3	22.2	10.7	38.0	25.2	14.5	44.7	30.3	22.0	52.6	30.1
All Ages	13.0	34.5	24.0	18.7	39.5	29.5	24.8	46.9	36.2	39.3	64.1	52.2
5 and above	15.3	40.4	28.3	22.0	45.9	34.5	28.5	53.5	41.4	39.1	64.0	52.0
10 and above	15.5	43.6	30.1	22.6	49.9	36.8	29.0	57.0	43.6	37.8	64.1	51.5
15 and above	13.2	41.5	27.8	19.4	47.7	34.1	25.7	54.9	40.8	33.7	61.6	48.2

Source : Registrar General, India, Census of India (various years); for 1981, figures exclude Assam State where census could not be conducted that year; 1991 figures exclude Jammu and Kashmir as census was not held in that State that year; age group 5 and above excludes "age not stated"; figures of 1991 are based on population 7 years and above.

Bihar, Madhya Pradesh, Rajasthan, Uttar Pradesh, Orissa and Andhra Pradesh were the six States with the lowest female literacy. These six States continue to have the lowest female literacy rates in the country.

The male-female adult literacy (of population aged 15 plus) divide comes into sharper focus, if State-wise data are seen. Data on adult literacy rates and literacy gender parity indices in respect of various States are presented in Tables 32 and 33.

The bottom 10 districts have a literacy level ranging from 19.01 per cent in the Jhabua district of Madhya Pradesh and 26 per cent in the Banswara district of Rajasthan. It is obvious that in these districts total female literacy rates would be much more dismal - considering the overall pattern of male female literacy divide. The top ten highest literacy Districts are in areas of Kerala where the proportion of SC/ST population is low and the bottom 10 lowest literacy districts are in the areas of Madhya Pradesh, Bihar, Orissa, Rajasthan and Uttar Pradesh where the SC/ST population proportions are high as shown in Table 29

Census 2001 has brought out a significant increase in literacy, particularly female literacy, with a 14 percentage point increase over the 1991 count. Even more significant than this is the decrease in the number of districts at the lower range of female literacy and increase at the higher range. The number of districts with female literacy of over 50 per cent has increased to over 335 in 2001 from 143 in 1991. Data on districts falling in different ranges of literacy are presented in Table 30.

The district with the highest female literacy in the country is Aizwal in Mizoram with a literacy rate of 96.06 per cent. The lowest literacy rate is in Kishanganj district in Bihar at 18.49 per cent, a slide from its previous level of 22-22 per cent.

There are large number of households with no literate female Members of age 15 plus in the country as a whole. The percentages of such household were 67.14 in rural areas and 26.26 per cent in urban areas (1998) [Table 31].

The National Literacy Mission (NLM) was launched on May 5, 1988. The NLM aims to make men and women, who have not been covered by the formal school system, functionally literate. According to NLM document, functional literacy implies:

Table 29. Literacy Rates in Top Ten and Bottom Ten Districts in India

S. No.	*Name of the District*	*Top Ten*	*Name of the District*	*Bottom Ten*
1	Kottayam (Kerala)	95.72	Jhabhua (MP)	19.01
2	Pathanamthitta (Kerala)	94.88	Kishanganj (Bihar)	22.22
3	Mahe (Pondicherry)	94.10	Koraput (Orissa)	22.66
4	Alapuzha (Kerala)	93.87	Barmer (Rajasthan)	22.98
5	Ernakulam (Kerala)	92.35	Jalor (Rajasthan)	23.76
6	Kannur (Kerala)	91.48	Bahraich (UP)	24.39
7	Kozhikode (Kerala)	91.10	Baduan (UP)	24.64
8	Kollam (Kerala)	90.47	Bastar (MP)	24.89
9	Thrissur (Kerala)	90.18	Rampur (UP)	25.37
10	Thiruvananthapuram (Kerala)	89.22	Banswara (Rajasthan)	26.00

Source : Selected Educational Statistics, 1998-99; Ministry of Human Resource Development.

Table 30. Distribution of Districts* by Range of Female Literacy Rates: 1991, 2001

Ranges	*No. of Districts*	
	1991	*2001*
Total	577	577
<10	3	NIL
10-20	100	2
20-30	125	40
30-40	122	76
40-50	84	124
50-60	74	136
60-70	36	117
70-80	17	59
80-90	11	16
90+	5	7

* Excludes J&K, Kinnaur District of Himachal Pradesh and Kachchh District of Gujarat.

Table 31. Percentage of Households with no Literate Female Member of Age 15 Years and Above According to Place of Residence

State	*NSSO[1] (1993-94)*		*Time Use Survey[2] (1998)*	
	Rural	*Urban*	*Rural*	*Urban*
Haryana	66.5	44.5	65.27	32.55
Madhya Pradesh	80.3	44.0	71.83	38.30
Gujarat	61.9	34.0	57.01	26.29
Orissa	77.0	42.8	61.46	32.93
Tamil Nadu	58.7	36.1	38.24	17.79
Meghalaya	44.9	23.1	31.73	11.41
Combined States/*All India	67.8	39.7	67.14	26.26

Note : * Combined States refers to Time Use Survey and All-India refers to NSSO (1993-94).

Source : 1. NSSO (1993-94): National Sample Survey Organisation, Department of Statistics, Government of India.

2. Time Use Survey 1998: Central Statistical Organisation, Ministry of Statistics and Programme Implementation, Government of India.

- achieving self-reliance in literacy and numeracy;
- becoming aware of the causes of their deprivation and moving towards amelioration of their condition through organisation and participation in the process of development;
- acquiring skills to improve the economic status and general well being;
- imbibing the values of national integration, conservation of the environment, women's equality, observance of small family norm, etc.

The target under NLM is imparting functional literacy to the "threshold sustainable level of 75 per cent by the year 2005".

The NLM had adopted a mass campaign approach for removal of illiteracy. The campaign approach may be briefly described as a concerted effort involving various social resources, with a high degree of voluntary commitment to addressing the problem of illiteracy, in a defined region and within a limited period of time. The main modalities under the campaign approach are: identification of a cor team based on consultation and consensus among political parties, teachers, students and cultural groups; implementation through autonomous district level literacy committees; preparation of district profiles of non-literates; mass mobilisation; development of improved teaching-learning materials; training of resource persons; imparting training for 200 hours over eight months; consolidation of literacy skills imparted in post-literacy phase; creation of continuing education system; provision of resource support by Jan Shikshan Sansthans, etc. It is estimated that 62 per cent of the learners and 40 per cent of the instructors are females. The SC and ST constitute 22 per cent and 12 per cent of the coverage, respectively.

According to the Ministry of Human Resource Development, Department of Secondary and Higher Education, by 1998, 448 Districts have been covered, 150 million non-literates accessed and over 72 million persons made literate. It is also their view that "besides achieving the required levels of literacy, women experienced a tremendous rise in their self worth and progress ahead to form groups, cooperatives and small businesses". They cite the example of the campaign in District Dumka in Bihar State where women have formed *Jago Behna* (Awake Sisters) Group and where women have set up *Didi Banks* (Sister Banks).

The Department-related Parliamentary Standing Committee on Human Resource Development does not, however, seem to consider the performance in the area of literacy and projections in respect of future achievements in literacy with any sense of credibility. In its 93rd report on Demands for Grants 2000-2001, the Committee has observed: "The Committee was informed that as a result of concerted efforts in the area of primary education, non-formal education and adult education, there has been some increase in literacy rate prevailing in the country. Results of the 53rd round of the National Sample Survey Organisation (NSSO) indicate that against the literacy rate of 52.2 per cent in 1991, this rate was 62 per cent at the end of December, 1997 and is projected to touch 64 per cent at the end of 1998. This increase of almost two per cent may be seen against the backdrop of an average decadal growth of only 8.5 per cent between 1951 and 1991. Keeping the growth of around 2 per cent per annum, it has also been expected that by the year 2005, we could reach a target of 75 per cent literacy. Therefore, the revised scheme of National Literacy Mission has put it at a practical level of 75 per cent by 2005. .... The Committee is inclined to believe that literacy/enrollmerit/dropout rates projected on the basis of surveys conducted so far do not seem to be realistic. There is a lot of difference between assessment made by grass-root level workers and the so-called independent surveys. The Committee views with serious concern the difference between male and female literacy ...".

Table 32. Literacy Rate of Population Aged 15+ (15 and above), and 15-24, and Literacy Gender Parity Index - 1991

State/UT	*Sex*	*Literacy Rate*		*Literacy Gender Parity Index*	
		15+	*15-24*	*15+*	*15-24*
Andhra Pradesh	Male	50.4	65.2		
	Female	26.4	41.0		
	Total	38.5	53.1	0.5	0.6
Arunachal Pradesh	Male	48.7	64.3		
	Female	23.6	42.4		
	Total	37.5	54.1	0.5	0.7

(Contd.)

(Contd.)

State/UT	Sex	Literacy Rate 15+	Literacy Rate 15-24	Literacy Gender Parity Index 15+	Literacy Gender Parity Index 15-24
Assam	Male	60.2	69.0		
	Female	37.6	52.9		
	Total	49.6	61.0	0.6	0.8
Bihar	Male	50.3	62.8		
	Female	18.5	28.7		
	Total	35.1	46.6	0.4	0.5
Goa	Male	81.2	92.4		
	Female	61.5	85.7		
	Total	71.5	89.2	0.8	0.9
Gujarat	Male	69.2	79.7		
	Female	41.6	58.4		
	Total	55.9	69.4	0.6	0.7
Haryana	Male	64.2	79.5		
	Female	31.2	50.5		
	Total	48.9	66.5	0.5	0.8
Himachal Pradesh	Male	70.9	89.2		
	Female	43.5	72.3		
	Total	57.3	80.8	0.6	0.8
Karnataka	Male	63.8	73.8		
	Female	37.5	54.8		
	Total	50.9	64.6	0.6	0.7
Kerala	Male	92.7	97.9		
	Female	83.6	96.8		
	Total	88.0	97.3	0.9	1.0
Madhya Pradesh	Male	55.9	69.9		
	Female	22.9	35.8		
	Total	40.0	53.5	0.4	0.5
Maharashtra	Male	74.4	85.9		
	Female	45.3	67.0		
	Total	60.4	77.0	0.6	0.8

(Contd.)

(Contd.)

State/UT	*Sex*	*Literacy Rate*		*Literacy Gender Parity Index*	
		15+	*15-24*	*15+*	*15-24*
Manipur	Male	70.6	81.1		
	Female	41.9	62.2		
	Total	56.6	71.7	0.6	0.8
Meghalaya	Male	54.1	60.6		
	Female	42.6	56.9		
	Total	48.5	58.7	0.8	0.9
Mizoram	Male	85.8	88.5		
	Female	77.4	87.2		
	Total	81.9	87.9	0.9	1.0
Nagaland	Male	66.6	77.4		
	Female	50.6	70.0		
	Total	59.3	73.9	0.8	0.9
Orissa	Male	62.0	71.6		
	Female	29.7	45.5		
	Total	46.1	58.4	0.5	0.6
Punjab	Male	61.3	74.8		
	Female	43.4	66.5		
	Total	52.9	70.9	0.7	0.9
Rajasthan	Male	52.5	69.0		
	Female	16.9	25.9		
	Total	35.5	48.6	0.3	0.4
Sikkim	Male	61.6	77.4		
	Female	37.8	61.7		
	Total	50.9	69.9	0.6	0.8
Tamil Nadu	Male	69.9	81.8		
	Female	43.9	63.9		
	Total	57.0	72.7	0.6	0.8

(Contd.)

(Contd.)

State/UT	Sex	Literacy Rate		Literacy Gender Parity Index	
		15+	15-24	15+	15-24
Tripura	Male	69.3	81.0		
	Female	44.1	62.4		
	Total	57.1	71.7	0.6	0.8
Uttar Pradesh	Male	53.9	66.5		
	Female	21.0	33.0		
	Total	38.6	51.1	0.4	0.5
West Bengal	Male	68.0	73.4		
	Female	43.0	56.1		
	Total	56.2	65.0	0.6	0.8
A&N Islands	Male	75.8	88.7		
	Female	58.4	81.3		
	Total	68.4	85.4	0.8	0.9
Chandigarh	Male	80.5	84.8		
	Female	68.6	79.7		
	Total	75.4	82.6	0.9	0.9
D&N Haveli	Male	49.5	63.5		
	Female	21.3	32.0		
	Total	35.9	47.9	0.4	0.5
Daman & Diu	Male	79.9	88.2		
	Female	51.7	75.0		
	Total	66.0	82.1	0.6	0.9
Delhi	Male	80.4	85.1		
	Female	61.8	75.0		
	Total	72.2	80.6	0.8	0.9
Lakshadweep	Male	89.3	96.9		
	Female	66.9	93.4		
	Total	78.4	95.1	0.7	1.0
Pondicherry	Male	81.3	91.0		

(Contd.)

(Contd.)

State/UT	*Sex*	*Literacy Rate*		*Literacy Gender Parity Index*	
		15+	*15-24*	*15+*	*15-24*
	Female	59.3	78.9		
	Total	70.4	84.8	0.7	0.9
India	Male	61.9	73.5		
	Female	34.1	49.3		
	Total	48.5	61.9	0.6	0.7

Source : 1. Registrar General of India, Government of India.
2. National Sample Survey Organisation : Attending an Educational Institution in India : Its Level Nature and Cost, 52 Round, July 1995-June 1996. Report No. 439(52/25.2/1).

Table 33. Literacy Rate of Population Aged 15+ (15 and above), and 15-24, and Literacy Gender Parity Index-1997

State/UT	*Sex*	*Literacy Rate*		*Literacy Gender Parity Index*	
		15+	*15-24*	*15+*	*15-24*
Andhra Pradesh	Male	58.0	74.0		
	Female	35.0	49.0		
	Total	46.6	61.6	0.6	0.7
Arunachal Pradesh	Male	64.0	85.5		
	Female	39.9	75.3		
	Total	52.9	81.0	0.6	0.9
Assam	Male	83.0	95.0		
	Female	60.0	77.0		
	Total	72.1	86.1	0.7	0.8
Bihar	Male	60.0	73.0		
	Female	27.0	43.0		
	Total	44.3	59.0	0.4	0.6
Goa	Male	92.0	91.1		
	Female	74.9	92.1		
	Total	83.6	91.6	0.8	1.0

(Contd.)

(Contd.)

State/UT	Sex	Literacy Rate 15+	Literacy Rate 15-24	Literacy Gender Parity Index 15+	Literacy Gender Parity Index 15-24
Gujarat	Male	77.0	87.0		
	Female	49.0	72.0		
	Total	63.4	79.8	0.6	0.8
Haryana	Male	71.0	90.0		
	Female	41.0	69.0		
	Total	57.1	80.5	0.6	0.8
Himachal Pradesh	Male	84.0	100.0		
	Female	63.0	92.0		
	Total	73.7	96.2	0.8	0.9
Jammu & Kashmir	Male	65.0	76.9		
	Female	35.0	63.1		
	Total	50.6	70.6	0.5	0.8
Karnataka	Male	63.0	73.0		
	Female	43.0	66.0		
	Total	53.2	69.6	0.7	0.9
Kerala	Male	95.0	99.0		
	Female	88.0	99.0		
	Total	91.4	99.0	0.9	1.0
Madhya Pradesh	Male	66.0	82.0		
	Female	32.0	52.0		
	Total	49.6	67.2	0.5	0.6
Maharashtra	Male	81.0	94.0		
	Female	56.0	83.0		
	Total	68.9	88.8	0.7	0.9
Manipur	Male	84.1	98.0		
	Female	57.9	88.0		
	Total	71.4	93.3	0.7	0.9
Meghalaya	Male	72.1	88.3		
	Female	64.0	91.9		
	Total	68.2	90.0	0.9	1.0

(Contd.)

(Contd.)

State/UT	*Sex*	*Literacy Rate*		*Literacy Gender Parity Index*	
		15+	*15-24*	*15+*	*15-24*
Mizoram	Male	95.8	94.7		
	Female	93.9	98.8		
	Total	94.9	96.6	1.0	1.0
Nagaland	Male	91.9	97.7		
	Female	71.9	89.9		
	Total	82.5	94.2	0.8	0.9
Orissa	Male	62.0	70.0		
	Female	32.0	47.0		
	Total	47.2	58.4	0.5	0.7
Punjab	Male	67.0	80.0		
	Female	53.0	75.0		
	Total	60.4	77.7	0.8	0.9
Rajasthan	Male	69.0	85.0		
	Female	27.0	45.0		
	Total	48.9	66.2	0.4	0.5
Sikkim	Male	85.0	100.0		
	Female	66.2	91.3		
	Total	76.2	96.1	0.8	0.9
Tamil Nadu	Male	77.0	92.0		
	Female	54.0	78.0		
	Total	65.6	84.9	0.7	0.8
Tripura	Male	77.0	100.0		
	Female	65.0	80.2		
	Total	71.2	90.9	0.8	0.8
Uttar Pradesh	Male	64.0	77.0		
	Female	32.0	53.0		
	Total	49.1	66.1	0.5	0.7
West Bengal	Male	80.0	83.0		
	Female	58.0	72.0		
	Total	69.6	77.7	0.7	0.9

(Contd.)

(Contd.)

State/UT	Sex	Literacy Rate 15+	Literacy Rate 15-24	Literacy Gender Parity Index 15+	Literacy Gender Parity Index 15-24
A&N Islands	Male	100.0	100.0		
	Female	93.0	100.0		
	Total	96.9	100.0	0.9	1.0
Chandigarh	Male	89.9	93.8		
	Female	67.8	81.2		
	Total	80.2	88.5	0.8	0.9
D&N Haveli	Male	64.3	78.9		
	Female	30.2	50.0		
	Total	47.7	65.7	0.5	0.6
Daman & Diu	Male	95.1	100.0		
	Female	67.5	91.7		
	Total	81.5	96.2	0.7	0.9
Delhi	Male	90.0	95.0		
	Female	72.0	87.0		
	Total	81.8	91.5	0.8	0.9
Lakshadweep	Male	100.0	100.0		
	Female	90.0	100.0		
	Total	95.1	100.0	0.9	1.0
Pondicherry	Male	92.0	98.1		
	Female	81.8	100.0		
	Total	86.9	99.0	0.9	1.0
India	**Male**	**70.5**	**82.7**		
	Female	**43.9**	**63.6**		
	Total	**57.7**	**73.6**	**0.6**	**0.8**

Source : National Sample Survey Organisation, 53rd Round, 1997.

3

Social Status

India, with a population of 989 million, is the world's second most populous country. Of that number, 120 million are women who live in poverty. India has 16 percent of the world's population, but only 2.4 percent of its land, resulting in great pressures on its natural resources. Over 70 percent of India's population currently derive their livelihood from land resources, which includes 84 percent of the economically-active women. India is one of the few countries where males significantly outnumber females, and this imbalance has increased over time. India's maternal mortality rates in rural areas are among the world's highest. From a global perspective, Indian accounts for 19 percent of all lives births and 27 percent of all maternal deaths.

There seems to be a consensus that higher female mortality between ages one and five and high maternal mortality rates result in a deficit of females in the population. Deaths of young girls in India exceed those of young boys by over 300,000 each year, and every sixth infant death is specifically due to gender discrimination. Of the 15 million baby girls born in India each year, nearly 25 percent will not live to see their 15th birthday.

The persistence of hunger and abject poverty in India and other parts of the world is due in large measure to the subjugation, marginalization and disempowerment of women. Women suffer from hunger and poverty in greater numbers and to a great degree then men. At the same time, it is women who bear the primary responsibility for actions needed to end hunger: education, nutrition, health and family income.

Malnutrition: India has exceptionally high rates of child malnutrition, because tradition in India requires that women eat last and least throughout their lives, even when pregnant and lactating. Malnourished women give birth to malnourished children, perpetuating the cycle.

Poor health: Females receive less health care than males. Many women die in childbirth of easily prevented complications. Working conditions and environmental pollution further impairs women's health.

Lack of education: Families are far less likely to educate girls than boys, and far more likely to pull them out of school, either to help out at home or from fear of violence.

Overwork: Women work longer hours and their work is more arduous than men's, yet their work is unrecognized. Men report that "women, like children, eat and do nothing." Technological progress in agriculture has had a negative impact on women.

Unskilled: In women's primary employment sector - agriculture - extension services overlook women.

Mistreatment: In recent years, there has been an alarming rise in atrocities against women in India, in terms of rapes, assaults and dowry-related murders. Fear of violence suppresses the aspirations of all women. Female infanticide and sex-selective abortions are additional forms of violence that reflect the devaluing of females in Indian society.

Powerlessness: While women are guaranteed equality under the constitution, legal protection has little effect in the face of prevailing patriarchal traditions. Women lack power to decide who they will marry, and are often married off as children. Legal loopholes are used to deny women inheritance rights.

India has a long history of activism for women's welfare and rights, which has increasingly focused on women's economic rights. A range of government programs have been launched to increase economic opportunity for women, although there appear to be no existing programs to address the cultural and traditional discrimination against women that leads to her abject conditions.

Malnutrition

The greatest tragedy facing humanity today is the persistence of chronic hunger - an intolerable phenomenon that takes the lives of 24,000 of us every day. For fully one-fifth of humanity, life is a daily struggle to survive in conditions of relentless poverty. Day after day, the lives of one billion individuals are cut short or terribly diminished by chronic, persistent hunger. Day after day, one billion people are denied the opportunities they need to lead healthy and productive lives.

People living with chronic hunger exist in conditions of severe poverty. What they lack is the chance to change their situation, to develop their own self-sufficiency. The most potent confirmation of this fact can be seen in the lives of women. They, along with their children, are the main victims of hunger, and they are also most lacking in opportunities to end their own and their families' hunger.

The Hunger Project has come to the recognition that the persistence of hunger in India - and elsewhere in the world where hunger is still an overriding social issue - is, to a large degree, due to the subjugation, marginalization and disempowerment of women. Furthermore, women's suppression is rooted in the very fabric of Indian society - in traditions, in religious doctrine and practices, within the educational and legal systems, and within families.

Although India was the first country to announce an official family planning program in 1952, its population grew from 361 million in 1951 to 844 million in 1991. India's total fertility rate of 3.8 births per woman can be considered moderate by world standards, but the sheer magnitude of population increase has resulted in such a feeling of urgency that containment of population growth is listed as one of the six most important objectives in the Eighth Five-Year Plan.

Since 1970, the use of modern contraceptive methods has risen from 10 percent to 40 percent, with great variance between northern and southern India. The most striking aspect of contraceptive use in India is the predominance of sterilization, which accounts for more than 85 percent of total modern contraception use, with female sterilization accounting for 90 percent of all sterilizations.

The Indian constitution grants women equal rights with men, but strong patriarchal traditions persist, with women's lives shaped by customs that are centuries old. In most Indian families, a daughter is viewed as a liability, and she is conditioned to believe that she is inferior and subordinate to men. Sons are idolized and celebrated. May you be the mother of a hundred sons is a common Hindu wedding blessing.

A study of women in the Swayam Shikshan Prayog (SSP),

based in 20 villages in four districts in Maharashtra state was introduced in this way: The primary issue all women in the SSP were struggling with was that of everyday survival. Insufficient incomes and the lack of employment were reported to be their most pressing concerns. Survival is a constant preoccupation and at its most basic, survival means food. The most common problems were the lack of basic amenities such as food, water, fuel, fodder and health facilities. In addition, the deterioration of the natural environment and the fact that many of their traditional occupations were no longer viable were conditions that were making it increasingly hard for women to continue sustaining their families, as they had done in the past.

The exceptionally high rates of malnutrition in South Asia are rooted deeply in the soil of inequality between men and women. "...the poor care that is afforded to girls and women by their husbands and by elders is the first major reason for levels of child malnutrition that are markedly higher in South Asia than anywhere else in the world." This point is made in the article, *The Asian Enigma*, published by Unicef in the 1996 Progress of Nations, in which the rates of childhood malnutrition in South Asia are compared with those in Africa. We learn that malnutrition is far worse in South Asia, directly due to the fact that women in South Asia have less voice and freedom of movement than in Africa. "Judgement and self-expression and independence largely denied, millions of women in South Asia have neither the knowledge nor the means nor the freedom to act in their own and their children's best interests."

"Gender disparities in nutrition are evident from infancy to adulthood. In fact, gender has been the most statistically significant determinant of malnutrition among young children and malnutrition is a frequent direct or underlying cause of death among girls below age 5. Girls are breast-fed less frequently and for shorter durations in infancy; in childhood and adulthood, males are fed first and better. Adult women consume approximately 1,000 fewer calories per day than men according to one estimate from Punjab. Comparison of household dietary intake studies in different parts of the country shows that nutritional equity between males and females is lower in northern than in southern states."

Nutritional deprivation has two major consequences for

women: they never reach their full growth potential and anaemia. Both are risk factors in pregnancy, with anaemia ranging from 40-50 percent in urban areas to 50-70 percent in rural areas. This condition complicates childbearing and result in maternal and infant deaths, and low birth weight infants.

One study found anaemia in over 95 percent of girls ages 6-14 in Calcutta, around 67 percent in the Hyderabad area, 73 percent in the New Delhi area, and about 18 percent in the Madras area. This study states, "The prevalence of anaemia among women ages 15-24 and 25-44 years follows similar patterns and levels. Besides posing risks during pregnancy, anaemia increases women's susceptibility to diseases such as tuberculosis and reduces the energy women have available for daily activities such as household chores, child care, and agricultural labor. Any severely anaemic individual is taxed by most physical activities, including walking at an ordinary pace."

Poor Health

Surviving through a normal life cycle is a resource-poor woman's greatest challenge. The practice of breast-feeding female children for shorter periods of time reflects the strong desire for sons. If women are particularly anxious to have a male child, they may deliberately try to become pregnant again as soon as possible after a female is born. Conversely, women may consciously seek to avoid another pregnancy after the birth of a male child in order to give maximum attention to the new son. A primary way that parents discriminate against their girl children is through neglect during illness. When sick, little girls are not taken to the doctor as frequently as are their brothers.

A study in Punjab shows that medical expenditures for boys are 2.3 times higher than for girls. As adults, women get less health care than men. They tend to be less likely to admit that they are sick and they'll wait until their sickness has progressed before they seek help or help is sought for them. Studies on attendance at rural primary health centers reveal that more males than females are treated in almost all parts of the country, with differences greater in northern hospitals than southern ones, pointing to regional differences in the value placed on women. Women's socialization to tolerate suffering and their reluctance to be examined by male personnel are additional constraints in their getting adequate health care.

Even a woman who has had difficulties with previous pregnancies is usually treated with home remedies only for three reasons: the decision that a pregnant woman seek help rests with the mother-in-law and husband; financial considerations; and fear that the treatment may be more harmful than the malady.

It is estimated that pregnancy-related deaths account for one-quarter of all fatalities among women aged 15 to 29, with well over two-thirds of them considered preventable. For every maternal death in India, an estimated 20 more women suffer from impaired health. One village-level study of rural women in Maharashtra determined on the basis of physical examinations that some 92 percent suffered from one or more gynecological disorder.

Women's health is harmed by lack of access to and the poor quality of reproductive services. About 24.6 million couples, representing roughly 18 percent of all married women, want no more children but are not using contraception. The causes of this unmet need remain poorly understood, but a qualitative study in Tamil Nadu suggests that women's lack of decision-making power in the family, opportunity costs involved in seeking contraception, fear of child death, and poor quality of contraceptive service all play an important role. Some estimates suggest that some 5 million abortions are performed annually in India, with the large majority being illegal. As a result, abortion-related mortality is high.

Although abortion has been legal since 1972 in India, studies suggest that although official policy seeks to make pregnancy-termination services widely available, in practice guidelines on abortion limit access to services, particularly in rural areas. In 1981, of the 6,200 physicians trained to perform abortions, only 1,600 were working in rural areas. The tasks performed by women are usually those that require them to be in one position for long periods of time, which can adversely affect their reproductive health. A study in a rice-growing belt of coastal Maharashtra found that 40 percent of all infant deaths occurred in the months of July to October. The study also found that a majority of births were either premature or stillbirths. The study attributed this to the squatting position that had to be assumed during July and August, the rice transplanting months.

The impact of pollution and industrial wastes on health is

considerable. In Environment, Development and the Gender Gap, Sandhya Venkateswaran asserts that "the high incidence of malnutrition present amongst women and their low metabolism and other health problems affect their capacity to deal with chemical stress. The smoke from household biomass (made up of wood, dung and crop residues) stoves within a three-hour period is equivalent to smoking 20 packs of cigarettes. For women who spend at least three hours per day cooking, often in a poorly ventilated area, the impact includes eye problems, respiratory problems, chronic bronchitis and lung cancer. One study quoted by WHO in 1991 found that pregnant women cooking over open biomass stoves had almost a 50 percent higher chance of stillbirth.

Lack of Education

Women and girls receive far less education than men, due both to social norms and fears of violence. India has the largest population of non-school-going working girls. India's constitution guarantees free primary school education for both boys and girls up to age 14. This goal has been repeatedly reconfirmed, but primary education in India is not universal. Overall, the literacy rate for women is 39 percent versus 64 percent for men. The rate for women in the four large northern states - Bihar, Uttar Pradesh, Rajasthan and Madhya Pradesh - is lower than the national average: it was 25 percent in 1991. Attendance rates from the 1981 census suggest that no more than 1/3 of all girls (and a lower proportion of rural girls) aged 5-14 are attending school.

Although substantial progress has been achieved since India won its independence in 1947, when less than 8 percent of females were literate, the gains have not been rapid enough to keep pace with population growth: there were 16 million more illiterate females in 1991 than in 1981. Parents' reluctance to educate daughters has its roots in the situation of women. Parents have several incentives for not educating their daughters. Foremost is the view that education of girls brings no returns to parents and that their future roles, being mainly reproductive and perhaps including agricultural labor, require no formal education. As more and more boys are engaged in education, there is a growing reliance on the labor of girls. Girls are increasingly replacing their brothers on the farm while carrying on their usual responsibilities in housework. A large proportion of the roughly 40 million nonworking girls who are not in school are kept at home because of responsibilities in housework.

The role of parents is to deliver a chaste daughter to her husband's family. Sonalde Desai goes on to point out that "another disincentive for sending daughters to school is a concern for the protection of their virginity. When schools are located at a distance, when teachers are male, and when girls are expected to study along with boys, parents are often unwilling to expose their daughters to the potential assault on their virginity."

Budgetary provisions for non-formal education have been cut by 17 percent, leading to closure of many night schools and adult education programs in which working-class women participate. Reduction in government expenditures on higher education and encouragement to private colleges will reduce women's opportunities for higher education since privatization in education promotes only male-dominated professional and technical courses, as they are lucrative."

Overwork

Women work longer hours and their work is more arduous than men's. Still, men report that "women, like children, eat and do nothing." Women work roughly twice as many as many hours as men. Women's contribution to agriculture - whether it be subsistence farming or commercial agriculture - when measured in terms of the number of tasks performed and time spent, is greater than men. "The extent of women's contribution is aptly highlighted by a micro study conducted in the Indian Himalayas which found that on a one-hectare farm, a pair of bullocks works 1,064 hours, a man 1,212 hours and a woman 3,485 hours in a year."

In Andhra Pradesh, the work day of an woman agricultural labourer during the agricultural season lasts for 15 hours, from 4 am to 8 pm, with an hour's rest in between. Her male counterpart works for seven to eight hours, from 5 am to 10 am or 11 am and from 3 pm to 5 pm. Another study on time and energy spent by men and women on agricultural work found that 53 percent of the total human hours per household are contributed by women as compared to 31 percent by men. The remaining contribution comes from children.

The anxiety of man to monopolize his skill in plough culture is reflected in the taboo that is observed almost all over India, against the women's handling the plough. In many societies, she is not even allowed to touch it. Whereas operations performed by men were those that entailed the use of machinery and draught animals, thereby using animal, hydraulic, mechanical or electrical energy, women almost always relied on manual labour, using only their own energy. Rice transplantations, the most arduous and labour intensive task in rice cultivation, is carried out entirely by women without the help of any tools.

Girls learn to assist their mothers in almost all tasks, and from the age of 10 years participate fully in the agricultural work done by women. Mies cites the case of Laxmi, a three-year-old infant who, along with her mother, pulled seedlings for transplanting. Boys on the other hand were seldom seen transplanting or weeding though they did help out in ploughing or watering the fields. Not only do women perform more tasks, their work is also more arduous than that undertaken by men. Both transplantation and weeding require women to spend the whole day and work in muddy soil with their hands. Moreover, they work the entire day under the intensely hot sun while men's work, such as ploughing and watering the fields, is invariably carried out early in the morning before the sun gets too hot. Mies argues that because women's work, unlike men's, does not involve implements and is based largely on human energy, it is considered unskilled and hence less productive. On this basis, women are invariably paid lower wages, despite the fact that they work harder and for longer hours than do men.

In contrast, a study in Uttar Pradesh reports that men only reluctantly conceded that their womenfolk really work. The researchers in this area were repeatedly told that women, like children, simply eat food and do nothing. Many maintain that women's economic dependence on men impacts their power within the family. With increased participation in income-earning activities, not only will there be more income for the family, but gender inequality should be reduced. This issue is particularly salient in India because studies show a very low level of female participation in the labor force. This under-reporting is attributed to the frequently held view that women's work is not economically productive. In a report of the National Commission on Self-Employed Women and Women in the Informal Sector, the director of social welfare in one state said, "There are no women in any unorganized sector in our state." When the Commission probed and asked, "Are there any women who go to the forest to collect firewood? Do any of the women in rural areas have cattle?" the director responded with, "Of course, there are many women doing that type of work." Working women are invisible to most of the population.

Any income generated from this work is generally controlled by the men. Such work is unlikely to increase women's participation in allocating family finances. In a 1992 study of family-based texile workers, male children who helped in a home-based handloom mill were given pocket money, but the adult women and girls were not. The shift from subsistence to a market economy has a dramatic negative impact on women. According to Sandhya Venkateswaran, citing Shiva, the Green Revolution, which focused on increasing yields of rice and wheat, entailed a shift in inputs from human to technical. Women's participation, knowledge and inputs were marginalized, and their role shift from being "primary producers to subsidiary workers."

Where technology has been introduced in areas where women worked, women labourers have often been displaced by men. Threshing of grain was almost exclusively a female task, and with the introduction of automatic grain threshers - which are only operated by men - women have lost an important source of income.

Combine harvesters leave virtually no residue. This means that this source of fodder is no longer available to women, which has a dramatic impact on women's workload. So too, as cattle dung is being used as fertilizer, there is less available for fuel for cooking.

Unskilled

Extension services tend to reach only men, which perpetuates the existing division of labour in the agricultural sector, with women continuing to perform unskilled tasks. A World Bank study in 1991 reveals that the assumption made by extension workers is that information within a family will be transmitted to the women by the men, which in actual practice seldom happens. "The male dominated extension system tends to overlook women's role in agriculture and proves ineffective in providing technical information to women farmers."

In the farm sector, the process of mechanization of agricultural activities has brought in tendencies for gender discrimination by replacing men for a number of activities performed by women and also by displacing the labor of women from subsistence and marginal households. Women are employed only when there is absolute shortage of labor and for specific operations like cotton-picking. To supply food-processing industries being set up with foreign collaboration, there has already been a major shift from subsistence farming method of rice, millet, corn and wheat to cash-crop production of fruit, mushrooms, flowers and vegetables.

A number of factors perpetuate women's limited job skills: if training women for economic activities requires them to leave their village, this is usually a problem for them. Unequal access to education restricts women's abilities to learn skills that require even functional levels of literacy. In terms of skill development, women are impeded by their lack of mobility, low literacy levels and prejudiced attitudes toward women. When women negotiate with banks and government officials, they are often ostracized by other men and women in their community for being 'too forward.' Government and bank officials have preconceived ideas of what women are capable of, and stereotypes of what is considered women's work.

Mistreated

Violence against women and girls is the most pervasive human rights violation in the world today. Opening the door on the subject of violence against the world's females is like standing at the threshold of an immense dark chamber vibrating with collective anguish, but with the sounds of protest throttled back to a murmur. Where there should be outrage aimed at an intolerable status quo there is instead denial, and the largely passive acceptance of 'the way things are.'

Male violence against women is a worldwide phenomenon. Although not every woman has experienced it, and many expect not to, fear of violence is an important factor in the lives of most women. It determines what they do, when they do it, where they do it, and with whom. Fear of violence is a cause of women's lack of participation in activities beyond the home, as well as inside it. Within the home, women and girls may be subjected to physical and sexual abuse as punishment or as culturally justified assaults. These acts shape their attitude to life, and their expectations of themselves.

The insecurity outside the household is today the greatest obstacle in the path of women. Conscious that, compared to the atrocities outside the house, atrocities within the house are endurable, women not only continued to accept their inferiority in the house and society, but even called it sweet. In recent years, there has been an alarming rise in atrocities against women in India. Every 26 minutes a woman is molested. Every 34 minutes a rape takes place. Every 42 minutes a sexual harassment incident occurs. Every 43 minutes a woman is kidnapped. And every 93 minutes a woman is burnt to death over dowry. One-quarter of the reported rapes involve girls under the age of 16 but the vast majority are never reported. Although the penalty is severe, convictions are rare.

The most extreme expression of the preference for sons is female infanticide and sex-selective abortion.A study of amniocentesis in a Bombay hospital found that 96 percent of female fetuses were aborted, compared with only a small percentage of male fetuses. Government officials event suspect that the disproportionate abortion of female fetuses may be a major underlying cause of the recent decline in the nation's sex ratio. In 1971 there were 930 females for every 1,000 males. A decade later this figure had increased to 934, but by 1991, instead of continuing to rise, the ratio dropped to 927, lower than the 1971 figure. This sex ratio is one of the lowest in the world.

Government has passed legislation to curb the misuse of amniocentesis for sex selection and abortion of female fetuses. Women activists have been critical of this act because of its provision that calls for punishing the women who seek the procedure. These women may be under pressure to bear a male child.

Powerlessness

Legal protection of women's rights have little effect in the face of prevailing patriarchal traditions. Exposure to and interactions with the outside world are instrumental in determining the possibilities available to women in their daily lives. The situation of women is affected by the degree of their autonomy or capacity to make decisions both inside and outside their own household.

The position of women in northern India is notably poor. Traditional Hindu society in northern rural areas is hierarchical and dominated by men, as evidenced by marriage customs. North Indian Hindus are expected to marry within prescribed boundaries: the bride and groom must not be related, they have no say in the matter, and the man must live outside the woman's natal village.

"Wife givers" are socially and ritually inferior to "wife takers", thus necessitating the provision of a dowry. After marriage, the bride moves in with her husband's family. Such a bride is "a stranger in a strange place." They are controlled by the older females in the household, and their behavior reflects on the honor of their husbands. Because emotional ties between spouses are considered a potential threat to the solidarity of the patrilineal group, the northern system tends to segregate the sexes and limit communication between spouses - a circumstance that has direct consequences for family planning and similar "modern" behaviors that affect health. A young Indian bride is brought up to believe that her own wishes and interests are subordinate to those of her husband and his family. The primary duty of a newly married young woman, and virtually her only means of improving her position in the hierarchy of her husband's household, is to bear sons."

In the south, in contrast, a daughter traditionally marries her mother's brother or her mother's brother's son (her first cousin). Such an arrangement has a dramatic impact on women. "In southern India, men are likely to marry women to whom they are related, so that the strict distinction found in the north between patrilineal and marital relatives is absent. Women are likely to be married into family households near their natal homes, and are more likely to retain close relationships with their natal kin."

"Over the past several decades, however, marriage patterns have changed markedly. Social, economic, and demographic developments have made marriages between close relatives less common, and the bride price has given way to a dowry system akin to that in the north. Nevertheless, as long as the underlying ethic of marriage in the south remains the reinforcement of existing kinship ties, the relatively favorable situation of southern Indian women is unlikely to be threatened."

A 1976 amendment to the Child Marriage Restraint Act raised the minimum legal age for marriage from 15 to 18 for young women and from 18 to 21 for young men. However, in many rural communities, illegal child marriages are still common. In some rural areas, nearly half the girls between 10 and 14 are married. Because there is pressure on women to prove their fertility by conceiving as soon as possible after marriage, adolescent marriage is synonymous with adolescent childbearing: roughly 10-15 percent of all births take place to women in their teens. Child marriages contribute to virtually every social malaise that keeps India behind in women's rights. The problems include soaring birth rates, grinding poverty and malnutrition, high illiteracy and infant mortality and low life expectancy, especially among rural women.

Women are kept subordinate, and are even murdered, by the practice of dowry. In India, 6,000 dowry murders are committed each year. This reality exists even though the Dowry Prohibition Act has been in existence for 33 years, and there are virtually no arrests under the Act. Since those giving as well as those accepting dowry are punishable under the existing law, no one is willing to complain. It is only after a "dowry death" that the complaints become public. It is estimated that the average dowry today is equivalent to five times the family's annual income and that the high cost of weddings and dowries is a major cause of indebtedness among India's poor.

A December 1997 article in *India Today*, entitled, *Victims of Sudden Affluence* states, "A woman on fire has made dowry deaths the most vicious of social crimes; it is an evil endemic to the subcontinent but despite every attempt at justice the numbers have continued to climb. With get-rich-quick becoming the new mantra, dowry became the perfect instrument for upward material mobility." A study done by a policy think-tank, the Institute of Development and Communication, states, "the quantum of dowry exchange may still be greater among the upper classes, but 80 percent of dowry deaths and 80 percent of dowry harassment occurs in the middle and lower stratas." The article goes on to state, "So complete is the discrimination among women that the gender bias is extended even toward the guilty. In a bizarre trend, the onus of murder is often put on the women to protect the men. Sometimes it is by consent. Often, old mothers-in-law embrace all the blame to bail out their sons and husbands."

Divorce is considered as a shameful admission of a woman's failure as a wife and daughter-in-law. In 1990, divorced women made up a miniscule 0.08 percent of the total female population. Maintenance rights of women in the case of divorce are weak. Although both Hindu and Muslim law recognize the rights of women and children to maintenance, in practice, maintenance is rarely set at a sufficient amount and is frequently violated. Both Hindu and Muslim personal laws fail to recognize matrimonial property. Upon divorce, women have no rights to their home or to other property accumulated during marriage; in effect, their contributions to the maintenance of the family and accumulation of family assets go unrecognized and unrewarded.

Women's rights to inheritance are limited and frequently violated. In the mid-1950s the Hindu personal laws, which apply to all Hindus, Buddhists, Sikhs and Jains, were overhauled, banning polygamy and giving women rights to inheritance, adoption and divorce. The Muslim personal laws differ considerably from that of the Hindus, and permit polygamy. Despite various laws protecting women's rights, traditional patriarchal attitudes still prevail and are strengthened and perpetuated in the home. Under Hindu law, sons have an independent share in the ancestral property. However, daughters' shares are based on the share received by their father. Hence, a father can effectively disinherit a daughter by renouncing his share of the ancestral property, but the son will continue to have a share in his own right. Additionally, married daughters, even those facing marital harassment, have no residential rights in the ancestral home.

Even the weak laws protecting women have not been adequately enforced. As a result, in practice, women continue to have little access to land and property, a major source of income and long-term economic security. Under the pretext of preventing fragmentation of agricultural holdings, several states have successfully excluded widows and daughters from inheriting agricultural land.

Since the creation of the quota system, local women-the vast majority of them illiterate and poor-have come to occupy as much as 43% of the seats, spurring the election of increasing numbers of women at the district, provincial and national levels. Since the onset of PRI, the percentages of women in various levels of political activity have risen from 4-5% to 25-40%.

According to Indian writer and activist Devaki Jain, "the positive discrimination of PRI has initiated a momentum of change. Women's entry into local government in such large numbers, often more than the required 33.3 %, and their success in campaigning, including the defeat of male candidates, has shattered the myth that women are not interested in politics, and have no time to go to meetings or to undertake all the other work that is required in political party processes...PRI reminds us of a central truth: power is not something people give away. It has to be negotiated, and sometimes wrested from the powerful."

Contrary to fears that the elected women would be rubber stamp leaders, the success stories that have arisen from PRI are impressive. A government-financed study, based on field work in 180 villages in the states of Uttar Pradesh, Rajasthan and Madhya Pradesh, and coordinated by the Center for Women's Development Studies in New Delhi, has found that a full two-thirds of elected women leaders are actively engaged in learning the ropes and exercising power. Says Noeleen Heyzer, executive director of UNIFEM, "This is one of the best innovations in grass-roots democracy in the world."

Women leaders in the Panchayati Raj are transforming local governance by sensitizing the State to issues of poverty, inequality and gender injustice. Through the PRI, they are tackling issues that had previously gone virtually unacknowledged, including water, alcohol abuse, education, health and domestic violence. According to Sudha Murali, UNICEF Communications Officer in Andhra Pradesh, women are seeing this power as a chance for a real change for them and for their children and are using it to demand basic facilities like primary schools and health care centres. The PRI has also brought about significant transformations in the lives of women themselves, who have become empowered, and have gained self-confidence, political awareness and affirmation of their own identity. The panchayat villages have become political training grounds to women, many of them illiterate, who are now leaders in the village panchayats. Says Sudha Pillai, joint secretary in India's Ministry for Rural Development, "It has given something to people who were absolute nobodies and had no way of making it on their own. Power has become the source of their growth."

By asserting control over resources and officials and by challenging men, women are discovering a personal and collective power that was previously unimaginable. This includes women who are not themselves panchayat leaders, but who have been inspired by the work of their sisters; "We will not bear it," says one woman. Once we acquire some position and power, we will fight it out…The fact that the Panchayats will have a minimum number of women [will be used] for mobilizing women at large." It is this critical mass of unified and empowered women which will push forward policies that enforce gender equity into the future.

Women Empowerment : Kerala as a Model State

In no Indian State is the demographic transition as advanced as in Kerala. The population density in this State is rather high, but its growth rate is now rapidly declining, with a high average age at marriage, a high level of family planning acceptance and fertility control, a moderate decline in mortality and a high degree of population mobility. The population is also fairly well advanced in terms of literacy and educational attainment and is moderately successful in introducing social change.

Kerala's women are way ahead of women nationally in terms of these indicators. Of the various States in India, the overall sex ratio (females per 100 males) in Kerala has been much higher throughout the present century than for any other State or the country as a whole. As a result, in no Indian State is the ageing of the female population as advanced as it is in Kerala. Kerala leads all other Indian States in its proportion of women above the age of 60 years. The proportion of elderly women in Kerala is 15 per cent higher than in the country as a whole. However, the distribution of elderly women among the three age-groups, 60-64 years, 65-69 years and 70+ years, is strikingly different in Kerala compared with most of the other States. While the proportion of women aged 60-64 years is 3.1 per cent for India as a whole, it is only 2.7 per cent for Kerala. By contrast, Kerala leads all other Indian States in the proportion of women over 65-69 and 70+.

Since 1961 the population of elderly women has exceeded that of elderly men. The absolute excess, which was 0.1 million in 1961, is expected to be 0.6 million in 2011, stabilising at 0.5 million from 2016 onward. Thus, while the total population of the elderly is estimated to have increased from 0.9 million in 1961 to 2.6 million in 1991, the elderly population is projected to reach 8.3 million in 2026. During the same 35-year period, the number of elderly female women will have increased from 0.5 million to 4.4 million. It is also of significance that, while the percentage of elderly men in the total male population will have increased during this period from less than 6 to over 17, the percentage of elderly women in the total female population will have increased from 6 to about 20. Thus, elderly women will continue to outnumber elderly men in Kerala.

Not only has the expectation of life at birth been consistently higher for women in Kerala compared with men, but the gap in recent years has been widening. By contrast, for the country as a whole, the male-female differential has been in favour of men and will remain so into the next century. Whereas in 1960-1965, the expectation of life for women in Kerala was higher by 3.8 years, in the quinquennium of 1980-1985, it was higher by 5.9 years. The expectation of life at birth in Kerala is projected to reach 76.9 years for men and 79.8 years for women during the period 2020-2025. With the projected faster improvement in the expectation of life of men, the difference between men and women with regard to expectation of life at birth is projected to decline from 5.9 years during 1980-1985 to 2.9 years during 2020-2025. For India as a whole also, the projections are that the gender differential will have turned in favour of women by the period 2020-2025, but at a distinctly lower level of life expectancy for both women (68.6 years) and men (67.2 years).

Heavy female concentration among the very old is a likely future trend. In terms of numbers, the elderly in Kerala over the age of 75 years will number 1.97 million in 2026; as many as 1.12 million of that number will be women. The preponderance of women at old ages, particularly among the very old, has important implications for policy makers.

In view of the fact that in Kerala women not only outnumber men but also outlive them, it is important to know about their likely marital status when they become old, because that could influence the overall level of care and support they receive both from their family and society.

While only 1 per cent of the total male population in Kerala is widowed, the proportion of the female population widowed is 9 per cent. The corresponding proportions for the country as a whole are 2 per cent and 8 per cent, respectively. The gender gap in the incidence of widowhood in Kerala is thus more than twice that for the country as a whole. While 19 per cent of men aged 70+ in Kerala are widowers, over 80 per cent of the women of that age were widowed in 1981. The corresponding percentages for the country as a whole during that period were 27 and 78, respectively.

With advancing age, the incidence of widowhood obviously accelerates regardless of whether people are living in rural or urban sectors. In the age group of 70+, over 92 per cent of the rural women in Kerala are widows as compared with almost 80 per cent in India as a whole.

The differences in the incidence of widowhood arise for several reasons, the most important of which are the following:

(a) sex differentials in the age at marriage,
(b) women having married men who are significantly older than themselves and therefore belonging to cohorts which are exposed to a higher risk of mortality,
(c) the higher expectation of life of women and
(d) the significantly higher rate of remarriage among men compared with women.

The age at marriage for both men and women has been consistently higher in Kerala right from the turn of the century than for the country as a whole. The mean age at marriage of women in Kerala was 17.1 years in 1901 when the corresponding figure for India as a whole was 13.2 years. In 1981, the age at marriage for women in Kerala was 21.9 years and that for women in India as a whole was 18.3 years. In terms of age differences between marriage partners, the sex differentials have come down more sharply in India as a whole than in Kerala. While for the whole of India, the sex difference in mean age at marriage has varied between 7.0 years and 4.4 years over the 80-year period.

In Kerala, the age difference, although quite high, has fluctuated between a narrower range, namely, 6.8 and 5.3 years. However, the higher age differentials of marriage partners combined with the higher expectation of life of women as compared with men contribute to the high incidence of female widowhood. Further investigation is needed to determine whether the significantly lower rate of male widowhood can be explained largely in terms of these two factors.

In this context, it is relevant to note that, in 1981 for both Kerala and India as a whole, the proportion of those currently married among men was at least twice as high as among women at higher ages (i.e. at 60+). Also, this position was somewhat more pronounced in Kerala than for India as a whole. This strongly suggests that remarriage is possibly more prevalent among men relative to women in Kerala than in the rest of India.

There are a number of different ways of looking at the exent to which elderly people become dependent on society. The old-age dependency ratio indicates the number of dependents above the age of 60 per 100 persons of working age, i.e. those between the ages of 15 and 60. The old-age dependency ratio for Kerala in 1981 stood at 13; by 2026, this ratio is projected to go up to 81.

If the number of total elderly is compared with only the female population of working age, in order to indicate the burden of day-care that the elderly place on women who normally are the ones who provide care for them, in the year 2026 every 100 women will have to take care of 63 older men and women. Of course, the elderly are not alone in depending on others for care and support. Children also need to be taken care of. In fact, it can be argued that, even when the elderly do not have any economic contribution to make, they still can, and do, partake in providing child care and this is especially so for elderly women.

The vast majority of the elderly do not have any independent means of support except for those who had a pensionable job during their working life. Those who are involved in agriculture or casual wage labour have access to income only during their working life. Once they cease working, they become totally dependent on their children or relatives for support. As a result, elderly men and women continue to work much beyond what is normally regarded as the working ages.

In 1981, while the work participation rate for men above the age of 60 was as high as 43 per cent, only 7 per cent of the women were engaged in work. Of course, recorded work participation among women was considerably lower than among men even at younger ages. Thus, for the age group 40-49 years, the work participation of women was only 27 per cent compared with men's 88 per cent in 1981. The drop in women's work participation at age 60+ is considerably more pronounced than for men. This clearly has implications with regard to the considerably higher dependency of elderly women in comparison with elderly men.

The problems of the elderly have traditionally been taken care of by the family network. The entire responsibility for the care and support of the elderly members still continues to be shouldered by the family irrespective of whether it is a matriarchal or patriarchal family. While the obligations of the family to look after the elderly and respect them still holds true in both India as a whole and Kerala, there are many factors which may make the practice of the ideal increasingly problematic. Thus, it is becoming necessary for the State to take initiatives in the matter of the care of the elderly.

When the Kerala State Government initiated a pension system for the destitute elderly and widows in 1967, the pensions were restricted to those who had no family to help them or who had been abandoned by their relatives, or whose family income was extremely low. In 1980, a separate scheme was introduced granting pensions to agricultural workers with a family income below a prescribed ceiling; the entire cost of these two schemes is met by the State exchequer. The pension rates have been revised upwards from time to time following escalations in the cost of living.

Nonetheless, the rates are very low in real terms and are just about adequate to cover the cost of minimal quantities of basic food items. In 1989-1990, the number of persons covered under the first scheme was 180,000 and under the second scheme 300,000. Of the pension schemes administered by Kerala State, none is specially addressed to elderly women.

Under the scheme for destitute people, there is a special provision made for pensions for widows and divorced or separated women. But the entitlement to a pension under this provision concerns the marital status of the women and their economic position, not their age. As far as the other scheme is concerned, it is quite likely that many elderly women may be left out, not because they are not in need of assistance, but because they do not qualify for it in terms of the occupational norms that had been adopted for the pension scheme.

The Committee on the Status of Women observed "The health status of women includes their mental and social condition as affected by prevailing norms and attitudes of society in addition to their biological and physiological problems. Societies delineate women's roles partly according to their biological function and partly from prevailing attitudes regarding their physical and mental capacity. These social attitudes also influence the provision and use of preventive and curative health care, including maternal care." The

CSWI underscored health as an important factor both in the achievement of status as well as an indicator of social status, particularly for women, whose health is conditioned to a great extent by social attitudes. The CSWI therefore saw a definite link between low status of women and deficiencies in the knowledge and utilisation of preventive health services.

Factors identified by the CSWI as affecting women's health were,

- attitudes to marriage,
- age of marriage,
- value attached to fertility and sex of the child,
- Pattern of family organisation and the ideal role demanded of the women by social convention as the cultural norms.

Specific health needs of women

"The health needs of females vary according to their biological needs and are distinct for the different age groups. The prevalent gender-bias in the society runs through all the different age groups and manifests itself differently. Analysis of the specific needs of each of these age groups has to be related to this social discrimination. The proportion of the female population of 407.8 million (1991 census) in five distinct age groups with specific requirements is as follows:

Girl children in the age group of 0-14 years account for 153.85 million (37.8%). They need special protection and care for survival, opportunities for development, which they are sometimes deprived of, due to gender bias and discrimination in nutrition, education, medical care as well as parental affection.

Adolescent girls in the age group of 15-18 years account for 38.70 million (9.5%) and require special planning of their care as this is the preparatory stage for future productive as well as reproductive roles in the family and society.

Women in the reproductive age group of 15-44 years account for 183.67 million (45.1%) who need special care and attention to meet their reproductive needs.

(Contd.)

(Contd.)

> Women in the economically active age group of 15-59 years account for 226.04 million (55.5%). Planning for their education and training, employment, income generation and participation in developmental processes including decision-making etc. is necessary.
> Elderly women in the age group of 60+ account for 27.17 million (6.7%). The needs relate to health care, financial and emotional security."
> (National Profile on Women, Health and Development, India, April 2000).

The situation in India has not changed very much since the Report of the CSWI.

Trends in Vital Statistics in India

There has been a decline in birth rates, total fertility rates, infant mortality rates, child mortality rates, age at marriage, percentage of females married in the age group 15-19 years as already discussed in Chapter III, the demographic profile of the population in India. There has been increase in couple protection rate and life expectancy over the last three decades. The data is given in Table 1. While in itself this is a positive sign, the rates of changes are far too slow for sustainable development and better quality of life for the people. Consequent on the slow changes, India still contributes to the majority of the poor of the world with her large population living with poor infrastructure amongst abundant resources. The impact of these are more on women, given the burden of child bearing in a patriarchal social mindset. Poverty mixed with a poor social status, and lack of access to social development, multiplies the burdens on women's health and living conditions.

Goals of Health Policy in India and Achievements

The NHP goals and achievements at different points in time are proof of the slackness of the efforts made in the country in terms of investment strategies and programmes in the health sector. The goals and achievements are given in Table 2.

While we should have reached an IMR of 56-50 for All India by the end of the Ninth Plan, we are just around the Eighth Plan goal of 70, having achieved 72 in 1998. We need to concentrate more

Table 1. Trends in Vital Statistics

Year	*1951*	*1981*	*1991*	*Current level*
Birth rate (per 1000 population)	39.9	33.9 (SRS)	29.5 (SRS)	26.1 (SRS, 99)
TFR	6.0	4.5 (SRS)	3.6 (SRS)	3.3 (SRS, 97)
IMR (Per 1000 live birth)	146	110 (SRS)	80 (SRS)	70 (SRS, 99)
Child mortality rate (0-4 year per 1000 children)	57.3 (1972)	39.1 (1982)	26.5 (SRS)	23.9 (SRS, 96)
*Age at Marriage Male	22.6 (1971)	23.5	24.0	24.9 (NFHS-2)
Female	17.2 (1971)	18.4	19.3	19.7 (NFHS-2)
+Proportion of females married in the age group 15-19 years	R 61.03('71) U 35.91('71)	R 48.92 U 27.89	R 40.68 U 21.32	R34.4(NFHS-2) U16.4(NFHS-2)
Couple protection rate	10.4 (1971)	22.8	44.1	46.2 (31.3.2000)
Expectation of life at birth				
Male	37.2	54.1	60.6	62.36 (1996-01)
Female	36.2	54.7	61.7 (1991-96)	63.99 (Projection)

Source : Page 204, Economic Survey, Government of India, 2000-2001

* Page 21, IIPS (1998-99)

\+ Census 1991, RGI Quoted in Women in India, Statistical Profile, 1997

intensively on neonatal and perinatal mortality, if we are to get nearer the goal for IMR. As it is, against NHP goal of 30-35 for perinatal mortality we have reached 44.3 in 1993. The NFHS-2 records post-neonatal (1-12 months) mortality at 25.3 which is encouraging. This goal can be reached only if there is greater quality of Health Service including antenatal and post-natal care in the high IMR States. It may be pertinent to point out that the higher rate of female mortality at the post neonatal stage is a serious matter reflecting the poor social status of the girl child in the family that should cause great social concern. The female juvenile sex ratio surfacing in the 2001 census is a pointer to this.

Similarly the same factors of antenatal and post-natal care are responsible for our being far off the mark with regard to maternal mortality which is not very significantly different from 1978. This summarizes the social status of women and concern for her health as pointed out by the CSWI. The achievement on life expectancy is significant. The higher life expectancy for the female has caused a slight increase in the overall female sex ratio in the 2001 Census for All India.

We are still far off the mark with regard to decreasing LBW babies to 10 per cent. It remains above 30 per cent and even higher at 47 per cent according to NHFS-2. The absence of nutrition for the mother and poor health care are writ large on this data. Significant proportion of girls in the 15-19 age group get married as shown in Table 1 and become teen age mothers with LBW babies.

The CBR, CPR and NRR (NRR has to come down to 1.0) are still far off the mark. The National Population Policy has sought to achieve these goals by 2010 only. The TFR that was aimed at 2.3 by 2000 has not been realized. These need multi-pronged action from various social development sectors.

While decline in IMR is substantially due to improvement on immunization we have not reached 100 per cent immunization that should have been attained long ago. We are just around 65 per cent. The way ahead is definitely long and weary.

The National Population Policy, 2000, was announced in 2000. The immediate objective of the Policy is to address the unmet needs for contraception, health care infrastructure and health personnel and to provide integrated service delivery for basic reproductive and child health care. The medium term objective is to bring the TFR

Table 2. National Health Policy: Goals and Achievements

Indicator	*Prior to NHP*	*EIGHTH PLAN Goal*	*EIGHTH PLAN Achievement (1996)*	*NHP Goal for 2000*	*Ninth Plan Goal*	*Most recent estimate*
IMR	125 (1978)	70	72	60	56-50	72 (1998)
Perinatal mortality rate				30-35		44.3 (1993)
CDR	12.5 (1981)		9	9	9	8.9 (1996)
MMR	4.5 (1976)		4.7 (1993)	Below 2	3	4.07 (1997)
Life, Expectancy						
(a) Male	52.6 (1976-81)		59.0 (1989-93)	64	62 (1996-2001)	63.0 (96-01)
(b) Female	51.6		59.7 (1989-93)	64	63 (1996-2001)	63.4 (—do—)
Babies with weight below 2.5 Kg.(%)	30%	30%	10%		30% (1993)	47% (98-99)[@]
CBR/1000	35	26	27.5	21	24/23	26.5 (1998)
CPR %	23.6 (1982)	56	45.4	60	51-60	46.2 (2000)[&]

(Contd.)

(Contd.)

Indicator	Prior to NHP	EIGHTH PLAN		NHP Goal for 2000	Ninth Plan Goal	Most recent estimate
		Goal	Achievement (1996)			
NRR	1.48 (1981)					
Growth Rate % (Annual)	2.24 (1971-81)		1.8	1.2	1.6/1.5	
TFR	4.4 (1975)		3.5	2.3	2.9/2.6	2.85 (96-98)
Immunisation						
BCG (Infants)		100	97(1996-97)	100	65$	
Polio (Infants)		100	90(1996-97)	100	65$	
DPT (children than 1 year)		100	89 (1996-97)	100	65$	
Measles		100		100	65$	
DT (new school entrants) (5-6 years)		100	48 (1995-96)	100		

(Contd.)

(Contd.)

Indicator	Prior to NHP	EIGHTH PLAN Goal	EIGHTH PLAN Achievement (1996)	NHP Goal for 2000	Ninth Plan Goal	Most recent estimate
T.T. (for school children)						
a) 10 years		100	47 (1995-96)	100		
b) 16 years		100	41 (1995-96)	100		
Immunisation by TT (%) (for Pregnant Women)	20	100	79	100	95	66.8 (98-99)@
Pregnant mothers receiving antenatal care (%)	40-50	100	76	100	90	65.1 (98-99)@
Deliveries by trained personnel (%)	30-35		13	100	45	76.7 (98-99)%
Institutional Deliveries %	–	–	–	–	35	

(Contd.)

(Contd.)

Indicator	Prior to NHP	EIGHTH PLAN		NHP Goal for 2000	Ninth Plan Goal	Most recent estimate
		Goal	Achievement (1996)			
Leprosy (% arrested cases among detected cases)	20			80		
Prevalence per thousand TB (% of arrested cases among detected)	57.3 (1981)**		5.8 (1995) 30 (1995)	90	1/10,000 85#	–

Source : GOI, Planning Commission, Ninth Five Year Plan 1997-2002
* National Health Policy
** Ministry of Health and FW
$ Fully immunized against 6 VPD by 1 year
# 85% cure rate in RNTCP districts
@ IIPS - NFHS-2 1998-99 "Economic Survey 2000-2001
% "Women in India – How free? How equal?", Kalyani Menon and A.K. Shivakumar

to replacement levels by 2010, through vigorous implementation of intersectoral operational strategies. The long term objective is to achieve a stable population by 2045, at a level consistent with the requirements of sustainable economic growth, social development and environmental protection.

National Socio-Demographic Goals for 2010

1. Address the unmet needs for basic reproductive and child health services, supplies and infrastructure.
2. Make school education up to age 14 free and compulsory, and reduce drop outs at primary and secondary school levels to below 20 per cent for both boys and girls.
3. Reduce infant mortality rate to below 30 per 1000 live births.
4. Reduce maternal mortality ratio to below 100 per 100,000 births.
5. Achieve universal immunization of children against all vaccine preventable diseases.
6. Promote delayed marriage for girls, not earlier than age 18 and preferably after 20 years of age.
7. Achieve 80 per cent institutional deliveries and 100 per cent deliveries by trained persons.
8. Achieve universal access to information/ counseling, and services for fertility regulation and contraception with a wide basket of choices.
9. Achieve 100 per cent registration of births, deaths, marriage and pregnancy.
10. Contain the spread of Acquired Immuno Deficiency Syndrome (AIDS), and promote greater integration between the management of reproductive tract infections (RTI) and sexually transmitted infections (STI) and the National AIDS Control Organisation.
11. Prevent and control communicable diseases.
12. Integrate Indian Systems of Medicine (ISM) in the provision of reproductive and child health services, and in reaching out to households.

(Contd.)

(Contd.)

13. Promote vigorously the small family norm to achieve replacement levels of TFR. 14. Bring about convergence in implementation of related social sector programmes so that family welfare becomes a people centred programme.

"Goals fixed for women's health have only been related to Family Planning and later for MCH (such as the number of beneficiaries, and the number of deliveries Ante and Post Natal Care and the number of women and children being immunised). However, there have been no targets for women's health in the context of Revised National Tuberculosis Control Programme (RNTCP) and National Leprosy Eradication Programme (NLEP). This situation needs to be changed by fixing special targets for covering women patients under all diseases."[1]

PLATFORM FOR ACTION OF THE FOURTH WORLD CONFERENCE ON WOMEN, BEIJING, 1995

In the Platform for Action brought out by the Fourth World Conference on Women, Beijing, 1995, one of the Critical Areas of Concern identified was "Inequalities and inadequacies in and unequal access to health care and related services".

The basic strategies spelt out in the Platform for Action to address this concern were:

- Increase women's access throughout the life cycle to appropriate, affordable and quality health care, information and related services;
- Strengthen preventive programmes that promote women's health;
- Undertake gender-sensitive initiatives that address sexually transmitted diseases, HIV/ AIDS, and sexual and reproductive health issues;
- Promote research and disseminate information on women's health; and
- Increase resources and monitor follow-up for women's health.

Indicators of Women's Health Status

CSWI analyses women's health status in India from two angles viz., (a) demographic trends and (b) access to health services. From the demographic trends, they identified mortality rates by sex and age and identified lower sex ratio at different age groups. They concluded "all the demographic indicators thus point to a low health status of women". They observed "child bearing in India, for the majority of women is more a health hazard than a natural function".

CSWI observation on age-specific death rates

Neglect of women was proved by customs like female infanticide then prevalent in certain parts of the country. Child marriage, pre-mature consummation resulting in early childbearing, over-work and malnutrition were cited as other causes of women's poor health. The census of 1931 drew pointed attention to the higher female mortality in the age group 5-10, and "at the reproductive age". The data collected by CSWI indicate the high increase in female deaths in the age group 15-29 for both rural areas and the whole country. It is significant that in the age group of 1-4, in spite of some fluctuations, the mortality figures are higher than the 1960 figures throughout. The data indicates that in total deaths under one year, female deaths increase with age group from one week to 6 to 19 months. This is true for all areas and over the time period.

The apparently low sex ratio of deaths (female deaths per thousand male deaths) is actually due to large under-reporting of female deaths as compared to male deaths. The doubtful accuracy of SRS data on age-wise and sex-wise mortality rates has been demonstrated in a recent study. The difference between estimated and reported deaths of females is sometimes said to be as high as 75.69 per cent for rural areas and 59.07 per cent for urban areas in the lowest age group.

Demographic Trends — Age Specific Death Rates

The CSWI observed: "All the available evidence leads us to conclude that female mortality in fact is higher for all the three age groups, namely, during infancy, childhood and during the productive age particularly in rural areas. The inference from this is that female mortality is due to the consistent neglect of female health".

A comparison of the distribution of deaths, and socio-cultural factors. While there has been tremendous achievement in the decline of death rates, life expectation at birth and infant mortality, the variation in terms of regional disparities, gender disparities and rural urban differences are serious concerns. At the All India level, the distribution of deaths in the 0-4 age-group and 60+ age group is almost similar. In the case of Kerala, major proportion of the deaths take place at the 60+ age groups, with its high life expectancy and low infant mortality. In Uttar Pradesh, major proportion of deaths take place at the 0-4 age group with lesser proportion at the 60+ age group with high infant mortality and comparatively lower life expectancy. In States with high infant mortality, a large proportion of deaths takes place at the earlier age periods causing wastage of a lot of human resource at younger ages. Attention is also invited to discussions on the sex ratio. Analysis in further sections will bring out the gender-wise distribution of deaths in different age groups which will speak volumes on the socio-cultural factors which impinge on women's health. As we have already discussed in the chapter on demographic perspectives, the higher proportion of female deaths in the earlier age groups including at the 0-4 age interval causes adverse female sex ratio. This also stands out as a major indicator of the social attitude to gender and access to various facilities and infrastructure.

An analysis of age specific death rates in major States shows a greater risk of, death for females during infancy, early childhood and during prime life, until age 30. This is especially in States like Bihar, Haryana, Madhya Pradesh, Orissa, Rajasthan and Uttar Pradesh as can be seen from the State-wise age specific death rates by sex Table 3.

Age specific death rates for males and females highlights economic deprivation and gender discrimination leading to higher mortality for females, lack of access to resources that assure survival and health as shown in Table 4. The variation in the female to male death ratio reveals a great deal of socio-cultural factors. It is above unity and increasing in children between 0-4, 5-9, 10-14, in adolescence and until age 29, it declines in subsequent age groups. The F/M Ratio which peaks to 1.43 for the age group 20-24 goes up to 1.50 for the urban area. Thereafter it declines to 1.30 for the next age group. It becomes significantly less than unity after age 30. Some writers refer to the syndrome of "missing women" to describe this phenomenon of high female death rates until age 30. The CSWI also observed that the maternal mortality rate is high enough to raise the overall death rate for females and account for the low sex ratio.

Observations of CSWI on contributory factors to women's ill health

Recent medical research has tried to identify particular contributory factors to the problem of women's ill-health and higher mortality. Since maternal mortality in India continues to be so high, it is understandable that the bulk of this research has concentrated on this aspect of women's health. The specific factor that have been identified by various studies are firstly pregnancy wastage, caused by abortions and still births. The incidence of this phenomenon has remained constant over the period 1957-68, a period which witnessed intensification of family planning activity. In fact there was even an increase in actual numbers. Such foetal wastage prevails more in low income groups. One study reported that pregnancy wastage of malnourished mothers was 30 per cent as late as in 1972. Still births are reported as constituting 11 per 1,000 live births. Much of this pregnancy loss and perinatal mortality is caused by premature births and malnutrition. Perinatal mortality and still births result from premature births, itself a consequence of maternal malnutrition, particularly iron deficiency during pregnancy. Haeomoglobin estimations carried out on about 5,000 pregnant women in different parts of the country show that 30 per cent of them are anaemic, i.e., they have haemoglobin levels below 10 per cent. There is evidence that this is largely due to iron deficiency. Premature births have consistently been a very high proportion among the causes of infant deaths.

A second group of causes for both infant and maternal mortality relate to higher birth orders. Frequency of pregnancies causes protein malnutrition of the mothers. As it is, the majority of Indian women are victims of

(Contd.)

(Contd.)

> malnutrition. 10-20 per cent of maternal deaths are known to be due to nutritional anaemia. This has been borne out by a series of studies of the National Institute of Nutrition. CSWI data indicates the gap between the actual and recommended intake of nutrition in the case of pregnant and nursing women.

Infant and Child Mortality

Higher infant mortality rates amongst female infants are seen in Andhra Pradesh, Arunachal Pradesh, Delhi, Gujarat, Haryana, Himachal Pradesh, Lakshadweep, Maharashtra, Rajasthan, Uttar Pradesh and in rural areas of Jammu and Kashmir, Pondicherry, Punjab, Tamil Nadu and urban areas of Karnataka, Manipur, Madhya Pradesh, Mizoram, and Orissa.

The first concern is the continued disparity between States in mortality rates, particularly infant mortality rates which is given in Table 5. This is despite significant improvement in infant mortality rates which have come down at the All India level from 140 in 1971 to 78.5 per 1000 live births in 1993 and has since declined to 72 in 1998. The second concern is the high proportion of neonatal and post neonatal mortality, which contribute to high infant mortality in many of the major States (Table 6).

Table 5 gives the estimated death rates for children aged 0-4 years by sex and residence in India and major States. It is clear that the mortality among the females is still high, especially in the rural areas, in Bihar, Gujarat, Haryana, Himachal Pradesh, Madhya Pradesh, Orissa, Punjab, Tamil Nadu, Uttar Pradesh and West Bengal, in spite of programmes for child survival over the years.

The highest infant mortality is in Meghalaya, followed by Uttar Pradesh, Madhya Pradesh, Orissa and Rajasthan. These States show high neonatal and post-neonatal mortality as shown in Table 7. The trend changes for child mortality with Madhya Pradesh recording the highest at 56.4 followed by Uttar Pradesh, Rajasthan, Arunachal Pradesh, Meghalaya and Bihar. Child mortality reduces for Orissa. Consequently, when the total figure for under-five mortality is considered, the ranking of the States change with Madhya Pradesh taking the first place followed by Uttar Pradesh, Meghalaya and Rajasthan (Table 7). Generally, mortality rates are higher in areas with substantial tribal population.

Table 3. Age Specific Death Rates by Sex, Major States - 1993

Major States	M/F	Death Rate															
		0-4	5-9	10-14	15-19	20-24	25-29	30-34	35-39	40-44	45-49	50-54	55-59	60-64	65-69	70+	All age
AP	M	18.7	1.7	1.5	2.4	1.4	2.1	3.0	2.9	6.1	7.0	11.1	20.4	39.2	49.2	93.4	9.0
	F	15.5	1.5	1.7	2.9	2.1	3.0	2.2	3.8	4.5	6.2	10.2	16.1	22.8	45.0	82.6	8.1
Assam	M	36.9	2.9	1.6	1.9	1.9	3.3	4.1	6.7	4.3	11.4	16.3	23.6	35.4	48.8	96.5	10.5
	F	35.3	4.4	2.2	1.8	3.1	3.9	3.4	4.3	5.4	5.6	19.4	22.8	36.3	45.7	110.5	10.3
Bihar	M	23.0	2.8	1.3	1.9	2.1	2.5	2.9	4.4	5.4	8.8	13.8	18.0	33.4	36.6	94.3	9.8
	F	27.7	4.2	1.8	2.9	4.1	4.2	3.6	4.3	4.8	8.1	14.8	21.0	28.4	39.7	90.5	11.5
Gujarat	M	20.3	1.4	1.8	2.3	2.5	1.9	3.1	5.3	5.9	9.9	14.0	20.9	33.1	48.5	92.0	8.8
	F	21.1	1.7	1.8	1.7	3.0	3.1	1.9	2.2	4.6	5.6	5.9	11.9	21.3	29.7	65.1	7.5
Haryana	M	17.6	0.5	0.8	1.3	2.4	2.2	3.2	3.9	1.7	4.9	9.4	13.1	20.9	36.9	99.5	7.9
	F	23.5	1.9	0.8	2.1	2.6	2.6	2.2	1.0	4.4	4.8	9.2	7.7	20.0	33.6	74.6	7.9
HP	M	18.3	0.6	0.4	1.2	3.4	3.0	3.3	3.4	4.5	7.5	12.4	19.4	29.5	27.8	105.0	9.9
	F	13.7	0.7	1.6	1.7	4.2	0.7	1.2	1.8	2.6	4.8	9.4	18.1	16.7	21.7	93.1	7.4

(Contd.)

(Contd.)

Major States	M/F	Death Rate 0-4	5-9	10-14	15-19	20-24	25-29	30-34	35-39	40-44	45-49	50-54	55-59	60-64	65-69	70+	All age
Karnataka	M	19.6	1.4	1.1	1.0	1.4	2.1	2.5	3.7	5.9	4.9	15.6	20.9	27.1	46.8	80.3	8.5
	F	20.5	1.8	0.9	1.8	2.6	2.8	3.1	1.7	3.0	5.7	6.1	12.1	21.3	31.5	64.6	7.5
Kerala	M	3.9	0.1	0.2	1.0	0.9	1.4	2.1	2.5	2.9	5.5	9.8	19.2	28.4	39.6	101.1	7.2
	F	2.8	0.2	0.4	0.5	0.8	0.8	1.4	0.9	1.9	2.8	5.2	6.0	15.5	17.2	73.3	4.9
MP	M	35.2	2.3	2.1	1.8	3.0	3.2	3.5	5.7	5.6	8.6	15.0	23.7	35.2	59.3	117.2	12.5
	F	38.7	3.2	2.5	3.0	4.3	3.9	3.3	3.3	5.0	6.9	9.8	16.7	26.4	39.4	103.0	12.7
Maharashtra	M	13.8	1.2	0.6	1.1	1.7	1.4	2.2	3.3	3.7	8.2	10.3	17.4	30.3	40.4	100.0	7.5
	F	14.5	1.7	1.4	1.7	2.4	1.8	2.6	1.9	3.6	4.0	6.1	11.8	1.5	32.3	73.7	7.0
Orissa	M	35.4	3.4	0.9	2.3	2.5	2.1	3.0	3.6	7.4	15.3	16.9	27.5	31.7	45.4	112.3	12.7
	F	31.9	3.5	2.7	2.0	4.2	3.3	4.1	3.9	5.0	10.2	10.5	18.9	32.6	36.6	105.4	11.7
Punjab	M	14.7	0.7	1.4	2.1	2.7	3.7	3.8	4.2	8.1	7.5	13.7	15.1	25.8	3.8	83.7	8.7
	F	17.6	1.6	1.9	1.1	1.2	2.1	1.1	1.1	2.4	2.7	8.6	10.3	16.8	27.4	68.7	7.0

(Contd.)

(Contd.)

Major States	*M/F*	*Death Rate*															
		0-4	*5-9*	*10-14*	*15-19*	*20-24*	*25-29*	*30-34*	*35-39*	*40-44*	*45-49*	*50-54*	*55-59*	*60-64*	*65-69*	*70+*	*All age*
Rajasthan	M	25.9	1.8	1.3	1.1	2.4	1 9	2.2	4.3	5.8	11 6	13.9	20.8	26.5	48.7	91.0	9.5
	F	26.5	2.3	1.4	2.6	2.8	2.7	2.3	3.2	2.5	2.6	7.5	11.4	24.8	27.2	64.9	8.5
TN	M	13.5	1.9	0.8	1.1	3.0	3.2	3.1	4.7	5.2	6.4	13.9	20.5	28.2	46.6	94.3	8.7
	F	13.7	1.4	0.9	2.6	3.1	2.4	1.8	2.2	3.7	4.7	7.5	14.5	26.1	33.8	98.0	8.7
UP	M	29.7	3.0	1.4	1.8	2.5	2.7	2.9	4.3	4.6	8.1	14.1	23.2	31.7	54.9	95.4	11.2
	F	36.7	3.4	1.5	2.3	3.7	4.8	3.7	3.8	4.1	4.7	8.6	15.2	26.9	36.2	80.8	11.7
WB	M	16.7	1.5	0.6	1.4	1.7	1.5	2.6	2.4	4.2	5.6	11.0	20.2	26.8	43.4	81.9	7.4
	F	17.2	1.6	1.3	2.0	2.9	2.0	2.1	2.1	3.8	3.9	9.2	13.3	22.4	37.7	77.2	7.4

Source : Sample Registration System, Fertility & Mortality Indicator 1993 Office of the Registrar General, India, New Delhi.

Table 4. Estimated Age Specific Death Rates by Residence, All India, 1993

Per '000

Age Intervals	Rural and Urban			Rural			Urban		
	Male	*Female*	*F/M Ratio*	*Male*	*Female*	*F/M Ratio*	*Male*	*Female*	*F/M Ratio*
0 to 4	22.7	24.8	1.09	25.3	27.9	1.10	13.4	13.3	0.99
5 to 9	2.0	2.5	1.25	2.6	3.1	1.19	0.4	0.5	1.25
10 to 14	1.2	1.6	1.33	1.3	1.7	1.31	1.1	1.3	1.18
15 to 19	1.6	2.2	1.38	1.9	2.6	1.37	1.0	1.2	1.20
20 to 24	2.1	3.0	1.43	2.4	3.4	1.42	1.4	2.1	1.50
25 to 29	2.3	3.0	1.30	2.6	3.5	1.35	1.6	2.1	1.31
30 to 34	2.9	2.7	0.93	3.1	3.2	1.03	2.2	1.5	0.68
35 to 39	4.0	2.8	0.70	4.4	3.2	0.73	3.0	1.9	0.63
40 to 44	5.1	3.9	0.76	5.4	4.4	0.81	4.4	2.6	0.59
45 to 49	8.0	5.3	0.66	8.8	6.1	0.69	6.2	3.0	0.48
50 to 54	13.2	9.0	0.68	14.2	10.1	0.71	10.7	5.3	0.50

(Contd.)

(Contd.)

Age Intervals	*Rural and Urban*			*Rural*			*Urban*		
	Male	*Female*	*F/M Ratio*	*Male*	*Female*	*F/M Ratio*	*Male*	*Female*	*F/M Ratio*
55 to 59	20.6	14.4	0.70	22.1	16.4	0.74	16.0	8.0	0.50
60 to 64	30.7	24.2	0.79	33.3	26.4	0.79	23.4	17.7	0.76
65 to 69	46.2	34.6	0.75	48.9	38.6	0.79	37.3	22.4	0.60
70+	94.5	81.1	0.86	101.1	89.8	0.89	75.7	55.8	0.74
ALL	9.5	9.1	0.96	10.6	10.5	0.99	6.3	5.2	0.83

Source : RGI, 1995.

Table 5. Estimated Death Rates for Children Aged 0-4 Years by Sex and Residence, India and Major States, 1994#

India and Major States	Total			Rural			Urban		
	Total	Males	Females	Total	Males	Females	Total	Males	Females
India	23.974	23.6	24.2	26.1	25.7	26.5	15.7	15.8	15.6
Andhra Pradesh	17.0	19.0	14.9	18.2	21.3	15.0	13.6	12.5	14.7
Assam	24.7	26.2	23.1	24.9	26.8	23.1	21.7	19.3	24.2
Bihar	24.9	24.5	25.3	25.1	24.8	25.4	22.7	21.1	24.5
Gujarat	22.2	20.6	24.0	24.8	22.6	27.4	16.6	16.6	16.6
Haryana	22.3	19.1	26.1	22.5	19.0	26.5	21.8	19.5	24.6
Himachal Pradesh	16.0	14.5	17.7	16.3	14.7	18.2	11.8	12.2	11.4
Karnataka	18.6	19.7	17.4	21.0	21.9	20.1	12.8	14.5	11.1
Kerala	3.4	3.6	3.2	3.2	3.3	3.1	4.1	4.7	3.4
Madhya Pradesh	34.8	34.6	34.9	38.7	38.6	38.7	16.9	16.2	17.7

(Contd.)

(Contd.)

India and Major States	Total			Rural			Urban		
	Total	Males	Females	Total	Males	Females	Total	Males	Females
Maharashtra	14.4	15.3	13.4	17.4	18.3	16.4	10.0	10.9	9.1
Orissa	31.6	31.2	32.2	33.2	32.3	34.1	19.4	21.8	16.9
Punjab	15.7	14.0	17.7	18.0	15.9	20.4	10.3	9.7	11.1
Rajasthan	27.4	27.4	27.3	28.6	28.8	28.3	21.4	20.6	22.3
Tamil Nadu	13.4	13.3	13.5	14.0	13.5	14.6	11.8	12.7	10.8
Uttar Pradesh	33.0	31.3	34.9	34.7	32.7	37.0	23.2	23.2	23.2-
West Bengal	19.8	18.5	21.2	20.9	20.0	21.8	15.6	12.7	18.6

Excludes Jammu and Kashmir and Mizoram

Source : RGI 1995.

Table 6. Female/Male Ratios in Under-Five Mortality, 1992-93

States & UTs	*Female/Male Ratios*		
	Neonatal	*Post Neonatal*	*Child*
Haryana	0.80	1.59	2.35
Punjab	0.82	0.97	1.81
Uttar Pradesh	0.96	1.24	1.70
Jammu and Kashmir	0.99	1.47	1.69
West Bengal	0.95	0.84	1.63
Rajasthan	0.99	1.20	1.59
Delhi	0.84	1.41	1.56
Bihar	0.78	1.14	1.55
Orissa	0.82	0.96	1.45
Himachal Pradesh	0.83	1.11	1.44
Gujarat	0.93	1.24	1.42
Karnataka	0.83	1.06	1.30
Andhra Pradesh	0.75	1.21	1.28
Maharashtra	0.62	1.21	1.24
Madhya Pradesh	0.78	1.18	1.22
Assam	0.76	0.96	1.13
Goa	0.65	1.11	1.11
Kerala	0.88	0.68	0.94
Tamil Nadu	0.73	0.87	0.80

Source: IIPS, various volumes

According to the analysis in the National Profile on Women, Health and Development, India:

"Low birth weight including premature birth is one of the major causes for infant mortality as this increases the susceptibility to infection. Respiratory infections like pneumonia, bronchitis etc., are the next major cause. Between 1991 and 1994, female deaths due to bronchitis and asthma increased. This could be due to increasing levels of pollution and allergies. Diarrhoea continues to be a major cause of death in infants reflecting poor nutritional and hygiene standards. Poor immunity of neonates and infants are other reasons for mortality. Unclassified conditions peculiar to infancy, anaemia and unclassified fevers are other major causes of infant mortality.

"The major cause of female and male infant deaths in rural areas is prematurity followed by a host of respiratory problems like pneumonia, bronchitis, asthma and respiratory infections. Anaemic pregnant women are more prone to give birth to premature and low birth weight babies. The incidence of neonatal mortality increases with premature birth.

"The other causes peculiar to infancy which are responsible for deaths in infancy are: cord infection, congenital malformation and birth injury[2]. Thus a combination of poor nutrition and inadequately treated infections cause preventable mortality during early childhood".

The analysis comes to the following conclusion.

"During the 1-4 age interval, in continuation of the broad trends that have already been established, deaths due to pneumonia and anaemia increase. Other causes include gastro-enteritis, dysentery, typhoid, malaria, influenza and unclassified fevers[3]. Thus, a combination of unsuccessfully treated infections and poor nutrition cause mortality during early childhood.

"The female/male death ratio in all States at the neonatal stage is lower. This ratio reverses with advancement of age altering the female/male death ratio in most of the States as evident from Table 6. States are listed in descending order of F/M ratios in the Table; child mortality refers to deaths between the ages of one and five and the mortality rates are based on decadal information before 1992-93 survey. The ratios vary for the three age-groups in Punjab, West Bengal, Orissa, Assam, Kerala and Tamil Nadu. As the age of the infant advances, the ratio becomes even more adverse for the female child. Only in Kerala and Tamil Nadu, it is favourable to the female child".

The under-five mortality data captured by NHFS-2 is given in Table 7. This does not give the sex-wise break up for the States, as

Table 7. Infant and Child Mortality by State Neonatal, Post-neonatal, Infant, Child, and Under-five Mortality Rates for the Five-Year Period Preceding the Survey by State, India, (NHFS-2 1998-99)

State	*Neonatal Mortality (NN)*	*Postneonatal Mortality*[1] *(PNN)*	*Infant Mortality* $({}_1q_0)$	*Child Mortality* $({}_4q_1)$	*Under-Five Mortality* $({}_8q_0)$
India	**43.4**	**24.2**	**67.6**	**29.3**	**94.9**
North					
Delhi	29.5	17.4	46.8	9.0	55.4
Haryana	34.9	21.9	56.8	21.2	76.8
Himachal Pradesh	22.1	12.3	34.4	8.3	42.4
Jammu & Kashmir	40.3	24.7	65.0	16.1	80.1
Punjab	34.3	22.8	57.1	15.9	72.1
Rajasthan	49.5	30.9	80.4	37.6	114.9
Central					
Madhya Pradesh	54.9	31.2	86.1	56.4	137.6
Uttar Pradesh	53.6	33.1	86.7	39.2	122.5
East					
Bihar	46.5	26.4	72.9	34.7	105.1
Orissa	48.6	32.3	81.0	25.5	104.4
West Bengal	31.9	16.8	48.7	19.9	67.6

(Contd.)

(Contd.)

State	*Neonatal Mortality (NN)*	*Postneonatal Mortality[1] (PNN)*	*Infant Mortality* $({}_1q_0)$	*Child Mortality* $({}_4q_1)$	*Under-Five Mortality* $({}_8q_0)$
Northeast					
Arunachal Pradesh	41.8	21.3	63.1	37.4	98.1
Assam	44.6	24.9	69.5	21.4	89.5
Manipur	18.6	18.4	37.0	19.9	56.1
Meghalaya	50.7	38.3	89.0	36.2	122.0
Mizoram	18.8	18.2	37.0	18.4	54.7
Nagaland	20.1	22.0	42.1	22.7	63.8
Sikkim	26.3	17.6	43.9	28.4	71.0
West					
Goa	31.2	5.5	36.7	10.5	46.8
Gujarat	39.6	23.0	62.6	24.0	85.1
Maharashtra	32.0	11.7	43.7	15.0	58.1
South					
Andhra Pradesh	43.8	22.1	65.8	21.0	85.5
Karnataka	37.1	14.4	51.5	19.3	69.8
Kerala	13.8	2.5	16.3	2.6	18.8
Tamil Nadu	34.8	13.3	48.2	15.9	63.3

1. Computed as the difference between the infant and neonatal mortality rates.

similar analysis for all the States is not yet available, but the trend is clear as brought out in Table 8. This emphasizes the cultural gender bias against female children in different parts of the country.

Neonatal mortality for males is expected to be higher than for females owing to their inherent greater biological vulnerability. All India figures for the 1998-99 period reveal a female to male death ratio of 0.88 during the neonatal period. Substantial reversals take place after this period. In the postneonatal period female mortality exceeds male mortality, the ratio going up to 1.10 during the postneonatal period and 1.47 between the ages of one and four[4]. There may be some changes in these ratios for the different States when the data of NFHS-2 are computed. The pattern that sets in this stage is crucial, since majority of female and male deaths (as many as 33 per cent in 1993) occur during this period[5]. The F/M death ratio is higher for rural India at the neonatal, post-neonatal and child stages compared to urban India. The ratio declines in the case of child death rate - Table 8. The phenomenon of female death rates exceeding male deaths at the neonatal and child stages are critical for the sex ratio in the country as 33 per cent of all deaths in 1993 occurred at this stage. The provisional data already available from Census 2001 is indicating a lower sex ratio at the juvenile stage. This is a strong reflection of the social mind set - namely, 'son preference'.

"Female mortality during the post-neonatal and early childhood years is high in Haryana, Jammu and Kashmir, Uttar Pradesh and Rajasthan. The situation is different in States like Kerala and Tamil Nadu[6]. There is remarkable homogeneity in the mortality patterns for 0-4 and 5-9 age groups in contiguous districts across different States. In particular, the North-Western Region of India comprising districts in Haryana, Punjab, Western Uttar Pradesh, North-Eastern Rajasthan and the ravines of Madhya Pradesh has consistently shown excess female mortality over time and among lower caste groups[7,8]. Gender inequalities in these States are more manifest through their low female labour force participation rates, poor literacy rates, restricted property rights, strong preference for a male child and widespread neglect of higher order female children[9,10]. In Haryana, the second female infant in the family has a higher risk of deprivation and mortality".

Table 8. Death Rates During the First Five Years, All India 1998-99 (NFHS 2)

Per '000

Mortality	*Rural and Urban*			*Rural*			*Urban*		
	Male	*Female*	*F/M Ratio*	*Male*	*Female*	*F/M Ratio*	*Male*	*Female*	*F/M Ratio*
Neonatal	50.7	44.6	0.88	54.3	49.0	0.90	37.8	28.8	0.76
Post Neonatal	24.2	26.6	1.10	26.4	29.7	1.12	16.0	15.5	0.97
Child	24.9	36.7	1.47	27.9	41.7	1.49	14.6	19.7	1.35

Source : IIPS, 1998-99.

Notes : Child Mortality refers to deaths between the ages of 1 and 5.

Gender bias in health care seeking behaviour

Gender bias in health care seeking behaviour is extremely pronounced. There is evidence to say that female children below four years displaying symptoms of pneumonia were not taken to a health provider or given any treatment at home as compared to similarly afflicted male children of this age group (IIPS 1995). Some 39% of female under-fours were not taken to a health provider as against 29% of male under-fours. Similarly, 22% of females were not given any treatment as against 17% of male children that were not treated. In general, levels of non-utilisation of health services increased among higher order babies. Disaggregated information by gender is not available (National Profile on Women, Health and Development-India, 2000).

The National Family Health Survey[11] observes that there is an average decline of 2 infant deaths per 1000 live births per year over a 10 year period. Neonatal, post-neonatal and child mortality rates have declined. Despite this decline, 1 in every 15 children still die within the first year of life and one in every 11 children die before reaching age five. The Survey has highlighted excess female mortality among children at ages beyond the first month of life.

- During the post neonatal period (age 1-11 months), female mortality exceeds male mortality by 10 per cent.
- After age one year, sex differentials in mortality are even greater. The female child mortality rate (the number of deaths at age 1-4 yrs. per 1000 children surviving to age 1 yr) is one and a half times the male child mortality rate.
- The female disadvantage in survival from age one to exact age five years is evident in both urban and rural areas but is much more severe in rural than in urban areas.

Specific Causes of Deaths - During Infancy

The status of women in the society has implications for antenatal and postnatal care. The qualities of antenatal and post-natal care influence the survival of the infant. The persisting high rate of infant mortality is a manifestation of the inadequate care given to the girl child during her adolescence and the mother during pregnancy and after childbirth. This is reflected in the high incidence of 'prematurity' as being a significant cause for infant mortality. The distribution of deaths by specific causes peculiar to infancy in the period, 1991-95 are given in Table 9.

Table 9. Percentage Distribution of Deaths among Specific Causes "Causes Peculiar to Infancy" All India 1991-1995

Rank	*Specific Cause Group*	*1991*	*1992*	*1993*	*1994*	*1995*
1.	Prematurity	48.2	50.5	46.4	50.2	53.5
2.	Respiratory infection of new born	15.4	13.5	14.4	16.3	17.0
3.	Diarrhoea of new born	6.8	6.9	8.0	8.7	7.4
4.	Cord Infection (including Tetanus)	5.0	3.8	4.5	3.4	3.1
5.	Congenital Malformation	4.3	4.0	4.6	3.3	3.0
6.	Birth Injury	1.2	2.0	3.0	2.8	2.0
7.	Not classifiable	18.9	19.3	19.1	15.3	14.0
	ALL CAUSES	100.0	100.0	100.0	100.0	100.0

Source: Survey of Causes of Death (Rural) India Annual Report, 1995 Office of the Registrar General, India.

In the predominant causes for death of males and females in different age groups, the influence of anaemia becoming more pronounced for females as they grow up can be seen from the ten major causes of female and male deaths (Table 10). Greater neglect of nutrition of the female and specific health care in all ages as noticed by CSWI gets further emphasis. This situation still continues.

Leading Causes of Mortality

The ranking of different causes of mortality for males and females in different age groups in urban and rural areas are given in Tables 33 and 34 in Annexure I.

"Low birth weight, respiratory infections and anaemia are the main causes for under-five mortality. Respiratory infections and anaemia become the major causes for the age group 5-14. Respiratory infections especially tuberculosis becomes the major cause of mortality in females after the age of 15. Cancer is one of

Table 10. Percentage Distribution of Deaths Due to Ten Selected Diseases by Age-group and Sex, India 1994

Diseases	*Below One Year*			*1 Yr. - 4 Yr.*			*5 Yr. – 14 Yr.*			*15+*			*Total*		
	M	*F*	*T*	*M*	*F*	*T*	*M*	*F*	*T*	*M*	*F*	*T*	*M*	*F*	*T*
Asthma & Bronchitis	3.2	4.6	3.8	1.3	2.2	1.6	0.9	1.6	1.2	94.6	91.6	93.4	100	100	100
Heart Attack	0.3	0.1	0.2	0.1	0.0	0.1	0.8	1.2	1.0	98.8	98.7	98.8	100	100	100
Pneumonia	54.7	47.3	49.6	24.0	31.3	27.5	5.6	9.0	7.2	18.7	12.4	15.7	100	100	100
TB of lungs	0.1	0.3	0.2	0.4	0.4	0.4	3.0	3.0	3.0	96.5	94.8	96.3	100	100	100
Cancer	0.0	0.0	0.0	0.8	0.4	0.6	1.8	1.3	1.5	97.4	98.3	97.8	100	100	100
Anaemia	21.9	15.0	18.1	15.1	17.3	16.3	5.4	7.9	6.8	57.6	59.2	58.8	100	100	100
Prematurity	100.0	100.0	100.0	–	–	–	–	–	–	–	–	–	100	100	100
Paralysis	0.1	0.0	0.1	0.0	0.2	0.1	0.8	1.7	1.3	99.1	98.1	98.6	100	100	100
Gastroenteritis	4.8	6.6	5.7	25.8	21.3	23.5	15.4	15.8	15.6	54.5	51.9	55.2	100	100	100
Vehicular Accidents	0.5	1.8	0.9	2.4	6.2	3.4	8.7	14.7	10.3	90.1	69.0	85.4	100	100	100

Source : Survey of Causes of Death (Rural), India, Annual Report 1994, Office of the Registrar General, India.

the major causes of death after the age of 35, steeply increasing after 50 years. After the menopause, the mortality in females due to heart attack is caused with the steep decrease in levels of estrogen hormones. Males have similar high rates of mortality after 55 owing to acute myocardial infarction"[12].

The first ten causes of mortality for women in the reproductive age group have been given in Table 3 in Annexure IV for fifteen years. The hierarchy of causes of mortality has distinctly changed over the period introducing new ones like suicide, heart attack, burns and cancer over the earlier causes. This data also brings out that Tuberculosis as a cause of death has declined from 13 per cent to 9.2 per cent and continues to be the leading cause of death of women in the reproductive age group.

The data brings out that "three quarters of all males with pulmonary tuberculosis were in the age group of 20-54 years. More than half of all female patients were in the reproductive age group as established from the epidemiological data collected from South India (Tuberculosis Prevention Trial 1980). Women in the reproductive age group tend to deteriorate more quickly from infection to diseases[13]. They are likely to have severe or complicated systems including extra-pulmonary tuberculosis. Tuberculosis of the female reproductive system is an important cause of infertility. This has particularly harsh implications for women who have not completed child bearing. The second commonest cause of death in females in reproductive age group in 1991 was burns and third commonest cause of death was suicides. The 1995 RGI figures show suicides in females in the reproductive age group becoming the second commonest cause of mortality and death from burns being reported as the fourth commonest cause. It is evident that greater attention needs to be given to prevention of suicides and burns besides other causes of death. Undefined problems associated with old age seem to be the leading cause of women's mortality in rural areas according to the data generated by the RGI. If deaths associated with old age are excluded, illnesses associated with poverty, poor sanitary living conditions, poor nutrition and overall poor health become the major cause of mortality."[14]

Maternal Mortality

The situation regarding maternal mortality has not changed since the report of the CSWI as evidenced by data collected by NHFS-

2 (1998-99). The reasons given by the CSWI for high levels of maternal mortality continue to hold good even today. In fact, there has been no substantial decline in maternal mortality rates over the last four decades. While there are differences between States and between urban and rural areas in the reported maternal mortality rates, accurate State level estimates are not available. Effective screening of all pregnant women to identify those at risk and give them access to referral services for appropriate care is a far cry despite the Integrated Child Development Services (ICDS) and network of Primary Health Services System. Cent per cent registration of births and deaths would build a firm database for initiating appropriate interventions to avert maternal mortality.

Observations of CSWI on Maternal Mortality

- Maternal mortality rate is high enough to raise the overall death rate for females and accounts for the low sex ratio. It was reported to be 252 per 100,000 live births in 1964 for the country as a hole, but for rural areas, it is as high as 573 in 968;
- Factors contributing to high-maternal mortality are pregnancy wastage due to abortions and still birth foetal wastages are more in low income groups);
- Pregnancy wastages are significantly due to malnourishment amongst mothers, as reflected in on deficiency; and caused by higher birth orders (frequent pregnancies) and even psychiatric morbidity;
- If causes of maternal mortality are eliminated, fmale mortality will decline substantially;
- Child bearing in India for majority of women is more a health hazard than a natural function.

The mid-term evaluation of the Ninth Five Year Plan (October, 2000) observes: "The prevailing high maternal and prenatal morbidity and mortality is a source of concern. It is noteworthy that there has not been any substantial decline in these indices in the last two decades".

The National Family Health Survey (NFHS-2, 1998-99) observes that the estimated maternal mortality ratio at the national level is 540 deaths per 100,000 live births. According to this estimate, more than 130,000 women die each year from causes related to pregnancy and childbirth.

Maternal mortality goals set out in the National Health Policy,1983 referred to earlier have been elusive as many other goals which have now been, postponed to 2010.

NUTRITION

The National Nutrition Policy

The National Nutrition Policy has considered poverty in terms of a self-perpetuating vicious circle - causative sequential links being low intake of food and nutrition – under nutrition with attendant nutrition related diseases and infections – faltering growth of children – small body size of adults – impaired productivity – low learning capacity – back to poverty.

According to the Policy, the problems of nutrition have to be addressed in terms of grounding an overall development strategy - nutrition being tackled both independently and alongside other development issues. Direct interventions are required in a short term for expanding the safety net, reducing the incidence of severe and moderate malnutrition, reaching the adolescent girls, ensuring better coverage of expectant women, fortification of essential goods, popularisation of low-cost nutrition food and control of micro-nutrient deficiencies among vulnerable groups.

Indirect and long term interventions would include actions relating to provision of overall food security, transfer of income for enhancing the purchasing power of the vulnerable groups, establishing effective public distribution system, health and family welfare, prevention of food adulteration, nutrition surveillance, etc.

Indices of Nutrition Status

Indices of nutrition status are birth weight and anthropometric details - weight, height and body mass. Studies have shown that birth-weights of babies born to women in poor income groups are rather low and have been so over the last 50 years. Mean birth-weight of babies born to such women is only 2.7 kg as against 3.2 kg of children born to women from higher income groups. Weight below 2.5 kgs for India babies is construed as low birth weight. One-third of the infants born in India has low birth-weight.

Indian women have relatively lower height and this by itself impacts on weight. A significant number of Indian women are under weight and anaemic. Their weight gain during pregnancy is not adequate enough and leads to low birth-weight of babies. Studies conducted by the Indian Council of Medical Research have shown that the mean weight of adult women has remained at just 42 kgs between 1955 and 1975.

Data of National Nutrition Monitoring Bureau (NNMB) indicate that stunting of the height has consistently been a problem for girls as well as boys. At the age of five years, there is a deficit of strature of 8 to 9 cms, at the age of 20 years, 12 to 13 cms, and at 55 years of age, there is a height loss of 2 cms due to osteoporosis. Nor is there any secular change for the better in the heights of those belonging to younger generation especially amongst poorer sections.

Body Mass Index (BMI) - (weight in Kgs divided by height in Mtrs squared only shows a small decrease in chronic energy deficiency over the period from 1975-79 to 1995-96. The National Family and Health Survey, NFHS-2 of 1998-99 observes "In India one out of three women age 15-49 is undernourished according to the BMI and 11 per cent are obese. While undernourishment is widespread among women in most population groups, obesity is common only among Jain and Sikh women, richer women and more educated women. Obesity is most common in Delhi and Punjab. Almost half of women in Orissa are undernourished and two out of five or more are undernourished in West Bengal and Maharashtra."

Under Nutrition

The National Nutrition Policy has brought out that under-nutrition among the people in the country manifests itself in protein energy malnutrition, iron deficiency, iodine deficiency, vitamin A deficiency and low birth-weight of children. People in hilly areas and industrial and migrant workers have special nutrition problems. Urbanisation as well as seasonal factors also impact on the nutrition status of the people.

Child Malnutrition

It has been found that malnutrition in children is rather rampant - 90 per cent of children have low weight relative to age and 45-55 per cent of them have malnutrition of moderate and severe types. Nor has there been any decline in malnutrition worthy of mention in the past twenty years. The severest incidence of malnutrition is in rural and slum areas.

Gender Discrimination against Baby Girls and Cumulative Effects

Gender discrimination in breast-feeding and feeding patterns against baby girls has been established by studies. It has been found that 47 per cent of 15 year old girls in the country have body weight of less than 38 kgs and 39 per cent have heights lesser than 145 cms. Women suffer from anaemia to the extent of 40-50 per cent in urban areas and 50-70 per cent in rural areas.

Observations of CSWI on gender bias in nutrition

Females having food after the males in the family is a matter of discrimination. In families affected by poverty, this would result in greater malnutrition for the women. The culture of subservience and self-effacement would affect the young girls also. This process starting at an early age had adverse consequences on women's health, particularly at the time of pregnancy and childbirth.

A study in the early 1980's showed that maximum differentials in allocation of food and medical care were found in the first two years of life. Twice as much was spent on medical care of male infants as on females. Male children were also given culturally more valued foods that were also more nutritious. Such patterns of discrimination became more apparent with fewer pregnancies and smaller families.[15]

"Adolescence is an important phase of child growth and development. The adolescent growth spurt accounts for a substantial increase in body weights and heights. Adolescence is the period when there is considerable accretion of calcium in the bones; a good part of skeletal development (including pelvic development) takes place during this period. A girl of 15 or 16 years is still a child; she enters adulthood only after she crosses 18 years. Growth is complete only between 18 and 20 years.

"It is obvious that a good part of pregnancies in our country today are teenage pregnancies. Indeed, teenage pregnancy appears to be the rule rather than the exception. We witness the sad spectacle of millions of 'children' (girls of 14 to 18 years) compelled to engage in child-bearing and child-rearing even before they have had a chance to complete their own physical growth and development and attain adulthood. This is 'child labour' at its worst - in more senses than one. It is 'labour' which carries far greater risks than some of the other forms of child labour over which there is public outcry".[16]

Nutritional Intake

The National Nutrition Monitoring Bureau has brought out through its surveys that despite passage of five decades after Independence, average intake of calories is substantially below the Recommended Dietary Allowance (RDA), largest deficits being experienced by pregnant and lactating mothers. Mean intake of calories by women is less than 2100 calories. Low calorie intake coupled with high work demand on women adversely affects their health and nutritional status. Within households, the girl children are discriminated against in nutrition intake.

A basic factor affecting nutrition security, particularly for the 36 per cent of the people living below poverty line, is the high price of food articles. Efforts at containing the fiscal deficit include cutting down subsidies. In order to address this issue in the food front, the Targeted Public Distribution System (TPDS) is introduced. But by now, experience has shown that TPDS has not been very effective, even as stated in the mid-term review of the Ninth Plan. This scenario has implications for the nutrition intake of people below poverty line, particularly women amongst them.

While breast-feeding of children, relative to feeding of commercial infant foods have several advantages in terms of cost, availability, safety and psychological satisfaction of the babies, baby food companies are making significant investments on promotional campaigns for their products. Home made weaning foods, it has been found, are also not inferior to the commercial baby foods in nutrition composition and are also significantly much cheaper.

Government of India have enacted two laws to promote breast-feeding: first is the Infant Milk Substitutes, Feeding Bottles and Infant Foods (Regulation of Production, Supply and Distribution) Act, 1992 and the second is related to providing time to lactating mothers during working hours for breast-feeding.

The Integrated Child Development Services (ICDS) has been designed to provide supplementary feeding to children of below six years of age and pregnant women. However, only children in the age-group of 3-6 are benefited. Nutrition needs of children below three years of age are not met under this programme.

Overall Nutrition Scenario as Seen by Planning Commission

The entire scenario regarding nutrition status of the people in the country in all its aspects has been scrutinised by the Planning Commission in the perspective of several of the direct and general developmental measures that have been, and are to be, taken up:

".... It is a matter of concern that while the cereal production has been growing steadily at a rate higher than the population growth rates, the coarse grain and pulse production has not shown a similar increase. Consequently, there has been a reduction in the per capita availability of pulses from 60.7 gms in 1951 to 34 gms per day in 1996. There has been a sharp and sustained increase in cost of pulses, so there is substantial decline in per capita pulses consumption among poorer segment of the population. This, in turn, could have an adverse impact on the protein intake.

".... Adolescents who are undergoing rapid growth and development are one of the nutritionally vulnerable groups who have not received the attention they deserved. In undernourished children rapid growth during adolescence may increase the severity of under-nutrition. Early marriage and pregnancy will perpetuate both maternal and child under-nutrition. It is a matter of concern that prevalence of low birth weight and under-nutrition in pregnant women and children between 6 and 24 months has not declined. India with less than 20 per cent global children accounts for over 40 per cent of under-nourished children.

"Pregnant and lactating women have been an identified priority group for receiving food supplement through ICDS. However, experience over the years indicates that very few needy, at-risk pregnant women regularly access and benefit from ICDS food supplements.

".... Low dietary intake is the most important cause of under-nutrition. .... Other major factors responsible for under-nutrition in children are poor infant feeding practices, infections due to poor sanitation, lack of safe drinking water and poor access to health care. In spite of higher average dietary intake, under-nutrition rates are higher in UP, MP and Orissa because of lack of equitable distribution of food and access to health care. .... Prevalence of anaemia among pregnant women ranges between 50 per cent to 90 per cent.

"..... Iodine Deficiency Disorders (IDD) have been recognised as a public health problem in India since mid-twenties. ..... Production of iodised salt has been short of requirements, quality control is inadequate and transportation bottlenecks remain.

"..... The National Nutrition Policy adopted in 1993 advocates a comprehensive inter-sectoral strategy for alleviating the multi-faceted problem of malnutrition and achieving an optimal state of nutrition for all sections of the society. Several of the sectors have since reviewed the progress achieved and have revised their targets for the Ninth Plan 2010 AD. ..... The goals set in National Plan of Action for nutrition may have to be reviewed accordingly."[17]

MORBIDITY PATTERN

Rates of Morbidity, Gender Differentials

The National Profile on Women, Health and Development, India, 2000, brings out that morbidity prevalence rates for females was 2 per cent higher than that for males in rural India in 1993, while the differential went up to 10 per cent for urban India Table 11. General socioeconomic development has an impact on the morbidity prevalence rates. While men and women reported high morbidity levels in Orissa, Kerala and Himachal Pradesh; in Orissa it was largely due to prevalence of communicable diseases and acute illnesses while in rural Kerala and Urban Himachal Pradesh, it was due to chronic illnesses.[18]

Table 11. Age Specific Morbidity Rates, 1993

Per '000

Age Intervals	*Rural*			*Urban*		
	Male	*Female*	*F/M Ratio*	*Male*	*Female*	*F/M Ratio*
Below 5	131.4	125.0	0.95	143.5	122.7	0.86
6 to 14	86.5	72.9	0.84	76.0	67.2	0.88
15 to 59	99.5	110.4	1.11	90.2	110.5	1.23
60 +	214.6	192.2	0.90	219.7	215.9	0.98

Source : Sundar 1995 quoted from National Profile on Women, Health and Development, India, 2000.

The two extreme periods of the life cycle periods viz., below age 5 and above age 60 are the most vulnerable periods for both males and females as shown in the Table 11. Female morbidity is higher than male morbidity during the reproductive age. The female to male ratios for the age group 15-59 was 1.11 for rural India and 1.23 for urban India[19]. Male morbidity is higher during childhood, i.e., before age of 15. The morbidity ratio for females is slightly higher than for males for all illnesses as shown in Table 12.

The National Profile on Women, Health and Development, India, 2000, observes "Men seem more vulnerable than women in the case of serious communicable diseases in both rural and urban areas, with higher incidence in rural areas. In the case of acute illnesses, the situation is near equal in rural areas except in the category of aches, indigestion, etc. and others. Men are more prone to accidents, injuries and skin diseases. In the urban areas, women are more vulnerable in all categories of acute illnesses except accidents and injuries. And the incidence is very high in the case of the category "others". Amongst chronic illnesses, weakness, dizziness and anaemia ranks high as the major cause of morbidity for women compared to men in the rural areas. In the urban areas, mental and psychological disorder ranks first as types of illness for women with a higher incidence for women followed by cancer and anaemia, weakness, dizziness, etc."

Principal Causes of Morbidity among Women

The top ten causes of morbidity among women as brought out in different studies as shown in Table 13 give a high position for fevers and gynaecological and reproductive causes.

The National Profile on Women, Health and Development, India, 2000, brings out:

"Coexisting with these diseases of poverty and under development, there are some typically female afflictions like gynaecological illnesses/reproductive complaints reported in another national study of 1990[20]. The district study in Maharashtra showed that reproductive problems, aches and pains and weakness together made up 47 per cent of all reported morbidity. Fever, respiratory problems, eye/ear/skin problems, gastrointestinal problems, mental stress, injuries, boils and burns made up the remaining load[21]. Generally, most health complaints were chronic-lasting for more than a year. Girl children tended to report fever and respiratory infections. Women in the reproductive age group tended to report other complaints most of the time[22]. The study on Madhya

Table 12. Gender Differentials in the Type of Morbidity

Types of Illnesses	RURAL INDIA				URBAN INDIA			
	Male	*Female*	*Gend. Diff.*	*F/M Ratio*	*Male*	*Female*	*Gend. Diff.*	*F/M Ratio*
Serious Communicable Diseases								
Typhoid, malaria, cholera, acute gastroenteritis, jaundice	12.5	10.4	20%	0.83	11.4	11.2	2%	0.98
Mumps, measles, chickenpox, TB	5.1	2.6	96%	0.51	2.7	2.2	23%	0.81
Acute Illnesses								
Diarrhoeal diseases	4.9	5.5	12%	**1.12**	5.0	6.8	36%	**1.36**
Respiratory infection	9.1	9.3	2%	**1.02**	10.1	12.3	22%	**1.22**
Non-specific fever	30.0	31.5	5%	**1.05**	21.7	26.1	20%	**1.20**
Eye/Ear problems	6.8	7.0	3%	**1.03**	4.9	6.1	24%	**1.24**
Headache/Body-ache Backache	4.1	9.0	120%	**2.20**	4.3	7.5	74%	**1.74**
Indigestion, Gas, Acidity, Constipation	6.9	11.5	67%	**1.67**	5.7	8.8	54%	**1.54**

(Contd.)

(Contd.)

Types of Illnesses	RURAL INDIA				URBAN INDIA			
	Male	*Female*	*Gend. Diff.*	*F/M Ratio*	*Male*	*Female*	*Gend. Diff.*	*F/M Ratio*
Others	2.6	7.2	177%	**2.77**	2.1	7.6	262%	**3.62**
Accidents and injuries	4.3	1.1	291%	**0.26**	5.0	1.5	233%	**0.30**
Skin diseases	3.7	1.7	118%	**0.46**	2.9	3.1	7%	**1.07**
Chronic illnesses								
Arthritis, Rheumatism	2.2	2.0	10%	**0.91**	2.3	3.1	35%	**1.35**
BP. heart ailments, paralysis	4.5	3.1	45%	**0.69**	9.0	7.7	17%	**0.86**
Diabetes, kidney problems	1.2	1.3	8%	**1.08**	3.3	2.7	22%	**0.82**
Breathing problems, asthma	2.8	4.1	46%	**1.46**	2.7	3.3	22%	**1.22**
Cancer	0.8	1.0	25%	**1.25**	0.5	0.7	40%	**1.40**
Weakness, dizziness, anaemia	2.7	5.1	89%	**1.89**	3.4	4.6	35%	**1.35**
Mental, psychological disorder	0.8	0.2	300%	**0.25**	0.8	1.3	63%	**1.63**
Others	3.0	3.0	0%	**1.00**	1.9	1.5	27%	**0.79**
All Illnesses	108.0	116.6	1%	**1.08**	99.7	118.0	18%1	**1.18**

Source : NCAER (1995).

Pradesh emphasises the chronic nature of female morbidity in the age group of 25 to 44"[23].

"A range of gynaecological complaints- like menstrual problems, reproductive tract infections, sexually transmitted diseases, pelvic inflammation disease, uterine or genital prolapse as well as lingering effects of contraception and operations have been revealed in Community based studies in a few selected areas[24, 25, 26, 27, 28]. Generally, women had at least one gynaecological complaint. Less than 5 per cent of women covered in these studies reported childlessness. There does not seem to be a uniform pattern in the clinical and pathological diagnosis of morbidity in the different States, as women are reticent about their gynaecological problems in some cases[29, 30]. Gynaecological morbidity can cause difficulties in the performance of domestic and occupational work owing to recurring backaches.

Morbidity and multiple roles of women

Higher ratio of female morbidity during the reproductive age is corroborated by micro level studies in Madhya Pradesh and Maharashtra. A study in Nashik District of Maharashtra* brought out greater morbidity amongst married women compared to unmarried women. Separated or widowed women reported higher morbidity. These findings reflect the multiple burdens of women. Fulfilling their roles as wife, mother, attending to other household chores with very little help from their spouses, leaves them with a lot of work. When they take up remunerative work additionally outside the home, the burden multiplies. Thus, relentless work at the cost of rest and nourishment takes its toll on women's health. The reproductive age becomes very vulnerable with the multiplicity of roles handled by women without an effective social support.

* Madhiwala, Neha, Sunil Nandraj, Roopashri Sinha and Amar Jesani (1998), House Hold Study of Utilisation and Expenditure on Women's Health. A Study of Nashik-District, centre for Inquiry in) Health abide Allied Themes (Personnel Communication).

"Infections of the reproductive tract are considered as one of

Table 13. Top Ten Causes of Morbidity Among Women

General Morbidity Surveys	*Location*	*Method*	*Cause 1*	*Cause 2*	*Cause 3*	*Cause 4*	*Cause 5*
1990 (NCEAR 1992)	Selected urban areas, All India	Without probes (PR=18.43)	Fever infection (PR=8.05)	Respiratory (P R = 4.93) (PR=4.46)	Aches & Pains illness (PR=3.90)	Gynaecological infection	Gastro-entric
	Selected rural areas, All India	Without probes	Fever (PR=21.28)	Gynaecological illness (PR=8.00)	Gastroentric infection (PR =7.79)	Respiratory infection (PR =6.94)	Aches & Pains (PR= 6.68)
1993 (Sundar 1995)	Selected urban areas. All India	Without probes	Non specific fever (PR=26.1)	Respiratory infection (P R = 12.3)	Typhoid, malaria, cholera, jaundice, acute gastro (10.4)	Indigestion, Gas, acidity, Constipation (PR=8.8)	Blood pressure, Heart ailments. Paralysis (PR=7.7)

(Contd.)

(Contd.)

General Morbidity Surveys	*Location*	*Method*	*Cause 1*	*Cause 2*	*Cause 3*	*Cause 4*	*Cause 5*
	Selected rural areas, All India	Without probes	Non specific fever (PR=31.5)	Constipation (PR=l 1.5)	Typhoid, Malaria, cholera, Jaundice, acute gastro (10.4)	Respiratory infection (PR =9.3)	Headache, Backache (PR = 9.0)
Before 1993 (Shatrugna et.al. 1993)	One city (Hyderabad), Andhra Pradesh	Without probes	Gynaecologi-cal (28.9 %)	Preg. & Operation related (18.4%)	General feeling of ill Health (13.7%)	Upper respiratory infection (12.9%)	Fever (10%)
1996-97 (Madhiwalla et.al 1998	One district (Nashik) Maharashtra	After probing	Reproductive (9.9%)	Aches & Pains (17.9%)	Fever (16.9%)	Respiratory problems (12.4%)	Eye/Ear/Skin problems (10.8%)

Source : Iyer Aditi, background paper on Leading Causes of Morbidity and Mortality for the National Profile on Women Development and Health.

Note : PR - Prevalence rates per 1000.

the major contributing causes of gynaecological morbidity. Reproductive tract infections include:

- Sexually transmitted diseases like chlamydial infection that can lead to infertility, even death and trichomoniasis that can cause vaginal infections. Gonorrhoea, syphilis, chanchroid and genital warts are other possibilities.
- A second group comprises endogenous infections caused by abnormal growth of organisms that are normally present in the vagina like bacterial vaginosis and vulvovaginal candidiasis.
- A third consists of infections arising out of harmful obstetric and gynaecological practices including unsafe methods of contraception, childbirth and abortion or an unclean material used to absorb menstrual flow.

"Reproductive tract infections have received greater attention due to HIV and AIDS. Anaemia continues to be a greater villain that increases gynaecological morbidity of women. Nearly 91 per cent of all women in a study in rural Maharashtra had haemoglobin levels equal to or below 11.5 Gms/dl[31]. In rural Karnataka, some 17 per cent of all participating women were severely anaemic with haemoglobin levels below 10 Gms/dl and 67 per cent were anaemic with haemoglobin levels below 12 Gms/dl[32]. In Bombay, 46 per cent of the women had haemoglobin levels below 11 Gms/dl and 23 per cent had levels between 11 and 12 Gms/dl[33]. These findings are important too as they reflect the great deprivation that poorer women continue to face through the years.

"The Bang study (1989) brought out that women suffering from gynaecological morbidity also suffered filariasis (12 per cent), leprosy (10 per cent), urinary tract infection (4 per cent), pulmonary tuberculosis (2 per cent) etc.

Such diseases surge during the reproductive age group when women's bodies are overworked, under-rested, undernourished. During pregnancy, non-specific suppression of cell mediated immunity cause women to run the risk of suffering leprosy relapses and serious deformities. For those on treatment, pregnancy can exacerbate the disease and complicate its treatments[34]. There is epidemiological evidence of a tendency for women to manifest the disease of tuberculosis increasingly during the reproductive age group and to succumb to it[35]. Deaths due to pulmonary tuberculosis have consistently been the foremost killer of women in the reproductive age group for at least 15 years. Women in the reproductive age group are particularly vulnerable to a host of health problems not necessarily linked to their reproductive system. Non-reproductive health problems do have significant impact on reproductive functions. Stigmatized afflictions like tuberculosis, leprosy and mental disorders severely affect women's - and men's - lives. Poor access to services accentuates the problem for women".[36]

HIV/AIDS : Global Scenario

- Out of the total number of 18.8 million AIDS deaths since the beginning of the epidemic 7.7 million are women and 3.8 million are children
- Sub Saharan Africa is the only region of the world in which more women than men are infected with HIV and dying of AIDS. In Sub Saharan Africa alone, there are estimated to be 12 million women infected compared to 10.1 million men and 12-13 women get infected for every 10 men
- The percentage of adults living with HIV/AIDS who are women has been steadily increasing. In 1997, 41 per cent were women; in 2000, 47 per cent were women
- In South and South East Asia 35 per cent of the HIV-positive adults are women. In Cambodia 33 per cent of the infected population is that of women (Report on the Global HIV/AIDS epidemic June 2000)

IMPACT OF HIV AIDS

Incidence and its Dimensions

In the last two decades the incidence of HIV/AIDS has become a serious health hazard. Impairment of the immune system with the affliction of HIV/AIDS becomes a harbinger of all opportune diseases. In an environment of poverty and poor access to health the burden of disease could become the greatest deprivation. The worry in the new century is the toll on life this will have with the rapidity with which it has been spreading. AIDS now ranks as one of the leading causes of death among women aged 20-40 in several cities in Europe, Sub-Saharan Africa cities in Europe, Sub-Saharan Africa and North America. In India, the first known case of HIV was reported in Chennai in 1986.

According to the National AIDS Control Programme (NACO) estimates in 2000 there were 3.7 million people in the country infected with HIV with about 0.7 million estimated to be in the rural areas.

Findings of various impact studies

It is obvious that Power Relations underpin all social and sexual interactions. Besides women's unpaid labour subsidizes the social, welfare and health costs within the family and community.

- Married women in monogamous relationships are at risk because of the sexual trespasses of their spouses. Men have more partners than women do and a recent study revealed that 90 per cent of the male clients of male sex workers were married. Studies in Tamil Nadu have also shown that 82 per cent of the male STD patients have had sexual relations with multiple partners and only 12 per cent have used preventive methods such as the condom.
- UNIFEM sponsored studies have shown that when women are infected there is fear of abuse and ostracism, as sexual disease merits a very negative reaction from the family and the community and keeps women in hidden spaces. One of the worst effects of being infected is being blamed for the infection or being accused of sexual trespass.
- Positive and affected women end up fending for the family, repay debts and afford the hospital costs of her spouse. Single-partner positive women, within the household bear a greater burden of the epidemic. In several cases, the natal family provided the much-needed economic support to their daughter and son-in-law, rather than the marital

(Contd.)

(Contd.)

family. This seems much in line as an extension of the dowry demands' made on the wife's family. As such the economic costs incurred by the natal family remain invisible in the social context.

- Studies among sex workers shows that though the use of condoms has increased with clients it is quite low with their regular partners (Babus).
- Women particularly suffer discrimination from the health care systems. A positive woman undergoing labour pains at the hospital ended up cutting her own umbilical chord. When the chips are down, the woman is the most dispensable, only further reinforcing the prevalent gender ideologies.
- Misconceptions, fears and beliefs accompanying the disease result in a high degree of secrecy. In some cases men do not inform their wives of their sero-status even when they had informed other male members of their families. There is a desire to protect the wife on the one hand and keep the so-called honour of the family intact on the other, especially where female members of the family (sisters/ daughters) are yet to be married. Families have experienced isolation and have had to shift homes.
- There is a gendered differential impact of the infection. While HIV positive men focus on themselves, women focus upon on their children. While men are entitled to care from their wives, mothers and even daughters and mothers-in-law it is taken for granted that the wife would stay and care for her husband when she becomes aware of his sero-status. However the most striking feature is that on the death of the husbands, the wives have been either thrown out or sent back to their natal families. Women experience dual stigmatization as a widow particularly a widow of a positive person.

(Contd.)

(Contd.)

- Women experience a great deal of anger with their husbands for infecting them accepting it as their fate. They experience deep depression, isolation, and loneliness.
- In another study conducted by UNICEF majority of the widow mothers (23) have become aware of their HIV positive status (and of the youngest children) after the death of their husbands. Such female-headed households cannot often afford even basic medicines to treat opportunistic infections. Demands of caring for the sick family member results in neglect of own needs or those of the other children. Providing for the health care needs of the infected child often means depriving the older children of a day's meals.
- Children also bear the brunt of the socioeconomic changes in the family with the girl child being hit the hardest - the first to leave school and take over household chores and the last to eat.

Source: Progress of South Asian Women, 2000, UNIFEM 2000; UPDATE, Regional Project on HIV and Development, Asia and Pacific, Vol. I, Issue 1, UNDP, April 1999: UNAIDS report on the global HIV/AIDS epidemic, June 2000; Women and Substance Abuse : WHO 1993; and UNICEF sponsored study in Manipur 2000.

- India's epidemic is stated to be following the so-called Type 4 Pattern, first described in Thailand. In this scenario, the epidemic shifts from the highest risk groups (commercial sex workers, drug users) to bridge populations (clients of sex workers. STD patients, partners of drug users) and then to the general population. The second decade of the epidemic is marked by heterogeneity. It is made up of a number of epidemics and in some places, within the state. There is a noted shift towards women and young people with an accompanying increase in vertical transmission and pediatric HIV.[37] The impact of HIV/AIDS on girls and women is even more daunting as it brings with it social stigma and alienation from the society. There is a growing global understanding that the epidemic is less about infection and more about social factors. The growing feminization of poverty, diminishing food security and sustainable livelihood options, increasing incidences of violence against women and young girls, early marriages and unsafe abortions and insufficient access to decision making resources increase vulnerabilities for girls and women.

- Risk of unprotected sex is two to four times that of men. Semen has higher concentrations of virus than the vaginal secretions. Male to female transmission is more efficient because of the bigger surface area of mucous membrane exposed during sexual intercourse.
- Adolescent girls are at even greater risk because of their immature genital tract and scant vaginal secretions are less of a barrier to HIV.
- Women undergo more blood transfusions during childbirth due to being anaemic - more than 50 per cent of all married women in India are anaemic.
- Women respond to alcohol and drugs differently than men because of their physiological characteristics, including body composition and hormonal level change.
- As with HIV, women acquire STDs at an earlier age than men. Gonorrhea and syphilis are symptomatic in 50-80 per cent of the women and often go untreated. Recent studies from population based studies suggest that rates of RTIs/STDs among women are as high as 20-30 per cent in some parts of the country.
- The risk of MTCT including transmission through breast milk is increased by recent infection with HIV, the progression to AIDS, Vitamin A deficiency, breast conditions which include breast abscesses and bleeding nipples. In India it is estimated that 10-30 per cent of babies acquire the virus from their mothers while still in the uterus. 40-60 per cent during labour and delivery and 30 per cent through breast milk.
- Close to 60 per cent of women in rural India get married before the age of 18 and the average age of marriage in India is 19.7 and 60 per cent of married women become mothers well before they are 19 years. The infection

increases maternal mortality, in turn pushing up child mortality rates.

- Women have scanty understanding of their reproductive system and low access to information and medical care. Cultural beliefs, practices and values keep women in silence over matters of knowledge about their own bodies, particularly sexual health and expressing their sexuality by dictates of the concept of a "good" woman who is expected to be ignorant about sex and passive in sexual interactions.
- Sterilization accounts for more than 75 per cent of total contraception and female sterilization accounts for more than 95 per cent of all sterilization. Abortion is a contraceptive method for many women.
- 19.7 per cent of the 40 per cent of women who have heard of AIDS know that using condoms prevents AIDS. It is near impossible for most families to initiate a discourse on condoms.
- The dowry demands in Indian marriage leads to continued harassment of women. Desertion of families by male heads, abandonment of women by their families when widowed, etc. may force women to be at sites of work which demand sexual favours or exchange sex for food security. Migrant, refugee, displaced women are particularly vulnerable since their social net is completely depleted and their ability to negotiate protection for themselves is very unlikely.
- Violence against women contributes both directly and indirectly to women's vulnerability to HIV. Reported studies predict that anywhere from 10 to over 50 per cent of women report physical assault by an intimate partner. In India it is estimated that every 26 minutes a woman is molested and every 34 minutes a rape takes place, every 42 minutes an incident of sexual harassment and every 93 minutes a woman is burnt to death over dowry.[38] In UP 7 per cent men said that they resorted to violence to get their wives to have sex with them.
- Thousands of women are sold in to prostitution and

marriage and sexual slavery. Most of them lack knowledge and mechanisms to negotiate safe sex.

- Legal discrimination results in women having unequal access to property and inheritance.
- Women are also affected by drug abuse, whether they are drug users or not[39]. Their subordinated status and gender roles result in unmet needs which are experienced both by the drug abusing women and female partners of drug abusers in various social, cultural and economic environments.
- Human rights issues are involved around mandatory testing, demands for isolation and detention. Oftentimes testing is without consent. Information on the test result is also not given to the person. Right to marry and bear children has also been violated. Invasion of privacy including publicizing the names and addresses of people destroys homes and results in displacement. Inadequate access to counselling and lack of information puts women and particularly pregnant women and lactating mothers in greater jeopardy as they are not aware of the infection to the baby through breast feeding. Besides poor women have no other choice but to breast-feed[40].

Issues of Confidentiality: The debate between the rights of the individual versus the rights of the community has fore-grounded the issue of whether public disclosure would stem the epidemic or whether protecting the rights of the individual would strengthen the community since it would encourage greater numbers for voluntary testing and counselling. Many a time woman's test result is not collected by her, but by a male member of the family. In these circumstances the question whether the healthcare worker should give the results to the relative or whether she should insist on the patient collecting the results are issues for consideration.

Beneficial Disclosure: Closely linked to the principle of confidentiality is the notion of beneficial disclosure. This implies disclosure that is made for the benefit of the affected individuals, his/her sexual and drug-injecting partners and family. Beneficial disclosure maintains individuals' human rights, prevents discrimination, and improves public health in the form of prevention and care efforts and promotes the creation of an enabling environment where people will come forward for testing, counselling, prevention and care.

The debate between the rights of the individual versus the rights of the community is not yet settled. It is not yet certain whether public disclosure would stem the epidemic or whether protecting the rights of the individual would strengthen the community since it would encourage greater numbers for voluntary testing and counselling.

National Initiatives to Tackle HIV/AIDS

The National Initiatives to tackle the problem of HIV/ AIDS have been the following:

- Modernising of the blood banks, setting up blood component separation units and Blood-Transfusion Councils were established. This resulted in reducing transmission through blood from 8 per cent to 4.5 per cent.
- Introduction of school and college education programmes by NGOs and CBOs with use of mass media which increased awareness levels from near zero to 60-80 per cent in urban areas and 13-64 per cent in rural areas.
- Targeted Intervention programmes for high risk behaviour.
- A comprehensive epidemiological surveillance system was set up at 180 sites in urban and rural areas to study the progression of the disease and its regional implications.

The Infrastructure for Health Services

India can take credit for designing a health services network in the public sector for preventive, curative and promotional health care of her people. Starting from the Bhore Committee, 1946, various Expert Committees have contributed to shaping the health infrastructure in the country. These efforts through the Five Year Plans are traced in Table 4 in Annexure IV. Unfortunately, a comprehensive effective structure has still not fallen in place to meet the massive health needs of the people in the country in general and women in particular.

Hospitals and Hospital Beds

The inadequacy of services including beds in the public sector has a serious impact on the access to health services by the poorer section of the population. It has even greater impact on the access of service for women. **CSWI opined that the impact of the primary health centres and sub-centres on the rural population has not been substantial.** They quote from the observations of an expert committee of 1973 "that apart from West Bengal and Kerala where there was utilization of 50 per cent, in other States like Bihar, Rajasthan, U.P., Orissa, Madhya Pradesh and Jammu and Kashmir, the bed utilisation in primary health centres was hardly between 5 to 15 per cent. The reasons for this underutilisation were (a) apathy of staff, (b) the status barrier that separates the doctor and his team from the village population, particularly the lower socioeconomic groups, and (c) absence of lady doctors in many centres. Emphasising the need to improve maternity and child health services, the Committee recommended that provision of domiciliary maternity services as essential". The existing primary healthcare institutions are functioning sub-optimally because of one or more of the following factors:

(a) Inappropriate location, poor access, lack of maintenance;
(b) lack of professional and paraprofessional staff at the critical posts;
(c) mismatch between the requirement and availability of health professionals especially physicians at PHC;
(d) lack of funds for essential drugs;
(e) lack of First Referral Units (FRUS) for linkage of referral services.

The Public Sector including local bodies are larger with more beds compared to hospitals in the private sector. Recently, the hospitals and beds in the private sector are registering a high rate of growth. A large number of these have not come to notice due to inadequacy of registration systems and compilation of data. It is estimated by 'Cehat' and NGO working in the health sector, that the total number of Hospital Beds are 12,17,427 with 64 per cent of them in the Private Sector. In recent years emphasis has shifted significantly on the Indian System of Medicine and Homeopathy. The infrastructure available under this system is given in Table 14.

There is great need to improve the quality of health service and access to them by giving priority in the allocation of resources for the purpose.

Table 14. Summary of Medical Care Facilities under Indian System of Medicine and Homeopathy as on 1.4.1997

Facilities	*Ayur-veda*	*Unani*	*Siddha*	*Yoga*	*Naturo-phathy*	*Homeo-pathy*	*Total*
Hospital	2199	183	122	13	25	315	2857
Beds	31291	3541	1636	251	770	8560	46049
Dispensaries	13690	974	335	7	17	6681	21730*

* Includes 26 Amchi Dispensaries. Figures are provisional.

Primary Health Care Facilities

The norms for the network of sub-centres, primary health centres and community health centres in rural areas is presented in Table 15. The actual number of centres and sub-centres and actual population served in different States is presented in Table 16. According to the Ministry of Health and Family Welfare, there is shortfall of 7,727 sub-centres, 1,966 Primary Health Centres and 2,966 Community Health Centres in the country by June, 1997 for the population as of 1991. The shortfall would be much greater according to current population (details given in Table 37 in Annexure I). The National Population Policy recognises the shortage in the health infrastructure as 23,190 Sub-centres and 4,212 PHCs for the projected population in year 2002 and a further shortage of 3,776 Community Health Centres for the projected population for the year 2000.

Table 15. Rural Health Centres - Average Population Served, 1996

Item	*Population Norm*	*Av. Population Served*
Sub-centre	3,000 to 5,000	4,737 (4-7 villages)
PHC	20,000 to 30,000	28,375 (25-27 villages)
CHC	100,000 +	260,000

Source : Director General of Health Services, *Bulletin on Health Statistics in India*, 1996.

As regards the infrastructure of health service for the urban areas, there is a great deal of inadequacy as shown in Table 17. The National Development Council (NDC) has emphasized the need to create well-structured organisation of urban primary health care aimed at providing basic health and family welfare services to the population within 1-2 kms of their dwellings.

Table 16. Primary Health Centres (PHCS) and Sub-centres (1996)

States	*PHCs Numbers*	*Rural Population/ PHC (Actual)*	*Sub-centres (Nos.)*	*Rural Population/Sub-Centre (Actual)*
Mizoram	38	9,784	261	1,425
Sikkim	24	15,394	147	2,513
Arunachal Pradesh	47	16,041	223	3,381
Meghalaya	88	16,417	337	4,287
Jammu & Kashmir	335	17,550	1,700	3,458
Manipur	72	18,493	420	3,170
Himachal Pradesh	246	19,194	1,908	2,475
Karnataka	1,459	21,295	7,993	3,887
Kerala	959	22,334	5,094	4,205
Tamil Nadu	1,436	25,614	8,681	4,237
Orissa	1,056	25,970	5,927	4,627
Rajasthan	1,572	27,590	8,692	3,905
Gujarat	957	28,280	7,284	3,715
Maharashtra	1,695	28,552	9,725	4,976
Punjab	484	29,522	2,852	5,010
Uttar Pradesh	3,761	29,648	20,153	5,533
Nagaland*	33	30,343	244	4,104
Haryana	397	31,257	2299	5,398
West Bengal*	1,556	31,729	7,873	6,271
Assam*	619	32,191	5,280	3,774
Goa	21	32,859	175	3,943

(Contd.)

(Contd.)

States	PHCs Numbers	Rural Population/ PHC (Actual)	Sub-centres (Nos.)	Rural Population/Sub-Centre (Actual)
Bihar*	2,209	33,962	14,799	5,069
Madhya Pradesh	1,376	36,949	11,936	4,260
Tripura	63	37,071	537	4,349
Andhra Pradesh*	1,283	37,896	7,894	6,159
A & Nicobar	17	12,100	96	2,143
Chandigarh	–	–	12	5,516
D & N Haveli	6	21,125	34	3,728
Daman & Diu	4	13,511	19	2,844
Delhi	8	1,18,627	42	22,596
Lakshadweep	7	3,228	14	1,614
Pondicherry	26	11,185	79	3,681
All India	21,854	28,768	1,32,730	4,737

Source : Director General of Health Services, *Bulletin on Health Statistics in India,* 1996. Arranged in ascending order of population served by primary health centres.
* Data for 1995.

Table 17. Urban Health and Family Welfare Centres and Posts as of 30.6.1996

	In position	Required
Urban health and family welfare post	871	19480
Urban health and family welfare centres	1083	952

Source : National Profile on Women, Health and Development, India, 2000.

Manpower for Health Services

The Bhore Committee had recommended one doctor for a population of 1,500 and one nurse for a population of 500. We have not still reached these proportions of population ratio or inter-professional ratio. There are still quantitative deficiencies of professional persons in the rural primary healthcare institutions.

Doctors

Unfortunately, the services of qualified doctors are very often not available to people in the rural areas. They often have to resort to healthcare by unqualified and unlicensed medical practitioners. It is estimated that the number of such persons could be anything between 10-50 per cent of all doctors in India. The issue still is the absence of an effective regulatory system for practice of medicine under different systems. The absence of data, quality standards and regulation of charges for services are areas requiring very serious attention.

The total number of doctors under all systems were estimated at 10,69,629 in 1997. The distribution of doctors under different systems of medicine is given in Table 18.

Table 18, Medical Professionals of Different Systems in Position

Category	*Existing No.*	*Training Instts No.*
Allopathic Graduates	4,74,270	160
Ayurveda Graduates	3,50,416	150
Unani Graduates	41,592	31
Siddha Graduates	12,528	2
Homeopathy Graduates	1,71,298	146
Dental Graduates	19,525	67
Total	10,69,629	556

Source : GOI, Planning Commission 1997.

The total number of doctors which stood at 2,41,502 in 1961 (Table 19) has now multiplied four times to 10,69,629 in 1997. Allopathic doctors had gone up ten times between 1961 and 1981, but since 1981 it has gone up from 1,96,554 to 4,74,270. It is interesting to point out that the number of doctors in the Ayurvedic system at 72,987 in 1961 was more than Allopathic doctors, but the growth in numbers has been much slower over the years and in 1997, their number at 3,50,416 is much less than allopathic doctors.

Table 19. Area-wise Distribution of Doctors Under Different Systems.

Year	Total	Allopathic	Homeopathic	Ayurvedic	Unani	Dentists	All Others
1961							
Rural	1,19,969	19,187	16,185	45,112	–	1,122	38,363
	(49.6)	(29.5)	(52.4)	(61.8)		(20.3)	(54.3)
Urban	1,21,533	45,837	11,075	27,875	–	4,407	32,339
		(70.5)	(40.6)	(38.2)		(79.7)	(45.7)
Total	2,41,502	65,024	27,260	72,987	–	5,529	70,702
	(100.0)	(100.0)	(100.0)	(100.0)		(100.0)	(100.0)
1971							
Rural	1,29,896	49,846	23,527	36,871	4,110	1,333	14,209
	(48.8)	(39.4)	(61.2)	(62.6)	(52.4)	(22.8)	(49.6)
Urban	1,36,083	76,507	14,917	21,994	3,736	4,507	14,420
	(51.2)	(60.6)	(38.8)	(37.4)	(47.6)	(77.2)	(50.4)

(Contd.)

(Contd.)

Year	*Total*	*Allopathic*	*Homeopathic*	*Ayurvedic*	*Unani*	*Dentists*	*All Others*
Total	2,65,979	1,26,353	38,444	58,865	7,846	5,842	28,629
	(100.0)	(100.0)	(100.0)	(100.0)	(100.0)	(100.0)	(100.0
1981							
Rural	1,52,047	53,407	31,916	36,503	2,600	1,471	26,145
	(41.2)	(27.2)	(63.7)	(57.3)	(38.8)	(18.5)	(59.7)
Urban	2,16,818	1,43,147	18,188	27,211	4,097	6,493	17,682
	(58.8)	(72.8)	(36.3)	(42.7)	(61.2)	(81.5)	(40.3)
Total	3,68,860	1,96,554	50,104	63,714	6,697	(7,964)	43,827
	(100.0)	(100.0)	(100.0)	(100.0)	(100.0)	100.0	(100.0)

Source : Census (1961, 1971 and 1981), Government of India.

Notes : (1) "All others" denotes all physicians and surgeons not covered separately. (2) Figures in parentheses are percentages. (3) Unani practitioners were not separately covered in 1961 Census. (4) Siddha medical practitioners were not covered separately by any of the Census.

The distribution of doctors by sex and qualification registered with State Medical Councils, India between 1990-95 is given in Table 20. The table brings out that women doctors are less than 25 per cent of the registered medical practitioners. Their numbers have come down in the five years as have those of males. One of the reasons could be emigration of professionals outside the country. The increase of doctors under different systems since 1961 is given in Table 19 showing the predominance of the traditional systems in the rural areas. The traditional systems of medicine are increasingly gaining ground. Village level micro studies show that majority of the rural population use the facilities available under the non-modern system of healthcare. These are not captured in the household level health surveys conducted at the national and district levels.

Table 20. Number of Doctors by Sex and Qualification Registered with State Medical Councils, India - 1990-95

Number of Registered Medical Practitioners

Year	*Graduates*		*Licentiates*		*Total*	
	Males	*Females*	*Males*	*Females*	*Males*	*Females*
1990	505013	153389	51430	5522	556443	158911
1991	408529	112647	41887	3831	450416	116478
1992	576340	1583999	84972	6439	661312	164838
1993	606011	170490	87319	6470	693330	176960
1994	496629	129542	75383	5236	572012	134778
1995	436287	127496	65590	4342	501877	131836

Note : Refers to position as on 31th December of Respective Year.
Source : Medical Council of India, New Delhi, and Women in India, A Statistical Profile, p. 53.

"It is worth noting that the basis on which the total numbers of midwives were estimated by the Bhore Committee was one midwife for the total of 100 births per year. For 10 million births each year, they estimated a total requirement of 100,000 midwives. The number of midwives required in 1961 would, thus, be 166,820. But the achievement was not satisfactory even in 1967. India had only about 55 per cent of the required midwives. At the end of 50 years, the infrastructure including trained staff comprising lady doctors to take care of women's reproductive and maternal and general health, lab technicians required to provide the back up diagnostic facilities for the national health programmes are grossly inadequate. Large number of posts remain vacant both due to slow recruitment and unwillingness of selected persons to report in the rural duty posts. The impact of this situation on the quality of rural health service is very significant."[41]

Nurses, Auxiliary and Other Para-medical Staff

The doctor-nurse ratio is less than the recommended level of 1:3, instead it is 2.1:1. The status of nursing is poor despite India being a major supplier of nursing professionals. It is estimated that the number of nurses have since increased to 7,41,899 in 1996 improving the doctor-nurse ratio to 1.4:1. Of all registered nurses 66.6 per cent were general nurse/mid-wife, 30.1 per cent were auxiliary nurse midwife (ANM) and 3.3 per cent were health visitors (Table 21). It is significant to point out that nursing in India is almost exclusively a female profession. Only 4.2 per cent of all general nurse midwives are males.

Table 21. Number of Nurses

Categories	*Population*	*Number*	*Person per Nurse*
All (1996)	843930861	6,74,946 (100.0)	1,250
General Nursing/ Midwifery	843930861	4,49,351 (66.6)	1,878
Auxiliary Nurse Midwife	843930861	2,03,451 (30.1)	4,178
Health Visitors	843930861	22,144 (03.3)	38,111

Source : "Manpower profile: India: Yearbook. 1997" New Delhi: IAMR).

There is a great shortage of qualified nurses in the country. Unqualified and unregistered nurses at low wages are substituted in the private sector. The spatial distribution of nurses has an urban bias as in the case of doctors as shown in Table 22.

The number of qualified nurses, mid-wives, ANMs and health visitors registered with the State Nursing Councils is given in Table 23. As already mentioned the growth of qualified nurses/

Table 22. Rural Urban Distribution of Nurses

Area	*Total*	*Nurses*	*Midwives & Health Visitors*	*Other Health Workers*
		1961		
Rural	1,11,657 (47.5)	29,098 (38.2)	33,980 (66.4)	48,579 (45.2)
Urban	1,23,141 (52.5)	47,111 (61.8)	17,214 (33.6)	58,816 (54.8)
Total	2,34,798 (100.0)	76,209 (100.0)	51,194 (100.0)	1,07,395 (100.0)
		1971		
Rural	1,09,181 (39.3)	31,711 (30.6)	23,714 (65.3)	53,756 (39.0)
Urban	1,68,569 (60.7)	71,899 (69.4)	12,606 (34.7)	84,064 (61.0)
Total	2,77,750 (100.0)	1,03,610 (100.0)	36,320 (100.0)	1,37,820 (100.0)
		1981		
Rural	1,93,049 (43.1)	52,275 (31.3)	29,705 (59.9)	1,11,060 (48.1)
Urban	2,54,956 (56.9)	1,14,913 (68.7)	19,874 (40.1)	1,20,169 (51.9)
Total	4,48,005 (100.0)	1,67,188 (100.0)	49,579 (100.0)	2,31,238 (100.0)

Source : Census, (1961, 1971, 1981), Government of India.

Notes : (1) "Other Health Workers" include other nursing, sanitary and medical and health technicians.

(2) Figures in parentheses are percentages.

mid-wives is very inadequate in India, compared to the requirement. Females dominate this profession. It is common knowledge that less qualified persons are employed at lower wages in private hospitals due to absence of adequate number of qualified persons.

Table 23. Number of Qualified Nurses, Mid-wives, Auxiliary and Health Visitors Registered with State Nursing Councils, India -1986-94

	Number of			
Year	*Nurses/Midwives*		*Auxiliary Nurses Midwives*	*Health Visitors*
	Males	*Females*		
1986	6179	385951	108511	13248
1987	6838	373107	110016	12741
1988	11290	234115	132923	16419
1989	14071	250433	141191	16635
1990	– 3,11,235 –		150431	17892
1991	16320	323888	150658	17302
1992	17985	367425	165143	17910
1993	18762	430589	203451	22144
1994	19119	493476	229304	24411

Note : 1. As at end of year.

2. For 1990 separate figures for males and females are not available in respect of nurses/midwives

Source : Indian Nursing Council, New Delhi, and Women in India, A Statistical Profile 1997, p. 55.

'The inadequacy of manpower in rural primary health care institutions, with vacancies and absence of critical posts has very serious implications for quality health care of the people. The availability of various health professionals and the shortage of positions are presented in Table 6 in Annexure IV. The total deficiency in all technical categories was estimated at 2,37,712 positions.

The National Population Policy 2000 recognises the shortages of manpower as given in Table 24. The utilisation of MTP (Medical Termination of Pregnancy) kits distributed under the CSSM (Child Survival and Safe Motherhood) Programme numbering about 1,748 have been rendered impossible owing to the shortage of trained manpower. The population policy emphasises convergence of training requirements as well as decentralisation to sub-district and village levels by mobilising additional resources.[42]

Table 24. Shortage of Manpower of Unmet Needs (Population Policy 2000)

Category of Manpower	*Numbers*
ANMs	27,501
Male Multipurpose workers	64,860
Lady Health Visitors	4,264
Health Assistants (Male)	5,126
Medical Officers in PHCs	2,475
Surgeons	1,429
Gynaecologists	1,446
Pediatricians	1,774
Specialists	6,635
Radiographers	1,171
Pharmacists	6,045
Lab Technicians	12,793
Nurse Midwives in the rural primary health care delivery system	18,851

Source : Population Policy, 2000.

Organising regular training for Dais has been taken up recently and there is a hope of making them more professional for the service of millions of rural women who would have to rely on them for many years to come.

The traditional birth attendants known as 'Dais' who are not part of the public health care delivery system in the country fill up the manpower gap in the rural area and are the only source of health care available to millions of women in the rural areas. They are the only help available for child birth to majority of rural women. They are paid token amounts for conduct of delivery. Up to March 1993, there is a record of training 6,09,501 dais countrywide, who were given a delivery kit. According to the data compiled by the Ministry of Health and Family Welfare, Government of India, on the average, a trained Dai would cover a population of 965 in approximately one village (0.9 villages). A village health guide would cover a population of 1,527 in 1.4 villages as given in Table 39 in Annexure I.

Access to Health Services

The scenario presented by CSWI on approach and access to health services seems to be virtually unchanged, particularly in the rural areas. According to an ICMR study of 1994: "Inadequate resources, family responsibilities, inadequate antenatal care, failure to identify high risk mothers, absence of adequate and appropriate transportation and communication facilities has resulted in failure of women accessing health facilities in time. It is, therefore, not surprising that most deliveries continue to take place outside institutions by untrained women including relatives and neighbours. In 1992-93, 80 per cent of deliveries in Rajasthan, Uttar Pradesh, Bihar, Orissa, Assam, Andhra Pradesh were conducted by persons other than doctors and nurse midwives." In 1998-99, 67 per cent deliveries were not in an institution and 58 per cent of deliveries were not conducted by a health professional (All India), as per NHFS-2.

CSWI on approach and access to Health Services

Medical care remains inaccessible to a large section of the population despite substantial achievements in the first four five year plans.

There has been deviation from the basic recommendation of the Bhore Committee in the pattern of health services, which emphasized preventive services in the rural areas as the keystone of public health. Expenditure on curative services was three times that on preventive services and most of it was concentrated in urban areas. The ten per cent of hospital beds meant for the four-fifths of the population living in rural areas were ill staffed; ill-equipped and ill-financed. While the expert committee emphasized greater attention to maternity services, the actual position showed wide regional variations in the provision of this crucial service. The availability and utilisation of medical care for women reflects the general social attitude to women in a

(Contd.)

(Contd.)

region. The female literacy rate is an important determinant for utilisation as well as supply of medical and health care. This is particularly true of maternity and child-care.

The accessibility of health services is also affected by rural-urban and social-economic differentials, including a broad pattern of sex differentials. For example, uncontaminated water is available to 40 per cent of towns, but only 9 per cent of villages. Since about two thirds of the total number of doctors and nurses, and most hospitals are concentrated in urban areas, the four-fifths of the population living in rural areas get a much smaller share of these services. The National Sample Survey (19th Round, 1964-65) found that 46% of all births in urban India are attended by trained medical personnel, as compared to 9 per cent in rural areas. The household consumption data of the same Round also shows that average per capita private monthly expenditure on medicines and medical services is Rs. 1.01 in urban areas, and about half that in rural areas. Majority of doctors in urban areas are private practitioners, charging high fees. Their services can be used only by the upper and middle-income groups. Private nursing homes and paying hospitals, like private doctors, are almost totally out of reach of the poorer sections of society.

Recognising the socio-cultural context of health, in a document of the World Bank viz., "Improving Women's Health in India"[43], it is mentioned "Poverty underlies the poor status of most of the Indian population and women represent disproportionate share of the poor. Women's relatively low status particularly in North India and the risk associated with reproduction exacerbates what is already an unfavourable overall health situation." It recognises "women's health in nutrition status is inextricably bound up with social, cultural and economic factors that influence all aspects of their life. It has consequences not only for the women themselves but also for the well being of all (particularly female), the functioning of the households and the distribution of resources."

The analysis in the National Profile on Women, Health and

Development, India, 2000, brings out that "the perception about the degree of seriousness of the illness is the major reason for non-utilisation" of health services; 75 per cent of all rural women were noticed to have given "non-seriousness' as the reason in the 1986-87 NSSO Survey. According to a study in Maharashtra,[44] neglect of treatment was highest between the ages of 18 and 45, and among working women in both rural and urban areas.

The major findings were:

- Lack of finances was a major reason for non-utilisation.
- Largely, women tended to leave untreated conditions that were chronic but not incapacitating like mental stress, reproductive, problems, weakness and aches and pains. The levels of non-utilisation were as high as 50-80 per cent.
- Medical care that would have no impact on illness or the illness was not serious enough to warrant medical care were among other reasons.

"In sum, the purchasing power of the individuals and households determines the level of utilisation of health care services during illness. In poorer groups, men may use the few resources available in the household to access medical care. Women may pay no attention to their own health due to the priority they give for the care of the others in the family. Sometimes, there may be denial of approach to health care providers overtly or covertly. The many subtle and obvious layers of discrimination that may operate in households thus complicate the access of women to health care.[45]

Reproductive Health-care

The Reproductive and Child Health Programme in India aims to provide pregnant women with at least three antenatal check-ups, two doses of tetanus toxoid vaccine, and iron and folic acid supplementation during pregnancy for at least three months. In addition, the programme encourages institutional deliveries or home deliveries attended by a trained medical professional, and three postpartum visits. The National Family Health Survey-2 observes that only 20 per cent of live births received all the required components of antenatal care. 44 per cent received three or more check-ups and 65 per cent received at least one check-up. Between 1992-93 and 1998-99, the first and second National and Family Health Surveys, improvement has been noticed in the administration of 2 or more doses of tetanus toxoid, and supplementation of iron and folic acid (Tables 25 & 26). "Coverage for these antenatal care services is much lower in rural areas and for older mothers, scheduled-tribe mothers, mothers who already have several children and poorer and less educated mothers. Goa, Kerala, Tamil Nadu, and Andhra Pradesh perform consistently well and UP, Bihar and Rajasthan perform consistently poorly on almost all indicators of antenatal care "(IIPS, 1998-99).

Table 25. Antenatal Care: Tetanus Toxoid Coverage of Pregnant Women, India and Selected States, 1992-93 and 1998-99

State	*% age Receiving Two Doses of Tetanus Toxoid Vaccine*	
	1992-93	*1998-99*
India	53.8	66.8
Tamil Nadu	90.1	95.4
Kerala	89.8	86.4
Punjab	82.7	89.9
Andhra Pradesh	74.8	81.5
Maharashtra	71.0	74.9
Karnataka	69.8	74.9
West Bengal	70.4	82.4
Haryana	63.3	79.7
Gujarat	62.7	72.7
Orissa	53.8	74.3
Madhya Pradesh	42.8	55.0
Uttar Pradesh	37.4	51.4
Bihar	30.7	57.8
Rajasthan	28.3	52.1

Source : IIPS (1995) and IIPS (1998-99).

Table 26. Anaemia Prophylaxis Coverage among Pregnant Women, India and Selected States, 1992-93 and 1998-99

State	*Percentage Receiving Iron and Folic Acid Tablets*	
	1992-93	*1998-99*
India	50.5	57.6
Kerala	91.2	95.2
Tamil Nadu	84.1	93.2
Andhra Pradesh	76.4	81.2
Karnataka	74.9	78.0
Punjab	73.6	79.6
Maharashtra	70.6	84.8
Gujarat	69.3	78.0
Haryana	59.9	67.0
West Bengal	56.3	71.6
Orissa	49.9	67.6
Madhya Pradesh	44.3	48.9
Uttar Pradesh	29.5	32.4
Rajasthan	29.2	39.3
Bihar	21.4	24.1

Source : IIPS (1995) and IIPS (1998-99).

The IIPS Surveys show marginal improvement for both rural and urban India on availability of antenatal check up by health professional at the all India level. It has gone up from 41.1 per cent in rural areas to 59.4 per cent and from 76.8 per cent in urban areas to 85.7 per cent. There is a decline in home visit by health worker during pregnancy in the same period as shown in Table 27. It is very significant to point out the variation between the high percentage of coverage of antenatal check up by health professional in Kerala which has been over 96 per cent to Rajasthan which was only 23 per cent in 1992-93 and increased to 47.5 per cent in 1998-99. Uttar Pradesh remained at 30.2 per cent in 1992-93 and 34.6 per cent in 1998-99. If infant mortality and maternal mortality are to be reduced and the national goals reached in the targeted time period, the States lagging behind need to pay very special attention to the social infrastructure for improving delivery of health services, including provision of training to health personnel.

Table 27. Coverage of Antenatal Care, India and Major States 1992-93 / 1998-99

State	*Received Ante-natal Checkups by Health Professional*		*Home Visit by Health Worker During Pregnancy*	
	1992-93	*1998-99*	*1992-93*	*1998-99*
India	49.2	65.4	21.0	13.0
Rural	41.1	59.4	24.3	14.0
Urban	76.8	85.7	9.8	10.0
Kerala	96.6	98.8	26.5	18.0
Punjab	85.9	74.0	7.8	1.6
Tamil Nadu	78.2	98.5	40.4	26.0
Maharashtra	69.4	90.4	23.2	23.4
West Bengal	68.4	90.0	13.7	18.1
Haryana	67.0	58.1	11.9	1.8
Andhra Pradesh	65.6	92.7	41.0	17.4
Karnataka	64.8	86.3	41.9	17.2
Gujarat	50.0	86.4	36.6	33.2
Orissa	38.4	79.5	30.5	9.0
Madhya Pradesh	36.3	61.0	19.7	8.9
Uttar Pradesh	30.2	34.6	16.5	3.2
Bihar	26.4	36.3	11.1	2.4
Rajasthan	23.1	47.5	11.5	11.8

Source : IIPS (1995) and IIPS (1998-99) . Compiled from NFHS-2, Table 9.5, p. 322.

Postpartum check-up within two months of birth is rarely available to women who do not have the delivery in a health facility, or has received 3 or more antenatal check-ups. NHFS records only 17 per cent postpartum check-up. Except for Tamil Nadu where 53 per cent of non-institutional deliveries received a postpartum check-up in all other States this was very poor. The Survey has recorded that only 14 per cent of rural women and 10 per cent of urban women have received a visit from the RCH workers in the past one year.

The SRS 1994 highlighted only 22.3 per cent of pregnant women received institutional attention at the all India level, and only 16.9 per cent in rural India. A small proportion, 27.7 per cent are attended by trained professionals and 50 per cent by untrained professionals and others. The data varies significantly for rural and urban areas in different States as shown in Table 28. This, as already mentioned, remains a major lacuna in the health system for women.

Only one-third of deliveries takes place in a medical institution as per NHFS-2. Though, it is a slight improvement from 25.6 per cent in 1992-93, it is far from what the picture should be, particularly with the strong measures conceptualised in the early Plan regime. NFHS-2 has noticed that traditional birth attendants attend half the deliveries at home, and fewer than one in eight are attended by a health professional. The range is between 14.6 per cent for Bihar and 93 per cent for Kerala. Uttar Pradesh, Orissa, Rajasthan and even Haryana need to improve the institutional facilities for delivery. The data is presented in Table 29. The table also gives information on proportion of deliveries assisted by health professionals. Except for Kerala, which has the high 94 per cent of deliveries attended by a health professional, the other States have much lower proportions of cases handled by health professionals.

There has been an increase in the proportion of all births attended by a health professional, from 33 per cent in NFHS-1 to 42 per cent in NFHS-2 "Older women, rural women, and the more socially and economically disadvantaged women are less likely than others to deliver in institutions or to have a health- professional present at the time of delivery. Only some States are close to meeting the National Population Policy, 2000, goal of having a health professional attend all births by the year 2010; Kerala (94 per cent), Goa (91 per cent), and Tamil Nadu (84 per cent). Meghalaya, UP and Bihar, by contrast, lag far behind; less than a quarter of deliveries in these States are assisted by a health professional."

Table 28. Percent distribution of live births by type of medical attention received by the mother at delivery by residence, India and major states, 1994

India and Major States	*Institutional*			*Attended by Trained Professionals*			*Attended by Untrained Professionals and others*		
	Total	*Rural*	*Urban*	*Total*	*Rural*	*Urban*	*Total*	*Rural*	*Urban*
India#	22.3	16.9	54.7	27.7	26.7	33.8	50.0	56.4	11.5
Andhra Pradesh	36.8	32.4	81.7	27.7	29.5	9.9	35.4	38.1	8.4
Assam	20.5	17.5	55.6	14.9	14.1	24.0	64.5	68.4	20.4
Bihar	14.6	12.7	36.0	18.3	16.6	37.7	67.1	70.7	26.3
Gujarat	25.7	21.8	75.1	40.9	42.7	17.8	33.4	35.5	7.1
Haryana	23.0	19.9	49.1	67.0	69.0	49.9	10.0	11.1	1.0
Himachal Pradesh	23.4	21.4	56.0	24.8	23.8	41.2	51.8	54.8	2.8
Karnataka	48.8	36.1	80.9	24.1	28.1	14.0	27.1	35.8	5.1
Kerala	95.2	94.1	98.5	2.9	3.8	0.3	1.9	2.1	1.2
Madhya Pradesh	12.0	7.7	59.6.	20.0	19.8	23.0	68.0	72.5	17.4

(Contd.)

(Contd.)

India and Major States	Institutional			Attended by Trained Professionals			Attended by Untrained Professionals and others		
	Total	Rural	Urban	Total	Rural	Urban	Total	Rural	Urban
Maharashtra	35.5	27.1	81.1	19.1	19.1	17.6	45.4	53.5	1.3
Orissa	11.6	9.7	42.3	20.9	20.3	30.6	67.5	70.0	27.0
Punjab	14.0	12.1	29.7	83.7	85.4	69.3	2.4	2.5	1.0
Rajasthan	8.1	3.8	32.5	24.4	22.0	37.8	67.5	74.3	29.7
Tamil Nadu	56.3	51.6	94.6	24.4	26.8	4.6	19.3	21.6	0.8
Uttar Pradesh	7.0	4.1	23.2	41.6	37.7	63.4	51.5	58.2	13.4
West Bengal	35.8	26.0	78.5	12.3	11.3	16.4	52.0	62.6	5.1

* Excludes Jammu & Kashmir and Mizoram.

Source : SRS-1994.

Table 29. Place of Delivery and Delivery Attendance, India and Selected States[&]

State	Per cent of Birth Delivered in a Medical Institution		Percent of Deliveries Assisted by Health Professional	
	1992-93	1998-99	1992-93	1998-99
India	25.6	33.6	34.7	42.3
Tamil Nadu	63.6	79.3	72.0	83.8
Gujarat	35.7	46.3	43.2	53.5
Maharashtra	44.1	52.6	53.9	59.4
Kerala	88.4	93.0	90.2	94.0
Punjab	24.8	37.5	48.4	62.6
Karnataka	37.6	51.1	51.4	59.1
Andhra Pradesh	33.0	49.8	50.2	65.2
Haryana	16.7	22.4	30.6	42.0
Bihar	12.1	14.6	19.2	23.4
Madhya Pradesh	16.0	20.1	30.5	29.7
West Bengal	31.5	40.1	33.8	44.2
Uttar Pradesh	11.3	15.5	17.5	22.4
Orissa	14.2	22.6	21.1	33.4
Rajasthan	11.6	21.5	22.3	35.8

Source **:** IIPS (1995; NHFS-1) and IIPS (1998-99; NHFS-2).

[&] Table compiled from, NFHS-1 and NFHS-2

The Integrated Child Development Services (ICDS) was started in 1975 on a pilot basis to cover immunization for children and pregnant women, supplementary nutrition, child development services including pre-school education, awareness generation for women. ICDS has since been universalized to cover all the Community Development Blocks and Slums in urban areas. Less than 500 Blocks remain to be covered. The reduction in infant mortality and expansive coverage of immunization is largely due to this.

The programme for maternity and child health has received

special attention in the programme of family welfare and has had various modifications which will be discussed in subsequent sections.

Family Welfare Services

The CSWI had recommended norms for infrastructure for improving the services for women, particularly for maternity and child-care and family planning. Since then the Department for Family Welfare was carved out separately from the Ministry of Health, and the network of Primary Health Care Centres placed under it. The Expert Group on Population Policy headed by Dr. M.S. Swaminathan (1994) recommended among other thing that the Department of Health and Family Welfare be merged as one department. This has however not found favour.

Recommendations of CSWI on Maternal and Child Health and Family Planning

The rank of the Chief Executive of the integrated MCH services including family planning should be that of an Additional Commissioner. This should be so at the Centre as well as in the States.

A separate budget head for MCH services should be created, drawing on the provisions made for family planning and general health services; provision under this separate head should also be enhanced.

At the level of the primary health centre (PHC), MCH services should be separated for purposes of administrative provisions, medical personnel and budget.

Facilities in terms of maternity beds, equipment for immunization of children and family planning for women should be allocated to the MCH Unit.

While PHC should be responsible for sterilization, operations for men along with other general health services, the MCH unit could co-ordinate nutrition and immunization measures, which form a basic component of the integrated child development programme. The MCH unit could also collect and maintain fertility and morbidity statistics for women and children for facilitating better research and evaluation in these fields.

There has also been a great deal of debate on providing incentives and disincentives for Family Planning. The Women's Movement has been strongly opposing this. Government and industry have removed maternity leave and benefits for the third child. Some of the States have provided a disqualification for members seeking election to Panchayati Raj Institutions if they have a third child after a certain cut-off date provided in the State Act. This has had a setback for some women candidates in Rajasthan and Orissa.

The analysis of health services for women through the Five Year Plans highlights that family planning was initiated by the progressive Women's Movement in the country for the emancipation of women from repeated and unwanted pregnancies. The National Family Planning Programme started in 1952, was modified as Family Welfare Programme in 1977, and in 1997 it was further modified as Reproductive and Child Health Programme.

Table 30. Awareness of Contraceptive Methods Among Currently Married Women of Reproductive Age, India 1992-93/98-99

Method	**1992-1993 %*	*@1998-1999 %*
Any method	96	99.0
Any modern method	96	98.9
Any modern temporary method	76	NA
Pill	66	79.5
IUD	61	70.6
Injection	19	NA
Condom	58	71.0
Female Sterilization	95	98.2
Male Sterilization	85	89.3
Any traditional method	39	48.9
Periodic abstinence	35	45.1
Withdrawal	20	31.2
Other methods	4	2.7

Source : * IIPS (1995); @ IIPS (2000).

Contraception

The major health service for women has been in the area of

contraception. The National Family Health Surveys of 1992-93 and 1998-99 have brought out that practically all married women in the reproductive age are aware of one or the other method of contraception, Table 30. **Sterilization is the most predominant contraceptive method in use.** There are, of course, variations across states in the use of modern contraceptive methods.

Despite this awareness, the utilisation of family welfare services is very inadequate. One of the major implications of this is the persisting high total fertility in many parts of the country. As of 1998-99, a little above half the eligible couples in the country is effectively protected by contraceptive methods as shown in Table 31. The predominant method over near three decades is

Table 31. Percentage of Couples Effectively Protected by Various Family Planning Methods

		Percentage of couples protected by				
Year	*Eligible Couples ('000)*	*Sterili-sation*	*IUD*	*Oral Pill*	*CC*	*All Methods*
1970-71	94489	8.0	1.4	–	1.0	10.4
1975-76	105239	14.2	1.1	–	1.7	17.0
1980-81	116033	20.1	1.0	0.1	1.6	22.8
1985-86	129432	26.5	3.7	1.1	3.6	34.9
1986-87	132572	27.9	4.5	1.4	3.7	37.5
1987-88	135710	29.0	5.2	1.5	4.2	39.9
1988-89	138850	29.8	5.9	1.7	4.5	41.9
1989-90	141990	30.1	6.3	1.9	5.0	43.3
1990-91	145140	30.3	6.7	2.1	5.1	44.1
1991-92	148430	30.3	6.3	2.2	4.7	43.6
1992-93	151720	30.3	6.3	2.0	4.9	43.9
1993-94	155020	30.3	6.8	2.7	5.6	45.4
1994-95	158310	30.2	7.2	5.4	3.0	45.8
1998-99		36.2	5.6	8.4	7.9	55.1

Source : Department of Family Welfare, Ministry of Health and Family Welfare

IUD : Intra Uterine Devices CC: Conventional Contraceptives

sterilisation. Actual numbers of acceptors of different family planning methods over a quarter century upto 1994 is given in

Table 8 in Annexure IV. It is very conspicuous that very few males accept vasectomy. As mentioned earlier, more than a third of the couples protected go in for sterilisation. Other methods, namely oral pill, conventional contraceptive methods and IUD, in that order contribute for couple protection.

The failure to significantly decrease the birth rate in spite of massive deployment of manpower and expenditure in the public sector has led to the increasing involvement of the NGO sector in population control.

Abortion

India has been progressive on the policy on abortion. Not only was the 1971 MTP Act a bold step, its implementation too has been active. The actual numbers of legal abortions, however, are estimated to be 2-5 times more than those reported.

Recommendations of CSWI on Family Planning

(a) The practice of providing financial incentives to promoters of family planning should be abolished.

(b) Incentives could be given to women who accept family planning in the shape of a token or certificate to gain greater priority in access to health care facilities (for both mothers and children).

(c) Compensation for loss of wages during sterilization operation should be paid to daily wage labourers, others being given paid leave for the purpose.

(d) The qualifications prescribed for recruitment of personnel for family planning services in rural areas need to be gradually raised. Until women of requisite higher qualification are available, the present requirements may continue, the same being reviewed and progressively increased after three years. Attempts should also be made to obtain the services of older and matured women for these services in rural areas.

(e) Research in the field of female disorders like puerperal psychosis and effects of family planning methods.

(f) Denial of maternity benefits after three children to women in government service as practised in some State Governments should be stopped.

(g) Campaign for family planning should also aim at correcting prevailing social attitudes regarding fertility and metabolic hereditary diseases disorder and sex of the child for which the woman is generally blamed.

(h) Considering the increase in the neglect of female life as reflected by factors such as female, maternity and infant mortality rates as indicators of access to medical care, family planning should be integrated with health services like maternal and child health (MCH), nutrition and improvement in the life expectancy of children and mothers.

In addition about 4 million illegal abortions have been estimated. According to other estimates, this number ranges between 3-6 million. The fact that 6-9 per cent of abortions are in adolescent girls and 16 per cent are contributed by women in the age group 20-34 years. There is urgent need for adolescent health care and the use of abortion as a Family Planning technique. A negative development has been its linkup with sex selected foetal destruction, and the growth of clinics which make use of abortion services for foeticide. This calls for a careful MTP Programme as a part of the Safe Motherhood strategy. It has to be strongly supported by provision of information and public education to build awareness regarding safe use of MTP This can be achieved only with the back up of a strong Primary Health Care programme.

The conversion of family planning as a coercive tool for pushing the demographically driven agendas for population control has annoyed the Women's Movement. The observation in the National Profile quoted below sums up the situation.

"Women's health needs and sharing of responsibility by the male partners remained inadequately addressed. The power and gender relations crucial for addressing family planning and sexual and reproductive matters remained totally unaltered, leaving the woman with no control over her body and her life. Reproductive rights have been viewed more as a demographic tool in terms of woman's right to choose the number of children, 'how often' and 'how soon', and the type of contraceptive. Her personal and social right to choose the father of her child/children needs recognition and priority. This is relevant in the context of social reality where large number of girls, with many of them below the legal age of marriage, have unhappy and unwanted marriages inflicted upon them. Religious and cultural compulsions make it compulsory for parents of girls to get their daughters married. Poverty, problems of demands of dowry, and social non-acceptance of 'single' status for girls/women accompanied by social insecurity are some of the other reasons making many unhappy marriages inevitable. The social conditioning of girls to look at marriage as the only option in life and an environment that denies them opportunities to develop alternate career options, traps many girls into unwanted, untimely and inappropriate marriages."[46]

Unfortunately, the emphasis in the health sector has been more on fertility control than on women's health concerns. Family Planning has been perceived as one of the most critical inputs in women's health without recognising their nutrition and food security and other health needs through their life cycle. Recent Reforms in health services for women include the introduction of Reproductive and Child Health (RCH) approach to ensure safe motherhood and reproductive health. It is target free in the sense that users and providers focus on the quality of MCH services and ANMs fix goals by self-assessment. The limitation still continues as it leaves out the major cause of women's mortality and morbidity - namely the communicable diseases.

"RCH therefore must take this final leap of integrating FPP, RCH, Nutrition and Communicable Diseases Control Programmes and take a holistic view of women's health."[47]

EXPENDITURE ON HEALTH

Public and Private Expenditure

In India, of the total expenditure on health, only 22 per cent is from the public sector and 78 per cent is private expenditure. This allocation in the public sector is very low against 85.2 per cent in U.K., 73.8 per cent in Japan; 74.7 per cent in Canada; 44.1 per cent in United States, which are economically prosperous countries. The Reserve Bank of India has acknowledged in its Credit Survey, that the major cause of indebtedness of households is expenditure on health. Most of the expenditure is for serious illnesses. As mentioned earlier expenditure on women's health are only for very serious health episodes, and ordinarily, they do not have access to treatment for socio-economic reasons.

The proportion of expenditure on health as per cent of GDP remains quite comparable with other countries in the range of 6 to 12.7 per cent, US being the highest at 12.7 per cent and India at 6 per cent. (Even U.K. and Japan have only 6.1 per cent and 6.5 per cent). As mentioned earlier, bulk of health expenditure flows from private sources in India. NCAER (1995) estimates at Rs. 204, the annual per capita expenditure with the urban expenditure being higher at Rs. 258 and rural at Rs. 184. Some other sources put the expenditure estimates much higher.[48]

Budget Allocations

The Budget allocations for health has been far below the level of 10 per cent of total allocations recommended by the Bhore Committee in 1946 and Mudaliar Committee in 1967. There has been a steady decline progressively, starting from 3.3 per cent and declining to 1.7 per cent, for the Central Government and State Government put together for health. The allocation for Family Planning/Welfare has been steadily increasing over the same period. The proportion of expenditure on health and family planning over the five-year plan periods is given in Table 32.

While the proportion of Budget allocations for health has come down, progressively the allocation for family welfare has risen and is almost close to the total allocation for health. It has been observed that despite this increase in allocations for family welfare, the proportionate expenditure on MCH has actually declined till 94-95. Only in 1996-97 it goes up to 22.5 per cent of the total expenditure on family planning. It has been estimated that the Government revenue expenditure on health per person per annum has risen from less than a rupee in 1950-51 to Rs.85 in 1994-95. The state-wise details on per capita revenue expenditure by Government is given in Table 9 in annexure IV. The per capita expenditure ranges between Rs. 52 in Uttar Pradesh in 1994-95 to Rs. 324 in Sikkim.

Health Programmes Through the Five-Year Plans

The health programmes have emerged increasingly as

vertical programmes without much integration or co-ordination between health sector programmes themselves and other sectoral programmes. A very major criticism is that the choices of intervention are not based on epidemiological criteria or perceived needs of women of different strata or regions "nor do the immediate health care providers have a hand in the design of health care". On the contrary, profit driven global enterprise and trade dictate health care priorities and strategies neglecting human interests.[49]

"The global health strategy actually medicalises a social problem and adds market value to it. Illnesses like mental illness rooted in rising social tensions due to economic pressures, migration, destabilisation of whole communities and break up of joint and nuclear families, cannot be tackled through a medical curative route alone. This again emphasises the need for preventive interventions and an enabling social and economic environment"[50].

"Techno-centric approach to fertility or mortality control without the basic structural societal and economic issues may bring limited demographic changes but not do gender justice or ensure quality of life for women. This is clear from the evidence of the use of the technology meant to decrease maternal mortality related to unsafe abortions for female foeticide and unwarranted abortions."[51]

In dealing with reproductive health of women, other dimensions such as general and occupational health are not addressed adequately.

The major national health programmes since 1952 are presented in Table 4 in Annexure IV. They are vertical programmes without linkage with different programmes in the health sector, and much less with other sectoral programmes.

Women's Health in the Five-Year Pplans

The two over-riding principles underlying the Bhore Committee recommendations were (1) the provision of health services was the responsibility of the State; and (2) comprehensive health care was the right of all people, irrespective of their ability to pay. Unfortunately, we are yet far from realising either of these goals. Health continues to be largely a private matter with all the social bias including gender bias.

Government of India recognised that there must be a centrallised authority to provide services for mothers and children, a national level minimum infrastructure, training of paramedical

Table 32. Pattern of Investment on Health and Family Welfare (Plan Outlays)

	Period	*Total Plan Investment (All Dev. Heads)*	*Health (Centre and States)*		*Family Welfare*	
			Outlay/Expd.	*% of 2*	*Outlay/Exp.*	*% of 2*
1.	First Plan (1951-56)	1960.00	65.20	3.33	0.10	0.01
2.	Second Plan (1956-61)	4672.00	140.80	3.01	2.20	0.05
3.	Third Plan (1961-66)	8576.00	225.90	2.63	24.90	0.29
4.	Annual Plans (1966-69)	6625.40	140.20	2.12	70.50	1.06
5.	Fourth Plan (1969-74)	15778.80	335.50	2.13	284.40	1.80
6.	Fifth Plan (1974-79)	39332.00	682.00	1.73	497.40	1.26
7.	Annual Plan (1979-80)	11650.00	268.20	2.30	116.20	1.00
8.	Sixth Plan (1980-85)	97500.00	1821.00	1.87	1010.00	1.04
9.	Seventh Plan (1985-90)	180000-00	3392.90	1.88	3256.30	1.81
10.	Annual Plans (1990-91 & 1991-92)	137033.55	2253.86	1.64	1805.52	1.32
11.	Eighth Plan (1992-97)	434100.00	7582.20	1.75	6500.00	1.50
12.	Ninth Plan (1997-02)[@]	859200.00	5118.19*		15120.50	1.76

Source : Planning Commission, [@] Mid Term Appraisal of Ninth Five Year Plan.

*Figure does not include outlay for States hence per cent of 2 is not given.

workers and traditional Dais to provide natal, ante natal and post natal services on the basis of the recommendation of the Sokhe Committee, 1948, (a Sub-committee on health under the National Planning Committee set up by the Indian National Congress). This formed the basis for a Maternity and Child Health Focus within general health services in India. The evolution of health services for women through the Five Year Plans in presented in Table 42 in Annexure I.

Policy on Women's Health

The National Health Policy proclaimed by the Government of India in 1983 (following the recommendations made by the Indian Council of Medical Research (ICMR) and Indian Council of Social Science Research (ICSSR), Joint Committee on Health Report 1981 (Alternative Strategies - Health For All)) did not give separate identity to health issues relating to women and formulate strategies and approach to address them. The reference to women's health became an incidental issue. The National Health Policy is currently under review. There is a strong demand to formulate a policy on women's health.

The National Profile on Women, Health and Development observes "The population policy with the initiation of the Family Planning Programme (FPP) from 1952 focussed on fertility control of women. The consequences of this were:

- entire responsibility of contraception fell on women with consequential side effects on their health;
- the role of men in family planning was overlooked;
- other health needs of women were ignored."

The World Health Report recognises that there is increasing disparities between the privileged and the under-privileged within the countries and between the countries. This has resulted in increase in extreme poverty globally as well as increases in diseases of extreme poverty - globally and nationally. These are tuberculosis, water borne and vector borne diseases etc.

The World Health Report 1995 has included in its International Classification of Diseases (ICD), a new category called Z59.5. This stands for extreme poverty.

"The resurgence of communicable diseases, epidemics and outbreaks of malaria, cholera, hepatitis, dengue haemorrhogic fever is due to several reasons. Amongst these is failure to pursue the comprehensive primary health care approach of the Alma Ata Charter of WHO. The dilution of the approach to selective primary health care involving "Growth Monitoring, Oral Rehydration Therapy, Breast Feeding, Immunisation, Family Planning, Food Supplement, Female Literacy (GOBIFFF)" which is just at an early stage is another reason. Equity in health seems to be a long way off in the absence of economic and political justice.

"The emergence of techno-centric market friendly solutions with focus on maternity and reproductive health aspects has overlooked other health needs of women. This probably is the result of the concentration on selective aspects of primary health care that looks at the biomedical roots of the health problems neglecting the socioeconomic and political dimensions of ill-health.

"The shift of WHO from its commitment to comprehensive primary health care based on socioeconomic, cultural and political approach towards increasingly biomedical, techno-centric approach to health has been a cause of great concern to the people in the developing countries. The influence of the Bretton Wood institutions related to trade, finance and debt on WHO is being increasingly recognised. The influence of the policies of these agencies on the health of the poor especially on women has been documented world wide, wherever such policies have been implemented. This then, cannot be the direction or nature of development for the Third World, particularly India, nor can it be the basis for health of the Indian poor, especially women."[52]

The presentation of data with a focus on reproductive health ignores the toll taken by communicable and non-communicable diseases. Even diseases that cause bulk of the health problems and are amenable to technological interventions are excluded from the analysis. Consequently, they do not receive any priority in policy formulation. This has serious implications for developing countries like India which require great deal of resources and priority for preventive care through public services. Further, greater focus in the health sector reform policies on cost recovery ignores women's access to health services. Health services get out of reach of the poor.

Women's groups in India have focussed attention on women's health issues and brought clearer understanding through their action research. They have to use opportunities for advocacy, be equipped adequately with methodologies of policymaking, and get familiar with the various dimensions and determinants of health and the processes and tools of planning. Without these, there is great danger of these groups being used to push inadequate strategies and methodologies.

Major Recommendations in the National Profile on Women, Health and Development, India, 2000

"Health that should cover preventive, promotional and rehabilitative aspects besides curative care has become limited to curative care dependent on drugs, doctors and dispensaries, and that too in a highly commercialized form. This has led to tremendous distortions in healthcare in India. In the absence of understanding and addressing the socio-cultural, socio-economic and epidemiological realities of health it has been the Western biomedical model with a reductionist approach that has influenced the thinking and operation in the area of health. A comprehensive understanding of health requires addressing of its various dimensions, that is, physical, psychological, social, ecological and spiritual well being rather than mere physical dimension as is the case at present....... The urgency is for greater emphasis and attention to :

- All development policies to address health issues arising from the impact of the developments in the sector;
- Health impact assessments of other sectoral policies, projects and programmes on health of the people with a view to modify these appropriately to remove the negative impacts;
- A comprehensive and holistic approach to National Health Policies and Health Programmes and their proper implementation;
- Address health issue as a human development issue;
- Development of health infrastructure and provision of quality health services and health care; Establishment of a strong integrated as well as

(Contd.)

(Contd.)

pluralistic development of health systems appropriately using the different systems of medicine;
- Higher budget allocations for health; and
- Bio-medical and sociocultural interventions.

Public debates on women's health issues currently are:

- The use of medical technology for reasons other than the welfare of women - like sex determination and the lack of control on this practice;
- The declining juvenile sex ratio and the socio-demographic implications of the dwindling size of the female population;
- Illegal abortion and its impact on women's health;
- The problem of child-abuse, particularly the girl child;
- The issue of rape and the legalities involved in the procedures adopted while verifying the case and consequent review of the procedures by the legislators.
- The use of dangerous contraceptives that have impact on the women's health like Norplant.
- A public interest litigation was filed and won to stop the use of Quinacrine. The contraceptive pellet has yet to be approved as a drug. It has harmful affect on direct use;
- The mounting cost of pharmaceutical items, particularly after liberalisation of the economy is a matter of great concern which would further limit the access of health services and drugs to women;
- The issue of recognition of prostitutes as "sex workers" for provision of social security and an assured health care system.
- The human rights issues of persons, particularly women, affected by HIV/AIDS.

Despite a number of initiatives to increase awareness and improve facilities, the social attitudes remain pretty much the same even after a quarter century. "To a great extent the lower health status of women can be attributed to inadequate attention in policies, programmes and approaches in the health as well as other sectors

Annexure I

Table 33. Age and Gender Distribution of Top Ten Causes of Mortality in Urban India, 1988

Top ten causes of mortality	*Age Intexrvals*									*Per Cent*
	0 to 4	*5 to 14*	*15 to 24*	*25 to 34*	*35 to 44*	*45 to 54*	*55+*	*NS*	*Total*	*of Total*
MALES										
Cause 1 All other signs, symptoms & Il-defined conditions	14.1	5.6	7.5	9.0	10.1	13.5	37.3	2.8	100.0	6.9
Cause 2 Acute myocardial infarction	0.3	0.5	0.7	3.1	9.8	22.0	62.8	0.9	100.0	6.8
Cause 3 Fulmonary TB	2.2	1.4	7.0	15.8	19.6	20.5	32.2	1.2	100.0	6.6
Cause 4 Slow foetal growth, foetal malnutrition and immaturity	100.0	–	–	–	–	–	–	–	100.0	4.7
Cause 5 Pneumonia	49.0	6.7	5.9	3.5	4.1	5.7	23.8	1.3	100.0	4.0

(Contd.)

(Contd.)

Top ten causes of mortality	Age Intexrvals									Per Cent
	0 to 4	5 to 14	15 to 24	25 to 34	35 to 44	45 to 54	55+	NS	Total	of Total
Cause 6 Infectious colitis, enteritis and gastroenteritis	58.1	6.4	3.2	2.6	3.6	4.4	18.7	2.9	100.0	2.7
Cause 7 Septicaemia	51.8	4.7	6.4	5.5	6.7	7.6	16.5	0.8	100.0	2.6
Cause 8 Hypoxia, birth asphyxia and other respiratory conditions	100.0	–	–	–	–	–	–	–	100.0	2.0
Cause 9 Bronchitis. chronic and unspec emphysema & asthma	5.6	1.5	1.4	3.0	6.5	15.0	66.1	1.0	100.0	1.9
Cause 10 All other causes of originating in perinatal period	100	–	–	–	–	–	–	–	100.0	1.9

40.1% of all male deaths

(Contd.)

(Contd.)

Top ten causes of mortality	*Age Intexrvals*									*Per Cent*
	0 to 4	*5 to 14*	*15 to 24*	*25 to 34*	*35 to 44*	*45 to 54*	*55+*	*NS*	*Total*	*of Total*
FEMALES										
Cause 1 All other signs, symptoms and ill-defined conditions	22.6	6.3	7.8	9.2	7.1	9.7	34.3	3.0	100.0	7.4
Cause 2 Slow foetal growth, foetal malnutrition and immaturity	100.0	–	–	–	–	–	–	–	100.0	5.2
Cause 3 Pneumonia	53.2	8.0	6.8	3.2	2.7	3.4	21.8	0.9	100.0	4.7
Cause 4 Acute myocardial infarction	0.4	0.6	1.1	2.8	5.0	13.9	75.5	0.7	100.0	4.4
Cause 5 Pulmonary TB	4.0	4.1	13.7	19.4	18.2	14.7	24.7	1.2	100.0	3.9
Cause 6 Infectious colitis, enteritis and gastroenteritis	64.2	7.3	3.7	4.0	2.7	3.0	12.4	2.7	100.0	3.5

(Contd.)

(Contd.)

Top ten causes of mortality	*Age Intexrvals*									*Per Cent*
	0 to 4	*5 to 14*	*15 to 24*	*25 to 34*	*35 to 44*	*45 to 54*	*55+*	*NS*	*Total*	*of Total*
Cause 7 Septicaemia	50.6	6.2	9.4	9.0	6.7	5.4	11.8	0.9	100.0	2.5
Cause 8 Anaemias	12.8	6.9	13.5	15.8	10.3	9.3	29.0	2.4	100.0	2.3
Cause 9 Senility without mention of psychosis	–	–	–	–	–	–	99.9	0.1	100.0	2.3
Cause 10 All other diseases of nervous system	28.0	17.7	9.5	9.2	6.8	6.0	20.9	1.8	100.0	2.0
38.8% of all female deaths										

Source : RGI, 1992.

Table 34. Top Ten Causes of Mortality in Rural India by Age and Gender, 1994

Per Cent

Top Ten Causes of Mortality	*Age Intervals*						
	0 to 4	*5 to 14*	*15 to 24*	*25 to 34*	*35 to 49*	*50 & above*	*Total*
MALES							
Bronchitis and Asthma	4.5	0.9	1.2	2.1	6.2	85.1	100.0
Heart Attack	0.4	0.8	2.5	5.8	18.1	72.4	100.0
Tuberculosis of lungs	0.5	3.0	6.3	11.3	28.5	50.5	100.0
Prematurity	100.0	0.0	0.0	0.0	0.0	0.0	100.0
Pneumonia	75.7	5.6	2.4	1.0	2.6	12.6	100.0
Paralysis	0.1	0.8	1.4	1.6	9.6	86.5	100.0
Cancer	0.8	1.8	3.8	6.9	17.7	69.0	100.0
Vehicular Accidents	2.9	8.6	25.3	19.7	25.2	18.3	100.0
Anaemia	37.0	5.4	2.4	4.8	6.8	43.5	100.0
Suicide	0.7	0.9	29.0	26.9	23.3	19.1	100.0

(Contd.)

(Contd.)

Top Ten Causes of Mortality	*Age Intervals*						
	0 to 4	*5 to 14*	*15 to 24*	*25 to 34*	*35 to 49*	*50 & above*	*Total*
FEMALES							
Bronchitis and Asthm	6.8	1.6	2.0	2.1	8.1	79.4	100.0
Prematurity	100.0	0.0	0.0	0.0	0.0	0.0	100.0
Heart Attack	0.1	1.2	6.4	8.9	14.0	69.4	100.0
Pneumonia	78.6	9.0	1.8	2.5	0.9	7.1	100.0
Cancer	0.4	1.3	5.7	7.7	20.9	64.0	100.0
Tuberculosis of lungs	0.7	3.0	10.9	19.0	28.2	38.1	100.0
Non-preg. Anaemia	32.3	7.9	6.6	7.9	7.9	37.4	100.0
Paralysis	0.2	1.7	2.3	4.0	8.9	82.9	100.0
Non-classifiable	35.5	12.0	6.0	7.7	6.2	32.6	100.0
Gastroenteritis	27.7	15.8	10.8	6.9	14.8	24.0	100.0

Source : RGI, 1997.

Table 35. Top Ten Causes of Mortality of Women in the Reproductive Age Group (15-44 Years)

	1981		*1982*		*1983*		*1984*		*1985*		*1986*	
Cause 1	TB of lungs	13.0	TB of lungs	12.5	TB of lungs	12.8	TB of lungs	11.5	TB of lungs	12.8	TB of lungs	11.0
Cause 2	Bronchitis/ asthma	5.7	Typhoid	6.3	Not classified lever	5.1	Not classified fever	5.6	Heart Attack	6.2	Not classified fever	6.9
Cause 3	Typhoid	5.6	Burns	4.2	Heart Attack	4.6	Cancer	5.4	Not classified fever	5.3	Burns	6.3
Cause 4	Non-preg. anaemia	5.2	Not classified fever	4.2	Bronchitis/ asthma	4.5	Non-preg. anaemia	5.2	Cancer	5.1	Heart Attack	5.0
Cause 5	Congestive heart	5.2	Non-preg. Anaemia	4.1	Cancer	4.1	Heart Attack	5.1	Burns	3.5	Cancer	4.9
Cause 6	Gastro-enteritis	3.6	Congestive heart	4.0	Non-preg. anaemia	3.9	Bronchitis/ asthma	4.8	Suicide	3.5	Bronchitis/ asthma	4.0
Cause 7	Burns	3.2	Cancer	4.0	Acute abdomen	3.7	Typhoid	4.4	Acute abdomen	3.5	Suicide	3.5
Cause 8	Bleed. of preg.	3.2	Acute abdomen	3.5	Bleed of preg.	3.5	Burns	3.5	Bronchitis/ asthma	3.3	Non-preg. anaemia	3.5

(Contd.)

(Contd.)

	1981		1982		1983		1984		1985		1986	
Cause 9	Drowning	3.0	Bleed of preg.	3.4	Burns	3.4	Preg. anaemia	3.2	Non-preg. anaemia	3.2	Acute abdomen	3.2
Cause 10	Cancer	2.9	Preg. anaemia	3.3	Typhoid	3.4	Suicide	3.1	Preg. anaemia	3.2	Typhoid	2.8
	TOTAL	50.6	TOTAL	49.7	TOTAL	48.9	TOTAL	51.7	TOTAL	49.7	TOTAL	51.1

Top Ten Causes of Mortality of Women in the Reproductive Age Group (15-44 years) ... Cont.

	1987		1988		1989		1990		1991		1994	
Cause 1	TB of lungs	9.9	TB lungs	11.0	TB of lungs	11.7	TB lungs	9.0	TB lungs	9.9	TB of lungs	9.2
Cause 2	Bronchitis	6.1	Burns	6.6	Burns	6.5	Burns	7.6	Burns	7.9	Suicide	6.8
Cause 3	Heart Attack	6.1	Heart Attack	5.4	Not classified fever	5.2	Suicide	6.4	Suicide	6.0	Heart Attack	6.2
Cause 4	Burns	5.9	Not classified fever	5.2	Suicide	5.2	Heart Attack	4.9	Heart Attack	4.6	Burns	5.8

(Contd.)

(Contd.)

	1987		1988		1989		1990		1991		1994	
Cause 5	Not classified fever	5.9	Cancer	5.1	Cancer	4.7	Cancer	4.8	Cancer	4.2	Cancer	5.7
Cause 6	Cancer	5.1	Non-Preg. Anaemia	4.3	Heart Attack	4.6	Not classified fever	4.7	Congestive heart	4.2	Non-preg. anaemia	4.7
Cause 7	Suicide	4.5	Suicide	3.7	Bronchits/ asthma	4.6	Bronchitis/ asthma	4.0	Acute abdomen	4.0	Bronchitis/ asthma	3.6
Cause 8	Bleed. of preg.	3.7	Bleed. of preg.	3.5	Non-preg. anaemia	4.4	Congestive heart	4.0	Non-preg. anaemia	3.9	Acute abdomen	3.5
Cause 9	Non-preg. abdomen	3.6	Typhiod	3.5	Congestive heart	4.2	Non-preg. abdomen	3.5	Bronchitis fever	3.6	Malaria	3.5
Cause 10	Acute abdomen	3.4	Oth. med. cert.	3.3	Acute abdomen	3.5	Acute abdomen	3.4	Not classified fever	3.6	Snake bite	3.4
	TOTAL	54.4	TOTAL	51.5	TOTAL	54.5	TOTAL	52.5	TOTAL	52.0	TOTAL	52.4

Source : RGI various years quoted by Iyer Aditi in background paper on Leading Causes of Morbidity and Mortality for the National Profile on Women Development and Health.

of development aggravated by the prevailing gender discrimination. Even as preventive and promotive health measures are critical, policies and programmes in all sectors that are conducive to health are vital to enhance the health status of men, women and children". The National Profile on Women's Health and Development emphasizes the need for an holistic approach from the perspectives of various sectoral policies and their impacts on health and the need to mainstream gender and recognize women's reproductive rights by changing societal attitudes and social behaviour.

The National Policy on Empowerment of Women has since been approved by the Government of India (March 2001) which makes specific mention of reviewing all national policies and incorporating specific gender concerns in them. It suggests inclusion of gender concerns as a mandatory provision in new sectoral policies that are yet to be formulated/finalised. Finally, it must be concluded that the issue of health is not merely the concern of the health delivery system but that of the entire society and all sectors of governance.

Table 36. Approach and Objectives for Health in the Five Year Plans

Five Year Plans	*Main Objectives for the Health Sector*
First Five Year Plan 1951-56	- Establishment of Department of Preventive and Social Medicine. - Launching of Primary Health Centres. - Launching of Community Development Programme 1956.
Second Five Year Plan 1956-61	- Nation wide coverage of Primary health centres. - Campaign to eradicate malaria by mid sixties launched. - National Venereal Disease Control Programme launched in 1956.

(Contd.)

(Contd.)

Five Year Plans	*Main Objectives for the Health Sector*
Third Five Year Plan 1961-66	- Designed plans for a self-reliant economy by 1975-76. - The Mudaliar Committee noted that the primary health centre network that had evolved bore no resemblance to that visualized by Bhore Committee. - Primary Health Centres were to be consolidated rather than expanding services especially related to Primary Health Centres. - Family Planning Programme emerged as the focus of planned development, and Clinic approach abandoned in favour of Extension approach for motivating small family norm and for provision of services.
Fourth Five Year Plan 1969-74	- Strengthening of facilities in existing public health units.
Sixth Five Year Plan 1980-85	- Introduction of National Health Policy. - Focus on strengthening, consolidation and operationalisation of the network. - Introduction of National Mental Health Programme in 1982.
Seventh Five Year Plan 1985-90	- National AIDS Control Programme was launched in 1987. - National Diabetes Control Programme was initiated in 1987. - Sought to eliminate poverty by the year 2000; achieve full year employment; satisfaction of basic needs and Health for All.

(Contd.)

(Contd.)

Five Year Plans	*Main Objectives for the Health Sector*
	- envisaged universal immunization of expectant mothers, and all eligible children by 1990. - Family welfare programme was implemented with greater vigour to achieve a couple protection rate of 42% by the end of Seventh Plan period. - 20 point programme was restructured.
Eighth Five Year Plan 1992-97	- Goal was on human development. - National Child Survival and Safe Motherhood Programme was launched in 1992 - Revised National Tuberculosis Control Programme (RNTCP) with DOTS has been introduced since 1993. - Department of ISM&H has also been established in the Ministry of Health and Family Welfare in 1995. - The Reproductive and Child Health Programme launched in October 1997.
Ninth Five Year Plan 1997-2002	- Optimize coverage and quality of health care. This is done by (a) Identifying and rectifying the critical gaps in infrastructure, manpower, equipment, essential diagnostic reagents and drugs; (b) Enhancing the efficiency of the health system.

Source : Planning Commission.

Table 37. Statement Showing Sub-Centres, PHCs and CHCs Required as per 1991 Population and in Position as on 30.06.1997

Sl. No.	State/UTs	Sub-Centres			Primary Health Centres			Community Health Centres		
		R	P	S	R	P	S	R	P	S
1	AP	10242	10568	–	1707	1335	372	427	207	220
2	Arunachal Pr.	220	223	–	37	47	*	9	9	0
3	Assam	4356	5280	*	726	619	107	181	105	76
4	Bihar	15825	14799	1026	2637	2209	428	659	148	511
5	Goa	138	173	–	23	18	5	6	5	1
6	Gujarat	6168	7274	–	1028	960	68	257	186	71
7	Haryana	2482	2299	183	414	397	17	103	64	39
8	Himachal Pr.	973	1980	–	162	260	*	40	42	*
9	J&K	1176	1700	–	196	335	*	49	45	4
10	Karnataka	6431	8093	–	1072	1509	*	268	232	36
11	Kerala	4325	5094	–	721	956	*	1800	80	100

(Contd.)

(Contd.)

Sl. No.	State/UTs	Sub-Centres			Primary Health Centres			Community Health Centres		
		R	P	S	R	P	S	R	P	S
12	MP	12122	11937	185	2020	1376	644	505	190	315
13	Maharashtra	10533	9725	808	1756	1695	61	439	300	139
14	Manipur	344	420	–	57	72	*	14	16	*
15	Meghalaya	464	337	127	77	81	*	19	10	9
16	Mizoram	122	324	–	20	38	*	5	6	*
17	Nagaland	325	244	81	54	33	21	14	5	9
18	Orissa	6374	5927	447	1062	1056	6	265	157	108
19	Punjab	2858	2852	6	476	484	*	119	105	14
20	Rajasthan	7484	9400	–	1247	1616	*	312	261	51
21	Sikkim	85	147	–	14	24	*	4	2	2
22	TN	7424	8681	–	1237	1436	*	309	72	237
23	Tripura	579	537	42	96	56	40	24	11	13

(Contd.)

(Contd.)

Sl. No.	State/UTs	Sub-Centres			Primary Health Centres			Community Health Centres		
		R	P	S	R	P	S	R	P	S
24	UP	22337	20153	2184	3723	3761	–	931	262	669
25	WB	10356	7873	2483	1726	1556	170	431	89	342
26	A&Nicobar	45	96	*	7	17	*	2	4	–
27	Chandigargh	13	12	1	2	–	2	1	1	–
28	D&N Haveli	40	34	6	7	6	1	2	–	2
29	Daman & Diu	12	21	*	2	3	*	1	1	*
30	Delhi	190	42	148	32	8	24	8	–	8
31	Lakshadweep	7	14	*	1	4	*	–	3	*
32	Pondicherry	58	80	*	10	43	*	3	4	*
	All India	134108	136339	7727	22349	22010	1966	5587	2622	2976

(Figures are provisional) R : Required; P: In position; – : Nil; * : Surplus Infrastructure; S : Shortfall.

Source : Rural Health Statistics in India, Directorate General of Health Services M/O HFW.

Table 38. Manpower Requirement in Rural Primary Health Care Institutions

	Category of Manpower	*Requirement for 1996*	*In position as on 30.06.96*	*Number of posts sanctioned 1995*	*Posts needed*
1.	Specialists (4/CHC)	24584	2751	4763	19821
2.	Doctors at PHCs (1/PHC)	24584	26930	32074	0
3.	Block Extension Educator/Health Educator	24584	5621	6287	18297
4.	Pharmacist (l/CHC+l/PHC)	30730	20022	21790	8940
5.	Lab Technician (1/CHC+l/PHC)	30730	9711	12371	18359
6.	X-ray Technician/Radiographer (1/CHC)	6146	1288	1596	4550
7.	Nurse midwife (7/CHC+l/PHC)	67606	12683	16754	50852
8.	Health Assistant (m) (1/PHC)	24584	15745	18323	6261
9,	Health Assistant	24584	18904	21658	2926
10.	Health Worker (m) (1/SC)	147519	62229	71165	76354
11.	Health Worker (FM) (1/SC+l/PHC)	172103	133773	140751	31352
	Total	577754	309657	347532	237712

Table 39. Average Population and Number of Villages Covered by a Trained Dai and a Village Health Guide

State/UT	*Dais Trained since inception of the programme*	*Average covered by a trained Dai*		*VHGs trained since inception*	*Average covered by a Village Health Guide*	
		Population (1991)	*Villages (Number)*		*Population (1991)*	*Villages (Number)*
Andhra Pradesh	38147	127500	0.7	35624	1365	0.7
Arunachal Pradesh	513	1470	7.1	–	–	–
Assam	14229	1400	1.7	20107	991	1.2
Bihar	56029	1339	1.2	11180	6710	6.0
Goa	178	3877	2.0	884	781	0.4
Gujarat	32091	843	0.6	28260	958	0.6
Haryana	13063	950	0.5	10280	1207	0.7
Himachal Pradesh	9811	481	1.7	5591	845	3.0
J & K	4244	1385	1.5	948	6202	6.8
Karnataka	33748	921	0.8	15128	2054	1.8
Kerala	2906	7370	0.5	–	–	–

(Contd.)

(Contd.)

State/UT	Dais Trained since inception of the programme	Average covered by a trained Dai		VHGs trained since inception	Average covered by a Village Health Guide	
		Population (1991)	Villages (Number)		Population (1991)	Villages (Number)
Madhya Pradesh	46037	1104	1.6	37000	1374	1.9
Maharashtra	61010	793	0.7	41983	1153	1.0
Manipur	2162	616	1.0	1695	786	1.3
Meghalaya	2380	607	2.3	2300	628	2.4
Mizoram	1402	265	0.5	815	456	0.9
Nagaland	–	–	–	548	1827	2.2
Orissa	36914	743	1.3	23297	1177	2.0
Punjab	40367	354	0.3	11510	1241	1.1
Rajasthan	30597	1109	1.2	29959	1133	1.3
Sikkim	321	1151	1.4	345	1071	1.3
Tamil Nadu	37226	988	0.4	–	–	–
Tripura	1507	1550	0.6	1931	1209	0.4

(Contd.)

(Contd.)

State/UT	*Dais Trained since inception of the programme*	*Average covered by a trained Dai*		*VHGs trained since inception*	*Average covered by a Village Health Guide*	
		Population (1991)	*Villages (Number)*		*Population (1991)*	*Villages (Number)*
Uttar Pradesh	145271	768	0.8	90111	1237	1.3
West Bengal	39571	1248	1.0	41232	1197	0.9
A&N Islands	221	931	2.3	346	595	1.5
Chandigarh	446	148	0.1	42	1576	0.6
D&N Haveli	235	539	0.3	74	1713	1.0
Daman & Diu	40	1351	0.6	–	–	–
Delhi	317	2994	0.6	127	7473	1.6
Lakshadweep	92	246	0.1	42	538	0.2
Pondicherry	412	706	0.6	270	1077	1.0
All India	651487	965	0.9	411629	1527	1.4

(Figures are provisional).

Source : Bulletin on Rural Health Statistics in India, June, 1997, Rural Health Division, Directorate General of Health Services. Ministry of Health and Family Welfare, Government of India, New Delhi.

Table 40. Family Planning Acceptors by Methods

(Figures in thousands)

Year	*Sterilisation*		*IUD Insertions*	*Equiva- C.C. Users*	*Equivalent Oral Pill Users*	*Total Acceptors*
	Vasectomy	*Tubectomy*				
1970-71	879	451	476	1963	–	3769
1975-76	1438	1230	607	3495	32	6804
1980-81	439	1614	628	3718	91	6490
1985-86	639	4262	3274	9387	1358	18920
1986-87	810	4234	3935	9825	1829	20632
1987-88	754	4186	4356	11342	2064	22702
1988-89	617	4061	4851	12422	2416	24368
1989-90	342	3847	4942	14159	2793	26082
1990-91	255	3871	5370	14735	3125	27356
1991-92	174	3916	4386	13875	3366	25717
1992-93	150	4136	4740	15004	3001	27031
1993-94	150	4347	6017	17283	4302	32099
1994-95	144	4436	6702	17707	4873	33862

Source : Department of Family Welfare, Ministry of Health and Family Welfare

: Programme was introduced in November, 1974

IUD : Intrauterine Device

CC : Conventional Contraceptives

Note : 1. The equivalent CC users is arrived at by dividing the offtake of condoms, diaphragms, Jelly/cream, tubes and foam tables by 72,2,7 (3 in the case of Deflin cream of increased capacity and efficacy, i.e., 100 gms with a dosage of 2.5 ml from the year 1987-88) and 72 respectively required on an average by a couple in a year to give complete protection.

2. Equivalent Oral Pill users is arrived at by dividing the offtake of Oral Pills Packet by 13 which is required on an average by a couple in a year to give complete protection.

Table 41. Government Revenue Expenditure on Health (in Rupees per capita)

Year	*50-1*	*55-6*	*60-1*	*65-6*	*70-1*	*75-6*	*80-1*	*85-6*	*91-2*	*92-3*	*93-4*	*94-5*
Jammu & Kashmir	–	–	2.92	4.90	10.02	13.54	32.84	61.35	122.13	149.77	162.08	152.99
Kerala	–	1.09	2.63	4.45	7.03	14.43	22.43	41.64	75.43	76.86	103.77	122.07
Punjab	0.85	2.10	3.78	6.73	7.26	12.90	23.06	45.55	87.53	93.68	102.09	105.03
Karnataka	0.02	0.75	1.97	2.70	5.44	11.37	16.28	33.81	64.30	76.80	88.49	103.84
Tamil Nadu	–	–	2.47	3.73	6.76	11.42	18.23	36.25	66.82	84.98	95.46	100.75
Rajasthan	–	1.56	2.23	4.04	8.23	9.87	16.61	31.36	61.76	71.30	77.62	92.56
Gujarat	–	–	1.55	3.57	8.01	11.24	18.83	39.35	67.25	69.09	76.01	80.00
Assam	0.76	1.58	2.74	4.55	5.12	7.39	11.69	30.67	49.51	59.37	61.56	79.93
Maharashtra	–	–	2.29	3.50	7.64	11.26	19.94	38.09	65.13	74.15	80.74	77.87
Haryana	–	–	–	–	7.53	11.13	18.43	40.89	56.39	62.49	71.32	76.22
West Bengal	1.41	1.70	2.52	3.72	6.02	12.03	20.08	32.89	55.82	59.85	68.71	71.90
Andhra Pradesh	–	0.60	2.10	3.15	5.96	8.20	16.36	30.36	55.09	60.51	65.06	68.91
Orissa	0.48	0.70	1.48	3.51	4.90	8.15	15.50	25.54	48.48	52.05	66.72	64.40
Madhya Pradesh	0.27	1.56	1.72	2.94	4.73	6.61	13.18	25.37	40.40	48.33	58.14	62.67
Bihar	0.42	1.33	1.41	1.72	2.88	3.96	7.78	15.82	30.69	42.62	49.35	58.51

(Contd.)

(Contd.)

Year	*50-1*	*55-6*	*60-1*	*65-6*	*70-1*	*75-6*	*80-1*	*85-6*	*91-2*	*92-3*	*93-4*	*94-5*
Uttar Pradesh	0.47	0.62	1.00	1.93	3.18	5.50	10.07	29.74	43.76	50.44	50.18	52.02
Sikkim	–	–	–	–	–	17.54	39.37	104.08	227.90	284.44	277.32	324.00
Pondicherry	–	–	–	12.86	23.30	4.46	58.37	119.44	219.12	250.76	286.43	285.36
Arunachal Pradesh	–	–	–	–	–	33.47	66.78	110.55	189.97	235.50	235.81	283.74
Goa, Daman & Diu	–	–	–	15.18	22.69	38.27	49.16	100.74	232.25	254.55	280.01	280.69
Mizoram	–	–	–	–	–	45.49	77.35	151.36	232.15	254.52	276.40	245.22
Himachal Pradesh	–	1.33	–	4.21	11.53	16.71	36.13	69.02	133.94	164.29	197.09	227.24
Nagaland	–	–	–	13.02	34.27	44.20	72.62	158.73	159.22	*	256.35	205.84
Meghalaya	–	–	–	–	10.54	15.99	49.67	80.61	127.08	145.98	185.16	182.78
Tripura	–	–	–	5.47	8.84	12.86	21.56	27.80	96.54	91.30	106.68	92.46
Manipur	–	–	–	4.55	10.18	16.10	37.77	59.20	114.57	122.65	109.68	92.46
All India	0.61	1.27	2.45	3.41	6.11	9.91	17.35	35.52	60.13	70.15	79.44	85.10

Notes : (1) – = Not applicable. (2) 1993-94 are Revised Estimates. (3) 1994-95 are Budget Estimates

Source : Up to 1985-66 Combined Finance & Revenue Accounts. Comptroller and Auditor General of India, respective years. Other years. Demand for Grants, respective states.

CEHAT – Health database

(State arranged in descending order according to expenditure in 1994-95)

Table 42. Women's Health in Five-Year Plans

Plan	*Key Components and Comments*
First Five-Year Plan (1951-56)	Bhore Committee had recommended irreducible minimum of 10 per cent for health outlay. 50 to 60 per cent resources allocated to curative care and medical education.
Second Five-Year Plan (1956-61)	Family Planning Initiated by All India Women's Conference in the interest of women. Family Planning given greater priority than maternal health. "Clinic" approach to family planning. Priority given to child health in MCH. IMR linked to fertility of mother. Maternal health and its link to maternal mortality given low priority than fertility control. At the rate of one mid-wife for 100 births per year, 1,00,000 midwives were required for the estimated 10 million births. Only 55 per cent of the required number of midwives were available.
Third Five-Year Plan (1961-66) and Annual Plans (1966 to 69)	Clinic approach abandoned. Mukherjee Committee Report recommended specific "targets" and "incentives". Extension education approach called the "Reorganised Programme" initiated. Propagation of IUCD of the Reinforced Programme added to the Reorganised Programme at the behest of International organisations. UN Advisory Mission recommended delinking of MCH from family planning. 1967 - MCH integrated with FPP but separated from health. Mudaliar Committee - Health Survey and Planning Committee. Additional FP workers at PHC recommended: 4-6 Auxiliary Nurse 4 Family Planning Health Assistants

(Contd.)

Plan	*Key Components and Comments*
	Block Extension Educator Consolidation of existing PHC. Mobile dispensaries for far flung rural areas. Paediatric and Maternity hospitals in urban areas. Emphasis on professional higher education. Trend of urban bias set in with target oriented FP work, MCH and communicable diseases neglected.
Fourth Five-Year Plan (1969-74)	Set back of IUCD programme because of side effects Thrust on vasectomy Camp approach promoted. First camp pioneered in Kerala. Camp approaches not successful in some places - death of 11 men in Gorakhpur camp. TT and anaemia prophylaxis added to MCH. Intensive District programmes initiated in most populous states. Contraceptive projects introduced in 1967 focusing on female contraception. Enactment of MTP Act, 1971. Failure of contraceptive included as a legitimate indication for MTP. Family Planning Programme overshadowed MCH. Kartar Singh Committee in 1973 recommended integration of family planning with MCFI and multi-purpose workers. MCH and family planning became a responsibility of female MPWs. ICDS initiative to strengthen nutrition and education of mothers.
Fifth Five-Year Plan (1974-78)	Attempt at integration of FPP, MCH, nutrition ser vices and ICDS. Launching of minimum needs programme. Population policy pronounced in 1976. Raise in age of marriage and increased female education to decrease birth rate emphasised Compulsory sterilisation during the 'National "Emergency" in 1976. 1977 - Family planning promoted as voluntary programme.

(Contd.)

Plan	*Key Components and Comments*
	Comprehensive policy covering education, health, MCH and nutrition initiated.
	Srivastava Committee recommended strengthening of rural health service.
	In 1977 also launching of Community Health Workers Scheme with the motto "peoples' health in peoples hands".
	1978 - primary health care, health for all, Alma Ata launched.
	Family Planning, MCH seen as parts of basic health services.
	Community Health Volunteer (CHV), Multi Purpose Workers (MPW).
	Reorientation of Medical Education (ROME)
	Expanded Programme of Immunisation (EPI)
	1979 - Child survival as part of MCH launched.
Sixth Five-Year Plan (1980-85)	Norms for peripheral health services declared.
	PHC 30,000 population
	Subcentre 5000
	Community Health Centre 30 bedded hospital with six basic specialties including obstetrics and gynaecology and paediatrics.
	EPI initiated to decrease IMR and MMR.
	Supplementary feeding under ICDS and anaemia prophylaxis programme initiated.
	1981 - ICMR, ICSSR joint report on "Alternative Strategy for Health for All" presented.
	1981 - Report of working group on population.
	1983 - National Health Policy formulated.
	Selective primary health care under the influence of UNICEF launched.
Seventh Five-Year Plan (1985-92)	Increased investment in FPP programme.
	Child survival emphasised in MCH.
	Poor performance of GOBI-FFF (selective primary health care) admitted.
	Raising health consciousness through education and communication proposed.

(Contd.)

Plan	*Key Components and Comments*
	Besides vertical programme of Malaria, Filaria, Leprosy Blindness control, non-communicable disease introduced.
Eighth Five-Year Plan (1992-97)	1986 - NACO launched with loans from World Bank and US. Structural Adjustment Programme (SAP) formally accepted. Privatisation of medical care. Opening up of public sector in health to private enterprise. Cuts in public sector allocation. Basic minimum facilities to all Health for all strategy to health for underprivileged. Strategy to consolidate and not expand PHC. Strengthening education, equipment, drugs. Poor States unable to raise 50:50 share to obtain central investment for national health programmes. Example: TB, Malaria, etc. Promotion of local accountability to Panchayats. Strengthening of referral system at secondary and tertiary level. Family planning programme resource allocation increased. Promotion of improved social health, nutritional status, female literacy, employment, increased age of marriage recognised. Health policy focussed on promotion of contraception, sterilisation, safe motherhood, and child survival. Unmet needs for spacing and terminal methods of RCH emphasised. 1994 - ICPD country statement called family planning basic need. To increase in choices of contraceptives for women, 'surer" but 'questionably safe' contraceptives introduced. Swaminathan Committee Report promoting removal

(Contd.)

Plan	*Key Components and Comments*
	of targets submitted recommending formation of Population and Development Commission. Merging of health and family welfare ministries. Prioritisation to basic needs: Literacy, Supplementary feeding, Population control given primacy. Legislative steps taken to make birth of more than two children as disqualification. 1995 - Country statement Beijing, GOI, expressed commitment to reproductive health and women's health. 1996 - Draft population policy with modifications and dilution of the positive features of Swaminathan Committee Report accepted by Government.
Ninth Five-Year Plan (1997-2002)	Address inter-regional disparities. Target underprivileged. Place participatory process at the centre of social planning. Improve quality of life and employment. Emphasise food security and basic minimum services. Sectoral planning for population, family welfare, and health. RCH programme to decrease IMR and MMR. Fill gaps in infrastructure and manpower. Increase efficiency of system. Provision of family welfare through private and other sectoral linkages. Health promotion of primary healthcare - particularly rural population and urban slums. Increase outreach for fertility control and focus on fertility control.

Source : National Profile for Women Health and Development, India, 2000.

Status of Tribal Women

The tribal population of India (67.6 million) is larger than that of any other country in the world. In fact, it is almost equal to the tribal population of nineteen countries with substantial tribal population. Mynamar, with a tribal population of 14 million, has the second largest tribal population of India is much more the four times that of Myanmar and more than six times of Mexico (10.9 million) which has the third largest tribal population in the world. The tribal population of India is more than total population of France and Britain and four times that of Australia. If all the tribals of India had lived in one state, it could have been the fifth most populous state after Uttar Pradesh, Bihar, West Bengal ad Maharashtra. Despite the protection given to the tribal population by the Constitution of India, it remains the most backward ethnic group in India, on the three most important indicators of development: health, education and income.

The tribals are more backward not only compared with the General Population, but also compared to the Scheduled Caste, the other acknowledged backward social group with constitutional protection. D'Souza has examined the effects of planned developmental intervention in the tribals from 1961 to 1981. He has concluded that twenty years of intervention has not made any significant impact in improving the conditions of the tribals. In fact, the conditions of tribals in post-independence India has, in many ways, worsened.

The pace of commercial exploitation of the resources of tribal land which accounts for nearly 20 percent of the country's space with 8 percent of its population living on it has assumed a disturbing dimension. The tribal's rights in basic resources such as land, forest and water in fact in the entire environment have been seriously eroded, as non-tribal peasants, traders, businessmen and other categories of aliens have moved into tribal land, with the opening up of tribal areas, and with industrilization. The tribals in India constitute 8.08 percent of the total population. The following are the main demographic characteristics of tribals in India: In some States and Union Territories (UTs) they constitute an overwhelming majority, e.g., Mizoram (94.75%), Lakshadweep (93.154%), Nagaland (87.70%) and Meghalaya (85.53%).

Even though the tribals constitute a majority of the populatio in these States/Uts, they contribute only a small proportion to the total tribal population in India. On the other hand, the States of Madhya Pradesh, Maharashtra, Orissa, Bihar, Gujarat, Rajastan, Andhra Pradesh and West Bengal account for 83 percent of the total tribal population, even though in these States the non-tribals constitute the majority population.

In terms of geographical location, the distribution of tribal population is classified into the following zones:

1) *North-Eastern region*: Comprising Arunachal Pradesh, Assam, Manipur, Meghalaya, Mizoram, Nagaland and Tripura.
2) *Eastern region*: Comprising Bihar, Orissa, Sikkim and West Bengal.
3) *Northern region*: Comprising Himachal Pradesh and Uttar Pradesh
4) *Central region*: Comprising Madhya Pradesh
5) *Western region*: Comprising Dadra and Nagar Haveli, Gujarat, Goa, Daman and Diu, Maharashtra and Rajasthan
6) *Southern region*: Comprising Andhra Pradesh, karnataska, kerala and tamilnadu.
7) *Island region*: Comprising Andaman and Nicobar Islands and Lakshadeep.

The tribals live in forests and mountains somewhat isolated from the general population. Because of this have been called Girijan and Vanvasi. There are four racial/genetic group among the tribal population: the Negroid, the Proto-australoid, the Mongoloid and the Caucasoid.

The tribals are predominantly rural (92.6%). They are overwhelmingly illiterate. The literacy rate of the tribals is 23.63. This is lower than that of the general population (52.21) and is even lower than that of the SC population (30.6), another backward social group with constitutional protection. The literacy rate of the rural tribal female is 12.74 percent, which is lowest of all the social groups.

The tribals are the poorest social group. In 1987-88, 52.6 percent of the tribals were below the poverty line as compared to 44.7 percent of the SCs and 33.4 percent of the general population. The health status of the tribals is lower and inferior compared to that of the general population. Several studies have suggested higher infant mortality rate, higher fertility rate and greater malnourishment. The tribal groups are engaged in various occupations: hunting, shifting cultivation to settled agriculture and rural crafts. A very negligible percent are engaged in non-agricultural activities.

The women in the tribal community, as in other communities,

constitute half of the tribal population. The well-being of the tribal community, as that of any other community, depends importantly on the status of their women. The popular image and perception of the tribal women is that of being better off than their non-tribal counterparts. There is no child marriage, no stigma on widowhood. She enjoys the right to decide about her marriage, etc. Instead of dowry there is bride price indicating high social status of the tribal woman. A tribal woman can divorce and remarry easily. She earns and is, therefore, to a great extent economically independent.

There are many facts which indicates a low status for the tribal woman. For example, she does not have property rights except in a matrilineal society which is a small proportion of the tribal population. She is paid less as wages than her male counterpart for the same work. Several taboos discriminating against tribal women exist in certain tribal groups implying impurity and low status. The tribal women cannot hold the office of a priest. There are taboos related to menstruation as in non-tribal communities. The Kharia women, cannot touch a plough nor can she participate in roofing of a house. The Oraon women is also prevented from touching a plough. The Todas of Nilgiri Hills do not touch a menstruating women for fear of destruction of harvest. In certain tribes only the males can participate in ancestor worship. The Toda and Kota women in southern India cannot cross the threshold of a temple. The Santal women cannot attend communal worship.

Rivers, Dalton and Grigson have reported low status of women among Todas, Kharies and Mariya Gonds with reference to certain taboos during certain periods and ceremonies. Majumdar has reported a higher status of tribal women on some indicators while lower on other, while Shashi has concluded that the status of tribal women varies from tribe to tribe. The development projects have adversely affected the tribal women. With deforestation they have to travel a longer distance to gather forest products. Incidentally this has been one of the reasons for the participation of tribal women in Chipko movement to save the tribal the trees. There are evidences of sexual exploitation of tribal women by forest and mining contractors. The incidence of sexual assualts on tribal women have increased.

The United Nations has declared 1993 as the International Year of the Indigenous Poeples, the Government of India has not signed the ILO Convention 169 of 1989 and has not accepted that the tribals in Indian are the Indigenous Peoples to the tribals of India have been discussed by K.S. Singh and B.K. Roy Burman in *Status of the Tribals in India*. Notwithstanding the political difficulties in the definition of the Indigenous Peoples, there is not doubt that the tribals are among the earliest settlers in India if not the original settlers. The Hindi word Adivasi, literally means the first habitants. The UN International Year of the Indigenous Peoples is an appropriate occasion to review the Status of the Tribals of India and also the Status of the Tribal Women.

The status of any social group is determined importantly by its levels of health-nutrition, literacy-education and employment-income. The tribal women, constitute as in any other social group, about half of the total population. However, the importance of women in the tribal society is more important than in other social groups in India, because of the fact that the tribal women, more than woman in any other social group, works harder and the family economy and management depends on her.

The factors which influence the health status of the tribal population in general, are also applicable to the tribal women, in fact, more so. For example, it has been found that illiteracy, in tribal, as also in non-tribal population, is positively correlated with ill-health. The tribal women, as women in all social groups, are more illiterate than men. The tribal women share, with women of other social groups, problems related to reproductive health.

The low educational status of tribal women is reflected in their lower literacy rate, lower enrolment rate and higher dropouts in the school. The literacy rate of the tribal population as well as Scheduled Castes and general population for three decades (1961-1991) are given in table 43. The following major trends can be seen from Tables 43 and 44:

Table 43. Literacy rates among General, SC and ST population

	General		*Scheduled Caste*		*Scheduled Tribe*	
	1981	1991	1981	1991	1981	1991
Total	36.23	52.21	21.38	30.06	16.35	23.63
Male	46.89	64.13	31.12	40.24	24.52	32.50
Female	24.82	39.29	10.93	19.03	8.04	14.50

- the literacy rate of tribals is lower than that of general as well as SC population.
- the literacy rate of the rural tribal female is the lowest of all groups.
- there is gender bias in the literacy of tribal population as in other groups, the female literacy being lower than the male literacy. Through there has been five-fold increase in the literacy of tribal females it still is much lower than the national average for the females.

Table 44. Literacy Rates Among Scheduled Tribes and General Population, 1961-1991

	1961	*1971*	*1981*	*1991*
Tribal Male	13.04	17.09	24.52	32.50
Tribal Female	2.89	4.58	8.04	14.50
General Male	34.44	39.45	46.89	64.13
General Female	12.90	18.70	24.82	39.29
Rural Tribal Female	2.62	4.06	6.81	12.74
Rural General Female	8.42	13.08	17.96	30.62
Total Tribal	7.99	10.89	16.35	23.63

The relative ratio of girls-tribal and non-tribal-enrolled for every 100 boys is given in Table 45. The data relates to four years: 1965-66, 1970-71, 1975-76, 1980-81). Though the enrolment ratio for girls has been increasing in both the tribal and non-tribal groups, the ratio for tribal girls is much lower than that for non-tribals at all given periods of time in classes I-V as well as classes VI-VIII.

Table 45. Relative Enrolment Ratios of Girls per 100 Boys for Tribals and Non-tribals

Year	*Classes I-V*		*Classes VI-VIII*	
	ST	*Non-ST*	*ST*	*Non-ST*
1965-66	38.6	57.9	27.3	37.3
1970-71	41.2	60.7	31.5	41.6
1975-76	45.9	62.5	37.2	46.2
1980-81	48.7	64.2	38.2	49.9

The drop-out rates for classes I-V,I-VIII and I-X for boys and girls are given for tribal and non-tribal population in Table 46. The drop-out rates for tribals are higher than those for the non-tribals at all three levels of schooling. The drop-out rates for girls are higher than those for boys in tribal as well as general population. The drop-out rate for tribals at the secondary level is as high as 87 percent and for the girls it is almost 90 percent. Consequently, there is a negligible percent (0.06%) of tribal women in institutions of higher education.

Table 46. Drop-out Rates of Girls and Boys for Tribals and Non-tribals, 1988-89

	Total Population			*ST Population*		
	Boys	*Girls*	*Total*	*Boys*	*Girls*	*Total*
Class I-V	46.74	49.69	47.93	61.94	68.73	64.53
Class I-VIII	59.38	68.31	65.40	76.21	81.45	78.08
Class I-X	72.68	79.46	75.36	84.87	89.91	86.72

There are wide variations in the literacy rates of various tribal groups. There are tribes with zero percent literacy and there are tribes with literacy rate as high as 40 percent (Nagas). The female literacy rates also vary from zero percent in some tribes to 33.4 percent in Khasis, Jaintias, etc.

The measures to improve educational status of tribal women are:

- On the basis of data related to education available from various sources, identifying tribal groups for initiating innovative educational programmes at the micro-level.
- Conducting Statewise and district-wise surveys of causes of non-enrolment of girl child in tribal communities in order to achieve the goal of universalisation of elementary education.
- Studying the problems of drop-outs, wastage and stagnation among tribal girls in school.
- Examining occupational mobility among tribal women as a result of modernisation, education and social change.
- Evaluating ongoing integrated tribal development programme in tribal areas under the tribal sub-plans through performance appraisal with reference to:

- improvement in social and economic status of the people,
- health modernity,
- use of science and technology in agricultural/ horticultural production, and
- environmental conservation.

- The role of mass media in educational development of tribals needs to be assessed.

A very large majority of the tribals are engaged in agriculture; their other economic activities being food gathering, pastoral, handicrafts, trade and commerce, and industrial labour. Rarely are they engaged in only one occupation. The employment status of tribal women may be considered in terms of their work participation, agriculture, forests, non-agricultural activities and impact of development programmes.

The work participation rates among tribals are higher than those among Scheduled Caste and general population.

Table 47. Work Participation Rates, 1981

	General	*SC*	*ST*
Male	51.62	52.60	56.66
Female	13.99	18.46	28.18

Through the work participation rate among tribal women has been increasing over a period of time (1997-1991), it is lesser than that for the tribal males, but higher than that for the general female.

Table 48. Work Participation Rates, 1971-1991

	1971		*1981*		*1991*	
	Male	*Female*	*Male*	*Female*	*Male*	*Female*
General	52.6	12.1	51.6	14.0	51.0	16.0
ST	55.0	20.8	56.7	28.2	53.7	30.0

Though the work participation among tribals is greater than among the general population, within the tribals it is again the males who have a higher work participation rate than the females, as in the general population.

Through an overwhelming majority of tribal men (85%) and women (91%) were involved in agriculture, there were more cultivators among tribal males while more tribal women were agricultural labourers. As compared to general females, the tribal females were engaged more as cultivators but less in occupations other than agriculture. The major role that women play in agricultural operations has been discussed by Roy Burman. In the slash and burn cultivation, women join in felling and burning trees, making holes with digging stick, sowing seeds, weeding and harvesting. In plough based cultivation, transportation , weeding, winnowing and dehusking is done entirely by women while harvesting and threshing are done by both men and women. Generally the ploughing is done by men but in some tribal societies, women do the ploughing too.

Minor forest produce forms a major source of income in many tribal communities, specially those having less than five acres of land. Women and children are almost exclusively involved in collection of minor forest produce, its storage, processing and marketing. Increased government control of forests has distributed tribal economy adversely affecting tribals lives, particularly that of women. Appointing of agents from outside for collecting forest produce has not only affected their livelihood, but has also made the work of women more difficult. Collection of fuelwood has become more difficult since it is less accessible and more time-consuming. The result has been less income combined with less fuelwood available for themselves and lesser nutrition. It also leaves them little time for earning wages. Government control over forests has also reduced hunting to a ritual.

Only less than 10% of the tribal women are involved in activities other than agriculture. This is less than half the percentage of females in the general population in similar occupations. This category includes livestock, forestry mining/quarrying, manufacturing/processing/servicing and repairs in household as well as non-household industries, trade/commerce and services.

The impact of development programmes has been different on different sections of tribal women. A small number of tribal women have taken advantage of education, new opportunities for employment and self-fulfilment. In a seri-culture project for tribal women in Udaipur a remarkable change in the quality of life of the tribal women was reported. Besides economic benefits they had more leisure, self-reliance, innovativeness, adaptability and a more aware social outlook.

However, there have been negative effects of development Programmes also, such as:

i) the workload of women has increased,
ii) with modem agricultural implements, unemployment of women has increased and they have been migrating to other areas as labourers,
iii) restrictions regarding exploitation of *forests* has marginalised women,
iv) exploitation of women in various ways:
    - with introduction of Rural Land Ceiling Act, Tribal Land Transfer Act, etc., the non-tribal men often marry tribal women to purchase land from tribal poor to avoid legal complications, or derive financial benefits received from Govt. but deny tribal women their position as wives;
    - lands are taken away by mine owners in the name of development and no land is given in lieu of it nor is any rehabilitation programme sponsored; when vacancies occur, jobs are given to menfolk who are inheritors/owners of land;
    - women are prohibited from working in nationalised mines in evening and night shifts; they are permitted in private mines but these don't employ women to avoid maternity benefits, equal remuneration, rest shelters and creches;
    - indirect retrenchment is done by introducing voluntary retirement programme for women : a woman may retire after 36 years and offer her job to any male member who continues with her Provident Fund number and gets all her PF benefits;
    - tribal women are used for immoral trafficking in collieries and mines and by labour contractors;
    - women labourers (rejas) are exploited socially and sexually. Almost half of them are unmarried and parents don't get them married fearing loss of substantial income. On the other hand, tribal men

prefer to marry non-rejas and even wires are deserted for doing this job.

References

1 Dr. Sarala Gopalan and Dr. Mira Shiva, National Profile on Women, Health and Development, 2000.

2. Registrar General of India (1995), Sample Registration system. Fertility and Mortality Indicators, 1993. New Delhi: Government of India.

3 RGI - SRS Bulletin 1997.

4 National Family Health Survey, (NFHS-2). 1998-99. IIPS, October, 2000.

5. Registrar General of India (1995), Sample Registration system. Fertility and Mortality Indicators. 1993. New Delhi: Government of India.

6. International Institute of Population Studies (1995) National Family Health Survey in India 1992-93. Mumbai : IIPS.

7. Dreze, Jean and Amartya Sen (1995) India, Economic Development and Social Opportunity, Delhi: Oxford University Press.

8. Agnihotri Satish (1996) "Juvenile Sex Ratios in India. A Disaggregated Analysis" in *Economic and Political Weekly*, December 28, 3369-82.

9 · Das Gupta, Monica (1987) "Selective Discrimination against female-Psychiatric Field Study of Culcutta, New Delhi.

10. Dreze. Jean and Amartya Sen (1995) India, Economic Development and Social Opportunity, Delhi: Oxford University Press.

11. National Family Health Survey (NFHS-2), 1998-99.

12. Dr. Sarala Gopalan and Dr. Mira Shiva. National Profile on Women, Health and Development, 2000.

13. Connolly and Nunn 1996 quoted by Iyer Aditi in background paper on Leading Causes of Morbidity and Mortality for the National Profile on Women Development and Health.

14. Dr. Sarala Gopalan and Dr. Mira Shiva, National Profile on Women, Health and Development, 2000.

15. Das Gupta, Monica (1987) "Selective Discrimination against female – Psychiatric Field Study of Calcutta", New Delhi.

16. Gopalan C. (1993). "Child Care in India - Emerging Challenges", Towards Better Nutrition - Probiems and Policies, Nutriton Foundation of India, New Delhi.

17. Mid Term Appraisal of Ninth Five Year Plan (1997-2002), Government of India, Planning Commission, New Delhi

18. Dr. Sarala Gopalan and Dr. Mira Shiva, National Profile on Women, Health and Development, 2000.

19. *Ibid.*
20. National Council of Applied Economic Research (NCAER) (1992), Household survey of Medical Care, New Delhi : NCAER.
21. Madhiwala, Neha, Sunil Nandraj, Roopashri Sinha and Amar Jesani (1998), Household Study of Utilisation and Expenditure on Women's Health. A Study of Nashik District, centre for Inquiry in Health abide Allied Themes (Personnel Communication).
22. *Ibid.*
23. George, Alex Illa Shah and Sunil Nandraj (1997), "Morbidity, Health Care Utilization and Expenditure : Madhya Pradesh 1990-91" in household health Expenditure in Two States. A comparative Study of Districts in Maharashtra and Madhya Pradesh, Pune/Mumbai: Foundation of Research in Community Health.
24. Bang R.A, A.T Bang M.Baitule Y Choudhary, S. Sarmakadam and O. Tale (1989) "High Prevalence of Gynecological Disease in Rural Indian Women" in Lancet (8629) 85-88.
25. BCC, CINI, SEWA Rural and Streehitakarini (Undated), Prevalence of Clinically Detectable Gynaecological Morbidity in India, Results from four Community based Surveys, Unpublished document.
26. Bhatia Jagdish. C. Clelend, John, Bhagvan, Leela and Rao, N.S.N (undated) Prevalence of Gynaecological Morbidity among Indian Women in South India, Unpublished document.
27. Parikh, Indumati, Taskar, Vijayalaxmi, Dharap, Neela, Mulgaonkar, Veena (Undated) Simple Comprehensive Study of Gynaecological Disorders in 15 to 60 or more years of age group of women from slums in Bombay in which Streehitakarini is working with an aim to ensure an on going programme for healthy womanhood, Unpublished Paper.
28. Koening M. Jeieebhoy, Shireen, Singh and Sridhar, S. (1996), Undertaking Community-based Research on Prevalence of Gynaecological Morbidity : Lessons from India, Unpublished document.
29. Bang R.A, A.T Bang. M. Baitule, Y. Choudhary, S. Sarmakadam and O. Tale (1989) "High Prevalence of Gynaecological Disease in Rural Indian Women" in Lancet (8629) 85-88.
30. BCC, CINI, SEWA Rural and Streehitakarini (Undated), Prevalence of Clinically Detectable Gynaecological Morbidity in India, Results from four Community based Surveys, Unpublished document.
31. Bang R.A., A.T. Bang M. Baitule, Y. Choudhary, S. Sarmakadam and O. Tale (1989) "High Prevalence of Gynaecological Disease in Rural Indian Women" in Lancet (8629) 85-88.
32. Bhatia Jagdish, C. Clelend, John, Bhagvan, Leela and Rao, N.S.N (undated) Prevalence of Gynaecological Morbidity among Indian

Women in South India, Unpublished document.

33 Parikh, Indumati, Taskar, Vijayalaxmi, Dharap, Neela, Mulgaonkar, Veena (Undated) Simple Comprehensive Study of Gynaecological Disorders in 15 to 60 or more years of age group of women from slums in Bombay in which Streehitakarini is working with an aim to ensure an ongoing programme for healthy womanhood, Unpublished Paper.

34. Duncan, M.E. (1996) "Pregnancy and Leprosy Neuropathy" in *Indian Journal of Leprosy,* Vol. 68(l): 23-33.

35. RGI, various years, Survey of Causes of Death - Rural, Annual Report 1994, New Delhi : Ministry of Home Affairs.

36. Dr. Sarala Gopalan and Dr. Mira Shiva, National Profile on Women, Health and Development, 2000.

37. (UNIFEM: Stephanie Urdang, 2001; Joshi & Prasada Rao : Changing epidemology of HIV/AIDS in India AIDS Res Review 1999; 2 : 7-9; Mehendale SM HIV infection amongst the persons with high risk behaviour in Pune city. AIDS Res Review 1998: NFHS 1999-2000, Women, Family and drugs: Vivekananda Education Society, 1992).

38. Progress of South Asian Women, 2000, UNIFEM 2000.

39. Women and Substance Abuse: WHO 1993.

40. Background material at the National Conference on Human Rights and HIV/AIDS, Nov. 2000/AIDS, Nov. 2000.

41. Dr. Sarala Gopatan and Dr. Mira Shiva, National Profile on Women, Health and Development, 2000.

42. Government of India, National Population Policy, 2000

43. World Bank (1996): "Development in Practice : Improving Women's Health in India", Washington, World Bank.

44. Madhiwala, Neha, Sunil Nandraj, Roopashri Sinha and Amar Jesani (1998), House Hold Study of Utilisation and Expenditure on Women's Health. A Study of Nashik District, Centre for Inquiry in Health and Allied Themes (Personnel Communication).

45. Dr. Sarala Gopalan and Dr. Mira Shiva, National Profile on Women, Health and Development, 2000.

46. Dr. Sarala Gopalan and Dr. Mira Shiva, National Profile on Women, Health and Development, 2000.

47. *Ibid.*

48. *Ibid.*

49. Dr. Sarala Gopalan and Dr. Mira Shiva, National Profile on Women, Health and Development, 2000.

50. *Ibid.*

51. *lbid.*

52. Dr. Sarala Gopalan and Dr. Mira Shiva, National Profile on Women, Health and Development, 2000.

4

Discrimination Against Women

The Indian Constitution gives equality of status and opportunity to women. Article 14 provides for equality in general and Article 15 (18) prohibits discrimination on special grounds of, *inter alia*, sex, Article 15(3) embodies the exception which permits the state to make special provisions for women. The 73rd and 74th Amendment in the Indian Constitution provides for reservation of seats of women in election to panchayats and municipalities. *Dasi* system has been held to be trafficking by the Supreme Court. Similarly Article 39 (a), (b), (c) and Article 42 and 44 of the Constitution provides provisions for the benefit of women. Article 44 gains importance in achieving the goals of gender justice. Article 15 A (e) in the chapter on fundamental duties makes it obligatory, *inter alia*, to renounce the practices derogatory to the dignity of women. However, the dynamic philosophy of the Constitution has been distilled by stagnant, changing and oppressive parallel regime of laws. Let us now discuss various types of crimes and violence against women which is linked to their disadvantageous position in the society and amounts to violation of human dignity and human rights. The violence can be categorised into sexual and domestic violence.

Sexual violences are the most brutal form of expression against not only the person of a women but against the entire society. Rape is a humiliating and the most shocking of the crimes against human conscience and morality. This crime occupies a significant place in the penal status of every country. The laws, relating to sexual offences do not have adequate provisions for the protection of female victims. Section 375 to 376 (D) of Indian Penal Code deal with the issue of rape. Section 375 defines the statutory offence of rape. It denotes the sexual intercourse with a woman first, against her will, secondly without her consent; thirdly with her consent obtained by putting her in fear of death or hurt; fourthly with her consent when man knows that he is not her husband and if consent is given under her misconception of his identity as her husband; fifthly with her consent when at the time of giving such consent she is under the influence of unsoundness of mind or administration of some substance to make her give consent; sixthly with or without consent when she is under of sixteen years age.

Law Commission

After the 84th report of Law Commission on rape and allied offences were submitted, certain amendments were introduced and section 376 A to 376 D were incorporated in the Indian Penal Code. These changes, include protection of the victim during investigation, change in the definition to remove the element of consent, addition of custodial rape as a crime and increase in the punishment of custodial, gang rape and rape of a pregnant women. In order to give teeth to the provisions of rape, Cr. P.C. and Evidence Act were also modified by the Amendment Act of 1983. When these amendments were introduced it was feared that more stringent punishment would result in fewer convictions but the judgments proved otherwise. The Amendments have not decreased the crime in any way. The devastating, dehumanising and brutal crime continues. However there is need to compensate the victim. In this scenario, the Supreme Court judgment in Delhi Domestic Working Women's forum Vs. Union of India suggesting the formulation of a scheme for awarding compensation to rape victims at the time of convicting a person when found guilty of rape is appreciable. The court suggested the setting up of a Criminal Injuries Compensation Board under Art 38 (1) of the Constitution. Even if, law remains in fact, the number of victims increases destroying the very soul of the helpless female. The concept of marital rape does not exist in our country. There is no time limit for the trial. It is a sad reflection on the attitude of indifference of the society towards violation of human dignity. Contrary to the popular belief rape is almost never perpetrated for sexual gratification.

The derogatory depiction of women in print or electronic media is rampant. The concept of obscenity was based on the 19th century notion which considered anything concerning sex as dirty and obscene. In the existing statutes Sec. 292, 293 and 294 of IPC deal with obscenity. Under these sections, the definition of obscenity was vague and the interpretation depended on the individual judges. As over the years the concept of obscenity has changed from depiction of sex *per se* to sex with crime or violence or sexually humiliating situation, there was thus a need for special enactment against indecent representation which was passed as the Indecent Representation of Women (Prohibition) Act 1986. This Act prohibits indecent representation of women through advertisements or in publications, writings, paintings, figures or in any other manner. Sec. 509 of IPC also deals with intention to insulting the modesty of any women and prescribing punishment for the same. If a man intending to outrage the modesty of a woman exposes his body indirectly to a woman or uses obscene words intending that she should hear them or exhibits to her obscene drawing, he commits this offence.

Sexual harassment at work place has increased with the increase in the number of working women. Each such incident results in the violation of fundamental right of gender equality and right to life and liberty. It is a clear violation of rights under Articles 14, 15 and 21 of the Constitution.

One of the logical consequence of such an incident is also the violation of victims' fundamental rights under article 19(1) (g) to practise any profession or to carry out any occupation, trade or business. The right depends on the availability of safe working environment. Right to life means right to life with dignity. The primary responsibility for ensuring such safety and dignity through suitable legislation and the creation of a mechanism for its enforcement is of the legislature and the executive.

When however the domestic law in the field is absent, there is a need to formulate effective measures and find an alternative mechanism to fill the legislative vacuum. The present civil and penal laws in India do not adequately provide for specific protection of women from sexual harassment in work places and that enactment of such legislation will take considerable time, the Supreme Court held it necessary and expedient for employees in workplaces as well as other responsible persons or institutions, to observe certain guidelines to ensure the prevention of sexual harassment of women.

Sexual Violence

Another noticeable type of sexual violence against women in

our society is incest. Incestuous relationship can be defined as sexual intercourse between two persons who are related closely or are within the prohibited degree of relationship. This prohibited degree of relationship includes full blood, half blood and uterine blood relationship and those by adoption. Although all personal laws prohibit marriage within the prohibited degree, the offence of incest is being committed rampantly within the four walls. Once initiated the incestuous activity continues unabated. This is more so because of the nature of the crime. Being closely related, the victims are forced to continue for fear or social ostracism. Incestuous offences are more heinous and action lies under the Indian Penal Code for rape.

Domestic violence is a term which refers to violence against women especially in matrimonial homes. As this type of violence increased day to day, there were pressures and protests against it. Since the police in a majority of cases refused to register cases, there was a demand for a special act under which the offenders could be punished. Generally complaints can be registered only after an offence has been committed but in a situation of domestic violence, a women needs protection even before the crime is committed as she apprehends danger to her life from the assaulter on whom she is dependent and the threat is constant. To meet this challenge of increasing domestic which highlighted on violence, the Criminal Acts were amended in 1983 and 1986 violence, special categories of offences dealing with cruelty to wives, dowry harassments and dowry death. The first amendment introduced a new section on cruelty to wives under 498-A of IPC.

Dowry Harassment

Although it aimed to deal with dowry harassment and suicide it was wide enough to cover the incidents of domestic violence also because the word dowry as such is not mentioned. It includes physical as well as mental violence or cruelty. The section is an effective deterrent to violent husbands if the judiciary and police interpret and enforce it in the right spirit. Denial of food, insistence on perverse sexual conduct, etc., were held to be examples of domestic violence for registering cases under IPC. Further the law of evidence was also amended to provide presumption in law against husband, his relatives if a married woman commits suicide within seven years of her marriage. The cases of dowry deaths or bride burning or suicide have become a common form of violence experienced by women in India. To curb the evil of dowry both – giving and taking – Dowry Prohibition Act 1961 was passed. In this Act, dowry was defined as any property or valuable security given or agreed to be given directly or indirectly by one party for marriage to other party. The act of giving and taking of dowry or abetting to take dowry became an offence with the punishment prescribed.

The Amending Act of 1986 made the law more stringent and the period for filing complaint was removed and the court was given powers to act *suo moto* or on a complaint by a registered welfare organisation. By the amendment, a new section 304-B on dowry murder was introduced in IPC. The Indian Evidence Act was amended to shift the burden of proof to the husband and his family, where dowry is demanded and the bride dies within seven years of marriage, otherwise than under normal circumstances.

Another act which is violative of human dignity is *sati*. *Sati* is an act of self-immolation by a widow on the pyre of the dead body of her husband. It is manifestation of the barbaric attitude of man in violation of the human rights of a woman. The practice has the social and religious sanctions. Incident of *sati* of Roop Kanwar in Deorala Rajasthan caused furore amongst various sections of the society. This led to widespread protests demanding legislative protection in matters relating to the practice of *sati*. The first legislation against the practice of *sati* was promulgated in 1827. A plea was made to the Privy Council to repeal the same on the religious grounds. The argument was countered on the ground that no freedom of religion could go beyond the claims of humanity and justice. The abetment of *sati* and *sati* itself could be brought under the Indian Penal Code and punished, a need was felt for a separate law to deal with the offence. The Roop Kanwar's incident added fuel to the fire and led to the promulgation of the Rajasthan *sati* (Prevention Ordinance) Act 1987. Ultimately federal legislation, the Commission of *Sati* (Prevention) Act 1987 (Act No. 4 of 1988) providing for stringent punishment including death sentence for abetment of *sati* was passed having application throughout the country. The Act stipulated punishment not just for practice of *sati* but also its glorification. The important component of the Act was establishment of special courts for trying offences under the Act.

Parliament, realising the consequences and implications of

such pre-natal diagnostic techniques and its abuse, passed the Pre-Natal Diagnostics Technique (Regulation and Prevention of Misuse) Act 1994 which came into effect only in 1996. The Act provided for the regulation of pre-natal diagnostic technique and prevent its misuse. It seeks, *inter alia*, to prohibit misuse of pre-natal diagnostic technique for determination of sex, prohibition of advertisements of such techniques for the determination of sex, permission to use such techniques only under certain conditions by registered institutions and prescribing punishment for violation of the provisions of the Act. Inspite of these provisions, causing miscarriage continued and forced the parliament in 1971 to pass an Act known as the Medical Termination of Pregnancy Act. This Act provided for termination of pregnancy in certain circumstances of risk to life of pregnant woman or unborn child by registered medical practitioners. Women thus obtained the right to safe, scientific and legal abortions.

The prostitution and the accompanying evil of traffic in human beings for the purpose of prostitution are incompatible with the basic human dignity and worth of human beings. The Supreme Court in Vishal vs Union of India ((1990) 3 SCC 318), said:

> Prostitution always remains as a running sore in the body of civilisation and destroys all moral values. The causes and evil effects of prostitution maligning the society are so notorious and fightful that none can gainsay it. This malignity is daily and hourly threatening the community at large slowly but steadily making its way onwards learning a back marked with broken hopes. Therefore, the necessity for appropriate and drastic action to eradicate this evil has become apparent.

Realising this bane, the state made efforts to abolish the pernicious system of flesh trade in the larger interest of society. Putting spirit in Art. 23 of the Constitution which prohibits trafficking in human beings Suppression of Immoral Traffic in Women Act, which was later renamed as Immoral Traffic Prevention Act 1986 was passed. This Act realised the fact that prostitution is not confined to females and children only. The purpose of the enactment was to inhibit or abolish commercial traffic in women, men and children for the purpose of prostitution as an organised means of living.

The practice of prostitution in or in the vicinity of certain places such as places of public, religious, educational institutions, hospitals, etc., is made punishable. The Act deals with prostitution not merely as a social problem but a socioeconomic problem. Therefore the provisions of the legislation are more preventive than punitive. The Supreme Court issued directions for the prevention of induction of women in various forms of prostitution. It said that women should be viewed more as victims of adverse socio-economic circumstances rather than as offender in our society.

In India, presently, debates are going on regarding licensing of prostitution. It is demanded by a section of the society that licence be given to sex workers so that various health and safety measures can be imposed. It is sincerely hoped that the Parliament will make suitable changes in the existing law so as to make it more effective for the purpose of eradicating prostitution as a scar on the society. In presenting crime against women, the role of police is very crucial. Police are still governed by the Police Act of 1861 and archaic pre-independence Police Manual. Too much emphasis is laid on the physical training and the sensitisation aspect is totally neglected. The result is that sometimes the protectors of the society or the guardians often become the perpetrators of the crime. The police force needs fundamental changes in concept, attitude and training. The legal requirements sometimes are a stumbling block for the enforcement machinery.

UN Commission

UN Commission on the Status of Women in its 25th report has recommended to all member states the establishment of National Commission or a similar body with a mandate to review, estimate and recommend measures and priorities to ensure equality between men and women and the full integration of women in all spheres of national life. Acting on this resolution and on the demands of several women organisations, the Government of India set up a Committee in 1971 known as the Committee on the Status of Women to evaluate the changes that had taken place in the status of women as a result of the constitutional, legal and administrative measures adopted since independence and to examine the impact or the complex process of social change on various sections of women, and suggest measures to enable women to play their full and proper role in building up the nation. In order to ensure the implementation of various measures, the committee recommended the constitution of a commission at the centre and in the states. It is indeed surprising to note that the government took sixteen years to give effect to the recommendation of the committee for a setting up a National Commission. The Commission has been entrusted to investigate and examine all matters relating to safeguards provided for women under the Constitution and other laws, presentation to the central government annually and at other times reports upon the working of those safeguards. Making recommendations in such reports for the effective implementation of safeguards for improving the conditions of women by the union or any state; reviewing of the existing provisions of the constitution and other laws affecting women and recommending amendments so as to suggest remedial legislative measures to meet any lacunae, inadequacies or shortcomings in such legislations.

It has taken up the cases of violations of constitutional provisions or other laws with the authorities; looking into complaints and taking *suo-moto* notice of matters relating to deprivation of women's rights, non-implementation of laws meant to provide protection to women and also to achieve the objective of equality and development, non-compliance of policy decisions, guidelines or instructions aimed at instigating hardships, ensuring welfare and providing relief to women and taking up issue arising out of such matters with authorities; calling for special studies or investigations into specific problems or situations arising out of discrimination and atrocities against women and identifying the constraints so as to recommend strategies for their removal. It has also undertaken promotional research; participating and advising on the planning process of socioeconomic development of women; evaluating the progress of the development of women under union and state; inspecting jails, remand homes, women's institutions or other places of custody of women; funding litigation involving issues affecting a large body of women; and making periodical reports to the government. It is very important that some legal assistance is given to women in need who went to have redress of their rights through court of law but their financial position does not permit them. In this context it is necessary to study the concept of legal aid.

The Legal Services Authorities Act is one of the most

important pieces of social legislation that the Indian Parliament adopted on the 40th anniversary year of Indian Independence. The government both at the centre and in the states instituted expert committees on legal aid to make recommendation for evolving proper schemes and policies for legal services, delivery to the women and poor among them. The report of the expert committee on legal aid titled "Processual Justice to the People" submitted to the Union Government in May 1973 provided the foundational guidelines for development of approaches, strategies and programmes in the matter of legal aid. In 1977 through the Constitution (Fortysecond Amendment Act) Parliament inserted Article 39-A as a directive principle of state policy which reads:

> Equal justice and free legal aid. The state shall secure that the operation of the legal system promotes justice, on the basis of equal opportunity . . . provide free legal aid . . . to ensure that opportunities for securing justice are not denied to any citizen by reason of economic or other disabilities.

Through a series of judicial decisions the Supreme Court amplified the nature and scope of legal aid to the poor and finally interpreted it a fundamental right which the state is constitutionally obliged to provide for any poor accused in criminal proceedings. Further, the court evolved the strategy of public interest litigation and allowed third parties to seek grievances on behalf of different classes of the poor. The Supreme Court and the High Courts even set aside technical rules of procedure, allowed invoking the judicial process through letters and telegrams, resorted to the Commission system for gathering facts and evidence on matters of public interest and issued directions in the nature of affirmative action dispensing meaningful social justice to the poor and the needy. This silent revolution in the judicial process brought about the activist judges, public spirited lawyers, journalists, teachers and social workers to a new poverty jurisprudence.

Article 21 of the Constitution has no meaning to her. Thus, where a wife leaves her husband on account of his ill-treatment, cruelty and violence and goes to her parents' home, the husbands have forcibly taken her away and law's arm has failed to provide protection to such women. We would proceed to look into the new laws passed for according protection to her. A new offence, the offence of cruelty to wife by her husband and in-laws have been created by inserting a new chapter—Chapter XX-A, and a new section-Section 498-A-in the Indian Penal Code. The section defines cruelty thus:

- Cruelty to married woman includes wilful conduct which may drive the wife to commit suicide or an attempt to commit suicide or may cause her injury or danger to her life, limb or health.
- Cruelty is defined to include such harassments of the wives which may coerce her or her parents or relations to meet any unlawful demands of dowry by her husband and in-laws.

Dowry Prohibition Act, 1961, a demand made for dowry is a dowry offence. According to probably it will be an offence even if the dowry is demanded after the marriage. Section 498-A of the Indian Penal Code specifically deals with a situation when coercion is exercised for demanding dowry by the husband or in-laws of the married woman after the marriage. The period during which this harassment of the married woman and her relations with a view to coercing her or her relations to meet any unlawful demand for dowry can be made extends to the first seven years of marriage.

A wilful conduct of the husband or her in-laws of such a nature as is likely to drive the woman to commit suicide or cause grave physical or mental injury to her, and harassment of a woman by her husband or by any relative of her husband with a view to coercing her or any of her relatives to meet any unlawful demand for property amount to cruelty under the section and is punishable as such. Probably the provision will not work, if left here and if the offence is not made cognisable. It has been made cognisable under certain circumstances.

Let us take the case of protection of a married woman against cruelty. The mother of the bride met the demand of dowry amounting to Rs. 30,000 by selling her property. But the lust for dowry remained insatiable. The wife and her mother were harassed endlessly, treated with cruelty and were tortured both physically and mentally. When the cup was full and the wife's suffering became intolerable, she filed the complaint bringing the case under Section 498-A, IPC leading to the chargesheeting of the husband. Since the husband challenged the constitutional validity of Section

498-A, the High Court held that the Section 498-A was valid and remanded the case for trial.

The cruelty as criminal offence means such harassment of the wife which may coerce her or her parents or relations to meet any unlawful demand for dowry made by the husband or her in-laws. The criminal offence of cruelty can lead to the punishment of the husband and in-laws to jail term which may extend to three years and a fine may also be imposed.

Dowry Deaths

During the 1990s, we have seen a growing number of murders of married women, variously called dowry murders or bride burnings. The burning of wives is neither an extension of nor culturally related to the notorious practice of *sati*, the voluntary immolation of Bengali widows on the funeral pyres of their husbands. The resonances are startling—the burning of women, the thin line between suicide and murder—but the differences are significant because they point to a serious further devaluation of women in present-day India in spite of a century of progressive legislation on women's rights. Sati was socially countenanced suicide because the widow was perceived as having failed in her ritual duties to ensure the longevity of her husband by using her special female power or shakti; bride burning, however, is murder and equally culpable by social and legal standards. The method of dying or killing, i.e., the immolation of women in both cases, is also a false parallel.

The rituals that are prescribed for *Sati* are adequately described elsewhere; suffice it to say that it was public act that generated social awe, status, religious merit, and even material gain for the woman's kin. Burning a wife is perhaps more appalling than the less sensational ways of getting rid of her by poisoning, drowning, strangling, shooting, or bludgeoning. It is chosen chiefly for the forensic advantage it has over the others. It virtually destroys the evidence of murder along with the victim and can easily be made to look like an accident. It is also relatively simple to commit. It occurs in the kitchen, where the lower middle-class housewife spends a large amount of time each day. Pressurized kerosene stoves are in common use in such homes; a tin of fuel is always kept in reserve. This can be quickly poured over the intended victim and a lighted match will do the rest. It is easy to pass off the event as an accident because these stoves are prone to explode, and the now ubiquitous but highly inflammable nylon sari easily catches fire and engulfs the wearer in flames. Signs of a struggle simply do not show up on bodies with 90 or more per cent third-degree burns. The bereaved widower, who has equipped himself with a cast-iron alibi, is soon in the marriage market again looking for a new bride with perhaps a more handsome dowry. Often it is the mother-in-law, with or without her son as accomplice, who will obligingly commit the murder.

Dowry serves as the foundation on which explanation for discrimination against women have been built; it has the conceptual richness to satisfy a variety of analytical tastes over time. The colonialists stressed its cultural roots in a benighted Hinduism; Marxists see it as an economic institution, feminists view it as gender discrimination for daughters did not traditionally inherit land. Today, the dowry system is seen as the prime motive for two other crimes akin to infanticide widely prevalent in the subcontinent. Female infant neglect was reflected in the worst adverse female to male sex ratios in the world today, and the abortion of female foetuses made possible by the abuse of recent advances in foetal diagnostic technology. Until recently, billboard advertisements in Bombay, for instance, made an unabashed appeal to pregnant women to take the expensive and some what risky amniocentesis test. It importuned them to spend Rs. 500 now on the test in order to save Rs. 50,000 in the future on a daughter's dowry. The cause of bride-burnings or dowry death in India was, indeed, dowry and indubitably a cultural problem. This alleged fact has found wide support expressed in both detailed historical and anthropological analyses of female infanticide, the oldest and most widespread form of murder believed to be related, even in other cultures, to the practice of dowry. Dowry, an integral part of Hindu high caste culture, appeared to be a timeless and pernicious custom that constructs women as a financial liability to their natal homes as infants and in their marital homes as brides. Its ban, by an act of the Indian Parliament in 1961, seems only to have entrenched the custom deeper. There were glaring contradictions in the explanations.

Culture was blamed on the one hand, but so were westernisation, which brought in gross materialism, greed, and a desire for consumer goods and modernisation, which put a cash value on everything and commercialised human relationships. Here was the puzzle: Was this violence against women related to the ancient custom of dowry or was it a product of acculturation to western and modern culture? But why then in the west, where dowries were once common, had the practice all but disappeared? Clearly culture does change; what made the culture of dowry gradually disappear in the west and change for the worse in India? When examining the evidence, particularly the colonial evidence on infanticide, the explanation that had hoped only to deepen and endorse began to unravel. Statistical evidence on sex ratios in the subcontinent point to a serious anomaly in the logic that underpinned the colonial verdict on the dowry system and made their figures suspect.

On close inspection a startling fact emerged. Several families from Hindu lower castes and religions, such as Islam and Sikhism, which did not follow the practice of dowry and even received bride price (bride price is paid in cash and/or gods to the bride's family by the groom's family), were found guilty of committing infanticide, so it was awkward to insist on either dowry or upper caste pride (as pronounced in the case of Rajputs [powerful landowning and ruling castes in North India]) to be the cultural justification of so heinous a crime. The convenient lie of branding dowry as the motivating culprit or finding barbaric practices particularly among the upper caste Hindus, was begun by colonial bureaucrats in the mid-nineteenth century.

Parliamentary inquires about the improverishment of the India peasantry had to be answered satisfactorily. It was expedient to lay the blame on culturally sanctioned "improvidence" and wasteful ceremonies and rituals, chiefly marriage celebrations and dowry, than to reverse the colonial land revenue policies that had uprooted the old system and transformed the basic relationship between peasants and their land. These official documents generated by colonial bureaucrats are laced with information that flatly contradicts their own assertions, and the net result was that the one clear fact about the nature of this timeless custom of dowry dissolved into a murky half-truth. The politics of the process of describing and attributing meaning to the cultures of the colonised became more important to understand than their unhappy social consequences.

Dowry in its menacing form for some women, as we know it today, was patiently the artifact not of an organically unchangeable and permanently constituted Hindu or Sikh culture but of acculturation in colonial time and space. This change, fortunately, did not occur evenly across castes and classes, and today, the majority of Hindu families practice what might be seen as a precolonial form of dowry. It is this process of change—sporadic, uneven, and regrettably irreversible—that this study endeavours to reconstruct from the very documents that claim otherwise.

After a careful rereading of colonial sources, dowry could be called on of the few indigenous feminist institutions in an overwhelmingly patriarchal and agrarian society. In the late nineteenth and early twentieth century, dowry was not the enemy but rather an ally of women, acting as an economic safety net in a setting where women always married outside their natal villages (village exogamy is still almost mandatory) and where they did not normally inherit land.

The dowry was the only independent material resource over which women had partial, if not total, control. It was viewed by a woman's natal family not only as a matter of pride but also as a means of securing for her the best possible match, while providing her with recourse in an emergency.

Dowry can be reckoned not only as the index of the appreciation bestowed upon daughters in their natal villages and the measure of their status in their conjugal villages, but the practical concern of familiar to unsecure for their daughters a husband from a comparable family in which her children would be raised.

How then did such a strongly spun safety net twist into a deadly noose? The time span studied covers the mid-nineteenth century to the present. The place is the Punjab, in the north-western part of the subcontinent, a varying and often partitioned space. In 1851, the Sikh Bedis were found guilty of female infanticide. This discovery became political capital for the British and justified their two unsanctioned bitter and bloody wars against the Sikh ruler of the Punjab, Maharaja Ranjit Singh, that led to the annexation of the Punjab only two years earlier.

The righteousness of British aggression was further underscored, in their own estimation, by the fact that Guru Nanak, the founder of the Sikh religion in the fifteenth century, was of the Bedi caste. The present-day Indian states of Punjab and Haryana (which was part of the Indian Punjab until 1966) continue to have the most adverse female to male ratios, or 879 and 870 per 1,000 males respectively in the 1981 census.

Female Infanticide

Female infanticide is treated as an aberration of the past because the British government set up a department to deal with it in 1870 and closed the department in 1906, claiming total success in their campaign to suppress the practice and make the Punjabis less improvident about dowries. They were wrong on both counts: Sex ratios have steadily worsened nationwide in the twentieth century. In 1901, there were 972 females for every 1,000 males, while in 1971 and 1991, the ratios have declined to 930 and 920 females per 1,000 males respectively.

The practice of killing female infants may have become less prevalent, but it was substituted by the less detectable practice of medical or nutritional neglect that achieved the same end more slowly. It was the current sex ratio in India and comparable ratios in Pakistan and Bangladesh that aroused my suspicion that female child mortality has little to do with dowry or Hindu culture, since the partition of the subcontinent had been on religious lines and removed Hindus from west Punjab and East Bengal in 1947.

Since dowries do not figure prominently in Muslim culture, why were the sex ratios not all that much better in these two Muslim nations? This suspicion began the quest for a new culprit and the reappraisal of this intriguing cultural whodunit. The rest of the investigation was not startling. Female infanticide was found among all castes and classes of people and the rationale for it was to have a planned family with the right number of children of the two sexes, in a convenient birth order. The bias in favour of boys was also universal, whether Hindu or Muslim or Sikh, and whether urban or rural.

By a careful rereading of colonial records not only on infanticide but also on variety of seemingly unrelated matters, such as land revenue, peasant indebtedness and foreclosures of agricultural property, it is possible to establish that the meaning of dowry changed drastically in the colonial period in qualitative and quantitative terms and that is stewed gender inequalities further.

The British charge of "improvidence" was not based on the expense for dowry but on wedding celebrations. These latter costs were strictly itemised and evaluated in cash for three economic tiers in society and became part of the bureaucrats' handbook for enforcement. Wedding expenses did not mean only a daughter's wedding expenses; many cases cited as evidence of prolificacy in the handbooks of reference to the weddings of sons. Yet the concerts about the escalating pressures of enhanced dowry in the late nineteenth and the twentieth centuries suggest that changes in this period affected the nature of this institution. The upward spiral in costs continued; cash and anever-increasing range of consumer goods that became available in the Punjab as imports from Europe made the increase especially steep.

Demands for Cash

Demands for cash at the time of betrothal, lavish feasting and entertainment of the wedding guests, gifts for the family of the groom, expenses for the celebration of annual fasts and festivals, and the birth of children and their naming and tonsure ceremonies changed in time the nature of the daughter-parent bond. This trend has steadily aggravated in the post-colonial period and in its extreme form it has been the cause for violence against women and, more recently, the burning to death of wives who brought inadequate dowries. What we are dealing with is not just a dowry problem but a pathology or a syndrome rooted in history and gender inequality in a patriarchal society. Colonialism and patriarchal values became meshed in an alliance against women, even when the avowed purpose of legislative reform in this period was to uplift the status of women in Indian society.

Since the issue of violence against women is not merely an academic puzzle, but a matter of life and death, a re-examination of contemporary evidence in the light of history and feminist theory is urgently warranted. In other words, although dowry is the centrepiece of this study, it cannot help but illumine the pervasive commercialisation of social relations in general and the central event in women's lives—marriage—in particular. This will help in assessing the loss of women's economic power and social appreciation even as they gained in legal and political rights through the process of changes unleashed in this period.

This complex interaction of local customs, such as dowry and colonialism has hardly been suspected to exist, let alone been adequately analysed. The widely accepted denunciation of dowry undergirds a host of corollaries that have blurred the thinking on the triangular relationship among marriage, gender, and property, which needs to be discussed in some detail.

Did colonial policies often create, or aggravate, the very problems they sought to ameliorate? "Social evils" was the common designation for Indian customs such as *sati* and *thuggee* (the practice of thugs, a criminal caste), "discovered" by the East India Company collectors and magistrates and described as part of the exotic and "barbaric" culture they encountered. Systematic legal and police measures were taken to eradicate these practices. It was in this context that Indian women and their status in Hindu society became a central preoccupation of the colonial powers.Were the social evils, such as accelerating chronic indebtedness, increasing drunkenness, and improvidence in the Punjabi countryside, the unwitting consequence of rules and regulations of the new regime rather than the consequences of Hindu or Muslim culture? What influence did the colonial codification of customary law (*rivaj-i-am*) and its implementation in the new colonial courts in the Punjab have on various customs, particularly on the definition of the rights of women and the notions of *dahej* (dowry) and *stridhan* (women's wealth)? These questions are explored in detail in the larger study to plumb the depths of social change and disruption under British rule. Now we have to explain the politics of two key terms, culture and colonialism and their interrelationship on which the arguments rest. Neither represents a permanently constituted entity; both are continually contested and negotiated sets of power relations, and history has constructed their meanings. Moreover, native and culture and British colonialism were in dynamic relationship with each other and not without mutual, albeit unequal, effect on each other.

It would be as narrow-minded to construe Hindu culture or tradition as a timeless, frozen entity as it would to think of the more than 250 years of British rule in India as a fully imagined and executed vision that can be called British colonialism. Both continually changed in the process of interaction and acculturation. Colonialism in mid-nineteenth century Punjab could not be mistaken for the colonialism that Bengal experienced when it was first overtaken in 1757; differing strategies produced different results in the two places. Colonial investment in the Punjab, although accomplished at little cost to the British, greatly expanded agriculture production. By building canals, communications and railway lines, this ultrafertile grain-producing region was linked to a thriving international market. The British extracted wealth from the countryside through heavy taxation and exports of wheat and other raw materials to Europe. Although this development was self-interested, it brought prosperity to this region along with enormous changes in the peasant's way of life. There was also an intensified colonial interest in understanding, describing, and ultimately reforming the varieties of cultures encountered among the subjugated people; this interest was not academic or philanthropic but political. The stubborn tendency to interpret indigenous culture as an organic entity with immutable values, symbols and belief systems was plainly self-serving. That the culture of the colonialists was dynamic and ever-changing and Indian culture was static, timeless and inflexible were representations enable bureaucrats to devise means of social control in addition to political and economic domination. It was colonialism's professed mission to improve civilise, and regenerate Indian society, but this could be done only after the serious flaws in the culture were located.

In the Punjab, for example, bride price and dowry simply exist and it is therefore untenable to argue that women's work in the fields alone determines the mode of marriage payments. Briefly, what happened under colonial rule to the Punjab countryside is recorded in a succession of revenue settlement reports. The British had pioneered the permanent settlement in Bengal presidency in 1793; its revolutionary feature was that it transformed land, in which all classes and castes of people had varying rights and shared unequally in its produce, into private property that could be bought, sold, or mortgaged. This created (very crudely and quickly) a class of zamindars with immense holdings on the one hand and landless peasants on the other. This is because the revenue payments were fixed in perpetuity and due on a certain fixed date every quarter. These amounts and dates had little sensitivity to seasonal variations in the quantity of produce or to delayed harvest times, both of which depended on the caprice of the weather.

In a bad year, there would be no recourse but to mortgage or sell the land to meet government demand, which was set at a higher, more "efficient" level than the past rulers had deemed fair. This created absentee landlords, for traders and moneylenders from Calcutta could now buy this land in government-sponsored auctions or foreclosures of mortgaged land. An army of landless peasants roamed the countryside for food, shelter and wage labour. The economic and social havoc this caused in Bengal has been adequately dealt with in the works of a large number of historians and economists. With land as collateral and with prices of land rising, the peasant was able to borrow far more than he could ever before: up to 70 per cent of the value of his land. He borrowed either in a bad year or in a year when the harvest was late, chiefly to pay his taxes on time. Chronic indebtedness became the other side of the coin of prosperity for the vast majority of these small peasant proprietors. The figures on foreclosures on the lands of the people who were not seen as the best cultivators, namely, Rajputs, and of the self-exploiting Jat, tell a painful story. Interests rates went up from an already high level around 18 to 24 per cent to an exorbitant 24 to 40 per cent range, with various other tricks and deceits built into the loans secured with land titles to hoodwink the illiterate peasant. Prices of land went up too, particularly as monetisation of the economy moved along apace with the building of canals, roads, railways and market facilities, and the price of grain increased as exports rose. Apart from the colonial government, the grain merchant and the money lender, not the peasant, were the most direct beneficiaries of this trend.

The dowry became a prize for men as much as their inherited rights in land had been. If anything, a dowry was the more versatile in a situation where land was barren. The other unfortunate effect of the canal was the spread of water- and vermin-borne diseases, such as malaria and typhoid, that claimed dark colonial plot—just tragic and unintended ecological disasters that undermined the ability of the peasants to pay their fixed dues. So, indebtedness and poverty grew in the midst of the new prosperity. This quiet desperation built pressure to exploit customary ways of obtaining cash or gold or silver to buy land elsewhere, or to replenish a herd—and dowry was a logical place to look. The will to obtain larger dowries from the families of daughters-in-law, to demand more in cash, gold, and other liquid assets, becomes vivid after leafing through pages of official reports that dutifully record the effects of indebtedness, foreclosures, barren plots, and cattle dying for lack of fodder.

The next thing the peasant would need was a further loan to marry off his pubescent daughter because the profits of the harvest were now pledged to the moneylender. What this spiral of events boils down to is that a daughter's marriage, which customarily could not wait too long past her puberty, became the last straw that broke the camel's back. A son's wedding cost as much as a daughter's wedding (and this is true even today in Punjabi urban and rural families), but a son's wedding could be postponed. While funeral expenses could be trimmed, wedding expenses that could be borne by the bride's family steadily climbed because of reasons that will emerge presently. The crucial fact, however, was that neither daughter's weddings nor funerals could wait; other ritual events could be postponed, particularly the son's betrothal or wedding day. So it was not the cost of the wedding but the constraints of time that made a daughter's wedding an exploitable condition in early colonial times. A daughter's wedding, therefore, necessitated a loan more often than a son's; and a possible demand for a bigger dowry from her in-laws would occasion an even bigger loan. In desegregating a farmer's debt, the amounts that pertained to a daughter's dowry were seen as inexcusable improvidence. This kind of circumstantial evidence against dowry finally indicated it as the killer. The British increasingly understood the devastating ramifications of their own revenue policies but they preferred to blame the culturally based dowry system, rather than their own rational reconstruction of the landholding and revenue system. The notoriety about dowries quickly gained currency, and women were the losers in both natal and affinal families. It can be asserted with confidence, because a plethora of evidence dots the journals, reports and other accounts of British officers, that in the colonial period the cost of a daughter's wedding went up as a result not just of higher tax levels but of other policy decisions as well.

The First Schedule to the Code of Criminal Procedure, 1973, the offence of "dowry death" has been made cognisable, non-bailable and triable by the Court of Sessions. The Supreme Court had dwelt on the subject in some decisions and had clarified the law, where death of a married woman was caused by burns. Dowry deaths occur not only when the husband or in-laws put the bride to death, but also when she is made to die by abetment to commit suicide. Everytime a case relating, to dowry death comes up, it causes ripples in the pool of the, conscience of this court. Nothing could be more barbarous, nothing could be more heinous than this sort of crime. The root cause for killing young bride, or daughter-in-law is avarice and greed. All tender feelings which alone make the humanity noble disappear from tire heart. Kindness which is the hallmark of human culture is buried. Sympathy to the fairer sex, the minimum sympathy is not even shown.

The seedling which is uprooted from its original soil and is to be planted in another soil to grow and bear fruits is crushed. In the case of bride burning, soon after marriage, the young bride was harassed by her husband and mother-in-law for not bringing dowry and ultimately she was put to death by burning; the defence was that it was a case of suicide and murder. The trial court acquitted both the accused. But on appeal to both the High Court and Supreme Court, an appreciation of evidence found both the accused guilty of murder.

Indian Penal Code

The Indian Penal Code will be cognisable if information relating to the commission of the offence is given to the officer in charge of a police station by the victim of the offence or a relative of the victim of the offence or, in the absence of any such relative, by any public servant authorised in this behalf by the state government. It is further provided that no court shall take cognisance of the offence except upon a police report of a complaint made by the victim of the offence or by her father, mother, brother, sister or her father's mother's brother or sister or with the leave of the court by any other person related to her by her blood, marriage or adoption. This has been achieved by inserting a new sub-section (3) to Section 174, Code of Criminal Procedure. Section 174 of the Code of Criminal Procedure already contains a provision which empowers a magistrate to make an inquiry into the cases of suspicious deaths. The new sub-section empowers the magistrate to hold such all inquiry when a woman dies while living with her husband and her in-laws or other relations of the husband during the first seven years of her marriage. That sub-section lays down the following:

- the case involves suicide by a woman within seven years of their marriage; or
- the case relates to the death of a woman within seven years of her marriage in any circumstances raising a reasonable suspicion that some other person committed an offence in relation to such woman; or
- the case relates to the death of a woman within-seven years of her marriage and any relative of the women has made a request in this behalf; or
- there is any doubt regarding the cause of death; or
- the police officer for any other reason considers if expedient to do so.

Under the new provision a similar suspicion arises when a married woman dies while living with her husband or in-laws during the first seven years of her marriage. "This is a warning to the husband and in-laws that the newly wedded wives coming to live with them for the first time is a sacred trust. If they violate the confidence reposed in them by the parents of the wives then their conduct would be judged by the same standard as the conduct of the police is judged in respect of person police custody. In both these cases the person in custody is under the overall powers of the custodians and it such a person dies in such custody then a suspicion arises that the custodian must have ill-treated her and this must have led her to commit suicide or the custodian must have murdered her." The new Section 198-A of the Code of the Criminal Procedure lays down that no court shall take cognisance of an offence punishable under Section 498-A of the Indian Penal Code except upon a police report of facts which constitute such offence or upon a complaint made by the person aggrieved by the offence or by her father, mother, brother sister or by her father's or mother's brother or sister or with the leave of the court, by any other person related to her by marriage, blood or adoption. Then the offence under Section 498-A of the Indian Penal Code is made non-bailable, and, as we have seen earlier, it is cognisable only it the information is lodged with the police of the commission of such offence by a relation of a deceased woman, or by a public servant authorised in this behalf. During the course of investigation, she was found to have poured kerosene on her and ignited it. She also admitted that her elder son might have burned the wife to death.

The investigation in this case did not proceed as it ought to and there appears to be soft-pedalling of the whole case. During investigation the appellant herself stated that her son Madan might have burnt Pushpa. He is the elder brother of Jagadish. Madan was seen by the neighbours behind the kitchen and running down the stairs at the time when Pushpa was in flames inside.

The police, however, did not prosecute him. Jagadish, the husband of Pushpa, appears to have no human qualities. He was a silent spectator for all the dastardly attack on his wife. He had not even the courtesy to take his wife to the hospital. He did not make arrangements for securing blood when Pushpa was struggling for life. He positively dissociated himself as if he had nothing to do with her. His tacit understanding with those who perpetrated the crime is so apparent that it could not be ignored. Yet he was not chargesheeted. This indifferent attitude of the investigating agency should be deprecated. Similarly, in Joint Women's Programme v. State of Rajasthan, the Supreme Court found the investigation made by the police in a dowry death case was totally inadequate. The Code of 1973 also amends the Indian Evidence Act by inserting a new Section 13-A. That section lays down, "When the question is whether the commission of suicide by a woman had been abetted by her husband or any relative of her husband, obviously, cruelty has to be looked as it is defined under Section 398-A Indian Penal Code. This provision is a meant to solve the problem of proof. It has been found to be one of the most difficult things to establish that it is the husband or his relations to who have abetted her to commit suicide. To raise the presumption under Section, 113-A of the Evidence Act the following two conditions should be satisfied:

— It must be shown that the married woman committed suicide within a period of seven years from the date of her marriage, and
— It must also be established that her husband or other relations of the husband subjected her to cruelty.

The word "cruelty" is to be under Section 498 given the meaning that has been given to it under Section 498-A, Indian Penal Code and not under the matrimonial law. The acts of cruelty by the husband or her in-laws should be such that the married woman was driven to commit suicide or inflict on herself grave injury or his or their acts or conduct caused injury or danger to her life, limb or health. Any demand of dowry by the husband or his relations would also amount to cruelty. Let us hope that these measurers would go a long way in solving the problem of battered wives of' cruelty to married woman. But to this author these measures appear to be no more than "first aid", what this malady needs is "intensive care" which these measures do not provide. Many a time culprits in dowry offences including dowry-death escape punishment because of non-availability of evidence beyond reasonable doubt.

A dowry death case in the trial court acquitted the accused mother-in-law as it considered the evidence before it not sufficient for conviction. The High Court, on the other hand, found the evidence sufficient to convict the accused. The Supreme Court agreed with the appreciation or the evidence by the High Court. The doctor who treated the young daughter-in-law clearly deposed that the latter had told him categorically that it was the mother-in-law who poured kerosene on her. The trial court said that since it did not fall in the category of dying declaration it was not sufficient to convict the accused, despite the fact that there was corroborative evidence. The Supreme Court said that Dr. Goel who received Pushpa (wife) and admitted her in the emergency ward had testified that neighbours brought Pushpa and no relative accompanied her. He had stated that Pushpa was in a serious condition. He deposed that upon his questioning, Pushpa told him that her mother-in-law had burnt her. It was true that Dr. Goel had not recorded this statement in the medical register but that was no ground to disbelieve him. Dr. Goel was a disinterested person. The High Court had accepted his version and there was no reason to reject it. Dr. Goel himself had treated the victim. Therefore, there was no question of finding out from the doctor whether Pushpa was in a position to give her statement or not. Moreover, the statement before the doctor was not recorded as a dying declaration. It was a communication by the patient to the doctor who treated her. He was a government doctor on duty in the hospital at that time. Nothing had been elicited from his cross-examination that at he was interested in or enemically disposed towards the mother-in-law.

Sexual Assualts

The amendment provides more stringent punishment and changes the burden of proof, by amending the Evidence Act. New

Sections 376B, 376C and 376D are inserted relating the various categories of custodial rape. Taking advantage of his position as a custodian to have sex with an inmate amounts to rape. Then new Section 114-A of the Evidence Act lays down that once a raped woman stated that she did not consent, there was presumption that she did not consent, if for the alleged rapist to prove that she consented. Let us see the case of police inspector who was charged with raping a girl in her teens.

One Shaminabanu, aged 19 years and Mahomed Shafi aged 25 years were neighbours in Nagpur and were in love with each other. They eloped to Bombay and contracted a marriage through a *Kazi*. They returned to Nagpur and took a lodge. The accused knocked at the door of the couple and took them to police station where he separated the couple, took Shaminabanu to the first floor, flirted with her, slapped her when she refused his overtures, and demanded that she should spend the night with him. He further wanted her to give her age as 15 years to facilitate the booking of Mahomed Shafi. Constable Chandra Bhan gave a beating to Mahomed Shafi. The accused inspector of police recorded all offence under Section 110 of the Bombay Police Act, read with Section 117 against Mahomed Shafi, on the allegation that he was misbehaving in front of Gujarat lodge. The husband Mahomed Shafi, who was released on bail, came to know about the incident through his wife. He lodged a complaint against C. K. Jain and the inspector. The trial court found the accused guilty of the offence of rape and convicted them. On appeal the High Court acquitted the accused as it found the testimony of the prosecution was uncorroborated.

Attempt to rape a women of easy virtue: Is raping or attempting to rape a woman of easy virtue an offence? Or is it a mitigating circumstances so that minimum sentence as prescribed under Section 376, IPC may be reduced. In the state of Haryana, the Supreme Court reduced the minimum sentence of 10 years for rape to five years on account of the "conduct" of the raped girl. The raped girl was a woman of easy virtue. This decision caused a stir, an agitation and a movement by the woman's organisations and other voluntary social organisations and led to gross criticism of the Supreme Court verging on brickbatting.

A review petition was filed. Although the review petition did not succeed, the Supreme Court tried to clarify its position. It said, "We have neither characterised the victim, Suman Rani as a woman of questionable character and easy virtue nor made any reference to her character or reputation in any pan of our judgment but used the expression "conduct" in the lexicographical meaning for the limited purpose of showing as to how Suman Rani had behaved or conducted herself in not telling anyone for five days about the sexual assault perpetrated on her.

In the State of Maharashtra, one Madhuker, a police inspector came on the night of November 13, 1965 at about 8.45 p.m., to the hut of one Banubi and entered it and demanded to have sex with her. On her refusal, he tried to force it on her. She raised a hue and cry which made neighbours and her husband rush in. Thereupon the 'valiant' inspector called the police and ordered that Banubi be taken to the police station. On Banubi's complaint an inquiry was made, and the inspector was dismissed. In the course of' inquiry it was revealed that Banubi was a woman of easy virtue. On the appeal of the inspector, the High Court observed that since Banubi was a woman of easy virtue, it would be unsafe to allow the fortune and career of a government official to be put in jeopardy upon the uncorroborated version of such a woman.

Gender Discriminations

The male-dominated system of high technology, rather than offering relief, has contributed to the intensification of discrimination against women. Parents can now detect the sex of a foetus within the first trimester, and, upon learning that the sex of the unborn child is female, many women choose or are forced to abort. Girl-children are fed less and for shorter periods and are not given foods like butter or milk, which are reserved for boys. Studies have shown a 12 per cent mortality rate among infant girls under a year old, and an eight per cent mortality rate among girls under five years old. While boys are sent to school, girls often stay home to look after younger siblings and to help with household chores. Even those girls who do receive some education must, at the same time, do washing and cleaning, as these are taboo chores for males. But only a little over half of all girls are enrolled in primary school, as compared with about 80 per cent of boys, despite the fact that the education level of mothers is inversely linked to infant mortality. Most Indian girls are married between the ages of 16 and 20, although some are married at significantly younger ages.

Marriage is almost always arranged by parents or brothers. The young bride must be obedient to her elders, loyal to her husband and his family, and never discuss her marital problems with outsiders. The model wife is taught that she must be ready to sacrifice her life for the honour of her husband and his family name. A major impediment to the human rights of women in India is the fact that laws relating to marriage, divorce, adoption, and inheritance are based primarily on religious law and tradition, with different laws for Hindus, Muslims, and Parsis. Any demand for equality based on sex is met with resistance on the grounds that such demands amount to interference with the right to freedom of religion.

The absence of any legislation relating to the right of the women to residence in the matrimonial home or to an equitable distribution of matrimonial assets on the dissolution of the marriage makes it legally possible for a husband to drive his wife out of her home. Divorce is taboo, and divorced women are treated as pariahs who, it is assumed, have failed to meet their husbands' needs. There are no viable alternatives to remaining in an abusive marriage—no group support, no support from relatives, no resources for a woman to live on her own. The long-standing demands of the women's movement for a general civil law against domestic violence have gone unmet. Judges are reluctant to grant injunctions restraining violent spouses from causing harm or injury to their wives. Sexual abuse of girls and women in families is common, but rarely reported. If a girl is raped, both she and her family are considered to have been shamed. Only rarely have rape cases come to public notice.

Despite the fact that serious sexual harassment is rampant in India, it usually goes unreported because women fear that complaining will attract negative attention. Although section 509 of the Indian Penal Code provides for prosecution of harassment, only a handful of cases are recorded; most are dismissed for lack of evidence. In one case, Rupan Bajaj Deol, a female senior officer of Indian Administrative Services (IAS), filed a formal complaint against the Director General of Police, K.P.S. Gill. The Indian government took no action against Gill, and the High Court merely dismissed her case, stating that the government could claim privilege against disclosure of police records.

Custom of Sati

The custom of *sati*, which involves the burning or burying alive of a widow along with the body of her deceased husband, persists. The practice, ostensibly intended to honour the devoted wife, was abolished in the last century, but the dramatic *sati* of Roop Kanwar in 1987 shocked the nation, and the central government felt obliged to enact the Commission of *sati* (Prevention) Act in 1987. The Act prohibits the glorification of *sati*, and includes prohibition of observing any ceremony or engaging in any processions in connection with *sati*; supporting, justifying, or propagating the practice of *sati*; arranging any function to eulogise the person who has committed *sati*; or the creation of any trust or collection of any funds, or the construction of a temple or place of worship with a view to perpetuating the honour or memory of any person who has committed *Sati*.

The constitutional validity of this Act has been challenged in the Supreme Court of India on the grounds that it violates the right of freedom of religion. The outcome of this challenge is yet to be seen. In the end, demographics provide what is perhaps the most telling indication of the status of women: the persistence of an adverse sex ratio, which declined from 934 females per 1,000 males in 1981 to 927 females per 1,000 males in 1991. And while bride burning, rape in police custody, and *sati* are shocking and visible forms of violence against women, the more silent and invisible forms of oppression that women face every day are as troubling. Fortunately, there have been strong women's movements to counter discrimination.

The oppression of women would be absolute public acknowledgment—governmental as well as societal—of the existence of widespread abuse and discrimination at every level of Indian society, both in India and in Indian communities abroad. Next, all girls must be sent to school, and the curriculum should include education in the equality of the sexes, beginning in the primary schools. Support groups should be established to help rape victims, the sexually exploited, harassed, and physically abused. But women must be empowered not only by cultural changes, which may be slow in coming, but also by enforced statutes.

The government must work to eliminate corruption at all

levels—in law enforcement, the legislature, and the judiciary so that those laws that are enacted may be enforced. Only then can the subcontinent address the fundamental human rights issue of violence against women. As long as cultural assumptions about the inferiority of women continue to exist, equality for women and freedom from discrimination based on sex will remain distant dreams.

Victims Physical Violence

Age at marriage does not differentiate battered from non-battered wives yet younger age at marriage puts a lot of stress for adjustment which may be exhibited in violent behaviour pattern on the part of young batterers. It can thus be assumed that women who are married at a younger age are at higher risk of physical violence. These women were more victims of physical violence by their husbands in contrast to those who got married at later age. Further, it was noted that there was a progressive decrease in the percentages of victims of physical violence from lower age at marriage category to higher age group. Out of 60 respondents who got married below the age of 18 years, 45 per cent were victims. In contrast to this who were married after the age of 21 years, only 24.71 per cent were the victims of physical violence. It is also interesting to note that median age at marriage of victims of physical violence was lower than those of non-victims. Therefore, class and situational factors may play an important role in determining the age at marriage which in turn may be associated with violence because young couples are under lot of stress to adjust to new role responsibilities. A few studies indicate that wives of younger age group are at higher risk of abuse as compared with those of older age group because older women are not prone to file assault charges either because of traditional attitudes or because of the possibility of divorce. The results of National Family Violence Survey conducted in America indicate that all forms of marital violence occur most frequently among those under 30 years of age.

The rate of marital violence among those under 30 years of age was found to be more than double the rate for the age for 31 to 50 years. The data for the present study were tabulated to find out association between the age of the wife and her being victim of physical violence. The respondents were distributed into four age categories. There was a progressive decrease in the percentages of victims of physical violence from lower age category to higher age category. In contrast to this those who were in the age group of 50 years above, only 18.18 per cent were the victims. Similarly, if the median age of the victims of physical violence is compared with non-victims, it was noticed that median age of victims was 35 years in contrast to 39.24 years median age of the non-victims. Physical violence against wives of younger age group was more frequent as against those of higher age groups. The data of the present study support the findings of studies cited above. Wife abuse can occur at any age but the data on age indicate that wives of younger age are at higher risk of being abused. It may be due to the fact that younger couples are still learning to make adjustment with each other and addition of children in the family puts enormous demands and stresses on the younger people. Presence or absence of children in the family is likely to affect the quality of relationship between husband and wife.

Physical Violence

The highest percentages of physical violence was found in those house-holds which had no child. It may be attributed to their younger age as well as wives' inability to have children because children are valued in the Indian society and those women who are unable to bear a child are ridiculed. In the patriarchal society like India, greater importance is given to the male child. The female child is not only considered a liability because of associated dowry problems but mothers who give birth to female children only do not get much respect in the family as compared with those who give birth to male children; lately with the help of amniocentesis the couples would like to know the sex of the child. In case the foetus is of the female sex, they go for abortion. The high female foeticide reinforces the sex preferences prevalent in our society.

The victims of physical violence were almost equally divided in the categories of those who had only male or female children of both the sexes. In the present study sex of the children in the family was not found to be associated with wife abuse. Wives living in extended and joint households are required to make adjustments with a large number of kin in contrast to those who are living in nuclear households. The men are more likely to act as sons rather than husbands. The parents-in-law and other kinsmen continue to have greater affiliation with the sons as compared with daughters-in-law. A number of cases have been reported where because of backbiting, the husbands have maltreated their wives. Hence presence of a large number of members in the family not only creates the problem of adjustment but they also act as instigators for wife abuse. Although there was no marked difference in the percentage of victims living in nuclear and extended households, yet among the victims a relatively higher percentage (36.67) were found to be living in joint and extended households in contrast to those living in nuclear households (32.94).

Among the non-victims no marked difference was found with regard to their pattern of living arrangement. Hence, the composition of household was not found to be associated with wife abuse. From the foregoing discussion on the demographic correlates of wife abuse, it was found that the younger age at marriage, young wives and those having no child or a large number of children were at higher risk of being victims of physical violence. However, no association was found between the sex of the children as well as living arrangement and wife abuse. Based on the results of this exploratory research the following hypotheses can be formulated for verification in future researches.

- The younger the age at marriage of the women, the greater is the possibility of their being battered.
- The younger the age of wife, the greater are the chances of her being victim of physical violence.
- The greater the number of children, a woman has the greater is the possibility of her being victim of physical violence of her husband.
- The absence of child is likely to result in wife battering.

Social behaviour is a function of the life situations which may be physical, economic, social or cultural or an interplay of these elements. It is assumed that persons having differential life situations would react differently to the same stimuli. It is, therefore, essential to explicate the role of these social variables for understanding the quality of conjugal relationship.

The social variables considered for the present study are educational and occupational status of the respondents, their social class background, their caste and religious background, their attitudes regarding traditional gender roles in the family and their value orientation in favour of use of violence for the resolution of conflict. Formal education helps an individual to know what is happening outside one's immediate surroundings. It also facilitates him to develop rational outlook towards life. Education widens the horizon and makes the individual more knowledgeable.

Education also helps an individual to get jobs of high prestige and with high economic returns. Further, higher education enhances one's social prestige. Efforts have been made to find out association between the level of education one has and the quality of interpersonal relations. A few studies indicate that the less education a person has, the more likely he or she is to approve of and support violence. Some other studies, however, contradict their findings and on the other hand, they are of opinion that couples with the lowest educational levels are less prone to violence than those who had attained higher education.

It is argued that low education level does not cause violence but it aggravates the frustration. The reason for more violence among those who have higher education, may be that women with high education may not endorse the traditional role relationship and this may be considered as threat to the dominant position by their husbands. However, education can provide people with alternatives for resolving family disagreements. It is, therefore, expected that with the help of education individual learns different mechanisms to resolve the conflict in the conjugal relationships.

The educational background of the victim wives indicates that those who have low educational attainment or higher educational attainment had over representation as compared with those who had moderate level of education. There is a progressive decrease in the percentage of the victims from illiterate educational category up to graduation with the exception of those who had higher education.

Occupation is an important indicator of a person's position in society. It is believed that the higher the education one has, the higher the occupation one holds and the higher the prestige he gets in society. Conversely, the lower the occupation, the lower will be the economic returns and as a consequence thereof, there are likely to be higher frustrations and greater marital conflicts. Many studies indicate that persons engaged in occupations of lower prestige are more likely to resort to physical violence against their wives to give vent to their economic stresses.

Wife beating is far less common in societies in which women have independent economic and social resources, perhaps because these resources are valuable enough to make a husband think twice before acting in ways that might force his wife to terminate the marriage. In the sample there are only 65 women respondents who were found to be engaged in paid work. Out of these 47.69 per cent were victims of physical violence of their husbands. On the other hand, out of those not engaged in paid work outside their homes, only 26.67 per cent were physically abused by their husbands. The results of the present study support the findings of Homung *et al.* who, in one representative sample, found housewives had a lower risk of violence than working wives.

The working wives may not accept the dominant position of the husband in family decision making and raise questions about asymmetrical conjugal relations. Such a situation may prompt the husband to use physical force to retain his dominant position. The general contention that working gives economic independence to women, hence, they would be relatively free dependence to be correct in the present from abuse is also not found to study on the other hand, it is the working women who are than the non-working women. The association abused more, status and her physical abuse will between wives' working which these become more clear if the type of occupation in which women are engaged in, is taken into consideration. The data reveal that the percentage of the victims goes on decreasing from low occupational prestige category to higher prestige category.

One salient feature of different definitions is that members of a class group have common style of living and value orientation. One set of studies maintains a positive association between lower class and wife battering. Whereas some researchers do not endorse their findings and they have contended that wife battering transgresses the boundaries of class. An attempt has been made to find out association between class background and wife beating. The class background of the respondents has been worked out based on education, occupation and income of the husbands of the respondents because a majority of the women respondents were not found to be working and hence, had no independent income of their own. While selecting the sample their living arrangement was taken into consideration and 50 cases from each house type were included in the sample, which were redistributed into different social classes. The class background of the respondent was also divided into lower, working, middle and high for the purpose of finding out differential behaviour pattern, i.e., wife abuse in different classes.

The data indicate that in contrast to 19.23 per cent victims of physical violence in the upper class, there were 51.85 per cent victims in the lower class. There is a progressive decrease in the percentages of victims of physical violence from the lower through the middle to the upper class. Similarly, among the non-victims the higher per cent (80.77) belong to the upper class. In short, women belonging to the lower class were at a higher risk of being physically abused by their husbands. The results of the study indicate inverse relationship between class background and wife battering. These findings support the contention of those researchers who found that women belonging to the lower class were at a higher risk of physical violence which was attributed to their way of life.

The use and approval of physical violence in the lower class has been attributed to what Lewis calls, the culture of poverty. The concept implies that the poor people have a distinct subculture. Due to common experiences they have developed certain attitudes and behaviour pattern which have been transmitted from parents to children. These include the casual resort to physical violence, an inability to plan for the future, seeking of immediate gratification, weak impulse control and fatalistic attitude towards the future. Davis, while describing the class-linked violence contends that physical violence in the lower class families is normal, socially approved and socially, inculcated type of behaviour. Similarly, Whitehurst, while making a distinction between the middle and the lower class families with regard to control over violence, maintained that violence-responses were much more built into lower class subculture as a means to achieve some goals to assert independence and masculinity.

The members of the lower class are subject to a lot of economic pressures and strains and they cannot show their resentment and frustration, against those who are highly placed and hence they give vent to their frustrations at the slightest provocation by beating their wives on whom they can exert their power.

On the other hand, members of the middle and upper classes have more resources and can keep their violence private and additionally, because of the sensitivity of the issue and embarrassment, the victims are not likely to admit its existence in their conjugal relationship. Individual's social status is determined by his ascriptive and acquired attributes. In the Indian society ascriptive attributes, like caste, determine not only his social milieu as castes are hierarchically placed but also his opportunities to acquire new attributes. Although an individual is now theoretically permitted to achieve any position and support any ideology yet caste plays an important role in influencing his behaviour pattern.

The distribution of the victims of physical violence according to their caste background indicates that respondents belonging to the lower castes group and those who have not specified their caste were more victims in contrast to the respondents belonging to the higher castes. Similarly, among the non-victims the higher percentages of respondents were found among the twice-born. The higher frequency of physical violence present among the members of the lower castes may be attributed to their lower class background.

Similarly, among those cases who have not specified their caste, most of them belonged to Muslim and Christian religion and these respondents were having lower socio-economic status. The association between caste background and physical violence would remain incomplete unless their economic status is also considered. Preceding analysis has indicated that members belonging to the lower class were more likely to resort to physical violence for the resolution of conjugal conflicts.

Role of Religion

Religion is an important institution which instils a particular philosophy of life in an individual. His outlook towards himself and others as well as his behaviour pattern are likely to be influenced by his religious belief system. Is wife abuse a characteristic of a particular religious group? To find out an answer to the question religious background of the respondents was considered. Among the two main religious groups present in Chandigarh, there was no marked difference in the percentage of victims.

In case of Muslims and Christians 50 per cent of the respondents belonging to these religious groups were the victims of husband's violence. This again may be attributed to the low economic status of the respondents. The results of the present study do not establish any association between religion and wife battering. The family as a social institution lays down norms and values to regulate the behaviour of the members of the social group. Family as a social group is structured in such a manner that one member, usually the husband, assumes the dominant position and the other members take up subordinate positions. The family provides a social setting where husband and wife play complementary roles. One of the conditions which maximises the cooperative elements in the family is the similarity of social values and ideologies which promotes not only cohesiveness and harmony but also helps in the proper functioning of the group. In the patriarchal traditional societies, like India, sex role expectations favour male dominance in the family.

Traditional ideology promotes and serves to justify male dominance as well as helps in cultivating a belief system among the husbands and wives as to how they should behave in the marital relationship. Motivated by traditional ideology, division of labour in the family was worked out into a male provider and a female to focus more narrowly on the domestic realm. The power structure in the family is maintained through the actions of the members involved in the relationships. Those at the top of the power structure behave in dominant ways and they do not hesitate to use coercive methods to retain their dominant position.

A number of studies have concluded that men who were more traditional in their attitudes towards women were more likely to become wife abusers. Some importance is also given to sex role orientation of the victims. Traditional sex role orientation of the respondents was worked out based on the responses to eight statements.

The level of traditionality was further divided into three: high, medium and low, to find out association between level of traditionality and wife battering. It is assumed that respondents who have low level of traditional role orientation are at higher risk of physical violence than those at high level of traditionality because wives with low level of traditional orientation are more likely to question asymmetrical power relations in the family. Data on traditionality and wife abuse reveal that there is a progressive decrease in the percentage of victims from low level of traditionality to high level of traditionality. In contrast to 22.86 per cent of the wives showing high level of traditional sex role orientation, 40.32 per cent wives indicating low level of traditionality were the victims of physical violence by their husbands. Similarly, among the non-victims, their percentages go on increasing from low to high level of traditionality.

The reason for wives showing less traditional sex role orientation being victims of physical violence may be attributed to their attempt in questioning the traditional power structure in the family. The husbands in such situation are likely to use physical force as the last resort to maintain their dominant position. The norms and values relating to intra-family violence indicate cultural contradiction.

On the one hand, there is a myth of family non-violence which reflects cultural norms for the family as a group characterised by love and harmony. On the other hand, there seems to be social norms which imply right of the family members to strike each other. The legitimation of violence in the family is explicit and mandatory—as in the case of rights and obligations of the parent to use a necessary and appropriate level of physical force to adequately train and control a child.

Violent wives as well as violent husbands express more approval of violence than do non-violent husbands and wives. The cultural norms and values permitting and sometimes encouraging husband to beat wife actually reflect hierarchical and male dominant type of society like India. The right to use force exists, to provide the ultimate support for the existing power structure of the family in which the wife assumes a subordinate position. Respondents' values in favour or against use of violence in the family were obtained from their reactions to 12 statements.

Their scores were divided into three categories depicting low, medium and high scores. This exercise was done with an assumption that the respondents with high score on values in favour of violence in the family would be at a higher risk of being victims than those with low score. The data did not depict any clearcut association. On the other hand, it was noted that those respondents who had medium score on values favouring use of violence to resolve family conflict were more victims in contrast to those who had high or low score.

The Indian society has placed women in a state of dependency as a daughter on her father, as a sister on her brother, as a wife on her husband and lastly as a mother on her son. Further, sexual division of labour and gender roles accentuate these differences. Additionally, patriarchal social norms not only grant control of family resources and property to men but also provide dominant position to them.

Dependency is also treated as a cause of physical violence in the conjugal relationships. Researches have utilised this explanation in two ways. In case, a wife is completely dependent, both physically and socially, her husband exploits her dependency and uses violence at whim to reinforce his dominant position in the conjugal relationship. A few scholars are also of opinion that when a husband is dependent upon his wife he resorts to physical violence as a last resort against his wife as he is afraid of losing his spouse or a person on whom he can exert his dominant position. Hence, dependency of husband over his wife is also treated as a cause of wife abuse.

As the present study is limited to wife abuse, the analysis is limited to wife's perception regarding the conditions which make her dependent upon her husband and how this state of dependency results into her being abused. To find out association between wife's dependency and her abuse, dependency has been divided into objective and subjective. It does not, however, mean that we can draw watertight compartments between the two. In certain cases objective dependency may lead to subjective dependency, whereas in other cases even though there is no objective dependency yet the individual remains subjectively dependent upon her spouse. For the purpose of analysis wife's objective dependency stands for conditions like not working, i.e., being economically dependent upon husband; not having any property in her name; not receiving any financial assistance from her family of orientation; inability to live alone; inability to do shopping alone, and inability to go outside the city alone. Further, level of objective dependency may vary from case to case hence, objective dependency was further divided into three levels: low, medium and high. The wives who are objectively dependent upon their husbands are at higher risk of being abused because it would be difficult for these women to come out of the abusive relationship as they do not have the resources to live alone.

Their objective dependency is also known to their spouses who may fully exploit the situation knowing fully well that their wives would not be able to leave them. It is further envisaged that wives who have high level of objective dependency are at greater risk of being abused. Wives with high level of objective dependency are physically abused more in contrast to those who have low level of objective dependency. This is evident in the percentages of the victims at different levels of dependency. Similarly, the percentage of non-victims goes on decreasing to high level. There were 33 respondents who had high level of objective dependency, out of which 60.61 per cent were not the victims of physical violence. The results of the study support the contention of a few scholars who are of opinion that high level of women's marital dependency is not associated with wife abuse because husbands of dependent wives can maintain their dominant positions without resorting to violence as their wives are in no position to question their dominance.

A few scholars contend that objective dependency of the wife *per se* does not result into her abuse but is mediated by her tolerance. One may, however, raise the question why she develops this tolerance to abuse? One reason may be that she remains subjectively dependent upon her husband because her social reality has not been constructed outside the marital relationship. In Indian society marriage is a must for every woman, unless she adopts a life of celibacy. Remaining unmarried or living a life of a divorcee is looked down upon. Hence, whether a wife is objectively dependent upon her husband or not she remains subjectively dependent. It is not, however, true in the case of husbands.

Re-marriage

Re-marriage after divorce or separation is more easily available to a man than a woman. Such a discriminatory practice perpetuate subjective dependency in the wives. Subjective dependency in the present study stands for, not leaving the husband even under adverse circumstances; divorce is not considered good; perception that married women even if abused enjoy higher status than divorced; lack of support from kin; greater commitment and more devotion to marital relationship. Depending upon their scores they are divided into three categories: low, medium and high. It is expected that wives having higher level of subjective dependency will be at higher risk of being physically abused in contrast to those having lower level of subjective dependency. In contrast to 23.94 per cent wives having low subjective dependency more than 42 per cent of the wives with high level of dependency are the victims of physical violence of their husbands. There was a steady increase in the percentage of abused wives from low level of subjective dependency through medium level to high level of subjective dependency.

Although, no positive correlation could be established between subjective dependency of wife and her being victim of physical abuse yet the high percentage of victims having high level of subjective dependency designate a partial association between subjective dependency and her being battered. The reason for high percentage of such victims can be attributed to wife's commitment to marriage and her inability to use alternative mechanisms to get out of the abusive relationships. Such a situation forces her to cultivate tolerance and continue living in the abusive relationship.

Similarly, the husband uses coercive methods to assert his dominant position in the familial network of relationship because he is confident that his violent behaviour would not be challenged and he can attain the desired goal, that is, subduing his wife.

The results of the present study on subjective dependency and wife abuse partially support the findings of other researchers. Subjective dependency in certain cases may be treated as a consequence of objective dependency. In other cases subjective dependency may not be the outcome of objective dependency. It was for this reason that these two facets of dependency were treated separately, however, to find out the impact of dependency on wife abuse both objective and subjective dependencies have to be combined.

In other words, to find out the validity of dependency framework to explicate wife abuse, both the facets of dependency are combined to find out their combined effect on physical violence. The total dependency scores of the respondents have been arranged into three categories—low, medium and high. The data indicate that wives with higher level of dependency are at higher risk of being abused in contrast to those with lower level of dependency. In contrast to 27.42 per cent of wives with low level of dependency more were the victims of husbands' physical violence. The percentage of non-victims goes on decreasing from lower level of dependency to higher level. Under these circumstances, though no clear cut correlations could be found between dependency and wife abuse yet it was found that with the increase in the level of dependency there was an increase in the percentage of victims.

Domestic Violence

In India, women conforming to the society's ideals have been hailed as *Sitas* and *Savitris*. Those who dared to defy have been victimised, scandalised and at times murdered, our history is replete with struggles against capitalism, caste system, feudalism and patriachy but it seems that struggle against patriarchy is left out in all broad struggles, e.g., one in class struggle, the men and women of different classes stand united against those of the other class. The evolution of women's movement world wide has thrown open questions which reveal the true nature of the sacrament institutions of marriage and family. It has also provided us analytical tools to understand the nature and causes of different forms of violence perpetrated over women and their interrelationships. In India, we have a unique situation of co-existence of all forms of violence, specially of elimination of women, e.g., selective female foeticide, female infanticide, bride burning and *sati*. The incidence of violence of all forms within family has also gone up. So has the awareness about it.

According to a study published by Peoples Union for Democratic Rights (PUDR), the number of unnatural deaths of women has been rising in the last few years most of these are a result of burns. Ninety eight per cent of these cases were married. During a period of eight months in 1982, the area falling under the jurisdiction of just two police stations in Bombay reported one death of a women due to burns every fifth day. Five women's organisations in Mumbai have been jointly monitoring the bum cases admitted to one of the municipal hospitals.

The burns ward consist exclusively women. A man may be admitted once in a month while a woman is admitted almost everyday in it. While the extent of burns (hence the possibility of death) is quite low in case of men, most women have burns over 50 per cent of their bodies. Experts feel that burns over 50 per cent cannot be a result of accidents, because in such cases, the victim and those nearby it would try to extinguish fire and hence would succeed in protecting a major portion of body from burns. What does the high incidence of women with more than 50 per cent burns indicate, not down right murder? It is true that mostly women work in kitchens and hence have greater chances of catching fire. Still, one hardly hears cases of male cooks working in restaurants and eating places of getting burnt in spite of the fact that they are exposed to a greater occupational hazard in form of open, large '*Bhattis*'.

Mental violence: All these experiences revealed the true nature of the system of married and family in our society. The stereotype rules of men and women are rigidly defined. While the material gains brought by the man are for everyone to see, the inputs provided by the women being distant are often invisible. The amount of time, energy and labour spent by women in performing her duties go unnoticed. Often she has to pay in terms of sacrificing her likings, interests and skills, while the society offers man many opportunities to go out of house and share with others his joys and sorrows such opportunities are much less for a woman. The society, the religion, her parents and in-laws, everyone expects her to become her husband's shadow. The worst thing is that all these come as a rude shock to her after marriage, because the institution of marriage in our society is highly glamorised. Hence, for a woman 'the union of souls' turning into a nightmare is a truly horrifying and shattering experience. The mental violence may be committed in such a subtle manner that others will never come to know of it. The woman in this case hailed from an educated, well-to-do family. She was bored of playing the role of a 'decorated doll' and 'ideal housewife' and wanted to do something of her own.The number for servants was cut down. All other members became much more busy in their activities outside home and hence contributed even less to domestic work. The elder members embarked on an eight month *Teerth-Yatra*. Thus it become almost impossible for her to pursue her study. It was as if she was foolish to take such a decision.

The character of domestic violence as a social phenomenon was first revealed and analysed by the women's movement. It also branched further to evolve support groups to take care of individual cases of domestic violence, at the same time focusing this issue on a macro level. When a woman approaches a group like 'Women's Centre' for help she feels that she is the only victim of such violence. She blames her bad luck; she blames herself or other women for what she had to suffer each one thinks that of all others are leading decent lives whereas she is the only one who is suffering.The first thing we do is to make her feel that her is not an isolated case. Even in suffering, she is one of the several thousands or lakhs of women who are the target of domestic violence. The centres regularly organise get-togethers of all women who approach them for help and initiate discussion on topics of everybody's concern.

Because our society believe that marriage is the primary occupation, the only way of life for all women for all such women, it is very difficult to make a fresh beginning. Another important problem is of finding suitable shelter. This problem is more acute in cities and towns. It haunts women. There are hardly any hostels and most of them do not accept women with children. The women belonging to minority groups feel much more insecure. They are insecure when they live with the members of their own communities because they have defied the norms of conduct followed by other members of the community. On the other hand, they do not have much faith in members of other communities, specially the males. In order to tackle the problem of women, specially those stepping out of their homes, a conference on 'Women and Shelter' was organised in Mumbai in December 1987. There are many problems which eat up the energy and drain the resources of women intending to lead dignified, independent lives. The laws do not offer much relief because it is mostly men who make and implement laws. They often tend to protect other man who violate such laws.

Moreover, the titled power balance in our society and the cumbersome legal procedures make justice almost impossible to achieve. Quite often women tend to give up their fight and go back to the husband's home. Such a compromise might ultimately result in murder of such a woman. The recent conference on 'Women, Religion and Personal Laws' organised by 'Women's Centre' shows that the women all over Asia are raising their voice against the existing laws which are highly biased against women. They are facing a lot of opposition from the growing fundamentalist forces. It is because these forces as well as the state realise women's potential as a force against all types of violence.

In some cases, the state is trying to cooperate, women's movement by showing sympathetic gestures towards it. In others there is confrontation between the state and women's groups on many issues. All these show that in spite of several limitations women's movement has the ability to cross barriers of caste. Class, community and even nations. Sisterhood can be a bond which unites all women irrespective of their differences. We should never forget that the fight against the domestic violence is just a part of our wide battle against patriarchy. There is a link between female foeticide, domestic violence, bride burning and *sati*. We have to fight on all fronts, while we are engaged in providing support to needy women, we should not lose sight of the action on the macro level.

Domestic violence as a form of social problem and social issue is being increasingly discussed by social scientists, social workers and activist groups and is given attention by media. This has resulted in some legislative changes and directives have been issued to the police department regarding this issue. In Pune city, 114 women met an accidental death (burns and poisoning) during the period of four months. Out of them 85 per cent women were newly married and were in the age group of 18 to 35 years. These figures indicate only those who could not escape death. Such kind of statistics is not merely statistics of accidents, but they are manifestations of malady in our socio-political system. Depending on the analysis of domestic violence various voluntary organisations are evolving different programmes and government is developing new schemes to tackle this issue.

Violence can be both physical and psychological. It indicates threat or aggressive behaviour towards her not only to her physical being but towards her self-respect andself confidence. Psychological violence is carried out with psychological weapons (threats/ insults/humiliating treatment/ denial of human existence) rather than physical attack. Physical violence includes all types of aggressive physical behaviour by husband or his family towards the women's body (victim). Sexual violence could include both passive (denial) or active violence.

The structural aspect is manifested in the hierarchical organisation of social institutions and social relation. It thus relegates power to certain individuals, groups or class and some form of subservience to others. The maintenance of this hierarchical structure and authority needs acceptance by many. The patriarchal ideology serves to reinforce this acceptance. It is a rationalisation of the inequality and subordination, which is accepted by those who are in a subordinate position. Quite often this is legitimised through religion and formal legislations.

Violence inflicted on women in the internal life of the family, in the so-called 'privacy' of the home extends beyond it, and so it should be understood in its total context. Even in wider political context violence runs along the lines of power in class-caste-gender stratified society. The ideology of subordination is required by material structure of production also. This subordination in material sphere leads to dependency of women. This gender-based disparity of our system (i.e., lower wages under reporting in labour force, discriminatory status of women in health and education) has been justified on the assumption that women's employment and existence is secondary to that of men. Practices which exclude women from inheritance of land are quite evident. All of us know the inadequacies of inheritance law, and in most of the cases daughters waive their property-rights in favour of their brothers. An argument is often made that 'dowry' is a form of her share in the property but over that also she has no so control. Secondly, land is very rarely given as dowry. Family has recently emerged as apolitical issue in India.

On the one side women's movement has raised the questions about, family structure and they have been questioning complex power relations in gender and violence. On the other side government policies indicate the planners' belief that unmistakable way to improve women's status is to improve the condition of the family. It continues to be the basic unit of development. Under the pressure of women's organisations and scholars a 'chapter entitled' Women and Development' has been added in the ninth five year plan. Thus efforts are being made to involve women in developmental process. On the other side they are being thrown out from economical sphere, and violence inflicted upon them both within and outside the family seems to be increasing. This violence is seen in the form of rape, dowry deaths, domestic violence, amniocentesis and female infanticide. The basic question asked by all women's groups and social scientists is why is so much of violence perpetuated against women? The answer to this question which connotes its widespread nature has to be found in its structural nature and not individualistic explanations. Usually we can identify three trends in theories related to domestic violence:

- Psycho-analytical theories
- Social learning theories
- Socio-political critique

Psycho analytical theories – These focus upon stress, anxiety, anger and guilt instilled during child rearing. They frequently depict the abused women as masochistic or exhibiting 'learned helplessness'. The men who suffer from this perspective are fearful and hateful towards women because of the child-rearing they have received. Men develop hyper-masculinity to overcompensate for their emotional insecurities.

Social learning theories – They consider the abuse to be an outgrowth of learned patterns of aggressive communication to which both husband and wife contribute, These theories consider family as "cradle of violence" where violent behaviour is intergenerational, i.e., bitterer a boy learns to be violent by watching or experiencing the violence of his parents. Similarly, a battered child learns to be recipient of violence. Especially in the Indian context most of the adults, rule and behaviour are learned where the aggressive and submissive behaviour by male and female respectively, has a social sanction.

Socio-political critique – These theories give emphasis on domestic violence as being manifestation of patriarchal and hierarchical (class+caste) social structure. It excludes women from political, business and religious leadership. Women are forced into subordinate position by two processes.

- Discrimination that block women from being in influential position.
- Ideology of innate inferiority which is often enforced by religious values, and glorification of feminine virtues. The aggression and dominance as masculine virtues and sacrifice tolerance, etc., as feminine virtues are emphasised right from childhood through plays, play materials, songs, sayings and idioms.

Especially the 'Mother-in law' emerges as dominating figure who inflicts violence or harasses the daughter-in-law. This also leads to the most popular myth that women are women's enemies 'or' women only are responsible for the harassment which closes all the discussion of power relations. Women as agents of patriarchy are hardly visualised. In India caste stratification and institution of family is very closely linked together. This was brought forward first in Maharashtra by Shri Ketkar and Dr. Babasaheb Ambedkar. The ban on sexual relations was much rigidly followed in case of higher case women than higher caste men or lower caste women. Men from higher caste were allowed to have the sexual relations with women of lower caste but not with the women of higher caste. At the same time the rigidity regarding sexual relations was women not so much enforced as low caste women were 'to be available' for upper castes. This was basically to ensure that father of the child was from the family only. This indicates direct linkage with in heritance and property. Such practices along with others such as *sati* and marriage before puberty were proved to be beneficial for maintenance of 'Purity' of the caste.

All these links between patriarchy, caste and class should be more clearly seen to understand the complexity of subordination of women. Unless there is significant change in the hierarchical and dominating structure of the society and family, the extent of women' freedom from structural violence would be limited. Many social scientists and theorists are theorising on these issues such as subordination, its origin, and links between patriarchy, class and caste; but still there are lots of gaps in the academic work done.

Condition of Elderly Women

Violence to the elderly women, whether in our country or abroad, remains, nevertheless, a hard fact, which unfortunately, has eluded attention of social scientist all these days. Elderly women, after their reproductive and gainfully remunerative stage, become, to all intents and purposes, a drag on the family, forfeiting their "entitlement", whatsoever, to all that is comfortable and cosy. Consequently there is earth and paucity of studies and even information on the state of females of the elder generation. It will take time to collect indicator-based data concerning this very poignant question. The family is the basic kinship unit, in its form consisting of a husband, wife, and children. In its widest sense, it refers to all relatives living together or recognised as a social unit, including adopted persons. The family is often called the basic social institution because of its important functions of procreation and socialisation, and because it is found, in some form, in all societies.

From the very definition, it appears that family is to be found, in some form or the other, in all societies, pre-literate and civilised, ancient, medieval and modern. Indeed, so far human knowledge goes, this basic social institution has been with us from time immemorial. This is not to say, however, that the types and patterns have remained the same and unchanged throughout the long stretch of the march of human civilisation. Consequently, classifications are really many more than we can think of, and this is based on different parameters like residence, pattern of inheritance, etc. When we have got a hang of this basic social institution, we shall have to go deep into it in the context of the present discussion. We shall deal with it both diachronically and synchronically. The historical and developmental study of the institution of the family, again, is not uniform.

Marxists take an altogether different view of the origin and development of this institution. The marxist framework may fit well with the subject "Violence in Family". The relationship between man and woman is antagonistic and not non-antagonistic. The term 'violence' has been used and also appropriated to situations from large-scale annihilation of human beings in wars, in conditions of revolutions, in human interactions of various categories like violence by insurgents, violence by terrorists and also violence by robbers, bandits and dacoits. Then the term has also been used to denote situations like violation of human rights, rights of citizens, rights of individuals in groups and institutions, etc.

There is, however, a fundamental difference between the corpus and the psyche-including personality with which the human kind differs from the rest of the species in the planet. From time immemorial, definitions and meanings of the term violence have been changing depending on the level of sensitisation and socialisation of the nations and societies in its twofold meanings. A foster-mother's breast-feed could be bought for the master's infant at the cost of the natural feed for her own infant in the transferred image of the bovine milkfeed for human infants. All the law givers the world over, from the earliest days of civilisation, thought of the human body and its sancity.

One may call it ecosystem and feminist approach to human nature relationship. This is the definition of the female which is being accepted for the present paper. The female has not to be equated with her reproductive role only, but her partnership in other productive processes has to be reckoned so that all the myths are done away with and reality is vindicated. This is wisdom derived from a diachronic understanding of the 'female'. For a synchropnic comprehension of the elder generation, they therefore, have to be understood in the general background of the formulations about the perception of females in general. There are two variations possible. Females of the age group starting from above 45 years could belong to the first category, female of an elder generation could also be a woman who got married at the age below 35 years. It is true universally, for the basic reason of the differential concept of generation *per se*, 25 years to reckon a generation which has come to prevail all over is because of the model of marriages at the later age. This may be true in variation in the developed world. But the developing world has its problems regarding this concept of generation. The quest of this chapter is to integrate these three aspects. The availability of data as well as studies are certainly the two limitations for any scholar to integrate concepts in both dischronic and synchronic studies. At the macro-level, the social science data is best available from the Census of India from 1901 to 1981. Seven indicators in their variables provide data which is the latest from the census of India, 1981. Population growth and sex ratio, migration, literacy and working population are the important indicators provided, concerning females in families and situations whereby the social and working conditions can perpetrate violence against them.

Since violence against females of the elder generation is not of the some variety and the same kind as that which is perpetrated to women of younger age, including teenage girls, newly married brides, new mothers and sons, the flashpoint of this chapter is that elderly women are subject to violence culminating into rejection by the family, by neighbourhood and by the society. The term elderly differs in rural and urban perception. In the rural areas where the average age of marriage is below 18 years, elder generation may, in those cases, include a female of 36 years when she marries off her daughter, however, in urban areas above 45 years could be the age for coming to be reckoned in the elder generation. Simultaneously, physical, biological component of a female, sometimes, is also responsible for giving a particular female to belong to the elder generation on account of her self-perception and perception by others around her during the menopause stage. So, these three categories of females of the elder generation, like any other set of categories, should find ramification in terms of population size, marital status, fertility, migration, literacy and as workers. Also, sociologically, they can be seen in terms of types of families they are in. The quantum of work in terms of statistical data has to be tabulated for three categories, in six situations, each situation to be subdivided into the two types of families—the nuclear and the extended.

Statistical data on categories in relation to the two types of families can only be derived from micro-studies, so as to design the matrix, accordingly. However, for the present paper, to illustrate from the macro-data. We have taken one situation in this paper. The situation of workers, we find, exciting enough for illustrating my point their other part of the work—the work they had been doing as women in the families/household. Also, mortality rates for females aged 50 and above who die in inactivity has a fairly high priority in order to plan for social security and pension schemes, but according to the expert, direct data is difficult; only estimations are possible. The coping-up mechanisms, so much talked about post-retirement adjustments, must be understood in this dual role context. The coping up mechanism for retiring from this field of work should necessarily determine their role perception by families, where this work takes place, as basic units of the societies changing very fast, and also their self-perception and evaluation. The latter goes a long way in letting them become empowered women for the old age as also belonging to the elder generation in a changing family nexus. Perpetration of crimes is both the function of the preparation of crime is both the function of the perpetrator and the one who willi-nilly accepts it succumbs to it because of some difficulty, physical, social emotional or thought-organisational. Total population figures show that 80 per cent of the females are in the rural habitat, whereas urban habitat is occupied by only 20 per cent of the females in the age groups of fifty to sixty years. Their break-up in terms of main-workers, marginal workers and non-workers brings certain very important points for consideration of the systemic violence against females as reflected in the family set-up.

The 40-49 years age group of women has been considered separately, on purpose, as elaborated in the preceding pages. Out of 78 per cent non-workers in the age group in India, 61 per cent are rural-based, whereas about 18 per cent are urban-based. This is a group which requires attention of a different kind so as to minimise overt and covert violence against them. In the aggregate, 16 per cent continue to be main workers. The break-up is 14 per cent for the rural and only two per cent for the urban areas. The state of their well-being depends on the way they are being treated. Are they being forced to be main workers? Who is forcing them? For what rewards? What are the social security provisions governing their future when they are getting sapped of their energies.? Out of the six per cent of marginal workers, almost all of them are rural-based, with a very all, from the futuristic trend-setter point of view two per cent in the urban areas. The type of crimes that are bring perpetrated against them could be indifferent sorts of inter-personal relationships:

- between the buyer of their services and their own selves;
- between the younger members of the families and these women, and above all,
- between their situation and the situation that is available to others in society at their age and at their level of economy.

One has to be conscious of the fact that the levels of economy do get generated by skills and by opportunities made available to a group of population. That by far would be the worst crime when neither the opportunities were ever made available to them nor could they ever improve their skills, and now, to top it all, family and society also ventilate themselves by different types of oppressions for them, certainly amounting to violence, which may not be a violence against a younger group of females in similar situations. Work is a reward in itself, it could never uphold its dictum in the face of deprivation of literacy and education and health services. These twin indicators are set against almost all of them, with 75 per cent females are literate in the rural areas, and when in some of the districts these rural women have been blessed with a literacy figure of one per cent only, we can very well infer their state and plight! Hence the Structure is set against them. Maternal and child care services would have cared for them. But to what extent the injury already caused to them, in case they have been saved from maternal mortality rates, would make them or leave them capable of looking after their personal needs. Since they have been used to being mothers to look after the needs of the members of the family, they would be left to fend for themselves much more extensively. In case of poor health, there would be terrible risks of violence; in case of better health, they might also add to the tensions in the families with the younger generation because without understanding the rapid change in mores and norms they may be able to adjust themselves. It is both ways necessary to look into this aspect. Planning for them at the rural level should be taken up as top priority along with population education programme and 'for of god'—the old age must also be added to other indicators set against early marriage and quick multiplication of offsptings. However, the number of the aging appear to be increasing as urban growth and growth of slums and squatters accelerate.

The plight of the elderly women in the tribal areas is, again a multidimensional one, different from those in rural and urban areas. As has been observed there are indicators and there are variables too; but there have to be carved out many more of them and put to benchmark surveys before we can reach scientific data for macro-planning macro-intervention and macro-alleviation. However, even before getting into the macro aspects, it would be necessary to have quick micro-studies conducted, just as has come out from Kerala and has been reported, both for understanding the depth of causes and the remedial measures to control violence against this generation. Till then, hypothesis building can be resorted to from the observation of perceptive sociologists and family-life counsellors. As in socialist countries and industrially developed capitalist countries of the west, social security measures could be extended to the elderly women in our country as well. To understand the nature of the social grouping as well as the quality of interrelationship that exists among the members, it is essential to understand their demographic background. Young children are expected to behave differently as compared with adult population. Similarly, the age at marriage determines the fertility span.

Marital status is also linked with differential role performance and evaluation. Additionally, the presence or absence of children in the family gives rise to different types of role responsibilities to which the couples have to make adjustments. To find out the correlates of wife abuse, the demographic variables which have been considered for the present study are: age at marriage; present age; number of children; sex of the children in a household composition. The age at marriage does not differentiate battered from non-battered wives, yet a younger age at marriage puts a lot of stress for adjustment which may be exhibited in violent behaviour pattern on the part of young batterers. It can thus be assumed that women who are married at a younger age are at higher risk of physical violence. The women who got married at a younger age were more victims of physical violence by their husbands in contrast to those who got married at a later age. Further, it was noted that there was a progressive decrease in the percentages of victims of physical violence from lower age at marriage category to higher age group. Out of 60 respondents who got married below the age of 18 years, 45 per cent were victims. In contrast to this of those who were married after the age of 21 years, only 24.71 per cent were the victims of physical violence.

The median age at marriage of victims of physical violence was lower than those of non-victims. It can, thus, be concluded that those women who married at a lower age were at a high risk of physical violence in comparison with those who got married at a later age in the Indian society. Although the age at marriage is increasing, yet in the rural areas it still remains quite low, that is, 17.81 years. Therefore, class and situational factors may play an important role in determining the age at marriage which in turn may be associated with violence because young couples are under a lot of stress to adjust to new role responsibilities.

A Survey

The results of National Family Violence Survey conducted in America indicate that all forms of marital violence occur most frequently among those under 30 years of age. The rate of marital violence among those under 30 years of age was found to be more than double the rate for the age group 31 to 50 years. The data for the present study were tabulated to find out the association between the age of the wife and her being victim of physical violence. The respondents were distributed into four age categories. There was a progressive decrease in the percentages of victims of physical violence from lower age category to higher age category. Among the victims of physical violence 45.45 per cent were below the age of 30 years. In contrast to this those who were in the age group of 50 years and above, only 18.18 per cent were the victims. Similarly, if the median age of the victims of physical violence is compared with non-victims, it was noticed that the median age of victims was 35 years in contrast to 39.24 years median age of the non-victims. In short, an inverse relationship was found between the age of wives and their physical abuse. Physical violence against wives of younger age group was more frequent as against those of higher age groups. The data of the present study support the findings of studies cited above.

Wife abuse can occur at any age but the data on age indicate that wives of younger age are at higher risk of being abused. Presence or absence of children in the family is likely to affect the quality of relationship between husband and wife. Further, presence of more children in the family would create problem of management and proper training of the younger ones. Researches on the impact of children on marriages consistently show that the level of marital satisfaction and marital adjustment goes down after the birth of the first child.

An additional child would imply a decrease in time for parents to pursue, their own interests. Further, each additional child increases the work load and conflicts. In the traditional societies like India, child care still remains under the domain of mothers and for any deviance on the part of the child it is the mother who is blamed. Further, more children put a lot of stress on the limited resources of the family. The highest percentages of physical violence was found in those households which had no child. It may be attributed to their younger age as well as the wives, inability to have children because children are valued in the Indian society and issueless women are ridiculed. In the patriarchal society like India, greater importance is given to the male child. The female child is not only considered a liability because of associated dowry problems but mothers who give birth to female children only do not get much respect in the family as compared with those who give birth to male children.

Lately with the help of amniocentesis the couples get to know the sex of the child. In case the foetus is of the female sex, they go for abortion. The victims of physical violence were almost equally divided in the categories of those who had only male or female children. In the present study sex of the children in the family was not found to be associated with wife abuse. Wives living in extended and joint households are required to make adjustments with a large number of kin in contrast to those who are living in nuclear households. Further, patrilocal residence and patriarchal structure of the family places women in a subservient position. The men are more likely to act as sons rather than husbands. The parents-in-law and other kinsmen continue to have greater affiliation with the sons as compared with daughters-in-law.

A number of cases have been reported where, because of backbiting, husbands have maltreated their wives. Hence, the presence of a large number of members in the family not only creates the problem of adjustment but members also act as instigators for wife abuse. Although there was no marked difference in the percentage of victims living in nuclear and extended households, yet among the victims a relatively higher percentage (36.67) were found to be living in joint and extended households in contrast to those living in nuclear households. Social behaviour is a function of the life situations which may be physical, economic, social or cultural or an interplay of these elements. It is assumed that persons having differential life situations would react differently to the same stimuli. It is, therefore, essential to explicate the role of these social variables for understanding the quality of conjugal relationship.

Education widens the horizon and makes the individual more knowledgeable. It also helps an individual to get prestigious jobs with high economic returns. Further, higher education enhances one's social prestige. Efforts have been made to find out the association between the level of education one has and the quality of interpersonal relations.

A few studies indicate that the less education a person has, the more likely he or she is to approve of and support violence. Some other studies, however, contradict their findings and, on the other hand, they are of the opinion that couples with the lowest educational levels are less prone to violence than those who had attained higher education. It is argued that low education level does not cause violence but it aggravates the frustration. The reason for more violence among those who have higher education may be that women with high education may not endorse the traditional role relationship and this may be considered as a threat to the dominant position by their husbands. However, education can provide people with alternatives for resolving family disagreements. It is, therefore, expected that with the help of education individual learns different mechanisms to resolve the conflict in the conjugal relationships. The educational background of the victim wives indicates that those who have low educational attainment or higher educational attainment had over representation as compared with those who had moderate level of education.

The women with low education designate their complete dependency because with low educational background they will not be able to have economic independence or would be engaged in occupations with low economic returns and low prestige. In the case of those who have higher education they may be in a better position to gain economic independence and with the higher education they may start questioning the dominant position of their husbands. Such a threat is not tolerated by husbands and they use physical violence as their ultimate resource to maintain their dominant position in the family. Many studies indicate that persons engaged in occupations of lower prestige are more likely to resort to physical violence against their wives to give vent to their economic stresses.

It is also argued that women who stay at home and are not engaged in paid work outside their homes are at somewhat greater risk of being physically abused than those engaged in paid work. This is probably because housewives are perceived to contribute less to family subsistence and are consequently valued less than women who are engaged in paid work outside the home. Wife beating is far less common in societies in which women have independent economic and social resources, perhaps because these resources are valuable enough to make a husband think twice before acting in ways that might force his wife to terminate the marriage. The reason as to why housewives are abused less than working wives is because keeping in view their economic dependency they may have "learned helplessness". The result is that they have developed tolerance to such violence and do not share with outsiders that they are being abused or they would endorse the traditional gender roles and would not question the authority of their husbands. Hence, they do not provoke their husbands to use physical violence to maintain their dominant position in the conjugal relationship. The working wives may not accept the dominant position of the husband in family decision-making and raise questions about asymmetrical conjugal relations. Such a situation may prompt the husband to use physical force to retain his dominant position. The general contention is that working gives economic independence to women, hence, they would be relatively free from abuse.The data reveal that the percentage of the victims goes on decreasing from low occupational prestige category to higher prestige category. There was inverse relationship between occupational prestige and physical violence, i.e., the lower the prestige of paid work, the greater was the violence against wives. The results indicate that it is not the working status *per se* which provides women freedom from physical violence of their husbands but it is the nature of the occupation and associated prestige and economic returns which facilitate women to be free from physical abuse.

Criminal Law

Act No. 46 of 1983, assented to on 25 December, 1983

An Act further to amend the Indian Penal Code, the Code of Criminal Procedure, 1973 and the Indian Evidence Act, 1872. Be it enacted by Parliament in the Thirty-fourth Year of the Republic of India as follows—

Short title—This Act may be called the Criminal Law (Second Amendment) Act, 1983.

Amendment Act 45 of 1960—In the Indian Penal Code, after Chapter XX, the following Chapter shall be inserted, namely:

Chapter XX-A

Cruelty by husband or relatives of husband

498-A. *Husband or relative of husband of a woman subjecting her to cruelty*—Whoever being the husband or the relative of the husband of a woman, subjects such woman to cruelty shall be punished with imprisonment for a term which may extend to 2 years and also be liable to fine.

Explanation—For the purposes of this section, "cruelty" means—

— any wilful conduct which is of such a nature that is likely to drive the woman to commit suicide or cause grave injury or danger to life, limb or health (whether mental or physical) of the woman; or

– harassment of the woman where such harassment is with a view to coercing her on any person related to her to meet any unlawful demand for any property or valuable security or is on account of failure by her or any person related to her to meet such demand.

Amendment of Section 174 – In the Code of Criminal Procedure, 1973 (hereinafter referred to as the Code of Criminal Procedure), in Section 174, in sub-section (3), for the words "When there is a doubt regarding the cause of death, or when for another reason the police officer considers it expedient so to do, he shall", the following shall be substituted, namely:

– the case involves suicide by a woman within seven years of her marriage; or
– the case relates to the death of a woman within seven years of her marriage in any circumstances raising a reasonable suspicion that some other person committed an offence in relation to such woman; or
– the case relates to the death of a woman within seven years of her marriage. and any relative of the woman made a request in this behalf; or
– there is any doubt regarding the cause of death; or
– the police officer for any other reason considers it expedient so to do, he shall."

Amendment of Section 176 – In Section 176 of the Code of Criminal Procedure, in sub-section (1). for the words "When any person dies while in the custody of the police," the words, brackets and figures.

Insertion of new Section 198-A – In the Code of Criminal Procedure, after Section 198, the following section shall be inserted, namely:

198-A. *Prosecution of offences under Section 498-A of the Indian Penal Code* – No court shall take cognisance of an offence punishable under Section 98-A of the Indian Penal Code except upon a police report of facts which constitute such offence or upon a complaint made by the person aggrieved by the offence or by her father, mother, brother, sister by father's or mother's brother or sister or, with the leave of the court, by any other person related to her by blood, marriage or adoption.

Amendment the First Schedule – In the Code of Criminal Procedure, in the First Schedule, after the entries relating, to Section 498, the following entries shall be inserted, namely:

Amendment cf Act 1 of 1872 – In the Indian Evidence Act, after Section 133, the following section shall be inserted, namely:

"113-A. *Presumption as to abetment of suicide by a married woman* – When the question is whether the commission of suicide by a woman had been abetted by her husband or any relative other husband and it is shown that she had committed suicide within a period of seven years from the date of her marriage and that her husband or by such relative of her husband had subjected her to cruelty the court may presume having regard to all the her circumstances of the case that such suicide had been abetted by her husband or by such relative of her husband.

Explanation – For the purposes of this section, 'cruelty' shall have the same meaning as in Section 498-A of the Indian Penal Code.

The Criminal Law Amendment Act, 1983

Act No. 43 of 1983, Assented to on 25 December, 1983

In Act further to amend the Indian Penal Code, Code 1, Criminal Procedure, 1973 and the Indian Evidence Act, 1872. Be it enacted by Parliament in the Thirty-fourth Year of the Republic of India as follow:

Short title – This Act may be called the Criminal Law (Amendment) Act, 1983.

Insertion of new Section 228-A. – In the Indian Penal Code (hereinafter referred to as the Penal Code), after Section 228, the following section shall be inserted, namely:

"228-A. Disclosure of identity of any person against whom an offence etc. – (I) Whoever prints or publishes the name or any matter which may make known the identity of any person against whom an offence under Section 376, Section 376-A., Section 376-B, Section 176-C or Section 376-D is alleged or found to have been committed (hereafter in this section referred to as the victim) shall be punished with imprisonment or either description for a term which may extend to two years and shall also be liable to line.

Nothing in sub-section (1) extends any printing or publication of the name or any matter which may make known the identity of the victim if such printing or publication is—

- by or under the order in writing of the officer in-charge of the police station or the police officer making the investigation into such offence acting in good faith for the purposes of such investigation; or
- by or with the authorisation in writing of the victim; or
- where the victim is dead or minor or of unsound mind, by or with the authorisation in writing of, the next of kin of the victim:

Provided that no such authorisation shall be given by the next of kin to anybody other than the chairman or the secretary, by whatever name called, of any recognised welfare institution or organisation.

Explanation—For the purpose of this sub-section, "reco-gnised welfare institution or organisation" means a social welfare institution or organisation recognised in this behalf by the Central or State Government.

Whoever prints or publishes any matter in relation to any proceeding before a court with respect to an offence referred to in subsection (1) without the previous permission of such court shall be punished with imprisonment of either description for a term which may extend to two years and shall also be liable to fine.

Explanation—The printing or publication of the judgment of any High Court or the Supreme Court does not amount to an offence within the meaning of this section.

Substitution of new sections for Sections 375 and 376—In the Penal Code, for the heading "Of rape" occurring immediately before Section 375 and for Sections 375 and 376, the following heading and sections shall be substituted, namely:

Sexual offences

375. *Rape*—A man is said to commit 'rape' who, except in the case hereinafter excepted has sexual intercourse with a woman under circumstances falling under any of the six following descriptions:

- Against her will.
- Without her consent.
- With her consent, when her consent has been obtained by putting her or any person in whom she is interested in

fear of death or of hurt.

- With her consent, when the man knows that he is not her husband, and that her consent is given because she believes that there is another man to whom she is or believes herself to be lawfully married.
- With her consent, when, at the time of giving such consent, by reasons of unsoundness of mind or intoxication or the administration by him personally or through another of any stupefying or unwholesome substance, she is unable to understand the nature and consequences of that to which she gives consent.
- With or without her consent, when she is under sixteen years of age.

Explanation—Penetration is sufficient to constitute the sexual intercourse necessary to the offence of rape.

Exception—Sexual intercourse by a man with his own wife, the wife not being under fifteen years of age, is not rape.

Punishment for rape

376. (1) Whoever, except in the cases provided for by sub-section (2), commits rape shall be punished with imprisonment of' either description for a term which shall not be less than seven years but which may be for life or for a term which may extend to ten years and shall also be liable to fine unless the woman raped is his own wife and is not under twelve years of age, in which case, he shall be punished with imprisonment of either description for a term which may extend to two years or with fine or with both:

Provided that the court may, for adequate and special reasons to be mentioned in the judgment, impose a sentence of imprisonment for a term of less than seven years.

Whoever,

- being a police officer who commits rape—
  - i) within the limits of the police station to which he is appointed; or
  - ii) in the premises of any station house whether or not situated in the police station to which he is appointed, or
  - iii) on a woman in his custody or in the custody of a police officer subordinate to him: or
- being a public servant, takes advantage of his official

position and commits rape on a woman in his custody as such public servant or in the custody of a public servant subordinate to him; or

– being on the management or on the staff of a jail, remand home or other place of custody established by or under any law for the time being in force or of a women's or children's institution takes advantage of his official position and commits rape on any inmates of such jail, remand home, place or institution; or

– being on the management or on the staff of a hospital, takes advantage of his official position and commits rape on a woman in that hospital; or

– being on the management or on the staff of a hospital, takes advantage of his official position and commits rape on a woman in that hospital; or

– commits rape on a woman knowing her to be pregnant; or

– commits rapes on a woman when she is under twelve years of age; or

– commits gang rape

shall be punished with rigorous imprisonment for a term which shall not be less than ten years but which may be for life and shall also be liable to fine:

Explanation 1—Where a woman is raped by one or more in a group of persons acting in furtherance of their common intention, each of the persons shall be deemed to have committed gang rape within the meaning of this sub-section.

Explanation 2—Women's or children's institution means an institution, whether called an orphanage or a home for neglected women or children or a widow's home or by my other name, which is established and maintained for the reception and care of women or children.

Explanation 3—'Hospital' means the precincts of the hospital and includes the precincts of any institution for the reception and treatment of persons during convalescence or of persons requiring medical attention or rehabilitation.

376-A. *Intercourse by a man with his wife during separation*—Whoever has sexual intercourse with his own wife, who is living separately from him under a decree of separation or under any custom or usage without her consent shall be punished with imprisonment of either description for a term which may extend to two years and shall also be liable to fine.

376-B. *Intercourse by public servant with woman in his custody* – Whoever, being a public servant takes advantage of his official position and induces, or seduces, any woman who is in his custody as such public servant or in the custody of a public servant subordinate to him, to have sexual intercourse with him, such sexual intercourse not amounting to the offence of rape, shall be punished with imprisonment of either description for a term which may extend to five years and shall also be liable to fine.

376-C. *Intercourse by superintendent of jail, remand home etc.* – Whoever, being the superintendent or manager of jail, remand home or other place of custody established by or under any law for the time being in force of a women's or children's institution takes advantage of his official position and induces or seduces any female inmate of such jail, remand home or other place of custody established by or under any law for the time being in force or of a women's or children's institution takes advantage of his official position and induces or seduces any female place or institution to have sexual intercourse with him such sexual intercourse not amounting to the offence of rape, shall be punished with imprisonment or either description for a term which may extend to five years and shall also be liable to fine.

376-D. *Intercourse by any member of the management or staff of a hospital with any woman in that hospital* – Whoever, being on the management of a hospital or being on the staff of a hospital takes advantage of his position and has sexual intercourse with any woman in that hospital, such sexual intercourse not amounting to the offence of rape shall be punished with imprisonment of either description for a term which may extend to five years and shall also be liable to fine.

Amendment of Section 327 – In the Code of Criminal Procedure, 1973 (hereinafter referred to as the Criminal Procedure Code), Section 327 shall he renumbered as sub-section (1) of that section and alter it, as so renumbered, the following sub-section shall be inserted, namely:

> Notwithstanding anything contained in sub-section (1), the inquiry into the trial rape or an offence under Section

376, Section 376-A, Section 376-13, Section 376-C or Section 376-D of the Indian Penal Code shall be conducted in camera:

Provided that the presiding judge may, if he thinks fit, or, on an application made by either of the parties, allow any particular room or building used by the court.

Where any proceedings are held under sub-section (2), it shall not be lawful for any person to print or publish any matter in relation to any such proceedings except with the previous permission of the Court.

Amendment to the First Schedule – In the first Schedule to the Criminal Procedure Code, under the Indian Penal Code, under the heading "1 – Offences under the Indian Penal Code".

Dowry Related Violence

Dowry is clearly a dangerous interdisciplinary problem, and this is reflected in the research conducted on the subject. Once a woman is perceived merely as property, or the bearer of property, any individual woman's rights to property given by her parents on the occasion of marriage is in a sense, assumed to be transferred to the ownership of the new family. When a mother-in-law virtually confiscates a new bride's possessions and gives them to her own daughters or to someone else, we find clear evidence of abuses of the dowry system which can have disastrous consequences. Again it would be too simplistic to blame traditions like the joint family system, for such abuses do not occur in all joint families. The dowry problem is an immensely complex and complicated phenomenon in South Asian societies and that no quick-fix solutions can be offered. One of the most worrying aspects of dowry-related violence among South Asian women has been that problems have been on the increase and now occur no longer only in South Asia, but also somewhere far away in South Asia, London, other British cities, and in the urban centres of North America.

All the international conferences on dowry and bride-burning generated fierce debates about different approaches to the dowry problem itself. If we want to protect South Asian women from dowry deaths, it is not enough to engage merely in polite talk or detached academic discourse. Many Asians in Britain and North America are not keen to talk about the problems surrounding dowry transactions. Their defensive reactions confirm that the dowry problem constitutes a huge social problem in the communities themselves. While we may respect the right of individuals not to talk about such problems, we cannot simply condone the fact that a growing number of South Asian women has been falling victim to dowry-related violence.

Instead of defining the problems away and closing our eyes to such disturbing aspects of current daily reality as the systematic murder of South Asian women, we have pursued the path of trying to understand how dowry-related violence is brought about and how such violence might be restricted. Speaking for a moment as someone with a specific interest in legal aspects of this problem, we want to highlight the fact that the various legal protection mechanisms developed by South Asian legal systems, in particular, have led to some prosecutions of murderers, but overall they have not been sufficiently effective to control, let alone stop, dowry murders. In contrast, North American legal systems and English law have only just begun to take notice of legal problems relating to dowry among South Asians in England, the USA and Canada. In these countries the absence of culture-specific knowledge about dowry problems among South Asians adds to the dangers for South Asian women in diaspora, increasing their isolation and helplessness in situations of crisis.

Dowry-related violence has a complex economic and social dimensions which need to be unravelled, and which any remedial strategy must not overlook. Significantly, it became impossible for participants in the three anti-dowry conferences so far to stick to tempting slogans like 'Dowry is bad! Abolish dowry!' As we heard again and again, the truth of the matter is that many South Asian women actually expect, want and more or less demand dowries or their equivalents.

While it would be foolish to deny that there may be elements of tradition which feed the roots of the dowry problems which south Asians face today, dowry as a phenomenon is too complex to yield to any one-dimensional explanation of its origin and development into a custom of questionable pedigree. Given the internal diversity and long history of Hindu traditions specifically, and South Asian traditions more generally, one could prove almost anything by reference to tradition.

Dowry and Bride-Burning

During the First Conference on "Dowry and Bride-Burning in India" at Harvard, Professor Michael Witzel showed that the ancient Sanskrit texts mention a number of relevant aspects and subjects which relate to the dowry problem. Witzel noted in particular the fact that brotherless daughters could inherit property and could also become an appointed daughter, which meant that such a daughter's son would then be acknowledged as continuing his grandfather's patriliny and would inherit the maternal grandfather's property. This was obviously a clever device, a legal fiction, as it were, to ensure the continuity of a bloodline which was in danger of being discontinued.

As a general statement on whether daughters can inherit property, it rather shows the opposite of what modernists would like to see, normally, a man's sons would inherit the family property, while the daughters, in classic patrilineal and patrilocal fashion, would move away to follow the husband. In normal circumstances, daughters did not inherit immovable property but took only movables with them into marriage. What the old classic fiction about the daughter's son also tells us, however, is that ancient Indian tradition was flexible enough to take account of emergencies and of difficult situations.

Old Hindu law is not a rigid rule system which cannot cater for change or is oblivious to pressures for finding a proper balance between patrilineal and matrilineal ideologies. Therefore, it would be wrong to claim in principle that a Hindu daughter could never inherit the family's property. What is for example, of the institution of the *gharjamai*, the son-in-law who agrees to move to the wife's home and who then takes on the business of looking after the family's economic affairs? There are many variations within South Asian traditions, Hindu, Muslim and others, so that no one regime of property relations was absolutely dominant. With regard to marriage and dowry, the old sources appear to be familiar with the concept of dowry in the sense that a bride would bring possessions with her to the new home. These possessions, crystallised in the rather wider term *vahatuni*, signifying all the things that are brought with the bridal procession, may be exclusively the woman's property, or they may not be.

Far from being owned by others as chattels, Hindu women were also perceived as individuals in their own right. After all they constituted the most precious element of human creation, since women alone could give birth and thus ensure the continuity of humanity. There seems to be much unspoken agreement in the specialist literature that the birth monopoly protected ancient South Asian women against annihilation. It had the effect that killing a woman, and certainly killing a bride at the point of entry to that phase of life in which she was supposed to be most productive, would be viewed as the most heinous of violations of the eternal order (*rita*).

In view of this conceptual context, Witzel argued that, within such traditional frameworks of reference, bride burning or dowry deaths, of course, do not occur at all. Such behaviour goes against the *Shruti* rule not to kill any woman. Later conceptualisations of this superhuman order do not stress the key role of women to the same extent. In a sense, the refusal of modern women to accept a predestined role as birth machines is matched by the relative de-recognition of the female birth monopoly.

We know quite a bit about ancient Indian society and its development, but it is apparent that new research is required to answer new question's that now arise about the relevance of traditions. Asking why South Asian women today are subjected to killings of the type we have seen, and being given explanatory models which contain references to the insufficiency of dowry, we need to know more about what dowry actually is and why it is considered so essential for the success of a marital relationship. On the First Dowry Conference at Harvard, R. N. Tripathi referred to the so-called eight forms of marriage among Hindus as a potential source of further information about the value attached to dowry transactions. In this context it is highly significant that the best form of marriage, the *brahma* form, is the one in which the bride herself is the sole consideration. In other words, the solemn transfer of the bride to her new home is for the sake of continuity undertaken not for any financial gain but for mankind, signified in the sacramental tie between a specific husband and wife.

The dominant ideal model within Hindu tradition is

therefore, it seems, the transfer of a virgin bride to the husband's family for no consideration at all. If we look at this contract in its social context, the absence of any direct consideration may well be a sign that the wife-giving family would, in turn, be entitled to expect that it was given wives from the other side. At this stage of our research on the dowry problem among South Asians today, far too little is known about why and to what extent brides were given something in marriage which we would call dowry.

Already the ancient material makes it clear, however, that there are various aspects of dowry transactions which can be distinguished. The treasure-chest of the old *vahatum* probably contains many different things. The idealised and idealising old texts appear to suggest that these were willingly given. But it is equally clear that women were not killed and maimed because the dowry they brought with them was insufficient. Thus, tradition involves South Asian women in some form of dowry transaction, but before one condemns this outright, one ought to reflect whether what we now refer to as dowry problem might not be a more recent phenomenon. At the same time, giving presents to a daughter on her wedding looks also like some kind of ancient, universal phenomenon. The firm conclusions on the role of tradition in this context may ultimately be possible, and we will not get any clearer answers unless a good deal of specific research is conducted on such questions. The resources for this, in the form of texts and material, are available in suffocating magnitude. What we need is researchers who can undertake this kind of painstaking work, and who are not merely excellent linguists but are mindful also of the social contexts within which the textual statements need to be interpreted.

The first two International Conferences on Dowry and Bride-Burning were held at Harvard. The two conferences were organised jointly by the International Society Against Dowry and Bride-Burning in India (ISADABB) in Boston, Massachusetts and by the Committee on South Asian Studies at Harvard University. The conferences in particular attracted much attention among North American South Asians as well as international participants. In the first conference, eighteen papers were presented and lively discussions continued throughout the three days of the event. A souvenir volume collecting the papers from the first conference was issued, but its circulation has been limited. Some of the papers, together with other work, have been published in the electronic *Journal of South Asia Women Studies 1995-97* but that journal does not focus particularly on the dowry problem and looks at South Asian women's studies more generally.

Recounting her own journey of discovery about the extent of the dowry problem in India Julia Leslie argued for serious thinking about the links between past and present, and called for more attention to be given to the connections between dowry and female property rights generally. Another keynote paper from the first conference seeks to provide an overview of the issues surrounding dowry-related violence and also offers a preliminary literature review. It is argued that, at the end of the day, dowry-related violence represents a breakdown of civilised behaviour, akin to a serious form of bullying. In other words, this becomes a form of domestic violence, ultimately denying the newly married woman even the right to live.

Professor Witzel showed clearly that ancient Hindu law did not underwrite dowry extortion, but that dowry in the sense of presents made to the bride by her parents and natal family, was known. In the ideal order of things the bride herself was the main consideration and the most precious asset on which all ritual and social attention was focused. What a contrast between this idealised depiction of tradition and a detailed presentation given during the same conference about an actual case of dowry murder affecting a South Asian family in the USA! Several papers focused on domestic violence generally and the marginalised position of women, arranged marriages and their consequences, as well as various marriage practices linked to dowry and gift-giving. Some of these papers could not be included in our present collection. Ms. Bandita Phukan emphasised in a brief paper that sons are not essential for the execution of Hindu rites and that daughters can act in their place, thus seeking to oppose the gender-based ideology according to which daughters are only burdens and no asset to a Hindu family. Uma Narayan examined the effects of modernisation on patterns of marriage arrangements in India and concluded that the process of modernisation, by itself, has not benefited women, that it has in fact made marriage arrangements more prone to hazards which could negatively rebound on women, making them more vulnerable to violence. Bisraam Rambilass presents the interesting argument that South African Indians did not and do not indulge in the demanding of dowry and claims that such practices are largely absent in his country. At the same time, he provides evidence of the inflation of expenses surrounding marriage, a theme which several other contributors have also picked up as an indicator of spiralling anxieties related to dowry problems.

The first Harvard Conference gradually shifted away from the classic approach of simply blaming the male side, or the husband's family, and began to look more closely at the roles played by the wife's family. It was found that the simply binary opposition of male-female does not make sense in this discussion since in most cases the wife-givers of today would be the wife-takers of tomorrow. Several contributors showed clearly that the dowry problem was integrated with many other socio-psychological issues and that an exclusive focus on dowry could not explain why South Asian women suffer dowry-related violence and continue to die. As a result of that first conference, it was even more obvious that further research was needed to explain and elucidate certain specific points.

The second Harvard Dowry Conference gave space to a more specific analysis of the economic and legal aspects surrounding dowry problems. Specialist papers had been produced for this conference and were discussed in detail. Our discussions focused in particular on the economic aspects surrounding dowry and the effectiveness of legal control mechanisms. Bisakha Sen's paper explained why dowry still persists in India, using economic models which show convincingly that the wife's family actually benefits from offering and giving dowry. This challenging paper, which we have included although it is primarily addressed to a more specialist readership of economists, confirmed the earlier preliminary view that one-sided blaming of male extortion might not be sufficient to explain why dowry problems have continued with such vigour among South Asians.

Finding that the socio-economic conditions in South Asia so strongly operate in favour of continuing the transfer of resources to the bride and the groom's family on the occasion of marriage, Bisakha Sen began to explore the next logical step, asking how it can be made more certain that any resources transferred in this way would actually benefit the woman. The suggestion that this is a law-job may be correct, but surely this is a matter not only for the law, but in the first instance for members of society? It will surely be useful to explore the economic rationales of Bisakha Sen's paper further and to contrast scenarios in which women do benefit economically from the dowry given to them on marriage with situations where such assets or their use are withheld from the woman because the husband or members of his family appropriated them as soon as they could. The law paper which presented at the Second Dowry Conference assessed and analysed in some detail how modern Indian law has sought to control the dowry problem. The almost universal perception that the Indian anti-dowry law has been a complete failure was correct until recently. However, beginning in the mid-1980s, the legal control and retribution mechanisms for dowry murder in Indian law have been strengthened by a number of new enactments which have gradually led to more strictly enforced judicial supervision.

Still, despite growing evidence of convictions for dowry murders, it was found that those strict legal deterrent's remained largely ineffective because only very few prosecutions for dowry murder or dowry-related violence were ever brought to the courts. It transpired that there are continuing problems of implementation of the anti-dowry laws at ground level, and it became evident that further research would be needed on this aspect of the legal control mechanisms.

The London Dowry Conference on 14–15 November 1997 had two major aims. It wanted to bring together our current knowledge about dowry-related violence among South Asians and to apply this to case studies reflection specifically on the British Asian experience. The morning session was devoted to a round-up on existing research on the dowry problem. The economic and legal aspects of the dowry problem were addressed through Bisakha Sen's paper on the economic dimensions of dowry. On the legal front, the detailed analysis of Indian case law on dowry was used as a basis for further discussion on legal strategies to combat dowry-related violence. It was confirmed that it is no longer correct to assert categorically that Indian courts currently do not convict dowry murderers.

A more updated analysis of the *Indian Dowry Prohibition Act, 1961* shows, however, that despite many amendments to the anti-dowry law in India, women continue to be killed. Is appears that the legal deterrents by themselves do not lead to a decline in dowry-related violence. The law has many loopholes, only some of which were plugged during the 1980s. While the legal definition of dowry has now been tightened, the giving as well as the taking of dowry are still crimes, and many participants in the discussion felt that this remains a major drawback. Most cases of dowry murder in South Asia never even go to court. Manjaree Chowdhary from India threw some light on the reasons for such legal inefficiency and anti-women collusion. The evident non-implementation of the anti-dowry law in India, presented as a powerful first-hand account, starkly illustrated why dowry crimes are still not pursued with the required vigour by Indian enforcement agencies. The special focus of the London Conference on dowry problems among Asians in Britain today led, as expected, to animated debates following two papers based on fieldwork, presented by Rohit Barot (Bristol) on dowry among British Gujaratis and Jagbir Jhutti (Oxford) on dowry among Sikhs in Britain.

The dowry conferences held so far have each identified a set of focal points of concern and established an agenda for further research, which will be pursued in a series of further conferences. We have begun to link dowry-related violence with studies on domestic violence generally, and the need for more fieldwork-related explorations of the subject has become very evident indeed. With particular reference to Asians in Britain, we need to explore further to what extent specific research on dowry-related violence could assist law enforcers in the UK, as well as the countries of North America, to gain better knowledge and awareness about the dowry problems among South Asians. The ultimate aim is to save thousands of young women from a gruesome death.

Dowry-related violence and the associated problems have continued to escalate, irrespective of various legal measures in the countries of the subcontinent, and despite much social censure against dowry-related violence in the overseas Asian communities of Britain and North America. As a group of socially-conscious academics and activists who seek to save lives, we have been painfully aware of such limitations. Simple sloganeering about the desirability of abolishing dowry altogether misses important points. Similarly, any laws which envisage a total ban on dowry or its outright prohibition are not going to be effective in social reality. If a total ban on dowry is not a realistic option, because the people with whom we are concerned want to have some form of exchange, gift-giving and transfer of property, what other avenues of curbing dowry-related violence can we think for many conference participants, there was a need to think about acceptable forms of exchange that fall under our definitions of dowry. As a leading Indian social activist with a focus on women's right, Madhu Kishwar initially tried to use techniques of public protest and boycott to highlight abuses of the dowry system to call for the total abolition of dowry transactions. She was then told by women who had benefited from dowry transfers that, in essence, she had no business to tell other women to renounce their dowry claims. The dowry conferences held so far have taught us similar lessons. When it comes to dowry, we cannot throw the baby out with the bath water; we have to co-exist with the fact that various dowry systems are operated by people in their respective social circles.

5

Women's Participation in Government

The British introduced local democracy in India by constituting municipal councils and the municipal corporations in the last quarter of the nineteenth century. They also provided a federal structure to the country with the Government of India Act, 1935. The country today has a quasi-federal structure.

Apart from the Government of India in New Delhi, there are twenty-five States with their own state governments. The Seventh Schedule to the Constitution of India divides the subjects of State activity between the Union and state governments. The Union (Centre) as well as State governments in India both have a parliamentary form of government based on the Westminster pattern. The executive powers of the central government are vested in the Council of Ministers with the Prime Minister at its head. Similarly, the executive powers in the State governments are vested in its Council of Ministers with the Chief Minister at its head. However, following the Westminister pattern, the Head of the State is not the Prime Minister but an indirectly elected President, who broadly performs the role as the Head of State. India has a bicameral parliament, with the Lower House directly elected by the people on the lines of the House of Commons in the UK. or the House of Representatives in the USA.

The Upper House is more like the US Senate. It is a permanent house with one-third members retiring every two years. Like in the USA, the Vice President of the country presides on the Upper House. Although local government in India is a subject of the State governments, the seventy-third and the seventy-fourth amendments to the Constitution of India now make it obligatory for the State governments to organise local bodies, to hold regular elections to them and to give them appropriate finances.

The urban local bodies are of three grades; municipal corporations for cities with a population of more than (0.3 million), municipal councils for towns smaller than this population limit and nagar panchayats for villages in transition to becoming towns. These bodies are elected on a universal suffrage basis, with all citizens above the age of eighteen years of age having a right to vote.

The rural local bodies are organised in three tiers, the village panchayat at the village level, the block panchayat samiti for about 100 villages and a district council for a district comprising about 1000 villages. The rural local bodies do not have many resources of their own. They actually spend the state government funds as implementing agencies.

Civil Service

The civil service in India is a closed system, with a very limited scope for lateral entry at senior level. Most permanent officials join the service as a lifetime career through an entrance examination/ interview conducted by the Public Service Commission. The age of entry is usually 21 to 30 years and the age of retirement either 58 or 60 years of age. The subject matter of the Government of India is divided between the Union Government and the State Governments. The respective governments recruit most of their employees independently. However, a unique feature of the Indian system is the existence of three All India Services, the Indian Administrative Service, the Indian Police Service and the Indian Forest Service.

The Government of India recruits the members of these services although they work with the States where they are allotted (their cadres) for most of their career. However, the Government of India obtains the services of these officers at higher and middle management levels through deputation for a period of about five years. This enables a regular exchange of officers between the field and the central levels. Senior Indian Administrative Service Officers who have had their initial grounding in different States of India thus man the top secretariat posts in most ministries of the Government of India. India is a democratic republic and full freedom of speech and religion is allowed to all its citizens.

The Constitution of India guarantees the following Fundamental Rights to the citizens of India.

Right to equality: This includes equality before law. Prohibition of discrimination on grounds of religion, race, caste, sex or place of birth and equality of opportunity in matters of employment.

Right to freedom: This includes protection of certain rights regarding freedom of speech etc., protection of life and personal liberty and protection against arrest and detention in certain cases.

Right against exploitation: This includes prohibition of traffic in human beings and forced labour and prohibition of employment of children in factories etc.

Right to freedom of religion: This includes freedom of conscience and free profession, practice and propagation of religion, freedom to manage religious affairs, freedom as to payment of taxes for promotion of any particular religion and freedom as to attendance at religious instruction or religious worship in certain educational institutions.

Cultural and educational rights: These include protection of interests of minorities and the right of minorities to establish and administer educational institutions. The Constitution of India further guarantees the right to move to the Supreme Court for enforcement of the above rights.

India has a multitude of political parties; some organised on economic ideology, some on religious ideology while some on local and linguistic aspirations. However, only three or four parties really have a presence at the National level; the Congress Party that was the ruling party for more than forty years, the Bharatiya Janata Party, the Janata Dal and the Communists. There are many religion-based parties like the Akali Dal, the Muslim League etc.

The regional parties like the DMK and AIADMK (Tamil Nadu), Shiv Sena (Maharashtra), Telugu Desam (Andhra Pradesh) and some parties in the smaller North-Eastern States have been contenders of powers in the State governments of their respective states. However, at the National level, only three parties have been able to provide the Prime Minister i.e. the Congress, the BJP and the Janata Party/Janata Dal in alliance with smaller parties.

Election Commission

An independent body called the Election Commission of India conducts elections to the parliament and the state legislatures in

India. The elections are based on a universal adult suffrage with voting rights to all citizens above eighteen years of age. The lower houses of the national and the state legislatures have a five-year term although elections are regularly held before this term expires.

The elections to the local bodies have been brought under the purview of a similarly constituted body called the State Election Commission. These bodies also usually have a five-year term. It is statutorily not possible to supersede the local bodies for long periods or to keep them under Government-appointed Administrators.

An age of more than twenty-one years is usually an eligibility condition for getting elected to an elective post in a local body. The eligibility for being a member of the Lower House of the National or state legislatures similarly prescribes the minimum age of twenty-five years.

A minimum age-limit of thirty years is similarly a qualification for membership of the Upper Houses of the National and State A minimum age-limit of thirty-five years is prescribed as a qualification for holding the post of the President or Vice-President of the Indian Republic. The elections to both the urban and rural local bodies in India are ward based. The local area is divided into wards of more or less equal population. Each ward sends one representative to the concerned local body. After the Seventy-third and Seventy-fourth Amendments to the Constitution of India, one-third of the wards are reserved for women candidates and only women candidates can contest elections from these wards. Apart from the reservation for women candidates, some other wards are reserved for candidates from socially underprivileged sections.

Political parties are allowed to take part in elections to all local bodies except the village panchayats in India. It is, however, not uncommon for locally influential politicians to form local fronts to contest and win elections to municipal councils and the smaller municipal corporations in the country. India became independent in the year 1947. In all the elections held since independence, women had the voting rights.

Women play a dual role in politics—as voters and political representatives. On the voting front, though adult franchise was granted in 1937, it was the progressive spirit that pervaded the making of the constitution that made it a reality. The Constitution of India guarantees equal rights to men and women as voters and citizens.

Usually, however, countries that do hold regular elections show an improved recognition of women as a political constituency and parties and candidates tend to adopt pro-women stances and appeal specifically to women's votes, especially at the time of elections. This becomes very evident when we look at consecutive elections in the Indian context, wherein there is a growing consciouseness of the need to woo the woman voter and the need to pay attention to the needs and issues of women, in the election manifestos of political parties.

Since Independence, due to exercise of their franchise, Indian women have been exposed to the political processes and are showing increasing awareness about not only lack of rights but also their utility. A majority of illiterate rural women are also politically sensitive and aware of the various issues confronting them. Women get easily mobilised in the political processes by the political parties who approach women very often for party issues and for short-term goals by winning elections, but not for long-term goals of bringing about social changes and gender equality in political power-sharing. In all the elections held since independence, women had the voting rights.

The percentage of seats won against the seats contested is showing a declining trend only because the number of women contesting elections has increased sharply. However, it may be seen that voting by women in all tiers of Government has always been a feature of the Indian Polity since 1947. Due to the parternalistic family and male dominated political structures which do not provide space for women in decision-making bodies, women constituted 3.1 per cent of the total contestants in 1996 election and did not occupy more than 6.10 per cent of the total seats in the state legislative assemblies and Parliament.

Women in Elections

The number of women contestants in Parliamentary elections has not increased significantly over the years. Political parties are still reluctant to field women candidates at national level.

In the early days of the Indian republic, the number of women representatives was a mere 22, which was a lowly 4.4 per cent of the total seats in the Lok Sabha. The sixth Loksabha in the year 1977 saw an all time low of just 19 woman representatives. The twelfth Lok Sabha had 44 women i.e. 8.8 per cent of the total.

Even as early as the 19th century Indian women had begun to appear on the national scene in public and political activity. Women were not only being accepted in public activity but were organising themselves to fight for their rights in different walks of life. Though women constitute nearly half of the population of the country, it was only after Independence that efforts were made to promote women's participation in public life.

Though the Constitution of India provides for the Government to make special provisions to safeguard the interests of women. It has not made any provision for reservation for women in respect of jobs and political offices. However 73rd and 74th Constitional Amendment Act mandated reservation of one-third seats in the village, block, districts, municipal elected bodies in India.

As a consequence, women had not advanced much politically and economically. From the records available of the past 50 years, since the independence, it is seen that the strength of women in the political field as reflected in State legislatures remained at an average of 3 per cent to 5 per cent of those elected. At the level of Parliament, the position of women members has varied between 5 to 7 per cent .

Women in large numbers have come out against atrocities on women, in defence of their traditional control over crucial resources, water., forests, and land, mass literacy drives and other issues. They are also coming out in large numbers over ecological degradation, price rise or protests against police repression, etc. While there is the increased participation in grass root political movements, it is not getting translated into a growing share of women in the formal political structure of the country.

Amongst the several reasons for such a situation is the growing money power and muscle power required to contest even the smallest of elections in India, the intimidation, violence and slander that a woman candidate has to face combined with the traditional male domination that seeks to keep her indoors. Narrow electoral arithmetic and the necessity of fielding a winning candidate makes most political parties shy away from fielding more than a token number of women candidates. And if they are fielded at all, kinship and affinity factors play a major role.

Increasingly, women have stood for elections and got elected as members of State Legislative Assemblies and the Parliament.

However, at the national level there is only one woman Cabinet Minister and 8 Ministers of State in a Cabinet of 70. There is only one woman Governor and one woman Chief Minister. Some studies of Parliamentary participation indicate that women members participate more actively in 'women's issues' - health, welfare, atrocities against women, crimes like dowry and violations of human rights. This participation is confined to the more articulate women. In issues such as defence, finance, politics, etc. their participation is relatively limited.

The 73rd and 74th Amendments to the Indian Constitution have served as a major break through towards ensuring women's equal access and increased participation in political power structures. This Amendment provided for reservation of one third of seats for women at level of local governance in urban areas.

There is also a one-third reservation for women for posts of chairpersons of these local bodies. This amendment has initiated a powerful strategy of affirmative action for providing the structural framework for women's participation in political decision-making and provided an opportunity to bring women to be forefront and centre of city development and develop new grass-root level leadership. There are about one million elected women representatives in Panchayats and Municipal Bodies in India.

After 1993, women's participation in local governments increased quite radically, with the enactment of the legislation providing 33 per cent reservation of seats for women in local bodies. The legislation and its implementation has added another level in political participation.

In Governments too, there has been limited representatives of women. A few eminent women have no doubt, occupied important administrative positions, such as Secretaries of Departments in the National Government as well as in State Governments. It is only 5.71 per cent of the total number of persons in administrative services are women. It is noteworthy that within the premier civil services of India, the representation of women is not that encouraging. Since relatively few women enter the civil services, several efforts have been made to improve the situation. The Department of Personnel and Administrative Reforms of the Government of India has also provided, wherever possible, women officers on the selection boards for posts and services.

The 74th Amendment to the Indian Constitution, 1992 has served as a major breakthrough towards ensuring women's equal access and increased participation in local government. The Constitution (74th Amendment) Act, 1992 aims at Constitutional guarantees to safeguard the interests of urban local self government to enable them to function as effective democratic and self governing institutions at the grass root level. This Amendment provides for reservation of 331/3 per cent of elected seats for women at local government level in urban and rural areas. There is also a one-third reservation for women of posts of chairpersons of these local bodies. A very active role for women in local governance is envisaged as compared to governance at the state and national levels in India. These provisions have provided great opportunities and challenges to women in India, particularly in the local government field. This is of great significance, since this grass-root level participation has considerably broadened the base of women's participation in politics at city level.

Involvement of women in the political arena and in decision-making roles is an important tool for empowerment as well as monitoring standards of political performance at local level. However, in the present political process of entry into decision making political institutions, there is growing influence of money and muscle power, backroom dealings, communalisation and criminalisation. In many respects women and men elected representatives face similar problems on election to office.

Above all there is a need to understand just how to be a good local politician. The role of political representatives at local level is demanding and all new 'recruits' need time to gain experience and to understand the rules, regulations and procedures governing the administrative bureaucracy with which they now have to work-often quite closely in the urban service delivery system. Some of the major constraints that prevent women from effective participation at local level are as follows:

1. Lack of orientation / training in urban development issues and municipal administration.
2. No proper knowledge/orientation about municipal acts and rules and regulations.
3. No prior experience about dealing with multidimensional urban development issues/civic

issues and its complexities.

4. Lack of knowledge about technical in-puts related to urban service delivery system.
5. Lack of support from senior male / female colleagues in the party / municipal body.
6. Less co-operation from municipal officials understanding about various facets of the budget, such as allocation of budget at ward level.
7. Lack of party support and poor organisational structure.
8. Lack of money and resources to sustain the electoral campaigns.
9. Discrimination in decision making at party level.
10. Specific notions towards politics and political atmosphere.
11. Fear and insecurity.
12. Lack of confidence in public speaking.
13. Criminalisation of politics and use of money power.
14. Family responsibilities.

Political system in India works through political parties who contend for power by invoking popular support. Therefore it is necessary that if women want to share power they have to make a place for themselves within the political parties through which the Indian democratic system operates. The experience of the last 52 years show an inability to create this space and recent studies show that there has been no significant change in either the nature of women's functioning or in the political parties' approach to women and women's issues. If we examine women's participation it is seen that the political parties have given less importance to women's issues in terms of ideology, either in priority in their party manifesto or in terms of the number and importance of the position that women occupied in individual political parties.

Women are not seen as a vote bank to be approached, and once the men are mobilised, women will merely endorse their choice of party and candidate. Male candidates rarely have access to the female electorate and there are not enough women involved in political campaigns to be able to reach out to a large section of women even in big cities. As a result, the exposure of women to political debates and issues has always remained indirect. According to women from all parties the political environment was not conducive to women's participation in politics.

Reservation of seats for women in Panchayats/Municipal bodies have shown that it has tremendous implications, not merely in terms of the number of women entering the public arena and holding public office, but also in terms of the social, economic and political impact that these reservations have had for the total system.

It is for these reasons that women are increasingly demanding political roles for themselves. They recognise that constitutional guarantees do not ensure effective participation and that these cannot ensure political equality. Hence the need to gain entry into political institutions and in the functioning of the state, and to share control over the power the state exercises. This alone would lead to a situation where women are able to reverse the existing situation, which has consistently been against their interests, and bring about the necessary changes in policy and the social structure so as to ensure a more equitable and humane order.

Role in Elected Bodies

The role of women's participation in elected bodies should not be undervalued. Elections are after all a forum for self government and democracy, they are significant in drawing the attention of the nation to the problems and needs of disadvantaged sections; the manifestos, campaigns, promises made by individual candidates, track record and future course of action of political parties are indicative of national concerns as well as mandates for action. Proper selection of candidates in an election is vital if this representative democracy is to function in the interests of a majority of the population that is depressed and disadvantaged. Hence, opportunities for participation at this level are significant for the adoption of politics and measures for women's development.

Strong and dynamic women who would not dream of appropriating privilege are today talking of reservation because they have come to recognise that they will not give easy entry in the corridors of power without reservation. This hierarchy is so rigid that the natural processes of democracy and constitutional guarantees have not been able to make a dent in these fortresses of power. The demand for reservation should not therefore be seen as either a gift or a privilege that women are seeking. For most women it is the last straw and a desperate measure to ensure their coming into the political mainstream.

Their participation becomes vital in the context of the adoption of development strategies that are negative and harmful to women. Today most of the political parties in India have initiated some initiatives to activate political participation of women and develop their capacities. However, most of the political parties have not yet developed any special programmes to meet the special requirements of women in urban or rural areas, despite the fact that most of the women activists felt that if planned efforts were made, they could be easily mobilised.

Different debates concerning struggles of women as well as various actions by women's groups and NGOs on local as well as national problems have forced the mainstream political parties to accept women's concerns in their political programmes. The political parties started changing their attitude towards women which is reflected in their election manifestos, their attitudes towards women candidates, speeches and slogans.

Statistics on women's participation in the electoral process are not very encouraging. It is important not only to pressurise the political parties but also to make the leaders understand the significance of organising systematic training of women possessing leadership qualities, of carefully selecting women candidates and ensuring financial, technical and human resources for affirmative action.

The need to strengthen womens' participation and leadership is constantly emphasised by various institutions viz, All India Institute of Local Self Government, NIUA, HSMI, Rambhau Mhalaji Prabhodini, etc., and several NGOs and Women's groups like SEWA, Working Womens' Forum, YUVA, Disha, Prayas, Astha, Winavani, SNDT University, Aalochana, Agni, FASDSP (Forum Against Sex-determination and Sex Preselection), Stree Mukti Sanghathana, etc.

Many NGOs / CBOs, Womens' groups have provided some training, however systematic training of women possessing leadership qualities is not enough and more concentrated efforts are required to facilitate the process of women's ascent to key positions in political field. It is essential that the women's groups and movement recognise the importance of women as a constituency and ensure their participation and representation in policy formulation. The movement must provide a support system for women who enter political processes to win elections.

The women's movement has been a powerful agent of

empowerment and has provided an alternative perspective for fundamental structural changes. The movement has created organisational strength of women, has focused on women's issues and mobilised them around these issues. The women in the movement, however, have shied away from active participation in politics. The women's groups and women activists thus aim to bring about a change in the women's perceptions, but not necessarily in the structures which subordinate women. If we want to bring about change in the lives of women and transform mainstream politics, there is no other way than to get involved in politics and transform it.

Women's Movement

The women's movement and groups have to recognise the importance of women as a constituency and ensure their participation and representation in policy formulation. This can be achieved through reorienting existing structures for entry into decision-making including the political party system and introduce quotas or reservation as a temporary means of women's representation. The movement should also provide a support system for women who enter political processes to win elections.

The women's groups working at the grassroots level are small and scattered and have diverse ways of empowering women. There are no infrastructural facilities of networking available that could bring them together and strengthen them while allowing autonomy in their functioning. It is important to create unity in diversity between women's groups, organisations and individuals involved with women's empowerment. They need to adopt a common strategy, informed by a common vision, to be able to bring about changes in the policies and structures that perpetuate their subordinate status.

Reservation for women in local government is not just a question of getting a certain number 'in'; it also develops their capacities to play their rightful roles in the development process and makes an important difference as the local governments deals mostly with the quality of life for citizens. Municipal responsibilities relate both to women's practical needs and their strategic needs. The better we meet women's strategic needs, the better they are able to contribute to good city governance. Good Local Governance, in turn, enables a better response to women's practical needs.

Most local governments have initiated orientation / training programmes to encourage women to participate in local governance by organising city-specific induction or theme-based training programmes, wherein intensive training is given in various subject areas, such as, municipal acts and its implementation, laws of meetings, municipal budgeting, budgeting at ward level, municipal taxation, mobilisation of resources, urban service delivery systems (solid waste management, water supply, sewerage, health care services, traffic and transportation), poverty alleviation schemes, community management, environment management, shelter programmes, new reforms in municipal administration, functioning of ward committees, motivation techniques, communication skills, women and development, handling the media etc.

The Ministry of Urban Development, Government of India and Urban Development Department of State Governments organise a number of training programmes, workshops, seminars for women elected representatives at local level through various training institutions. Many municipal bodies have initiated a series of in-house training in municipal administration and urban development, in collaboration with premier training institutions in India.

State governments through their State Training Centres organise capacity building programmes for women elected members from municipal bodies in their States. Special training / orientation programmes are organised by Ministry of Urban Development and Poverty Alleviation, Government of India under the UNICEF assistance and government's funds in the area of poverty alleviation schemes and its implementation in urban areas.

Local governments are using sex-desegregated data for policy and programme formulation. It is an obligatory duty of municipal governments in India to collect, compile and maintain vital statistics in their city limits. Sex-disaggregated data is in use in many cities of the States in India for policy programme formulation and implementation of some special programmes and projects at local city level.

The Government of India regularly collects, analyses and disseminates quantitative and qualitative data on the number of women and men employed at various levels in government on an annual basis and many mechanisms have been set up within governmental structures for monitoring progress in this field.

The Department of Women and Child Development,

Government of India is collecting and using gender-disaggregated data to evaluate development from a gender perspective. The Department is also developing a Gender Development Index (GDI) for the construction of EDI and Gender Empowerment Measure (GEM).

Government departments, other institutions, non-governmental organisations, and women's organisations have undertaken several programmes to sensitise local governments about the issues and needs of women in their cities. Law enforcement is a critical factor for bringing about enduring changes in gender perceptions. Several initiatives have been taken by the Government of India and the voluntary sector to sensitise law enforcement personnel and policy makers.

Gender sensitisation of police personnel and urban administrators in the National and State level training centres is now a regular programme. A National Centre for Gender Training and Research has set up in the National Academy of Administration in Mussourie with the objective of sensitising young administrators and policy makers on gender issues.

The Election Commission of India maintains updated information on women representatives in each Parliament, including categorised information on the number of scheduled castes women representatives. With the recent revolution in information technology, the entire information is available not only in print but also on the internet in the Parliament and Election Commission websites. This increases out-reach and access of this information to the general public.

The Ministry of Rural Development, Government of India maintains updated information on the representation of women in local self-government or Panchayati Raj. The Department of Women and Child Development, Government of India also has come out with publications like 'Women in India – A Statistical Profile' in 1997, which compiled information on all aspects related to women in India. The Planning Commission, which is mooting the process of collection of gender desegregated data by all concerned departments in various Ministers, has included information on women's representation in power and decision-making in its Ninth Five Year Plan Document.

Besides these, several independent organisations are carrying out their own research and surveys that provide updated information on the same. These are also widely used and are quoted in different public documents. Sensitising the leadership of people's movements in the country to gender issues need to be prioritised. Prior to 1990, the women in local politics were generally either politicians who had lost membership of higher institutions, and those who were given such an opportunity to serve the purpose of publicity. In many cases, the motive was partially also to satisfy the aspirations of these few women, since they could be kept under virtual control and denied higher aspirations.

The 74th Amendment of the Indian Constitution in 1992 ushered in a new era in the democratic process of the country as it not only provided constitutional status to the municipal bodies but also provided an enabling environment for women to a direct part in the local self government and brought women to the forefront and centre of local development. Sharing power and responsibilities with immense control over resources for development and social change will be an empowering instrument for women.

Different political parties in India have shown great reluctance to field women candidates. Reservation of seats at Municipal level has put pressure on political parties to identify and field more women candidates.

Attention is being given to the training and capacity developing skills and capacities of all elected representatives in local government, including women. They are trained to acquire skills, knowledge and orientation needed to carry out the onerous responsibilities given to them. A time bound, systematic and comprehensive training programme has been drawn up which will be funded by the Central Government.

Role of IGNOU

The Indira Gandhi National Open University has been associated with the preparation of a syllabus on women and development. The Government of India is also committed to capacity building efforts by organising and funding training programmes for women elected to municipal bodies in India. A large number of such kind of training programmes for elected members are handled by All India Institute of Local Self Government which is a premier training institution in local government field (established in 1926) in India. Ministry of Urban

Development (MUD) supports several such kind of training programmes through Regional Centre for Urban and Environmental Studies (RCUES) which are functioning in all the regions of India.

Apart from this, some of the theme-based training programmes are organised by State Training Institutions in several States for women elected members in municipal bodies. Human Settlements Management Institute (HSMI) of HUDCO organises some specialised training for women elected representatives in India.

The examination indicates that women elected to local governments have not formed any formal associations, groups and forums. However, all women mayors meet during meetings organised by All India Council of Mayors (AICM), which is an association of mayors representing all cities in India. These meetings give women mayors an opportunity to interact with each other and with other male Mayors and exchange ideas, information about effective urban service delivery, good governance and also provide issue based support.

Similarly, various seminars, workshops, training programmes organised by Government of India, State Governments and National and Regional institutions provide wide opportunities for women elected members to meet and inter act with elected women members from different municipal bodies in India.

Similarly, events organised by political parties, women's groups, non-governmental organisations also provide an opportunity for women elected members for experience sharing, networking and sometimes lobbying for some specific purpose in urban development and good governance. It is also observed that in many cities women elected members have close links with local NGOs, CBOs or Residents' Associations or action groups and through such networking women members support each other and initiate networking among themselves about governance at local level or any issues related to women and development.

The following institutions undertake training or appointed officials:

i) Urban Development Department, Government of India and Urban Development Departments of various State Governments in India have initiated several capacity building or training initiatives to train women working at various levels of municipal administration.

ii) National Academy of Administration in Mussourie is actively involved in training senior government officers from Indian Administrative Services in India. The Academy has set up a National Centre for Gender Training and Research to further issues related to women and development. Apart from this, several State. Training Centres in various states organise training-cum-orientation and workshops for women appointed in local government.

It is observed that women officers from the Indian Administrative Service (IAS), Police (IPS), and Foreign Services (IFS) have their associations in all the States of India. These associations organise periodic meetings and get together which provide an opportunity for the women officials to interact with each other. The City Managers' Association of Gujarat State also provides opportunities for women officials in local government in Gujarat State. 'Metro Forum' an association of Municipal Commissioners of Metro Cities will also provide an opportunity for women municipal commissioners to meet and interact on issues related to civic governance and any other issues related to women and development. Similar efforts are underway to establish an association of women officials in all municipal bodies in India.

All India Institute of Local Self Government, through its various Centres in India imparts training in the field of municipal administration. Besides short-term specialised programmes, it also organises full time diploma courses on various aspects of municipal administration for junior and middle level municipal personnel.

These courses are attended by large number of women employed at junior and middle and senior levels in municipal bodies in India. The following main institutions also offer several need-based or tailor-made specialised programmes for women working at different levels of municipal administration in India.

The main purpose of urban management training is to develop capacities of officials to deal with the complex urban problems in a holistic manner to achieve efficiently the aim of municipal bodies and of the urban sector as a whole. One of the variables that go into the Gender Empowerment Measure, as depicted in the Human

Development Report, is the proportion of men and women at senior levels of government.

In this context the study initiated in 1996 by the Department of Personnel and Training (DoPT), as part of a project Capacity Building for Civil Services, was a significant step. In order to crystallise the problems faced by women in Civil Services as well as to isolate areas which needed to be addressed through policy guidelines, a survey was carried out across a cross section of the services, among men and women officers, to ascertain the issues on which guidelines would have to focus. The survey questionnarie was formulated keeping in mind different areas of concern for women officers like Gender Image in workplace and in the family to stress factors.

A national level Project Steering Committee was set up for carrying out the Capacity Building project, and a Focal Point was identified in the DoPT for examining the sphere of Women's Issues in the Civil Service. The Lal Bahadur Shastri National Academy of Administration (LBSNAA) was appointed as consultant for developing a curriculum for Gender Sensitisation Programmes and ten Regional Seminars were conducted at nine State Administrative Training Institutes. The Focal Point identified in the DoPT will begin work towards framing guidelines on women's issues by reviewing existing rules / regulations of various services. The task that has emerged for the Focal Point is as follows :

i) Review of existing rules and regulations for possible gender bias and discrimination against women and suggest corrective action.

ii) Co-ordinate output flowing from various activities of the project related to the issues requiring policy formulation.

Women's organisations or other civil society organisations have taken some initiatives in some states of India to encourage women to stand in local government elections, however, these groups or organisations are small and scattered and have diverse ways of empowering women. There are no infrastructural facilities of networking that could bring them together and strengthen them while allowing autonomy in their functioning. It is important to create unity in diversity between women's groups and civil society organisations involved with women's empowerment. Political participation would make a significant different if it came from those who are at the helm of affairs of political parties, and if women are there wielding power, the situation can improve to a great extent and political participation would give every woman a sense of dignity as a individual.

The women's movement and groups have to recognise the importance of women as a constituency and ensure their participation and representation in policy formulation. This can be achieved through reorienting existing structures for entry into decision-making including the political party system and introduce quotas or reservation as a temporary means of women's representation.

The movement should also provide a support system for women who enter political processes to win elections. The women's groups working at the grassroots level are small and scattered and have diverse ways of empowering women. There are no infrastructural facilities of networking available that could bring them together and strengthen them while allowing autonomy in their functioning. It is important to create unity in diversity between women's groups, organisations and individuals involved with women's empowerment. They need to adopt a common strategy, informed by a common vision, to be able to bring about changes in the policies and structures that perpetuate their subordinate status.

The 33 per cent for women in municipal bodies has brought into focus the fact that there is a need to bring more and more women into the party. But the problem is that many women are often not equipped to become members of the political parties, as the party expects a certain level of consciousness for membership— not everybody can become a member. Also, women have difficulty in attending party meetings, study circles or demonstrations because of their timings and the pressure of housework.

Most of the parties have not yet developed any special tailor—made programme to meet the special requirements of women in urban areas, despite the fact that most women activists felt that if such an effort was made, they could easily be mobilised.

Party workers at times exhibit a sense of lack of gender equality because they carry with them their traditional value systems which are often feudal and patriarchal, into the party. Much of the discrimination against women in the party is because of the attitudes of these individuals. But at the same time women assert that the party does not try to change the attitude of both men and women who come to the party or make them more gender sensitive.

The nature of electoral politics in India also marginalises women and women's issues from the political agenda. Many women feel that electoral politics, at times limits the kind of support women politicians would like to extend to members of their own sex, since they realise that they cannot win elections on women's issues alone. Most of them are still hesistant to identify themselves with women's issues, claiming that women form only one section of their constituency and till recently not the determining section. Also, elections are largely conducted by men and with men's support. Electoral expediency requires women participants to compromise to survive in the man's world of politics.

All parties recognise the need to win women's votes, but often seem unsure of the best way to gain support among women. The type of leadership required is of transformational type. Women's entry into processes of governance should create change in the very institutions of governance. In order to effect such change, leaders have to emerge which can occur only through participatory processes.

The participation allows empowerment, which then generates leadership. It is only through their leadership, and their implied changes in the hierarchy of party and power that they may provide that they can justifiably participate in governance as representing something 'different'. This leadership can emerge only through active participation.

Therein lies the role of the political parties in creating an enabling environment for active leadership generating participation. Prior to 1992, political parties have not been initiating any special initiatives or programmes to encourage women to stand in local government elections.

The number of women in politics at the local level has been very small, and their influence negligible. After 1993, women's participation in local governments increased quite radically with the enactment of the legislation providing one-third reservation of seats for women in local bodies. The effective implementation of this legislation has added another level in political participation. According to women from all parties the one third reservation for women in local governments has brought into focus the fact that there is a need to bring more and more women into the local government field and develop their capacities.

This particular 74th Amendment of the Indian Constitution ushered in a new era in the democratic process in India as it not only provided constitutional status to the municipal bodies but also provided an enabling environment for women to take direct part in the process of local self government and brought women to the forefront of city development.

The 74th Amendment mandated reservation of one - third seats in municipal bodies for women. There is also one third reservations for women in position of chairpersons of these local bodies in India. A very active role for women in local governance is envisaged as compared to governance at the state and national levels in India. These provisions have provided great opportunities and challenges to women in India. The challenge now is to transfer this large presence of women at local government level supported by the real delegation of power and responsibilities.

Women's role in decision making is one of the most important questions for consideration in the movement for their empowerment. Reservation of seats for women in local bodies has shown that it has tremendous implications, not merely in terms of the number of women entering the public arena and holding public office, but also in terms of the social, economic and political impact that these reservations have had for the total system.

Recognising various constraints such as present day politics, elements of criminatisation, corruption, muscle power, violence, lack of awareness of political participation, preparation to fulfil the role and responsibilities as elected representative, etc, the Government, NGOs, Womens Groups and activist's have been actively involved in providing necessary in-puts to women. Women have been mobilised to participate in elections as candidates and voters, and to be vigilant citizens where elections are held. Communities have received gender sensitisation to facilitate acceptance of the new roles assigned to women. Leadership and organisational training of women has been conducted to enable them to be dynamic change agents. Networks have been interacting, to influence mass based political structures to prove more space to women.

6

National Policy

After the establishment of All India Women's Conference (AIWC) in 1926, the agitation for improvement of status of women in India took an upward swing and became well organised. Enlightened Hindu opinion ever since 1919 had begun to feel that Hindu laws regarding women's right to property and laws and customs concerning marriage needed immediate reform. In 1919 V. J. Patel introduced the Hindu Marriage Validity Bill in the Imperial Legislative Council. Education, travel, contact in cities with people of other castes and various other factors widened the outlook of the younger generations, when ideas of marriage, home and life were generally broadened. Education and communication are the most potent factors of modernisation in the society.

Many Hindu intellectuals strongly felt that the time had come to bring about radical changes in Hindu laws to suit the needs of the society. Various women's organisations were also demanding reforms in Hindu marriage laws. The Mumbai women's council passed a resolution recommending registration of marriages.

As a matter of fact the All India Women's Conference and associations attached to it had been doing immense service to Indian womanhood.From 1937 onwards, a number of private bills or resolutions were brought up in the central legislature for improvement of the status of women in society. Dr. G.V. Deshmukh, a great champion of women's rights, had tabled a number of resolutions in central legislative assembly for upliftment of women. Hindu public opinion was moving rapidly in the direction of monogamous marriage.

Divorce Bill

Dr. Deshmukh tabled the Hindu women's divorce bill in the

central legislative assembly in November 1940. His intention was to make a second marriage by a husband as one of the grounds of divorce for a woman. He also brought another bill giving women the right to separate residence and maintenance in case of a second marriage by a husband. Some measures had already been passed due to his efforts in respect of women's right to property, particularly of widows in Hindus society.

Till then they were at the mercy of the other members of the household even for a morsel of food. But their position improved when the widow got a right in her husband's property. The first was the pursuit of out of date customs and the tendency to maintain inherited traditions and the second was the preservation of archaic Hindu laws by judicial decisions. The remedy against the first was education of public opinion by means of the press, the public platform and social meetings.

The laws of inheritance and marriage in Hindu society had become fixed and rigid as a result of judicial rulings and these rulings were in force throughout the country. The only remedy against the mischief caused by archaic.laws preserved by judicial decisions was through legislation. The stage was now set for the government to come forward to undertake a legislation for improvement of Hindu women's social and legal status. The government appointed the Hindu women's rights committee consisting of Sir B. N. Rau, D. N. Mitter and Principal J. R. Gharpure of Poona Law College to examine the whole matter and to make recommendations which would help the legislature to pass an act which would cover the whole of India.

Accordingly, the Hindu law bill on marriage and interstate succession was introduced in the central legislative assembly on 23 March 1943. Mrs. Renuka Ray was nominated as a member of the Central Legislative Assembly as a representative of AIWC for participation on the discussion regarding Hindu Code Bill. She observed:

> women did not succeed in changing social laws before but they had won a psychological victory, an important section of public opinion was convinced that change was essential. Gandhiji had pointed out the necessity for changing social attitude. His encouragement of women's emancipation and women's own participation in the

national movement brought this about.

A campaign for the uniform civil code for women was undertaken by the AIWC and other leading organisations in the thirties. To achieve this a vigorous campaign was started by AIWC. To mould public opinion in its favour, meetings were organised and processions were taken out throughout the country with Calcutta and Mumbai as the major centres of the campaign. They were in many ways in the forefront of women's emancipation.

An insistent demand for changes in the Hindu law in support of women's rights was voiced in the central legislative assembly which ultimately sought to remedy the disabilities from which women suffered. There was a spate of private bills on the anvil of the central legislative assembly.

Consequently, the government had to appoint the Hindu law committee under the chairmanship of Sir B.N. Rau. Sir Sultan Ahmad, the then law member, took interest in the matter. Their labours resulted in the introduction of bills on Hindu marriage and Hindu intestate succession in the central legislature in March 1943. Six associations of women wanted these bills to be passed as they were all in agreement so far as the broad principles were concerned.

All branches of organisations of women had accepted the bills in *toto*. The national planning committee had also agreed with the main principles of the bills. Both the Bengal and Bihar governments were of the opinion that the bills might be postponed till after the war because the time was not opportune for such radical legislation. Renuka Ray countered it by saying that the Bill would not come as surprise to anyone. The vast majority of opinion on the Bills was in their favour. The Hindus were not only willing to support the Bills but they would also go much further. A four-day conference was organised by National Council of Women to discuss the legal status of women.

Mrs. Sarojini Naidu in a message urged that the conference should demand for a complete and radical revision of the Hindu law which was outworn, unwieldy, too intricate and too rigid a system that acts frequently as a boulder of obstruction in the stream of modern progress. M. R. Jayakar was looking forward to the day when there would be one legislation for all women of India because religion had little to do with the property rights.

The Divorced from religion a civil bill of property rights

covering all communities would be an ideal one. He hoped that in the not too distant future India would have a simplified law governing marriage and inheritance. He urged the national council of women to wait for some time more when the legislature would be completely repre-sentative of the community. He feared that the bill then in the legislature would emerge in the most defective form.

Rau Committee

As a matter of fact, the Rau committee had done a great service to Indian womanhood by providing rules of inheritance and marriage which were in consonance with justice and equity. Jawaharlal Nehru too thought that a uniform civil code for the whole of India was essential. But this could not be imposed on unwilling people. The urgent need was the extension of the civil marriage act to cover marriages between any two persons, to whatever religion they might belong without any renunciation of religion, as at present. No change could be imposed from the top. It was the duty of the government of the time to try to educate public opinion so as to make it accept the changes proposed.

As a matter of fact the Hindu law committee wanted codification of the Hindu law by stages, beginning with the law of succession and the law of marriage. The government accepted this view. The bill was circulated for eliciting public opinion. Some of the opinions were critical and even hostile.

On the whole the opinions were in favour of the principles of the bill. The controversy mainly centred round the question of introducing monogamy and the application of sagotra marriage. The government did not contemplate any precipitate action on so important a matter touching the Hindu community.

The general opinion even among women appeared that daughter's share should be half of a son. The chief virtue of the bill was that it was merely a pointer in the proper direction and nothing more. It touched only a small proportion of Hindu property. It did not touch the ancestral property of a Hindu governed by Mitakshara law. The bill was not revolutionary in character. It was not going to disturb the fundamentals of Hindu society or materially change its structure. There was only one reform of any significance and that was the abolition of polygamy and insistence on monogamy. Sir Sultan Ahmad considered it a privilege that he brought forward a legislation (Hindu code) which was found to improve the status of the country both internally and internationally. Mrs. Renuka Ray, while supporting the bill observed:

> "Hindu law, if it is to be preserved, must get rid of the deadly influence of outworn customs which like dead wood are choking up the very life springs of Hindu society.

Women in general desired that polygamy should be prohibited not only because it was wrong and caused much suffering but also because it was highly detrimental to the peace and happiness of family life. The Indian press as a whole had given full support to the bill. But most of the judges found that this new code would undermine Hindu law and create a sort of revolution in the Hindu society, which it had not experienced for the last thousand years. They took it as a kind of revolution in the change of the fundamental principles of Hindu society.

One of the judges went so far as to say that the object of the bill was to satisfy those persons who were fond of slogans such as complete independence for women and sex- equality between men and women. Despite such orthodox opinions, there was a strong feeling growing in the country at that time that marriage laws should be simplified and be less expensive. The Congress election manifesto of 1937 stood for removal of all sex disabilities whether legal or social in any sphere of public activity.

Act of 1935

Under the act of 1935 women got special representation in provincial legislatures and some of them became ministers too. They stood for reforms in Hindu society. The result of the election in the provinces proved that the country supported the policy in an overwhelming manner. Even in remote villages the urgency and importance of the legislation for social reform was recognised. Some members of the house wanted to make the Bill more comprehensive by providing for dissolution of marriage on certain definite grounds and for the residence and maintenance of the divorced partner and for the custody of children. It was erroneous to think that such legislation would lead to disintergartion of the family.

As a matter of fact Hindu public opinion was moving rapidly in the direction of monogamous marriage. As the war neared its end, political matters engrossed the attention of the government and the people. Moreover, the government feared that the axis powers might use this to influence the minds of the Hindus against the British. The Bill was allowed to lapse and could not be enacted in law. When India became independent the same was taken up by Dr. B. R. Ambedkar with some modifications. Hence, the credit now goes to him for getting the Hindu code Bill enacted in law. The background had been prepared by the colonial government. During the whole of 1940s women's organisations in India were very active in the agitation for removal of disabilities of women.

Second World War

During the time of Second World War women too had to come forward to participate in the war effort in different capacities. There were about 5,00,000 British women in armed forces, another 2,00,000 in the women's land army and well over 3,00,000 in the civil services. Almost similar was the case with Russian women. Almost all able-bodied males in Russia were drafted for military services and the civil services were mostly handled by women.

In America, more than two million women had volunteered for Red Cross work during the war. Women had to take to trousers for war work. Consequently, women's purchases of trousers in the USA jumped five times since the beginning of the war. Large shops were opening departments for trousers for women. This indicated the extent to which women were going into war work.

Women working in war plants needed to make this sensible change of clothing. Mrs. Roosevelt congratulated women of the USA for the way in which they had come forward and taken their place in industry, often undertaking jobs which seemed beyond their strength or known skills to perform.

In India the situation was different because there was no dearth of male-power in the country. Still some educated women came forward to participate in war efforts. Previously women doctors were not admitted into the army medical service. After a considerable hesitation the government agreed to admit women doctors to the army medical service on the same terms as men. British as well as Indian women doctors were declared to be eligible for selection but they were liable to serve both in and outside India.

During the war there was a demand for trained nurses in the armed forces. A number of nurses had volunteered for military service in India and overseas. Among the tribals of northeast India the Khasi girls were the first to volunteer for nursing service abroad and joined the auxiliary nursing service. Many tribal women joined the women's voluntary service also.

The Indian military nursing service was constituted and by March 1943, 288 girls had joined it. The auxiliary nursing service was also constituted to provide a reserve of nurses sufficiently trained to be immediately useful in case of emergency in military or civil hospitals. The war provided a good opening for Indian girls to join the nursing service but only the tribal and Christian girls came forward to avail of this opportunity.

The women's voluntary service was also organised in India. They rendered useful service in organising canteens which served refreshments to troops. They also served army families, looked after soldiers in hospitals and helped with other odd jobs. When the auxiliary nursing service was started in 1941, over 15,000 applications were received for admission to the course.

Madras presidency had contributed nearly one-third of total number of nurses and Bombay nearly one-fifth. 603 were Europeans, 543 Indian Christians, 143 domiciled Europeans, 123 Hindus, 24 Parsis, 5 Sikhs and 11 Muslims. At that time there were fewer nurses in the whole of India than there were in London.

Many women of good social status from Punjab came forward to volunteer for the post of *Fauji Sevadarni* – women military welfare worker. Their work was voluntary and unpaid. They maintained contact with families of soldiers in the villages under their charge. They were to keep up the spirit of soldiers families and persuade them to write encouraging letters frequently to their relatives overseas.

About 500 *Sevadarnis* were appointed in an area which covered the districts of Jullunder, Ferozepore, Ambala, Ludhiana and Hosiarpur. They were chiefly ladies whose husbands or other relatives were in the army and who could command respect and confidence of village women.

In March 1942, the Women Auxiliary Corps (WAC) was started in India. It was recruited on voluntary basis. They were paid but their service was for the duration of the war only and limited to the confines of India. They were whole time workers. All women between the ages of 18 and 50 who were British subjects or subjects of Indian states, were eligible for enlistment.

Among the duties they might undertake were those of switchboard operators, telephone orderlies, wireless operators, clerks, drivers of staff cars, dieticians etc. These covered 45 distinctive types of occupation. Eighteen hostels had been set apart for them. Their number grew up rapidly because there was a rising demand for WAC(I) in all three services—Army, Navy and Air Force. Not a single new post was created to accommodate them. They merely replaced men who were released for service abroad. By September 1942, the strength of the WAC(I) was 90 officers and 200 auxiliaries. This scheme gave women of all races and creeds in India an opportunity for national service.

The WAC(I) was unique in having women from nearly every part of the world united together in common cause. Women of 27 different nationalities were represented there. Not only were all castes and creeds of India represented and of neighbouring countries, like Burma, Malaya, Ceylon, Java, and China, but also serving by the side of their Asiatic sisters were women from UK, Russia, Canada, Australia and several European countries.

Despite their differences of culture and outlook these women formed a union of loyalty and service to a common cause. They played their part as individuals in a great team. The strength of WAC(I) reached a peak of 11,000 consisting of all ranks. Women of all castes and creeds found it possible to work together in this corps. There were Hindus, Muslims, Parsis and Christians working together. Several persons levelled charges against the corps but general Auchinluck countered them forcefully. With War nearing its end in 1945, the problem of disbandment of WAC(I) loomed large.

The fear of demobilisation hung like the Damocle's sword. They feared that 50 per cent of the Indian girls would have to walk straight from the disbanded corps into brothels, being uneducated, unprepared, unequipped for any decent means of livelihood. During the War they had become used to a higher standard of life. As a consequence of demobilisation, they were likely to be thrown on streets. They appealed to the government to undertake the responsibility of peace time reconversion of the corps. Their principal charge, however, concerned the absolute irreparable mess this war time organisation had made of the lives of young Indian girls.

The government took steps to train them in various professions likely to absorb them in the mainstream of society. But in general the Indian society looked with suspicion on the girls who had served in the WAC(I).

More than one thousand anglo-Indian girls had joined the corps. Mrs. Hansa Mehta in her presidential speech at the AIWC in 1945 expressed her deep anxiety and concern for these girls who were likely to be thrown out of employment after demobilisation. She appealed to the AIWC to appoint a special committee to investigate into their problems and to find out ways and means to help these women. She advised that services of these women should be utilised for education and social work in rural areas. War had a liberating influence on women all over the world.

The AIWC and other women associations continued to play their part in general awakening of women in India. Educated women, instead of being tied to their homes began to take active interest in social and political work in a way that was really astonishing. All this produced a wider field for their talents, broke the relative segregation of women as a sex, relaxed the restrictions that otherwise narrowed their functions.

Men and women had been struggling to rectify this for half a century or more as a joint battle for the betterment of whole society. She struck a new note by affirming human value of a housewife in economic and social terms. Women's contribution is a basic cohesive element in the family and therefore society and the nation needed recognition; whether she held a job and contributed monetarily or not she was entitled to an equal status with her husband.

The women's movement in India was essentially a social movement and part of the process of enabling a constituent part of society to adjust itself to the constantly changing social and economic conditions.

Major reasons for lower participation of women in economic activities are identified as illiteracy and ignorance. Women are at a disadvantage to men in their access to employment and earnings for a number of reasons, namely, lower job mobility due to responsibility of child care, vulnerability to class or caste barriers, and more limited in their access to information on job opportunities.

Another important feature which governs employment of women is the age group of such women. Comparatively women who are young say below 30 years of age, for social reasons prefer jobs and employment by way of self-occupation rather than going for employment. However, this particular trend is changing and indications are now available to show that even young women would like to take jobs to support their family.

The provision of productive assets in the hands of women working in the informal sector has led to qualitative improvement in their lives, and they demonstrated higher productivity and better record of repayment of loans. The strategies suggested for their development and relating to the banking field, *inter alia,* propose strengthening their employment by providing appropriate support in the areas of skill, training, credit and marketing.

DWCRA

Development of Women and Child in Rural Areas (DWCRA) programmes has been adopted the strategy of group information mainly because it was felt that the women interact better in a group. The group approach not only helps in bringing women together for an economic activity suitable to their abilities and skills in planning and implementation, but also for inculcating in them a spirit of Community approach. The target group of DWCRA is families having an annual income of less than Rs. 11,000. The financial provisions under DWCRA are available only for this group. DWCRA was started as a pilot project in 50 selected districts in all states in 1982-83. The programme is being extended to more districts every year.

NABARD

National Bank for Agriculture and Rural Development's (NABARD's) credit facilities cover almost all types of activities for which loan or investment credit is given by banks under the refinance schemes. The activities can be taken up individually or in groups such as, individual loans, group loans, loan for industrial cooperatives, loans for worksheds, infrastructural development and common facilities.

NABARD can also, under the existing schemes, assist women activists through voluntary agencies and registered institutions for generating assured wage employment. Also grants, on selected basis, are available for technological upgradation and for setting top training-cum-production centres (TPC). One such TPC had been sanctioned to the Women Development Corporation Maharashtra for resettlement of' Devdasis.

NABARD also assists voluntary agencies and women groups on pilot project basis for developing replicable models, which could trigger large number of schemes for women within the banking fold.

Under automatic refinance facility, covering composite and integrated loans for non-farm activities, loans can be had by women entrepreneurs and artisans up to Rs. 10 lakhs per individual borrower; composite and integrated loans also cover working capital requirements. In case of difficulty in providing margin money, the borrower can avail of soft loan assistance for margin money from the NABARD, through the financing bank, at the concessional interest rate of one per cent per annum. Repayment period ranges between three to 10 years, including initial grace/ moratorium period of 12 to 18 months.

In the case of group loans, NABARD also provides assistance by way of grant for entrepreneurial development and technical training needed for efficient running of the enterprises financed. Eighteen such programmes are stated to have been sanctioned so far. However, despite the available line of credit and specific purpose grants, it is observed that adequate number of projects of group activities for women were not submitted by banks.

NABARD set up a women's cell in its Head Office at Mumbai and also constituted an Advisory Committee which included leading activists of women organisations and representatives of Government of India and Reserve Bank of India to coordinate its women schemes, and guide it on policies and programmes pertaining to rural women.

Assistance to Rural Women in Non-Farm Development (ARWIND) aims to provide Assistance to Rural Development in Non-Farm Development with the objective to encourage leading to rural women preferably organised in groups supported by Non-Governmental Organisations (NGOs), Women's Development Corporations, KVIC/KVIB or cooperatives, trusts, etc.

The scheme has a credit and grant component. Refinance is also available to Mother Units/Common Services Centres under normal schemes, even for loans in excess of Rs. one million and up to SSI level in respect of commercial banks and state cooperative banks, and up to Rs. one million in the case of Regional Rural Banks (RRB's).

NABARD also considers need-based grant assistance, subject to the availability of promotional funds, to meet the sponsoring agency's expenditure for organisation of groups, sensitisation, training and other related expenditures. In case the sponsoring agency provides services such as supply of raw materials, quality control, marketing, etc., such services undertaken by it will also be eligible for financial assistance under NABARD's promotion linked credit scheme such as Mother Units/Common Service Centres for providing common services for promotion and development of product design, quality control, training, marketing of products, supply of raw material, etc.

Under the flexible approach model it is intended that instead of suggesting, a pre-defined concept in all details to the NGOs, etc., their own programmes fitting into the goals of NABARD will be supported financially.

The main objective is to test the validity of promoting rural non-farm activities and enterprises, for creating sustainable employment opportunities in rural areas in a cost effective manner through voluntary agencies with a proven track record. The project concept, methodology and operational details are entirely left to the implementing agency, the only precondition being the cost effectiveness and credit linkage in achieving the results. NABARD's support will be for a programme to be implemented within a period of five years aimed at facilitating establishment or modernisation of rural non-farm enterprises of different types through production and marketing support, market information, technology transfer, supply of raw materials, training and extension credit linkage or any other similar services or a combination thereof.

NABARD's support could also be in the form of salaries to professionals with expertise in technology, marketing management, etc., to be appointed by the agency along with expenditure incidental to their services. The programme should lead to credit flow to enterprises through banks Under refinance support from NABARD and thereby generate sustainable employment opportunities in rural areas in a cost effective manner.

While NABARD will provide refinance for the credit component, the grant component will be linked to the number of rural employment opportunities generated on a sustainable basis and the quantum of credit. The implementing agency is required to contribute a share in any form including land, manpower, etc., to the extent of at least ten percent of the project cost. The project will include a strong component of participative monitoring and documentation.

NABARD has constituted an Agricultural and Rural Enterprise Incubation Fund (ARIEF) with an initial amount of Rs. five crores for supporting new technologies and also NGOs in critical spheres in providing backward and forward linkages both under farm and non-farm sectors. The fund is expected to act as a catalytic agent spurring growth and development of innovative and risk ventures.

SIDBI

To create opportunities of self-employment and wage employment for women, as well as to support their entrepreneurial capabilities, Schemes of Small Industries Development Bank of India (SIDBI) has been operating two special funds, namely, Mahila Udyam Nidhi (MUN) and Mahila Vikas Nidhi (MVN). An exclusive scheme of assistance to provide refinance for term loans granted to women entrepreneurs for setting up small industrial units is also operated. By way of extension services, financial support is extended to Entrepreneurship Development Programmes (EDPS) and other management development programmes specifically meant for women.

All new industrial projects in the small scale sector, as well as service activities which are eligible as per SSI norms and set up by women entrepreneurs, qualify for assistance, provided the project cost does not exceed Rs. one million. Assistance out of Mahila Udyam Nidhi is provided to women entrepreneurs to meet a gap in the equity for setting up new industrial projects in the small scale sector. Seed money assistance is provided in the form of soft loans to meet gap in the equity after taking into consideration the promoter's contribution which may be up to a maximum of 15 per cent of the project cost.

The assistance carries nominal rate of interest by way of service charge of one percent per annum with a provision to raise the same depending on the performance of the unit. No security, including collateral, is insisted upon by SIDBI. Assistance aggregating Rs. 51.8 million has so far been provided under the scheme to 753 units promoted by women.

A special development fund called 'Mahila Vikas Nidhi' with an initial capital of Rs. 30 million has been set up to extend support to specific proposals for income generating programmes of accredited Non-Governmental Organisations (NGOs) with strong support to the poor at the grassroots level and a proven track record of performance in managing economic programmes.

Activities such as setting up of Training-cum-Production Centre (TPCs), skill upgradation programmes, extension of marketing assistance and such other income generating pursuits as would improve the economic status of women, are eligible for support under MVN. Assistance is made available both by way of grant and soft loan and is mainly for capital expenditure, the recurring expenses being met by the NGOs out of their funds or grants/donations from government or other agencies.

Most of the cases which have been sanctioned assistance are related to setting up TPCs in diverse areas like spinning, weaving, printing, electronics assembly, knitting, embroidery, shoe-making, mat-weaving, garment stitching, mirror embroidery, patchwork, block printing, handloom projects, bamboo-handicraft products, woollen carpets, rexin/canvas bags, bakery products and catering. These are located mainly in rural areas in different parts of the country.

NGOs and SHGs

Non-Governmental Organisations (NGOs) in India have been working with the underprivileged and poor women, offering to them an accessible, flexible and non-exploitable informal credit system in the form of Self-Help Groups (SHGs) which address themselves to solving socio-economic problems and promoting self-reliance. The major credit models adopted by the NGOs are in the form of facilitating the formation of such groups, training the women and their leaders in principles of savings and credit and, lit times, giving one-time grant or revolving fund to supplement the funds of the SHGs.

At times, the NGOs created a separate cell for credit programme and advanced loans directly to the members of SHGs pending development of SHGs on a firm footing. NGOs have also been playing a catalytic role to help the banks in spreading awareness of bank schemes, training of the borrowers, preparation of small projects for income generation activity and applications for loans and assistance to banks in marketing, recovery, etc.

Another development observed in the NGO credit relates to formation of companies or separate societies for the proper management of surplus funds of SHGs and providing other services of deposits and loans. Over the past few years, these organisations have gained strength. In all the above, the basic principle is organising the women into groups which work on the basis of joint and several liability in all their financial dealings and transactions.

The ultimate aim is to strengthen the SHGs and make them stand on their own. The factors that seem to have influenced NGOs involvement in credit are obviously the non-availability of credit to the poor from the formal sector, improper working of the cooperatives which are alienated from the target group and expiatory practices adopted by the moneylenders, traders and landlords.

According to the Study Report published by NABARD on Self-Help Groups working in the area of credit the following features were noted. Self-Help Groups were able to mobilise savings from persons and effectively recycle them among the members. Sometimes the initial savings generated were supplemented by external resources loaned or donated by NGO.

The activities of the group received serious attention as a possible alternative or complementary mechanism for meeting the credit needs of the pool. Most of the groups evolved flexible systems for governing their working, managing their common resources in a democratic way with participation of every member in decision making. The groups made innovations in promoting thrift, pooling resources and meeting emergent and essential credit needs.

The loans were given for small amounts, but repeatedly, and they were for short periods of one to three months carrying an interest rate of two to three per cent per month. Longer term loans, which form a small proportion, were repayable in 12 to 18 months and carried a lower interest of 1 to 1.5 per cent per month. The credit needs of members were assessed by the group and all collections and disbursements were made in group meetings. Defaults either in loan amount due or in participation in group meetings carried stiff penalties, but such occasions were rare.

A healthy trend is emerging in NGO credit sector where registered and unregistered federations are being formed out of Self-Help Credit Group to attend to the common problems of the groups and render services relating to audit, accounts management of community assets and for providing a platform for sharing of experience and qualitative knowledge. The federations also help in solving inter-group disputes. Apart from the federations, which are normally at the district level, there are cluster committees at block or taluqa level to attend to the type of problems indicated above. With the formation of these federations, the NGOs are getting relief from the day-to-day operations of credit schemes and, thus, are able to attend to more important problems and issues relating to development.

Savings is an integral part of the SHGs. The poor women members of these groups save small amounts, but regularly, and these go to make up comfortable common funds. At times, the SHGs use these funds for lending purposes or keep these funds with the bank if the bank has given a line of credit to the group. However, as far as women entrepreneurs are concerned, they provide their own resources as margin money for seeking credit limits from banks.

Another practice followed by banks while lending to women entrepreneurs is to ask them to arrange some deposits either in their names or in the names of their relations, which is a condition not formally stipulated but generally followed. Thus presently there is no proper system of linking savings with lendings by banks in a formal manner as in the case of Self-Help Groups. This is an area where efforts will have to be made to develop a system which would generate savings out of the income generation activities undertaken with the assistance of loans from banks. If savings are properly linked and systems observed, it can be safely assumed that Rs. 10 to 15 billion could be generated as savings out of a total lending requirement estimated at Rs. 127.5 billion.

Another scheme Rashtriya Mahila Kosh (RMK) has been set up for the purpose of dissemination of credit mainly through NGOs/SHGs to poor women both in rural and urban areas. Loans are given particularly to women in the unorganised sector for undertaking self-employment/income generation activities to improve their quality of life. The NGOs extend loans to borrowers through simple/flexible procedures with no insistence on collateral.

Group dynamics is the main basis of all loan operations at the level of ultimate borrowers. Corporations running on sound lines and having experience in thrift and credit administration of at least three years will be eligible to borrow loans from RMK for on-lending to eligible poor women. The recovery performance of the NGOs/organisation should have exceeded 90 per cent during each of the last three years.

The loans drawn from RMK will be used by the borrowers for undertaking income generating activities except to the extent so sanctioned for other purposes. Loans for short term (ST) purposes up to Rs. 2,500/- per borrower will be supported by RMK. Loans could be given repeatedly if necessary. ST loans drawn from the RMK will be required to be repaid in quarterly instalments. The period of ST loans will not exceed 15 months.

The lending rate of the RMK will be at eight per cent per annum. The ultimate borrowers, whether financed directly by NGOs or through SHGs, will be charged interest not exceeding twelve per cent. The interest will be payable quarterly. Interest spread of four per cent will be available to NGOs and SHGs to meet their transaction costs. The borrowers will have to provide compulsory thrift at 10 per cent of the loan taken by them. RMK commenced its operations in November 1993. It started as an innovative intervention in credit delivery to poor women undertaken by the Government of India. By 1995 RMK had sanctioned credit support to several NGOs all over the country for a total amount of Rs. 56.5 million covering about 43,000 women borrowers. The scheme is progressing slowly but steadily.

The long term objective of the Seventh Plan with respect to women's development was to create greater employment opportunities for women so as to bring them into the mainstream of national development. Based on early state level initiatives in Tamil Nadu and Andhra Pradesh, the Department of Women and Child Develop-ment, Ministry of Human Resources Development, formulated a scheme to assist other state governments to establish Women's Development Corporations (WDCs).

The WDCs were intended to provide in institutional base for the promotion of women's economic advancement, in contrast to the traditional programme run by the state-level Departments of Social Welfare, whose focus has been the provision of welfare services.

The scope of WDCs is to identify women entrepreneurs, prepare viable projects, facilitate the availability of credit from banks and financial institutions, establish marketing linkages, provide training, technical skills in conjunction with polytechnic and financial management through relevant institutions, as well as provide technical consultancy services. They are also charged with the promotion and strengthening of Women's cooperatives and organisations. The focus of WDCs is to help poor and needy women including single women and female-headed households. Safeguards are sought to be provided to ensure that women who are relatively better off do not appropriate the advantages under this programme.

The funds for WDCs are to be drawn from existing schemes of the state and central governments. Loans are to be given to groups of women or women's cooperatives from IRDP funds and the responsibility for their recovery rests with WDC's field staff. Funds for training, research, evaluation etc., are to be drawn from the Department of Rural Development, Women Development CAPART, etc.

The stress is on the fact that WDCs shall only facilitate the setting up of income generating units, but not directly set up their own. Whenever the corporation has to set up a unit directly, it forms a cooperative and hands over the management of the unit to it. WDCs are currently functioning in sixteen states, of which those in Andhra Pradesh, Punjab, Maharashtra, Kerala and Tamil Nadu are reported to be successful. Information regarding their actual functioning is limited and there does not appear to be a fixed format for reporting by the WDCs. The Andhra Pradesh and Tamil Nadu WDCs, which were the first to be established and have provided the model for the national programmes, are worth a special mention.

DEW has a scheme for transfer of assets—milch animals and sheep units of women. Fifty per cent of the initial cost of the asset is met by a subsidy from DEW and the remaining fifty percent is a term loan from banks repayable over a period of five years. Banks have expressed satisfaction over women's repayment performance. IFAD has decided to finance a project worth $ 30 million in which DEW will assist women for income generating activities in the agricultural and allied sectors.

A number of studies have been carried out for evaluating bank procedures for credit to poor women and the issue has been discussed in several workshops and seminars held from time to time. Studies conducted by the Society for Participatory Research in Asia and NABARD on enhancing women's participation in rural credit programmes identified some of the important barriers in the outreach of credit to women. These are as under:

- Banks were too busy with trade advances and they have yet to develop attitudes and gender sensitisation for surveying the needs of women;
- The procedures and systems were rigid;
- Institutional structures prevented direct dialogue with beneficiaries, especially women who do not come to the banks;
- Extension approach of the banks was lacking in pre-project planning, i.e., identification of feasible economic activities, modification and skill training, etc., for women;
- Bank documentation and formalities of obtaining no dues certificates were time consuming which caused inordinate delays in processing the loan applications;
- Some banks required husband's signatures on documents executed by a woman borrower and also if a family member was a defaulter, a woman could not obtain a loan;
- There was urban bias of branch managers of banks and officials which led to ad hoc approach to assessment of credit needs for poor women;
- There was no involvement of the people of the area in the banks programme and there was lack of coordination with other agencies serving the cause of women;
- District and block level plans were prepared without consulting the target group, voluntary organisations and resource agencies. The role of voluntary agencies was limited. Explicit planning within a gender perspective was absent in the programmes of banks;

- Women were not able to access credit due to low mobility, literacy, training and other socio-religious taboos inhibiting them from undertaking employment. In addition, the women were mostly in the unorganised low paid sectors;
- Banks were hesitant in financing group activity of women or unregistered groups of women;
- Monitoring and evaluation was not up to the desired level;
- Recoveries of loans under directed credit were low. The underlying reasons for the high overdues of the formal structure are usually classified into those which are internal to the banking system and those which are external. Among the internal factors, defective loan policies and procedures involving under/over financing, improper choice of beneficiary and activity, inability to link credit with marketing, non-recognition of the need for consumption finance, especially of the poor section of the beneficiary spectrum, and ineffective credit supervision are some of the reasons often cited. The factors external to the system comprise the weaknesses inherent in the uncertainties of the agricultural and rural economy, natural calamities leading to losses in enterprises, the vitiating impact of target pressures and subsidies, and to some extent the politicisation of credit business; and
- Interest rates being low, the banks were hesitant to provide funds to target groups, especially when they had to deal with large member of borrowers which resulted in higher transaction costs.

The National Commission on Self-employment of Women has studied the problems of self-employed women, there has been no systematic and detailed study or benchmark survey of the total requirements of the credit by women in the rural and urban areas by self-employed women and women entrepreneurs in difficult income groups. It is high time that such a benchmark survey is undertaken which will help in initiating appropriate policies for the development of women through credit. The government has to play an important role in laying down policies aimed at economic development of the women, with great amount of flexibility built into such policies in order to take care of gender differences.

The Government of India has some policy formulation for empowerment but they should now weave credit and credit reforms as important components in their pro-grammes. Conscious policies have to be drawn for providing entrepreneurship development to eligible women, especially in areas where there are social taboos coming in the way of' taking up self-employment/wage employment.

Departments of Women and Child and of Banking, Government of India, should frame policies and fix targets for giving credit to women under each programme on the lines of IRDP, and also a certain percentage for women's credit in the overall limit of forty per cent for priority sector lendings by banks. The achievement of these targets should be reviewed by the Department of Banking along with the review of' the priority sector's performance every quarter.

The government should provide income tax relief for three-five years to all women, whether self-employed or otherwise employed. There should be at least one woman Director on the Board of every nationalised bank, including Reserve Bank, NABARD and State Finance Corporations, IDBI, SIDBI, ICICI, etc., so that proper focus can be given to the problems of access to credit by women. On the same lines, the constitution of the State Level Bankers Committee, District Level Committee and Regional Level Committee of Banks should provide for a minimum number of women representatives.

The central government budget for women's develop-ment as well as state government budgets for this purpose should contain an element by way of grant and subsidies for the promotion of group dynamics among women, providing interest subsidy and other facilitative activities parallel to credit like technology transfer, labour saving alternatives, marketing support, production training etc.

Assistance could be routed through the NGOs/Banks or Other related agencies. The central government should initiate suitable action on the various recommendations made by the National Commission on Self-employment of Women and also in the Perspective Plan for Women.

Steps should be initiated to strengthen the NGO credit movement particularly in the following areas: The central government should find an acceptable semi legal/legal framework for recognising the unregistered SHGs to enable banks to come forward for lendings to these groups. Exemptions need to be given to the NGOs undertaking savings and credit programme on the income arising out of the on-lending business in matters of income-tax, stamp duty, etc. The central government may consider providing counter guarantees to the banks for their bulk lendings to the NGOs for the purpose of making loans to the women borrowers.

The central government/state governments should provide for suitable risk fund contributions to the NGOs Undertaking lending work, which could be, say five per cent of the total loans made by the NGOs to the poor women. The new economic policies and the consequences of socio-economic adjustment may impose a severe burden which is not gender-neutral. The central government needs to take special precautions in this regard and integrate the concerns, needs and perceived threats to women and to strengthen the social support network for women.

There is a standing Advisory Committee in NABARD to advise the Bank on matters relating to women's credit in the rural areas. The committee should be broadbased and located in RBI as an Advisory Committee to guide the Reserve Bank on various facets of credit requirements of women. The committee should work both for urban and rural areas and specially look into the rigidities of procedures of endings adopted by banks in advancing credit to women, so as to make the procedures simple and more acceptable to women, particularly the poor women.

Each of the commercial banks should have a separate women's cell in its corporate office to look into the various problems of women's credit in that bank and find out solutions. Bigger branches should have exclusive women's counters to provide services to women customers.

On the lines of SIDBI, each of the nationalised banks/State Finance Corporations should have a 'Mahila Udhyam Nidhi' for giving special loans to women entrepreneurs for margin money, seed capital, etc., for undertaking non- traditional activities. The terms and conditions of' investment credit for women should be flexible to give some concessions in matters of rates of interest, gestation period, repayment schedules, etc.

Clear instructions should be issued by the RBI to identify the woman borrower as an independent entity and not linked with her husband's or family member's defaults in loan repayments. The RBI should arrange for special evaluation of various targeted credit programmes of the government being implemented through banks for women, like IRDP, SUME, etc., so as to find out the reasons for their slow progress, quality of lendings, utilisation of funds, impact on the quality of life, etc., of women borrowers.

The scheme of linking SHGs with banks is the right way to reach credit to poor women. It needs to be implemented in a big way by proper publicity, training of bank staff and other facilities required for its adoption in banks. RBI should introduce gender desegregated data in all its statistics relating to the deposits, loans and other related matters. Similarly, NABARD should introduce gender classification in all its statistical statements relating to cooperative credit/non credit societies.

All Service Area Plans of banks and potential linked credit plan for each district prepared by NABARD should contain explicit details of the economic activities and credit requirements of women in that area which should be monitored by the head offices of the banks. RBI should come out with special refinance schemes to provide further support to banks and other financial institutions providing loans for economic development of women. The conditions of this refinance should be liberal and also concessional. The Deposit Insurance and Credit Guarantee Corpora-tion should formulate schemes for extending deposit insurance for NGOs/SHGs, and providing better risk cover at a higher rate for on-lendings made by banks to women within certain income groups. The present trends in opening exclusive branches for women or exclusive banks for women, with female staff need to be encouraged so that many such institutions are created for providing credit, and other banking facilities to women.

After stabilising its procedures and lending operations, Rashtriya Mahila Kosh (RMK) needs to take up promotional and developmental activities and arrange its business on professional lines, taking its constituents/partner NGOs in full confidence in all its policy formalities. The RMK should one day grow to be the chief spokesperson of women's credit in India. The interest rate policy, presently aimed at a commissional rate, needs to be reviewed to cover all transaction costs, projected loan defaults, impact of inflation etc.Systems and procedures for registering women societies should be made simple and flexible so as to facilitate formation of such societies. Proper arrangements should also be made for providing management support to such societies by subsidising the cost of employing experts/professionals.

A separate quota should be fixed for membership of women in the primary agricultural credit societies and also for their minimum representation in the management committees of these societies so that the interest of the women could be taken care of. The women cooperatives now functioning are very weak in many parts of the country. State governments should draw special rehabilitation plans for putting the women cooperatives on a strong footing by providing both funds support and/or training for upgradation of management skills of office bearers/members. Industrial cooperatives of women should be encouraged for undertaking group economic activity by women and special finance schemes developed by banks to support such cooperatives.

Of late there have been some policy initiatives taken by the Reserve Bank and other banks to give a push to the availability of credit for women. NABARD has created a separate advisory committee in its head office for giving advice to it for increasing the access of credit to women in the rural areas. Separate cells for women credit have also been set up in some of the nationalised banks, particularly the State Bank of India, Canara Bank etc.The Reserve Bank of India and NABARD have formulated schemes for linking SHGs with the banks and also for providing bulk finance to them. A few of the State Finance Corporations give special consideration while sanctioning projects for women entrepreneurs in terms of providing longer gestation period, repayment schedules, etc. This apart, a few financial corporations and banks are reported to have created 'Venture Capital Fund' as part of their operations to provide seed capital and margin money loans assistance to the women entrepreneurs for innovative/new projects with suitable moratorium on repayment in the initial stages.

The Industrial Finance Corporation of India has also formulated a scheme to provide interest subsidy for small units run by women entrepreneurs. The RBI issued instructions for not insisting on husband's signatures while giving loans to the women borrowers and also for de-linking women borrowers from the default committed to a bank by her husband or family member. It has appointed a high level committee to look into the working of IRDP programme and offer recommendations for making a more effective and people oriented, with a special focus on women's credit.

The setting up of a Ladies Cell in the Federation of Indian Chambers of Commerce and Industry is a development which may assist women entrepreneurs in a big way. Similarly, the formation of association of women entrepreneurs in states like Karnataka, Maharashtra, etc. are good signs for the development of women's credit in the country as these associations can take up the common problems faced by women in getting credit from banks/other financial institutions.

7

Women in Politics

The political and administrative structure of the country is largely inherited from the British. The British introduced local democracy in India by constituting municipal councils and the municipal corporations in the last quarter of the nineteenth century. They also provided a federal structure to the country with the Government of India Act, 1935. The country today has a quasi-federal structure. Apart from the Government of India in New Delhi, there are twenty-five States with their own state governments. The Seventh Schedule to the Constitution of India divides the subjects of State activity between the Union and state governments. The Union (Centre) as well as State governments in India both have a parliamentary form of government based on the Westminster pattern. The executive powers of the central government are vested in the Council of Ministers with the Prime Minister at its head. Similarly, the executive powers in the State governments are vested in its Council of Ministers with the Chief Minister at its head. However, following the Westminister pattern, the Head of the State is not the Prime Minister but an indirectly elected President, who broadly performs the role as the Head of State. India has a bicameral parliament, with the Lower House directly elected by the people on the lines of the House of Commons in the UK. or the House of Representatives in the USA.

The Upper House is more like the US Senate. It is a permanent house with one-third members retiring every two years. Like in the USA, the Vice President of the country presides on the Upper House. Although local government in India is a subject of the State governments, the seventy-third and the seventy-fourth amendments to the Constitution of India now make it obligatory for the State governments to organise local bodies, to hold regular elections to them and to give them appropriate finances.

The urban local bodies are of three grades; municipal corporations for cities with a population of more than (0.3 million), municipal councils for towns smaller than this population limit and nagar panchayats for villages in transition to becoming towns. These bodies are elected on a universal suffrage basis, with all citizens above the age of eighteen years of age having a right to vote.

The rural local bodies are organised in three tiers, the village panchayat at the village level, the block panchayat samiti for about 100 villages and a district council for a district comprising about 1000 villages. The rural local bodies do not have many resources of their own. They actually spend the state government funds as implementing agencies.

The civil service in India is a closed system, with a very limited scope for lateral entry at senior level. Most permanent officials join the service as a lifetime career through an entrance examination/ interview conducted by the Public Service Commission. The age of entry is usually 21 to 30 years and the age of retirement either 58 or 60 years of age. The subject matter of the Government of India is divided between the Union Government and the State Governments. The respective governments recruit most of their employees independently. However, a unique feature of the Indian system is the existence of three All India Services, the Indian Administrative Service, the Indian Police Service and the Indian Forest Service. The Government of India recruits the members of these services although they work with the States where they are allotted (their cadres) for most of their career. However, the Government of India obtains the services of these officers at higher and middle management levels through deputation for a period of about five years. This enables a regular exchange of officers between the field and the central levels. Senior Indian Administrative Service Officers who have had their initial grounding in different States of India thus man the top secretariat posts in most ministries of the Government of India. India is a democratic republic and full freedom of speech and religion is allowed to all its citizens. The Constitution of India guarantees the following Fundamental Rights to the citizens of India.

Right to equality: This includes equality before law. Prohibition of discrimination on grounds of religion, race, caste, sex or place of birth and equality of opportunity in matters of employment.

Right to freedom: This includes protection of certain rights regarding freedom of speech etc., protection of life and personal liberty and protection against arrest and detention in certain cases.

Right against exploitation: This includes prohibition of traffic in human beings and forced labour and prohibition of employment of children in factories etc.

Right to freedom of religion: This includes freedom of conscience and free profession, practice and propagation of religion, freedom to manage religious affairs, freedom as to payment of taxes for promotion of any particular religion and freedom as to attendance at religious instruction or religious worship in certain educational institutions.

Cultural and educational rights: These include protection of interests of minorities and the right of minorities to establish and administer educational institutions. The Constitution of India further guarantees the right to move to the Supreme Court for enforcement of the above rights.

India has a multitude of political parties; some organised on economic ideology, some on religious ideology while some on local and linguistic aspirations. However, only three or four parties really have a presence at the National level; the Congress Party that was the ruling party for more than forty years, the Bharatiya Janata Party, the Janata Dal and the Communists. There are many religion-based parties like the Akali Dal, the Muslim League etc.

The regional parties like the DMK and AIADMK (Tamil Nadu), Shiv Sena (Maharashtra), Telugu Desam (Andhra Pradesh) and some parties in the smaller North-Eastern States have been contenders of powers in the State governments of their respective states. However, at the National level, only three parties have been able to provide the Prime Minister i.e. the Congress, the BJP and the Janata Party/Janata Dal in alliance with smaller parties.

Election Commission

An independent body called the Election Commission of India conducts elections to the parliament and the state legislatures in India. The elections are based on a universal adult suffrage with voting rights to all citizens above eighteen years of age. The lower houses of the national and the state legislatures have a five-year term although elections are regularly held before this term expires. The elections to the local bodies have been brought under the purview of a similarly constituted body called the State Election Commission. These bodies also usually have a five-year term. It is statutorily not possible to supersede the local bodies for long periods or to keep them under Government-appointed Administrators.

An age of more than twenty-one years is usually an eligibility condition for getting elected to an elective post in a local body. The eligibility for being a member of the Lower House of the National or state legislatures similarly prescribes the minimum age of twenty-five years.

A minimum age-limit of thrity years is similarly a qualification for membership of the Upper Houses of the National and State A minimum age-limit of thirty-five years is prescribed as a qualification for holding the post of the President or Vice-President of the Indian Republic. The elections to both the urban and rural local bodies in India are ward based. The local area is divided into wards of more or less equal population. Each ward sends one representative to the concerned local body. After the Seventy-third and Seventy-fourth Amendments to the Constitution of India, one-third of the wards are reserved for women candidates and only women candidates can contest elections from these wards. Apart from the reservation for women candidates, some other wards are reserved for candidates from socially underprivileged sections.

Political Parties

Political parties are allowed to take part in elections to all local bodies except the village panchayats in India. It is, however, not uncommon for locally influential politicians to form local fronts to contest and win elections to municipal councils and the smaller municipal corporations in the country. India became independent in the year 1947. In all the elections held since independence, women had the voting rights.

Women play a dual role in politics—as voters and political representatives. On the voting front, though adult franchise was granted in 1937, it was the progressive spirit that pervaded the making of the constitution that made it a reality. The Constitution of India guarantees equal rights to men and women as voters and citizens.

Generally, in India, registration and participation of women as contestants is less than that of men. In recent past, records show that there has been an increase in the percentage of women who vote. Such participation is also contingent on the mobilisation efforts made by political parties, NGOs, Action Groups and the general awareness among the community of the importance of women exercising their franchise. Again, a note of caution is required, lest it be assumed that political participation always indicates political awareness on the part of the woman voter.

Usually, however, countries that do hold regular elections show an improved recognition of women as a political constituency and parties and candidates tend to adopt pro-women stances and appeal specifically to women's votes, especially at the time of elections. This becomes very evident when we look at consecutive elections in the Indian context, wherein there is a growing consciouseness of the need to woo the woman voter and the need to pay attention to the needs and issues of women, in the election manifestos of political parties.

Since Independence, due to exercise of their franchise, Indian women have been exposed to the political processes and are showing increasing awareness about not only lack of rights but also their utility. A majority of illiterate rural women are also politically sensitive and aware of the various issues confronting them. Women get easily mobilised in the political processes by the political parties who approach women very often for party issues and for short-term goals by winning elections, but not for long-term goals of bringing about social changes and gender equality in political power-sharing. In all the elections held since independence, women had the voting rights.

Percentage of Seats

The percentage of seats won against the seats contested is showing a declining trend only because the number of women contesting elections has increased sharply. However, it may be seen that voting by women in all tiers of Government has always been a feature of the Indian Polity since 1947. Due to the parternalistic family and male dominated political structures which do not provide space for women in decision-making bodies, women constituted 3.1 per cent of the total contestants in 1996 election and did not occupy more than 6.10 per cent of the total seats in the state legislative assemblies and Parliament.

The number of women contestants in Parliamentary elections has not increased significantly over the years. Political parties are still reluctant to field women candidates at national level. In the early days of the Indian republic, the number of women representatives was a mere 22, which was a lowly 4.4 per cent of the total seats in the Lok Sabha. The sixth Loksabha in the year 1977 saw an all time low of just 19 woman representatives. The twelfth Lok Sabha had 44 women i.e. 8.8 per cent of the total. Even as early as the 19th century Indian women had begun to appear on the national scene in public and political activity. Women were not only being accepted in public activity but were organising themselves to fight for their rights in different walks of life. Though women constitute nearly half of the population of the country, it was only after Independence that efforts were made to promote women's participation in public life.

Though the Constitution of India provides for the Government to make special provisions to safeguard the interests of women. It has not made any provision for reservation for women in respect of jobs and political offices. However 73rd and 74th Constitional Amendment Act mandated reservation of one-third seats in the village, block, districts, municipal elected bodies in India.

As a consequence, women had not advanced much politically and economically. From the records available of the past 50 years, since the independence, it is seen that the strength of women in the political field as reflected in State legislatures remained at an average of 3 per cent to 5 per cent of those elected. At the level of Parliament, the position of women members has varied between 5 to 7 per cent .

Women in large numbers have come out against atrocities on women, in defence of their traditional control over crucial resources, water, forests, and land, mass literacy drives and other issues. They are also coming out in large numbers over ecological degradation, price rise or protests against police repression, etc. While there is the increased participation in grass root political movements, it is not getting translated into a growing share of women in the formal political structure of the country.

Amongst the several reasons for such a situation is the growing money power and muscle power required to contest even the smallest of elections in India, the intimidation, violence and slander that a woman candidate has to face combined with the traditional male domination that seeks to keep her indoors. Narrow electoral arithmetic and the necessity of fielding a winning candidate makes most political parties shy away from fielding more than a token number of women candidates. And if they are fielded at all, kinship and affinity factors play a major role.

Increasingly, women have stood for elections and got elected as members of State Legislative Assemblies and the Parliament. However, at the national level there is only one woman Cabinet Minister and 8 Ministers of State in a Cabinet of 70. There is only one woman Governor and one woman Chief Minister. Some studies of Parliamentary participation indicate that women members participate more actively in 'women's issues' - health, welfare, atrocities against women, crimes like dowry and violations of human rights. This participation is confined to the more articulate women. In issues such as defence, finance, politics, etc. their participation is relatively limited.

Analysis of trends of womens' participation to contest elections to the State Legislatures indicate that there is a gender discrimination which is responsible for poor representation of women in India. Women's role in decision making is one of the most important questions for consideration in the movement for their empowerment.

The 73rd and 74th Amendments to the Indian Constitution have served as a major break through towards ensuring women's equal access and increased participation in political power structures. This Amendment provided for reservation of one third of seats for women at level of local governance in urban areas.

There is also a one-third reservation for women for posts of chairpersons of these local bodies. This amendment has initiated a powerful strategy of affirmative action for providing the structural framework for women's participation in political decision-making and provided an opportunity to bring women to be forefront and centre of city development and develop new grass-root level leadership. There are about one million elected women representatives in Panchayats and Municipal Bodies in India.

Local Governments

After 1993, women's participation in local governments

increased quite radically, with the enactment of the legislation providing 33 per cent reservation of seats for women in local bodies. The legislation and its implementation has added another level in political participation.

In Governments too, there has been limited representatives of women. A few eminent women have no doubt, occupied important administrative positions, such as Secretaries of Departments in the National Government as well as in State Governments. It is only 5.71 per cent of the total number of persons in administrative services are women. It is noteworthy that within the premier civil services of India, the representation of women is not that encouraging. Since relatively few women enter the civil services, several efforts have been made to improve the situation. The Department of Personnel and Administrative Reforms of the Government of India has also provided, wherever possible, women officers on the selection boards for posts and services.

The 74th Amendment to the Indian Constitution, 1992 has served as a major breakthrough towards ensuring women's equal access and increased participation in local government. The Constitution (74th Amendment) Act, 1992 aims at Constitutional guarantees to safeguard the interests of urban local self government to enable them to function as effective democratic and self governing institutions at the grass root level. This Amendment provides for reservation of 331/3 per cent of elected seats for women at local government level in urban and rural areas. There is also a one-third reservation for women of posts of chairpersons of these local bodies. A very active role for women in local governance is envisaged as compared to governance at the state and national levels in India. These provisions have provided great opportunities and challenges to women in India, particularly in the local government field. This is of great significance, since this grass-root level participation has considerably broadened the base of women's participation in politics at city level.

Involvement of women in the political arena and in decision-making roles is an important tool for empowerment as well as monitoring standards of political performance at local level. However, in the present political process of entry into decision making political institutions, there is growing influence of money and muscle power, backroom dealings, communalisation and criminalisation. In many respects women and men elected representatives face similar problems on election to office.

Above all there is a need to understand just how to be a good local politician. The role of political representatives at local level is demanding and all new 'recruits' need time to gain experience and to understand the rules, regulations and procedures governing the administrative bureaucracy with which they now have to work-often quite closely in the urban service delivery system. Some of the major constraints that prevent women from effective participation at local level are as follows:

1. Lack of orientation / training in urban development issues and municipal administration.
2. No proper knowledge/orientation about municipal acts and rules and regulations.
3. No prior experience about dealing with multidimensional urban development issues/civic issues and its complexities.
4. Lack of knowledge about technical in-puts related to urban service delivery system.
5. Lack of support from senior male / female colleagues in the party / municipal body.
6. Less co-operation from municipal officials understanding about various facets of the budget, such as allocation of budget at ward level.
7. Lack of party support and poor organisational structure.
8. Lack of money and resources to sustain the electoral campaigns.
9. Discrimination in decision making at party level.
10. Specific notions towards politics and political atmosphere.
11. Fear and insecurity.
12. Lack of confidence in public speaking.
13. Criminalisation of politics and use of money power.
14. Family responsibilities.

Political system in India works through political parties who contend for power by invoking popular support. Therefore it is necessary that if women want to share power they have to make a place for themselves within the political parties through which the Indian democratic system operates. The experience of the last 52

Indian democratic system operates. The experience of the last 52 years show an inability to create this space and recent studies show that there has been no significant change in either the nature of women's functioning or in the political parties' approach to women and women's issues. If we examine women's participation it is seen that the political parties have given less importance to women's issues in terms of ideology, either in priority in their party manifesto or in terms of the number and importance of the position that women occupied in individual political parties.

Women are not seen as a vote bank to be approached, and once the men are mobilised, women will merely endorse their choice of party and candidate. Male candidates rarely have access to the female electorate and there are not enough women involved in political campaigns to be able to reach out to a large section of women even in big cities. As a result, the exposure of women to political debates and issues has always remained indirect. According to women from all parties the political environment was not conducive to women's participation in politics.

Women in India today are agitating at the doors of Parliament, demanding reservation for 33 per cent of the seats. The issue at stake here is more complex than it may seem. It is not only a question of a few more or a few less women in the corridors of Parliament and legislatures but also a response to the fact that a large section of society has historically been denied its legitimate share in the exercise of political power, power that ultimately determines its destiny. In this demand for reservation, women are also raising their voice against a system, which has consistently denied them space by harnessing the forces of tradition in order to marginalise and trivialise their role.

Indira Gandhi

Indira Gandhi belonged to the family of Motilal Nehru and Jawaharlal Nehru. The Nehru family was considered to be very rich, who came from Kashmir. Jawahar Lal's image was that of a prince who had sacrificed all the comforts of life, for the sake of struggling for the independence of India. Indira grew up in that atmosphere in which she was respected like a Princess. But she was a lonely child having no other brothers or sisters. Her father was busy in politics and remained shuttling between prison and home.

Her mother got seriously ill and died early in a foreign land.

Indira Gandhi was different from her father Jawaharlal Nehru in several ways. While the latter looked at the problems of the nation in a long-term perspective, Indira Gandhi was content to address herself to the issues of immediate concern. Indira Gandhi was a practical politician, expert in the art of wielding power, Nehru was an idealist and a philosopher.

About Indira Gandhi, Madhu Limaye had observed that (Dutt, Vishnu, 1986, 30). She was Nehru's daughter and as such she carried with her as heritage, some of his political acumen and intuition. But as his hostess and constant companion at home and abroad, she met and listened to the great men with whom her father conversed. The concentrated wisdom of this experience was one of her prize-possessions. This referred not only to political policy or tactics but also to the manner in which her personality had been tempered – a process of course, in which many other factors entered.

The qualities of courage and determinations in Indira Gandhi were outstanding. She had lofty vision of India. But her vision underwent a drastic change after she acquired a firm grip over the state apparatus, as a consequence of her victories, in Indo-Pakistani war, the creation of Bangladesh and success in the Lok Sabha elections of 1971. After Shastri's sudden death in Tashkent, the problem of finding a successor arose before the Congress party. There were complicated maneuvering among two candidate viz. the Gandhian right winger Morarji Desai (Nehru's ex-Finance Minister) and Nehru's daughter Indira Gandhi. The strong man from south, Kamraj, considered a King-maker, organized support for the latter. This syndicate of Congressmen headed by Kamraj, viewed Indira Gandhi as a person whom they could control and through whom they could indirectly rule. But once installed as Prime Minister Indira Gandhi asserted her supremacy and disillusioned them. She could perform that feat, even though those years were difficult and hard.

The initial assessment of her capacity by the syndicate, hurt her, Indira Gandhi became secretive and rarely shared feelings with others. In Indira Gandhi's biography, Popul Jaykar, who was very close to her, observed that she seldom discussed politics with her.

Indira Gandhi assumed the Prime Ministership of India for four terms first on January 24, 1966, second on March 13, 1967, third... 1972 and fourth on January 7, 1980. The only interregnum during the eighteen years between the periods of her Prime Ministership was during the years 1977 and 1980. It was the Janata interlude. Thus Indira Gandhi ruled as the Head of the Government for about sixteen years.

Her rapport with common people was extraordinary. She was the most charismatic leader after Gandhi and Nehru. Her strength lay in her relationship with the common man. Because of this she could ignore her political opponents and could appeal over their heads directly to the people. She by passed even her own party men during the midterm poll of 1971. In 1969, the Congress had split. Here it would be sufficient to note that the ruling Congress of Indira Gandhi became a minority in the Lok Sabha (first chamber of the Parliament). She wished to get a clear mandate from the people. Hence she advised the President to dissolve the Lok Sabha on 27th December, 1970. Thus Lok Sabha was dissolved and Mid Term elections for 1971 was announced.

In the mid-term elections of 1971, the Organisation Congress (the section which opposed ruling Congress), Jansangh, Swatantra Party and the Samajwadi Dal came together to form a four-party front against Indira Gandhi's ruling Congress. It had also secure the co-operation of the Communist Parties and the Dravida Munetra Kazagam. In spite of this combination, Indira Gandhi secured two third seats in the Lok Sabha in this election, In fact the factors behind Indira Gandhi's overwhelming victory were many. First, this election affected the mass psychology. The people came to believe that Indira Gandhi did not wish to remain seated in her power position without their approval. Moreover the people wanted stability at the centre, which according to them could only be provided by Indira Gandhi. In the light of the four party slogans of "Indira Hatao' (remove Indira) and 'Loktantra bachao' (save democracy), masses became sympathetic with Indira Gandhi whose slogans was to remove poverty (Garibi Hatao). She knew the mass-psychology and refrained from any personal attach.on the opposite parties, or on the leaders opposed to her.

The Socialist Image

The 1967 elections, in which though Congress received a major set back, demonstrated the organizing capacity of Indira Gandhi. It was the first election campaign by her. In spite of Congress pitfalls, her popularity was established beyond doubt. In the states various opposition parties came to form alliances. In Madras and West Bengal they came to hold power. In centre the support for Congress was reduced. In election campaign Indira Gandhi adopted a left wing posture and enlisted the support of the youth. In her foreign policy she became more inclined towards the USSR than the USA. For promoting her ten-point programme in order to achieve socialism, Indira Gandhi nationalised private banks, commercial banks and general insurance agencies. She also abolished the privy purses of India's ex-princess. In 1969, when the erstwhile President Fakruddin Ali Ahmad suddenly died, the old bosses of the Congress known as the "Syndicate" attempted to control Indira Gandhi. They proposed a candidate for Presidency who would oppose her Presidential candidate. She called upon the electoral college for "conscience voting" which would make them free from the binding of the syndicate and their Congress. Indira Gandhi's candidate was Mr. V.V. Giri, one time a Trade Union leader. He was elected by a narrow margin over the syndicate's nominee.

In spite of bitter criticism against her "wasteful" electronic media policy, Indira Gandhi held on to her scheme. She know that her imprint on Indian system could be made very strong, if the electronic media like television reached the far off corners of the nation, intertwining them into one network. Far eastern states of north India, which had remained aloof uptil now from the main stream of the nation, were brought in by this audiovisual strong media. It provided the same information, same entertainments and the same training programmes for all the Indians.

Indira Gandhi's environmental interest revealed her as one of the first true planetary leaders.

Maurice F. Strong, the Executive Coordinator, United Nations Office for Emergency Operation in Africa, wrote about Indira Gandhi. "She was the first leader of any great nation to appreciate that the concerns for environment which had been so dramatically manifested in the late 1960s and early 1970s in industrialized societies had a profound relevance to developing countries. At that time most of the developing world regarded the emergence of the environmental issue as a preoccupation of the rich which threatened to divert attention and resources from the development needs of the poor, but Indira Gandhi saw the indispensable need to force an alliance between environmental and development concerns in meeting these needs." Indira Gandhi Commemorative Volume, 409).

Indira Gandhi demonstrated her firm convictions regarding preservation of ecological balance in Kerala. She declared not to proceed with the Silent Valley hydro-electric power project, which would have destroyed the unique ecosystem there. She also took steps to eliminate the threats to the Taj Mahal from the harmful emissions from Mathura Oil Refinery and other industrial plants. The tiger population of India could be saved because of her strong support for "Project Tiger". The Department of Environment of the Government of India was established in 1981. The International Union for the Conservation of Nature and Natural Resources (IUCN) recognized Indira Gandhi's contributions to sustainable development and bestowed upon her its highest award. (Indira Gandhi Commemorative Volume, 420).

When one speaks about Indira Gandhi as image of courageous, dynamic and attractive woman emerges before one's eyes. Her place is among selective few of the world's political leaders. At home the events of success as well as failure in elections, she efficiently wielded the campaign machine, utilised ably the resources of her party and organized her activities in such a way that people felt attracted towards her. She was the most precious jewel of her party. Even during the Janata days in 1977, she prevailed in the minds of her people. It was she who could turn trend of voting when she indicated that the general elections were in reality elections for the Prime Minister. Hence she asked the people to cast their votes for those contestants who would in their turn support their candidates for Prime Ministership in Parliament.

As mentioned elsewhere Indira Gandhi was an acclaimed world leader. She elevated the international position of India among the Third World countries, western countries and the socialist nations. Pandit Jawaharlal Nehru was one of the founder members on Non-Aligned Movement along with Nasser of Egypt and Tito of Yugoslavia. All the three provided the ideological base for NAM. The successor of Pandit Nehru - Lal Bahadur Shastri stressed peaceful co-existence, nuclear disarmament and peaceful settlement of disputes among the nations. Indira Gandhi added an economic dimension to the NAM in the Algiers Summit of 1978, and provided it a positive and creative base. That Third World nations should get better facilities for exports began to be stressed. The Third World gave importance to economic issues in their relations with other nations. In the Colombo Summit of Nam, Indira Gandhi stressed on a new economic world order and the unity of the Third World in world politics. It was Indira Gandhi who saved NAM from the communist tilt and held its upright position by not recognising Soviet Union as its "natural friend". The term was proposed by Fiedel Castro. It was she who repaired the cracks in NAM at that time (Sharan Sarojini, 1989, 197-198)

In the year 1971 Indo-Pakistani war had resulted into a high drama of the birth of a new sovereign-state viz. the People's Republic of Bangladesh. During this period the programmes chalked out by Indira Gandhi, in the mid-term election of 1971, focused on proposals which were to be implemented only by the centre, thus giving greater scope for power wielding to the national government.

Indira Gandhi was successful in projecting her images as a socialist and well wisher of the common man. The common man felt important and centre of attention of the ruling party. They voted Indira Gandhi to power, with as overwhelming majority. It made her "ruling" Congress stronger after the split. The masses felt that the Congress was now more pure because the unwanted elements were purged out.

Centralization and Personalization

There was a rise in the number of religious parties during Indira Gandhi's regime. Demand for greater autonomy by the states and other sub-national groups began and became vociferous. Her personal supremacy came to be challenged which made her so insecure that she interpreted these as threats to the territorial integrity of India. She demonstrated intense intolerance to all partymen who questioned her dominance. She toppled the non-Congress I Government in the states and maintained a direct hold on the governmental apparatus in those status, through President's rule.

Indira Gandhi decided to hold elections in 1971, which was one year earlier than scheduled. She enlisted the youth bodies to campaign for her. It was a step for personalizing Indian politics.

Since the Congress I organisation had no grassroots, she had to depend upon the youth bodies, who would carry her socialist image to the rural areas. She created the impression that the opposition parties and some of her own party members, had vested interest in politics. They all had combined against her. She was fighting alone against their vested interest. The slogans of "Garibi Hatao" (banish poverty) checkmated the communists. She could get two-third majority in Lok Sabha. Her popularity surpassed even Nehru's.

Strikes, gheraos, rallies and demonstrations became order of the day. Trade Unions became aggressive and law and order touched the lowest. In 1974, the railway workers became determined to implement their decision for a general strike when negotiations broke down with the railway workers. Indira Gandhi used her unprecedented powers under the Preventive Detenment Act and crushed the spirit of the working class.

In the recent history of modern democracy. Indira Gandhi had few parallels, in leaving strong impact upon the whole tenor of a country's (Indian) politics. She was a political phenomenon. She brought economics to the core of political agenda. She convinced the masses that socialist programmes and secular path were inevitable for the Indian society. These were the catalytic doctrines, with which she came forward and caught the imagination of the people. Indira Gandhi had successfully projected her image as a radical. She outwitted even the left wingers in her radicalism. The latter gave a call for a distant revolution on imported ideas of class war. Won the hearts of the rural poor, the Muslims and other religious minorities, the tribals and other ethnic groups in the north as well as in the south. Her popular rhetoric of "Garibi Hatao" (banish poverty) appealed to all of them.

She was the Prime Minister for sixteen years and during her long tenure she faced very complex problems of political, socio-economic and religious nature. She took army action in Golden Temple to counteract the political opposition. Soon after she was shot dead by one of her bodyguards and was succeeded by her son, Rajiv Gandhi, as Prime Minister of India. .

8

The Assessment

The Constitution not only grants equality to women, but also empowers the State to adopt measures of positive discrimination in favour of women. Within the framework of a democratic polity, our laws, development policies, Plans and programmes have aimed at women's advancement in different spheres. From the Fifth Five Year Plan (1974-78) onwards has been a marked shift in the approach to women's issues from welfare to development. In recent years, the empowerment of women has been recognised as the central issue in determining the status of women.

The National Commission for Women

The National Commission for Women was set up by an Act of Parliament in 1990 to safeguard the rights and legal entitlements of women. The 73rd and 74th Amendments (1993) to the Constitution of India have provided for reservation of seats in the local bodies of Panchayats and Municipalities for women, laying a strong foundation for their participation in decision making at the local levels. India has also ratified various international conventions and human rights instruments committing to secure equal rights of women. Key among them is the ratification of the Convention on Elimination of All Forms of Discrimination Against Women (CEDAW) in 1993. The Mexico Plan of Action (1975), the Nairobi Forward Looking Strategies (1985), the Beijing Declaration as well as the Platform for Action (1995) and the Outcome Document adopted by the UNGA Session on Gender Equality and Development & Peace for the 21st century, titled "Further actions and initiatives to implement the Beijing Declaration and the Platform for Action" have been unreservedly endorsed by India for appropriate follow up. The Policy also takes note of the commitments of the Ninth Five Year

Plan and the other Sectoral Policies relating to empowerment of Women.

The women's movement and a widespread network of non-Government Organisations which have strong grassroots presence and deep insight into women's concerns have contributed in inspiring initiatives for the empowerment of women.

However, there still exists a wide gap between the goals enunciated in the Constitution, legislation, policies, plans, programmes, and related mechanisms on the one hand and the situational reality of the status of women in India, on the other. This has been analysed extensively in the Report of the Committee on the Status of Women in India, "Towards Equality", 1974 and highlighted in the National Perspective Plan for Women, 1988-2000, the Shramshakti Report, 1988 and the Platform for Action, Five Years After- An assessment"

Gender disparity manifests itself in various forms, the most obvious being the trend of continuously declining female ratio in the population in the last few decades. Social stereotyping and violence at the domestic and societal levels are some of the other manifestations. Discrimination against girl children, adolescent girls and women persists in parts of the country.

The underlying causes of gender inequality are related to social and economic structure, which is based on informal and formal norms, and practices. Consequently, the access of women particularly those belonging to weaker sections including Scheduled Castes/Scheduled Tribes/ Other backward Classes and minorities, majority of whom are in the rural areas and in the informal, unorganised sector – to education, health and productive resources, among others, is inadequate. Therefore, they remain largely marginalised, poor and socially excluded.

Goal and Objectives

The goal of the Policy is to bring about the advancement, development and empowerment of women. The Policy will be widely disseminated so as to encourage active participation of all stakeholders for achieving its goals. Specifically, the objectives of this Policy include

i) Creating an environment through positive economic and social policies for full development of women to enable them to realise their full potential

ii) The *de-jure* and *de-facto* enjoyment of all human rights and fundamental freedom by women on equal basis with men in all spheres – political, economic, social, cultural and civil

iii) Equal access to participation and decision making of women in social, political and economic life of the nation

iv) Equal access to women to health care, quality education at all levels, career and vocational guidance, employment, equal remuneration, occupational health and safety, social security and public office etc.

v) Strengthening legal systems aimed at elimination of all forms of discrimination against women

vi) Changing societal attitudes and community practices by active participation and involvement of both men and women.

vii) Mainstreaming a gender perspective in the development process.

viii) Elimination of discrimination and all forms of violence against women and the girl child; and

ix) Building and strengthening partnerships with civil society, particularly women's organisations.

Judicial Legal Systems

Legal-judicial system will be made more responsive and gender sensitive to women's needs, especially in cases of domestic violence and personal assault. New laws will be enacted and existing laws reviewed to ensure that justice is quick and the punishment meted out to the culprits is commensurate with the severity of the offence.

At the initiative of and with the full participation of all stakeholders including community and religious leaders, the Policy would aim to encourage changes in personal laws such as those related to marriage, divorce, maintenance and guardianship so as to eliminate discrimination against women. The evolution of property rights in a patriarchal system has contributed to the subordinate status of women. The Policy would aim to encourage changes in laws relating to ownership of property and inheritance by evolving consensus in order to make them gender just.

Decision Making

Women's equality in power sharing and active participation in decision making, including decision making in political process at all levels will be ensured for the achievement of the goals of empowerment. All measures will be taken to guarantee women equal access to and full participation in decision making bodies at every level, including the legislative, executive, judicial, corporate, statutory bodies, as also the advisory Commissions, Committees, Boards, Trusts etc. Affirmative action such as reservations/ quotas, including in higher legislative bodies, will be considered whenever necessary on a time bound basis. Women-friendly personnel policies will also be drawn up to encourage women to participate effectively in the developmental process.

Gender Perspective in the Development Process

Policies, programmes and systems will be established to ensure mainstreaming of women's perspectives in all developmental processes, as catalysts, participants and recipients. Wherever there are gaps in policies and programmes, women specific interventions would be undertaken to bridge these. Coordinating and monitoring mechanisms will also be devised to assess from time to time the progress of such mainstreaming mechanisms. Women's issues and concerns as a result will specially be addressed and reflected in all concerned laws, sectoral policies, plans and programmes of action.

Economic Empowerment of Women

Poverty Eradication

Since women comprise the majority of the population below the poverty line and are very often in situations of extreme poverty, given the harsh realities of intra-household and social discrimination, macro economic policies and poverty eradication programmes will specifically address the needs and problems of such women. There will be improved implementation of programmes which are already women oriented with special targets for women. Steps will be taken for mobilisation of poor women and convergence of services, by offering them a range of economic and social options, along with necessary support measures to enhance their capabilities

Micro Credit

In order to enhance women's access to credit for consumption and production,. the establishment of new, and strengthening of existing micro-credit mechanisms and micro-finance institution will be undertaken so that the outreach of credit is enhanced. Other supportive measures would be taken to ensure adequate flow of credit through extant financial institutions and banks, so that all women below poverty line have easy access to credit.

Women and Economy

Women's perspectives will be included in designing and implementing macro-economic and social policies by institutionalising their participation in such processes. Their contribution to socio-economic development as producers and workers will be recognised in the formal and informal sectors (including home based workers) and appropriate policies relating to employment and to her working conditions will be drawn up. Such measures could include reinterpretation and redefinition of conventional concepts of work wherever necessary e.g. in the Census records, to reflect women's contribution as producers and workers.

Globalisation

Globalisation has presented new challenges for the realisation of the goal of women's equality, the gender impact of which has not been systematically evaluated fully. However, from the micro-level studies that were commissioned by the Department of Women & Child Development, it is evident that there is a need for re-framing policies for access to employment and quality of employment. Benefits of the growing global economy have been unevenly distributed leading to wider economic disparities, the feminisation of poverty, increased gender inequality through often deteriorating working conditions and unsafe working environment especially in the informal economy and rural areas. Strategies will be designed to enhance the capacity of women and empower them to meet the negative social and economic impacts, which may flow from the globalisation process.

Women and Agriculture

In view of the critical role of women in the agriculture and allied sectors, as producers, concentrated efforts will be made to ensure that benefits of training, extension and various programmes will reach them in proportion to their numbers. The programmes for training women in soil conservation, social forestry, dairy development and other occupations allied to agriculture like horticulture, livestock including small animal husbandry, poultry, fisheries etc., will be expanded to benefit women workers in the agriculture sector.

Women and Industry

The important role played by women in electronics, information technology and food processing and agro-industry and textiles has been crucial to the development of these sectors. They would be given comprehensive support in terms of labour legislation, social security and other support services to participate in various industrial sectors. Women at present cannot work in night shift in factories even if they wish to. Suitable measures will be taken to enable women to work on the night shift in factories. This will be accompanied with support services for security, transportation etc.

Support Services

The provision of support services for women, like child care facilities, including creches at work places and educational institutions, homes for the aged and the disabled will be expanded and improved to create an enabling environment and to ensure their full cooperation in social, political and economic life. Women-friendly personnel policies will also be drawn up to encourage women to participate effectively in the developmental process.

Social Empowerment of Women

Education

Equal access to education for women and girls will be ensured. Special measures will be taken to eliminate discrimination, universalise education, eradicate illiteracy, create a gender-sensitive educational system, increase enrolment and retention rates of girls and improve the quality of education to facilitate life-long learning as well as development of occupation/ vocation/ technical skills by women. Reducing the gender gap in secondary and higher education would be a focus area. Sectoral time targets in existing policies will be achieved, with a special focus on girls and women, particularly those belonging to weaker sections including the Scheduled Castes/ Scheduled Tribes/Other Backward Classes/Minorities. Gender sensitive curricula would be developed at all levels of educational system in order to address sex stereotyping as one of the causes of gender discrimination.

Health

A holistic approach to women's health which includes both nutrition and health services will be adopted and special attention will be given to the needs of women and the girl at all stages of the life cycle. The reduction of infant mortality and maternal mortality, which are sensitive indicators of human development, is a priority concern. This policy reiterates the national demographic goals for Infant Mortality Rate (IMR), Maternal Mortality Rate (MMR) set out in the National Population Policy 2000. Women should have access to comprehensive, affordable and quality health care. The social, developmental and health consequences of HIV/AIDS and other sexually transmitted diseases will be tackled from a gender perspective. To effectively meet problems of infant and maternal mortality, and early marriage the availability of good and accurate data at micro level on deaths, birth and marriages is required. Strict implementation of registration of births and deaths would be ensured and registration of marriages would be made compulsory.

In accordance with the commitment of the National Population Policy (2000) to population stabilisation, this Policy recognises the critical need of men and women to have access to safe, effective and affordable methods of family planning of their choice and the need to suitably address the issues of early marriages and spacing of children.

Interventions such as spread of education, compulsory registration of marriage and special programmes like BSY should impact on delaying the age of marriage so that by 2010 child marriages are eliminated.

Nutrition

In view of the high risk of malnutrition and disease that women face at all the three critical stages viz., infancy and childhood, adolescent and reproductive phase, focused attention would be paid to meeting the nutritional needs of women at all stages of the life cycle. This is also important in view of the critical link between the health of adolescent girls, pregnant and lactating women with the health of infant and young children.

Special efforts will be made to tackle the problem of macro and micro nutrient deficiencies especially amongst pregnant and lactating women as it leads to various diseases and disabilities. Intra-household discrimination in nutritional matters vis-a-vis girls and women will be sought to be ended through appropriate strategies. Widespread use of nutrition education would be made to address the issues of intra-household imbalances in nutrition and the special needs of pregnant and lactating women. Women's participation will also be ensured in the planning, superintendence and delivery of the system.

Drinking Water and Sanitation

Special attention will be given to the needs of women in the provision of safe drinking water, sewage disposal, toilet facilities and sanitation within accessible reach of households, especially in rural areas and urban slums. Women's participation will be ensured in the planning, delivery and maintenance of such services.

Housing and Shelter

Women's perspectives will be included in housing policies, planning of housing colonies and provision of shelter both in rural and urban areas. Special attention will be given for providing adequate and safe housing and accommodation for women including single women, heads of households, working women, students, apprentices and trainees.

Environment

Women will be involved and their perspectives reflected in the policies and programmes for environment, conservation and restoration. Considering the impact of environmental factors on their livelihoods, women's participation will be ensured in the conservation of the environment and control of environmental degradation. The vast majority of rural women still depend on the locally available non-commercial sources of energy such as animal dung, crop waste and fuel wood.

In order to ensure the efficient use of these energy resources in an environmental friendly manner, the Policy will aim at promoting the programmes of non-conventional energy resources. Women will be involved in spreading the use of solar energy, biogas, smokeless chulahs and other rural application so as to have a visible impact of these measures in influencing ecosystem and in changing the life styles of rural women.

Science and Technology

Programmes will be strengthened to bring about a greater involvement of women in science and technology. These will include measures to motivate girls to take up science and technology for higher education and also ensure that development projects with scientific and technical inputs involve women fully. Efforts to develop a scientific temper and awareness will also be stepped up. Special measures would be taken for their training in areas where they have special skills like communication and information technology. Efforts to develop appropriate technologies suited to women's needs as well as to reduce their drudgery will be given a special focus too.

Women in Difficult Circumstances

In recognition of the diversity of women's situations and in acknowledgement of the needs of specially disadvantaged groups, measures and programmes will be undertaken to provide them with special assistance. These groups include women in extreme poverty, destitute women, women in conflict situations, women affected by natural calamities, women in less developed regions, the disabled widows, elderly women, single women in difficult circumstances, women heading households, those displaced from employment, migrants, women who are victims of marital violence, deserted women and prostitutes etc.

Violence against women

All forms of violence against women, physical and mental, whether at domestic or societal levels, including those arising from customs, traditions or accepted practices shall be dealt with effectively with a view to eliminate its incidence. Institutions and mechanisms/schemes for assistance will be created and strengthened for prevention of such violence, including sexual harassment at work place and customs like dowry; for the rehabilitation of the victims of violence and for taking effective action against the perpetrators of such violence. A special emphasis will also be laid on programmes and measures to deal with trafficking in women and girls.

Rights of the Girl Child

All forms of discrimination against the girl child and violation of her rights shall be eliminated by undertaking strong measures both preventive and punitive within and outside the family. These would relate specifically to strict enforcement of laws against prenatal sex selection and the practices of female foeticide, female infanticide, child marriage, child abuse and child prostitution etc.

Removal of discrimination in the treatment of the girl child within the family and outside and projection of a positive image of the girl child will be actively fostered.

There will be special emphasis on the needs of the girl child and earmarking of substantial investments in the areas relating to food and nutrition, health and education, and in vocational education. In implementing programmes for eliminating child labour, there will be a special focus on girl children.

Mass Media

Media will be used to portray images consistent with human dignity of girls and women. The Policy will specifically strive to remove demeaning, degrading and negative conventional stereotypical images of women and violence against women. Private sector partners and media networks will be involved at all levels to ensure equal access for women particularly in the area of information and communication technologies. The media would be encouraged to develop codes of conduct, professional guidelines and other self regulatory mechanisms to remove gender stereotypes and promote balanced portrayals of women and men.

Operational Strategies

All Central and State Ministries will draw up time bound Action Plans for translating the Policy into a set of concrete actions, through a participatory process of consultation with Centre/State Departments of Women and Child Development and National / State Commissions for Women. The Plans will specifically including the following:

i) Measurable goals to be achieved by 2010.
ii) Identification and commitment of resources.
iii) Responsibilities for implementation of action points.
iv) Structures and mechanisms to ensure efficient monitoring, review and gender impact assessment of action points and policies.
v) Introduction of a gender perspective in the budgeting process.

In order to support better planning and programme formulation and adequate allocation of resources, Gender Development Indices (GDI) will be developed by networking with specialised agencies. These could be analysed and studied in depth.

Gender auditing and development of evaluation mechanisms

will also be undertaken along side. Collection of gender desegregated data by all primary data collecting agencies of the Central and State Governments as well as Research and Academic Institutions in the Public and Private Sectors will be undertaken.

Data and information gaps in vital areas reflecting the status of women will be sought to be filled in by these immediately. All Ministries/Corporations/Banks and financial institutions etc., will be advised to collect, collate, disseminate and maintain/publish data related to programmes and benefits on a gender desegregated basis. This will help in meaningful planning and evaluation of policies.

Institutional Mechanisms

Institutional mechanisms, to promote the advancement of women, which exist at the Central and State levels, will be strengthened. These will be through interventions as may be appropriate and will relate to, among others, provision of adequate resources, training and advocacy skills to effectively influence macro-policies, legislation, programmes etc., to achieve the empowerment of women.

National and State Resource Centres on women will be established with mandates for collection and dissemination of information, undertaking research work, conducting surveys, implementing training and awareness generation programmes, etc. These Centres will link up with Women's Studies Centres and other research and academic institutions through suitable information networking systems. While institutions at the district level will be strengthened, at the grassroots, women will be helped by Government through its programmes to organise and strengthen into Self-Help Groups (SHGs) at the Anganwadi/Village/Town level. The women's groups will be helped to institutionalise themselves into registered societies and to federate at the Panchayat/Municipal level.

These societies will bring about synergistic implementation of all the social and economic development programmes by drawing resources made available through Government and Non-Government channels, including banks and financial institutions and by establishing a close interface with the Panchayats/Municipalities.

Resource Management

Availability of adequate financial, human and market resources to implement the Policy will be managed by concerned Departments, financial credit institutions and banks, private sector, civil society and other connected institutions. This process will include:

a) Assessment of benefits flowing to women and resource allocation to the programmes relating to them through an exercise of gender budgeting. Appropriate changes in policies will be made to optimise benefits to women under these schemes;

b) Adequate resource allocation to develop and promote the policy outlined earlier based on (a) above by concerned Departments.

c) Developing synergy between personnel of Health, Rural Development, Education and Women & Child Development Department at field level and other village level functionaries'

d) Meeting credit needs by banks and financial credit institutions through suitable policy initiatives and development of new institutions in coordination with the Department of Women & Child Development.

The strategy of Women's Component Plan adopted in the Ninth Plan of ensuring that not less than 30 per cent of benefits/ funds flow to women from all Ministries and Departments will be implemented effectively so that the needs and interests of women and girls are addressed by all concerned sectors.

The Department of Women and Child Development being the nodal Ministry will monitor and review the progress of the implementation of the Component Plan from time to time, in terms of both quality and quantity in collaboration with the Planning Commission. Efforts will be made to channelise private sector investments too, to support programmes and projects for advancement of women.

Legislation

The existing legislative structure will be reviewed and additional legislative measures taken by identified departments to implement the Policy. This will also involve a review of all existing laws including personal, customary and tribal laws, subordinate legislation, related rules as well as executive and administrative regulations to eliminate all gender discriminatory references. The process will be planned over a time period 2000-2003.

The specific measures required would be evolved through a

consultation process involving civil society, National Commission for Women and Department of Women and Child Development. In appropriate cases the consultation process would be widened to include other stakeholders too. Effective implementation of legislation would be promoted by involving civil society and community. Appropriate changes in legislation will be undertaken, if necessary. In addition, following other specific measures will be taken to implement the legislation effectively.

a) Strict enforcement of all relevant legal provisions and speedy redressal of grievances will be ensured, with a special focus on violence and gender related atrocities.
b) Measures to prevent and punish sexual harassment at the place of work, protection for women workers in the organised/ unorganised sector and strict enforcement of relevant laws such as Equal Remuneration Act and Minimum Wages Act will be undertaken,
c) Crimes against women, their incidence, prevention, investigation, detection and prosecution will be regularly reviewed at all Crime Review fora and Conferences at the Central, State and District levels. Recognised, local, voluntary organisations will be authorised to lodge Complaints and facilitate registration, investigations and legal proceedings related to violence and atrocities against girls and women.
d) Women's Cells in Police Stations, Encourage Women Police Stations Family Courts, Mahila Courts, Counselling Centers, Legal Aid Centers and Nyaya Panchayats will be strengthened and expanded to eliminate violence and atrocities against women.
e) Widespread dissemination of information on all aspects of legal rights, human rights and other entitlements of women, through specially designed legal literacy programmes and rights information programmes will be done.

Gender Sensitisation

Training of personnel of executive, legislative and judicial wings of the State, with a special focus on policy and programme framers, implementation and development agencies, law enforcement machinery and the judiciary, as well as non-governmental organisations will be undertaken. Other measures will include:

a) Promoting societal awareness to gender issues and women's human rights.

b) Review of curriculum and educational materials to include gender education and human rights issues.

c) Removal of all references derogatory to the dignity of women from all public documents and legal instruments.

d) Use of different forms of mass media to communicate social messages relating to women's equality and empowerment.

Panchayati Raj Institutions

The 73rd and 74th Amendments (1993) to the Indian Constitution have served as a breakthrough towards ensuring equal access and increased participation in political power structure for women. The PRIs will play a central role in the process of enhancing women's participation in public life. The PRIs and the local self Governments will be actively involved in the implementation and execution of the National Policy for Women at the grassroots level.

Partnership with the voluntary sector organisations

The involvement of voluntary organisations, associations, federations, trade unions, non-governmental organisations, women's organisations, as well as institutions dealing with education, training and research will be ensured in the formulation, implementation, monitoring and review of all policies and programmes affecting women. Towards this end, they will be provided with appropriate support related to resources and capacity building and facilitated to participate actively in the process of the empowerment of women.

International Cooperation

The Policy will aim at implementation of international obligations/commitments in all sectors on empowerment of women such as the Convention on All Forms of Discrimination Against Women (CEDAW), Convention on the Rights of the Child (CRC), International Conference on Population and Development (ICPD+5) and other such instruments. International, regional and sub-regional cooperation towards the empowerment of women will continue to be encouraged through sharing of experiences, exchange of ideas and technology, networking with institutions and organisations and through bilateral and multilateral partnerships.

Bibliography

Alice W. Clark (ed), *Gender and political economy: explorations of South Asian systems*, Delhi; New York : Oxford University Press, 1993.

Asia Watch/Human Rights Watch, Rape for Profit: Trafficking of- Nepali Girls and Women to India's Brothel, New York, NY Asia Watch, 1995.

Badhwar, I. and Rai, R., "Wedding of the Dolls", *India Today*, June 15, 1986.

Gail Omvedt, Chetrla Gala and Govind Kelkar, (eds.), "Women and Struggle: A Report of Nari Mukti Sangharsh Sammelan", Patna, New Delhi, 1988

, *Women and Rural Revolt in India*, Irvin: Program in Comparative Culture, UCLA, 1978.

, *Women in Popular Movements: India and Thailand during the Decade of Women*, Geneva: United Nations Research Institute for Social Development, 1986.

, *Violence Against Women: New Movements and New Theories in India*, New Delhi: Kali for Women, 1990.

Joanna Liddle and Rama Joshi, (ed), *Daughters of independence: gender, caste and class in India*, London: 1986.

Kurnkum Sangari and Sudesh Vaid, (eds.), *Recasting Women: Essays in Colonial History*, New Delhi: Kali for Women, 1989.

Lateef, S., *Muslim Women in India: Political and Private Realities*, New Delhi: Kali, 1990.

Mani, Lata, "Contentious Traditions: The Debate on Sati in Colonial India", *Cultural Critique*, 7 Fall 1986, Page 119-156.

Michael Allen, and S. Mukherjee, (eds.), *Women in India and Nepal*, Canberra, ANU Press, 1982,

Neera Desai and Maithreyi Krishnaraj, (eds.), *Women and Society in India*, Delhi: Ajanta Books International, 1987.

Patricia Jeffery, Roger Jeffery, Andrew Lyon., (ed), *Labour pains and labour power : women and childbearing in India*, London: Atlantic Highlands, N.J., USA: Zed Books, 1989.

Phulrenu Guha, Vina Mazumdar, et al. (eds.), *Towards Equality: Report on the Committee on the Status of Women in India*, New Delhi: Mnistry of Education and Social Welfare, Govt. of India, 1974

Saskia Wieringa., (ed), *Subversive Women: historical experiences of gender and resistance*, New Delhi: Kalki for Women, 1995.

Index

O

P

Q

R